Play Directing

Play Directing

Analysis, Communication, and Style

SIXTH EDITION

Francis Hodge

University of Texas, Austin

Michael McLain

University of California, Los Angeles

Boston New York San Francisco
Mexico City Montreal Toronto London Madrid Munich Paris
Hong Kong Singapore Tokyo Cape Town Sydney

Series Editor: *Molly Taylor*
Series Editorial Assistant: *Michael Kish*
Senior Marketing Manager: *Mandee Eckersley*
Production Administrator: *Michael Granger*
Editorial-Production Service: *Omegatype Typography, Inc.*
Composition and Prepress Buyer: *Linda Cox*
Manufacturing Buyer: *JoAnne Sweeney*
Cover Administrator: *Kristina Mose-Libon*
Electronic Composition: *Omegatype Typography, Inc.*

For related titles and support materials, visit our online catalog at www.ablongman.com.

Library of Congress Cataloging-in-Publication Data

Hodge, Francis.
Play directing : analysis, communication, and style / Francis Hodge, Michael McLain.—6th ed.
p. cm.
Includes bibliographical references and index.
ISBN 0-205-41923-2
1. Theater—Production and direction. I. McLain, Michael. II. Title.

PN2053.H6 2005
792.02'33—dc22

2004057261

Printed in the United States of America

10 9 8 7 6 5 4 3 2 1 09 08 07 06 05 04

Credits appear on p. ix, which constitutes an extension of the copyright page.

Contents

Dedication and Credits for Photographs

This sixth edition of *Play Directing* is dedicated to the many students, both graduate and undergraduate, at the University of Texas, Austin, and the University of California, Los Angeles, with whom we have worked over the years in the study of directing. Our work with so many fine students has been rewarding, and without their vital engagement, dedication, and energy, the explorations that have gone into this book would not have been possible.

We wish to acknowledge the contributions made by all the directors, actors, designers, technicians, and photographers whose work appears in the photographs throughout the book. Each photograph is credited here in the order of its use with the following notation: number of the photograph; title of the play and its author; specific director, designer, photo credit, and, where appropriate, actor credits; and the place of production.

1 *The Crucible* (Arthur Miller); director, Word Baker; William Larsen as the Rev. Parris; Martinique Theatre, New York.
2 *Idiot's Delight* (Robert Sherwood); director, Francis Hodge; set design, Laszlo Funtek; costumes, Ilse Richter; Banff School of Fine Arts, Banff, Canada.
3 *Hair* (Rado, Ragni, and McDermott); director, Mel Shapiro; scenery, Emily Philips; costumes, Jeannique Prospère; lighting, Jane Hall; University of California, Los Angeles; photograph by Craig Schwartz.
4 *Oliver!* (Lionel Bart); director, Margaret Elizabeth Becker; scenery, Gerhardt Arceberger; costumes, Karen Hudson; lighting, Alfred Stanley; Zachary Scott Theatre Center, Austin, Texas.
5 *Saint Joan* (George Bernard Shaw); director, Francis Hodge; scenery, Clayton Karkosh; costumes, Paul Reinhardt; University of Texas, Austin.
6 *True Love* (Charles Mee, Jr.); director, Michael McLain, co-director, Brian Kite; scenery, Daniel A. Ionazzi; costumes, RoseMarie Fabiano; lighting, Jane Hall; University of California, Los Angeles; photograph by Craig Schwartz.
7 *Orestes 2.0* (Charles Mee, Jr.); director, Michael McLain, co-director, Brian Kite; scenery, Daniel A. Ionazzi; costumes, RoseMarie Fabiano; lighting, Jane Hall; University of California, Los Angeles; photograph by Craig Schwartz.
8 *Curse of the Starving Class* (Sam Shepard); director, Michael McLain; scenery, Rich Rose; costumes, Miye Matsumoto; lighting, Joanne T. McMaster; University of California, Los Angeles.

9 *Look Back in Anger* (John Osborne); director-designer, Mark Ramont; University of Texas, Austin.

10 *The Resistible Rise of Arturo Ui* (Bertolt Brecht); director, Heinz-Uwe Haus; University of Kansas.

11 *Rosmersholm* (Henrik Ibsen); director-designer, Lawrence Peters; University of Texas, Austin.

12 *Black Comedy, the Wacky Side of Racism* (Nancy Giles); director, Ellie Covan; scenery, George Xeros; costumes, NIA; lighting, Greg MacPherson; photo, Valerie Brea Ross; Dixon Place, New York.

13 *School for Wives* (Molière); director, Michael McLain; scenery, Rich Rose; costumes, John Brandt; lighting, Joanne T. McMaster; University of California, Los Angeles.

14 *The House of Blue Leaves* (John Guare); director, Celena Sky April; scenery, Sean Cortemanche; costumes, Bobby Russo; lighting, Alex Molnar; Salem State College, Salem, Massachusetts.

15 *Dementia* (Evelina Fernandez); director, José Luis Valenzuela; scenery, Laura Fine; costumes, Helene Siebrits; lighting, Kwang-Sub Kim; Latino Theatre Company, Los Angeles Theatre Center, Los Angeles; photograph by Carol Petersen.

16 *Curse of the Starving Class* (Sam Shepard); director, Michael McLain; scenery, Rich Rose; costumes, Miye Matsumoto; lighting, Joanne T. McMaster; University of California, Los Angeles; photograph by Emmet Loverde.

17 *La Victima* (El Teatro de la Esperanza); director, José Luis Valenzuela; lighting, Kwang-Sub Kim; University of California, Los Angeles; photograph by Carol Petersen.

18–19 *Romeo and Juliet* (Shakespeare); director, Michael McLain; scenery, Rich Rose; costumes, John Brandt; lighting, Greg Sullivan; University of California, Los Angeles.

20–21 *Orestes 2.0* (Charles Mee, Jr.); director, Michael McLain, co-director, Brian Kite; scenery, Daniel A. Ionazzi; costumes, RoseMarie Fabiano; lighting, Jane Hall; University of California, Los Angeles; photographs by Craig Schwartz.

22 *Orestes* (Euripides); director, Don B. Wilmeth; scenery designer, John R. Lucas.

23 *Measure for Measure* (Shakespeare); director, James Thomas; scenery, Randy Wishmeyer; costumes, Elizabeth Kaler; Florida State University.

24 *Death of a Salesman* (Arthur Miller); director, Donovan Marley; scenery and costumes, Robert Blackman; lighting, Steph Storer; PCPA/theaterfest, Solvang, California.

25 *Othello* (Shakespeare); director-designer, Nancy Keystone; Georgia Shakespeare Festival; photograph by Yvonne Boyd.

26 *Jack, or The Submission* (Eugène Ionesco); director, Brian Frishman; scenery, Kip Marsh; costumes, Julie Kim; lighting, David Levy; University of California, Los Angeles.

27 *Orestes 2.0* (Charles Mee, Jr.); director, Michael McLain, co-director, Brian Kite; scenery, Daniel A. Ionazzi; costumes, RoseMarie Fabiano; lighting,

Jane Hall; University of California, Los Angeles; photograph by Craig Schwartz.

28 *Doctor Faustus* (Christopher Marlowe); illustration of open staging; director, Francis Hodge; scenery, John Rothgeb; University of Texas, Austin.

29 *Antigone* (adaptation by Nancy Keystone); director-designer, Nancy Keystone; Portland Center Stage; photograph by Owen Carey.

30 *Saint Joan* (George Bernard Shaw); director, Francis Hodge; scenery, Clayton Karkosh; costumes, Paul Reinhardt; University of Texas, Austin.

31 *Book of Days* (Lanford Wilson); director, Wendy C. Goldberg; scenery, Michael Brown; costumes, Annie Kennedy; lighting, Nancy L. Schertler; Arena Stage, Washington, D.C.

32 *The Illusion* (Tony Kushner); director, Alice Wilson; scenery and costumes, Michael Raiford; lighting, Robert T. Whyburn; Zachary Scott Theatre Center, Austin, Texas.

33 *Curse of the Starving Class* (Sam Shepard); director, Michael McLain; scenery, Rich Rose; costumes, Miye Matsumoto; lighting, Joanne T. McMaster; University of California, Los Angeles.

34 *The Misanthrope* (Molière); director-designer, Nancy Keystone; Actors Express, Atlanta; photograph by Yvonne Boyd.

35 *Elektra Fragments* (adaptation by Michael Hackett and Anna Krajewska-Wieczorek); director, Michael Hackett; scenery, Kazuko Kadogawa; costumes, Milsa Watson; lighting, Kristie Roldan; University of California, Los Angeles; photograph by Craig Schwartz.

36 *The Divorce Court* (Cervantes); director, Francis Hodge; scenery, John Rothgeb; costumes, Paul Reinhardt; University of Texas, Austin.

37 *Dementia* (Evelina Fernandez); director, José Luis Valenzuela; scenery, Laura Fine; costumes, Helene Siebrits; lighting, Kwang-Sub Kim; Latino Theatre Company, Los Angeles Theatre Center, Los Angeles; photograph by Kwang-Sub Kim.

38 *Doctor Faustus* (Christopher Marlowe); the heavens and upper above; director, Francis Hodge; scenery, John Rothgeb; costumes, Paul Reinhardt; University of Texas, Austin.

39 *The Price* (Arthur Miller); director, Dennis Razze; scenery, Michael Sullivan; costumes, Gaye Bowen; lighting, Donald Day; Zachary Scott Theatre Center, Austin, Texas.

40 *Blood Wedding* (García Lorca); director, Rafal Klopotowski; scenery, Chris Kerins; costumes, Abra Berman; lighting, Elizabeth Greenman; University of California, Los Angeles.

41 *Ghosts* (Henrik Ibsen); director, Chris Coleman; scenery, Dex Edwards; costumes, Susan Mickey; Alliance Theatre, Atlanta, Georgia.

42 *K2* (Patrick Meyers); director, Wendy C. Goldberg; scenery, Ming Cho Lee; costumes, Noel Borden; lighting, Allen Lee Hughes; Arena Stage, Washington, D.C.

43 *Tobacco Road* (adaptation by Jack Kirkland); director, Jack Wright; University of Kansas.

44 *School for Wives* (Molière); director, Michael McLain; scenery, Rich Rose; costumes, John Brandt; lighting, Joanne T. McMaster; University of California, Los Angeles.

45 *The Collection* (Harold Pinter); director, Michael McLain; scenery, Michael McLain; costumes, Judith Burke; lighting, John Lutterbie; Actors Theatre, Austin, Texas.

46 *Orestes 2.0* (Charles Mee, Jr.); director, Michael McLain, co-director, Brian Kite; scenery, Daniel A. Ionazzi; costumes, RoseMarie Fabiano; lighting, Jane Hall; University of California, Los Angeles; photograph by Craig Schwartz.

47 *The Council of Love* (Oskar Panizza); director, Jim Fritzler; setting, Niki Psomas; lighting and costumes, Jim Fritzler; photo, Bill Leissner; Big State Productions, Capitol City Playhouse, Austin, Texas.

48 *House of Bernarda Alba* (García Lorca); director, Cholseung Kim; scenery, Will Pellegrini; costumes, Cycy Lambert; lighting, Kwang-Sub Kim; Culver City Academy of Visual and Performing Arts; photograph by Kwang-Sub Kim.

49 *The Play's the Thing* (Ferenc Molnar); director, Jon Jory; scenery, Allen Mayer; costumes, Nanz Adzina; lighting, T. J. Gerkens; photo, Richard C. Trigg; Actors Theatre of Louisville.

50 *Kitty Hawk* (Len Jenkin); director, Garland Wright; William Larsen as Wilbur Wright; The New Playwright Series, Stratford, Connecticut.

51–52 *True Love* (Charles Mee, Jr.); director, Michael McLain, co-director, Brian Kite; scenery, Daniel Ionazzi; costumes, RoseMarie Fabiano; lighting, Jane Hall; University of California, Los Angeles; photographs by Craig Schwartz.

53 *The Wonderful Wizard of Oz* (Polish version, Jan Skotnicki); director, Lewin Goff; scenery, costumes, lighting, Adam Kilian; Plock, Poland.

54 *Lady from the Sea* (Henrik Ibsen); director, Francis Hodge; scenery, Clayton Karkosh; costumes, Paul Reinhardt; University of Texas, Austin.

55–56 *The Effect of Gamma Rays on Man-in-the-Moon Marigolds* (Paul Zindel); director, Sally Russell; scenery, Lee Duran; costumes, Eve Bull; lighting, Beki Willis; Gaslight Theatre, Austin, Texas.

57 *Jack, or The Submission* (Eugène Ionesco); director, Brian Frishman; scenery, Kip Marsh; costumes, Julie Kim; lighting, David Levy; University of California, Los Angeles.

58 *Beehive* (a composite musical); director, Edward Stern; scenery, Joseph P. Tilford; costumes, Elizabeth Coney; lighting, Kirk Bookman; photo, Sandy Underwood; Cincinnati Playhouse in the Park.

59 *Cowboy Mouth* (Sam Shepard); director; Kim Kovac; scenery, Kim Kovac; costumes, William Pucilovsky; lighting, Jack Halstead; photo, Dennis Deloria; Paradise Island Express and The Independent Theatre Project, Washington, DC.

60 *Suicide in B*^{b} (Sam Shepard); director, Kim Kovac, scenery, Kim Kovac; costumes, William Pucilovsky; lighting, Jack Halstead; photo, Dennis Deloria; Paradise Island Express and The Independent Theatre Project, Washington, DC.

61 *Summer and Smoke* (Tennessee Williams); director, James Thomas; scenery, Lyle Miller; costumes, Elizabeth Kaler; Florida State University.

62 *Tobacco Road* (adaptation by Jack Kirkland); director, Jack Wright; University of Kansas.
63 *The Little Foxes* (Lillian Hellman); Patrick Husted as Oscar Hubbard; Carol Schultz as Birdie; Robert S. Marx Theatre, Cincinnati, Ohio.
64 *The Akhmatova Project* (Nancy Keystone and Critical Mass Performance Group); director-designer, Nancy Keystone; Critical Mass Performance Group at The Actors' Gang, Los Angeles.
65 *Les Cenci* (Artaud); director, René Migliaccio; scenery, Dipu Gupta; costumes, Sungmin Kim; University of California, Los Angeles and Black Moon Theatre Company; photograph by Craig Schwartz.
66 *Heartbreak House* (George Bernard Shaw); director, Ray Keith Pond; costumes, Joseph Adams; University of Texas, Austin.
67 *Antigone* (adaptation by Nancy Keystone); director-designer, Nancy Keystone; Portland Center Stage; photograph by Owen Carey.
68 *The Adding Machine* (Elmer Rice); director-designer, Ray Keith Pond; University of Texas, Austin.
69 *The Crucible* (Arthur Miller); director, Francis Hodge; scenery, Laszlo Funtek; Banff School of Fine Arts, Banff, Canada.
70 *Rhinoceros* (Eugène Ionesco); director, Francis Hodge; scenery, John Rothgeb; University of Texas, Austin.
71 *Sticks and Bones* (David Rabe); director-designer, Mike Wheeler; University of Texas, Austin.
72 *True West* (Sam Shepard); director, Sally Russell; scenery and lighting, Whitney White; costumes, Douglas Garland; Salem State College, Salem, Massachusetts.
73 *Othello* (Shakespeare); director-designer, Nancy Keystone; Georgia Shakespeare Festival; photograph by Yvonne Boyd.
74 *Hedda Gabler* (Henrik Ibsen); director-designer, Tim Kovac; University of Texas, Austin.
75 *Orestes 2.0* (Charles Mee, Jr.); director, Michael McLain, co-director, Brian Kite; scenery, Daniel A. Ionazzi; costumes, RoseMarie Fabiano; lighting, Jane Hall; University of California, Los Angeles; photographs by Craig Schwartz.
76 *Ghosts* (Henrik Ibsen); director, Chris Coleman; scenery, Dex Edwards; costumes, Susan Mickey; Alliance Theatre, Atlanta, Georgia.
77 *Fuente Ovejuna* (de Vega); director, Francis Hodge; scenery, John Rothgeb; costumes, Paul Reinhardt.
78 *Elektra Fragments* (adaptation by Michael Hackett and Anna Krajewska-Wieczorek); director, Michael Hackett; scenery, Kazuko Kadogawa; costumes, Milsa Watson; lighting, Kristie Roldan; University of California, Los Angeles; photograph by Craig Schwartz.
79 *Doctor Faustus* (Marlowe); director, Francis Hodge; scenery, John Rothgeb; costumes, Paul Reinhardt.
80 *The Beaux Strategem* (George Farquhar); director, Francis Hodge; scenery, John Rothgeb; costumes, Lucy Barton; University of Texas, Austin.

Preface

The distinguishing difference from previous editions of this book is the association with Dr. Michael McLain of the University of California, Los Angeles, as coauthor. As Professor of Theater in UCLA's School of Theater, Film, Television and Digital Media, Dr. McLain teaches primarily in the areas of directing and acting. As founding Artistic Associate and Literary Director of the Geffen Playhouse in Los Angeles, he oversaw the development of numerous productions as well as master classes, internships, and symposia in the advanced training programs cosponsored by the theater and UCLA.

In this sixth edition of *Play Directing*, the intention of the first edition has remained the same: to guide students through the whole process of work on a play, from analysis to style, in the hope of freeing them to their own flight as creative and dedicated leaders. Many points throughout the text have been clarified or developed in greater detail, with new chapters added on directing actors and the relationship between the director and the dramaturg. Examples are updated to keep the text alive and in the present. New photographs with related questions enliven the progress of the text to help explain the points under discussion. A new bibliography gives an updated survey of a diverse range of works that relate to directing. Students are encouraged throughout the book to give full concentration to doing the exercises associated with the many points in the directing process.

We wish to thank the numerous students, both undergraduate and graduate, who have helped with the exercises that appear throughout the text, and the directors at all levels who helped illustrate it with photographs of their productions. We are also grateful to the readers who have offered comments concerning areas they would like to see amplified, many of which we have sought to respond to in this new edition. Finally, we thank the reviewers of this edition: Kevin M. Mace, North Georgia College and State University; Eric Somers, Dutchess Community College; Steven Marc Weiss, Coe College; and David Wohl, West Virginia State College.

F.H.

M.M.

1

Why the Director?

This book is about leadership—specifically, the leadership of an artistic enterprise: the play director in today's theatre. Although there is a brief discussion of doing musical theatre and opera in Appendix 1, the concentration throughout the basic text is on work with plays as the oldest (2,500 years) continuing form of live theatre in Western culture. When you are a director, on some days you might think of yourself as a football coach, managing a team and calling in plays from the sidelines; on other days, you might see yourself as a conductor of an orchestra, emphasizing and blending the sounds made by the violins, horns, and drums in front of you. But most of the time, you will see yourself as a *leader* (not a dictator) of multiple craftsmen, all with individual skills who are open to the energy of new ideas.

As you look at the table of contents you should note that the process of directing set out here has two major approaches: First, Chapters 1 through 22 are all about the *mechanics* of bringing a play alive on a stage with actors. Second, Chapters 23 through 29 are about *refining those mechanics* through the study of style in such a way as to individualize both the playscript and your own approaches to making it work on the stage. Some inexperienced would-be directors find the latter more attractive than the former and think they can do it without the hard work of understanding the former. Don't let this happen to you: Don't run before you can walk. Making a play's production *your own thing* can wait on an explicit understanding of the mechanics; reading through the text here is not sufficient. That is why each section of the mechanics has its exercises. Do them seriously and explicitly, and they will move you from a general approach in a play's production to specific ways to illuminate and individualize it.

Although this book is about the process of directing, it is also intended for playwrights, actors, and designers, for it is their work that the audience sees and hears. The director may give them the impetus to express their fullest, most creative talent, and the director may help shape their products, but unless these individuals know about and work as active collaborators toward what the director's imagining intends, they will merely be carrying out mechanical projects. The goal is always synthesis, and by working together under the director-coordinator, these craftsmen will find it.

This text is also written for those directors who make productions at the high school level. After all, there is no part-way point in this study of directing—that is, less for the beginners, more for the others. Directing is directing: You either know how to do it or you don't. Once you learn something of the whole process, you will see how it can be applied at all levels of production—beginner, intermediate, advanced, and even professional. What you bring to it from your previous study of dramatic literature, your basic courses in scenic materials, your acting classes, and just doing plays in production has already called extensively on your imagination. With directing you are about to plunge into one of the theatre's most specific and demanding areas of study. Yet the intention throughout the text is not that of selling a *system*—that is, a specific and correct way of doing things; rather, the goal is to provide an intense look at the *structure* of plays, of acting and actor-ownership, and all the other crafts that make a produced play. When you understand the whole, you can devise your own intimate and creative approach. This study about directing, then, is a format for piercing the process, not a rule book to be followed. Once you perceive directing as an enlightened form of leadership of other creative craftsmen, you will be liberated to undertake your own creative ways and not be tied up in a specific way of doing your job.

Although the *process* of directing is the subject here and not the history of directing, as you proceed in this study you will learn that directors, though they lead others, did not appear on the theatre scene in America until the late nineteenth century. In fact, they did not take hold until after 1915 when the "new" theatre of that day threw out the business-oriented, machine-made stagings of the old theatre and took a fresh, creative stance in playwriting. With the Provincetown Players and the New York Theatre Guild leading the way, came such American playwrights as Eugene O'Neill along with the art-theatre concept and subsequently such directors as George Cram Cook, Orson Welles, Harold Clurman, Elia Kazan, and a host of new American playwrights. Previously, "stage managers" had supervised the jobs of helping actors in their roles and the use of the stage, and arranged with the stage carpenter, also a scene painter, the conventional and limited scenery. The actors usually provided their own dress. But after 1915, in step with the European pattern, the director headed a producing organization as a creative executive who was knowledgeable about all the crafts. The director thus became recognized in the theatre in his own right, because it was out of his vision and feeling that audiences would see plays in a coordinated ensemble with actors moving before an artistically arranged staging. The director had established his mainstay as the primary theatricalist and set the pattern for the teaching of theatre crafts in the schools. A great deal more could be written about the history of the director in America, but this is enough to get you started in the process itself.

The Director's Job

You will also note as you proceed in this study that directors have four drives that guide all their work: a *vision* of the play that can dominate all the aspects of production from acting to staging; a *comprehensive knowledge* of the dynamics of plays—their rises and falls, their louds and softs, their slow beats and their fast ones; *skills in communication* that can help actors and designers give their most creative attention to a play; and a very *strong desire to entertain* audiences by exciting their minds, their hearts, and their spirits.

It is precisely because the director has so much power in the theatre that so much is expected of her or him. The curious paradox is that, like the playwright, the director is not actually seen *on* the stage but only *through* the actors and the physical staging provided by the designers. In contrast, symphony and opera conductors, and even football coaches, have a physical presence. They visibly run the performance, with the obvious capability of directly affecting coordination, rhythm, and mood. But the director's work can be measured only in what happens when the actors and designers work on the audience. In this sense, the director is a silent partner, though his work beforehand is anything but silent. To the contrary, the director is a talker, a verbal imagist, *for his primary work is communication*—not directly to the audience but to *actors and designers* who then transmit ideas and energies to the audience.

The director's job, then, is to be a communicator of the highest order. The director may have very strong feelings about a playscript, but sensitivity, though it will help, will not define the would-be director's directing capabilities. Because the transfer of ideas must be made through the minds and feelings of others, the challenge for a director lies in the talent for touching the magic wellsprings in others with what the director so vividly imagines and feels.

This challenge is the director's paradox. All artists operate within some balance of their subjective-objective selves, but it is the subjective that customarily dominates. The director is an exception, for most of his work is done on the conscious side of the scale. Herbert Blau in *The Impossible Theatre,* a stimulating and soul-searching study of the director's function, contends that "the director must be a brain." This statement does not mean that the director works only in a coldly objective, intellectual way. What it does mean is that *directors must trust their feelings to react primitively and vigorously to what they help make on the stage.* As the practicing critic in the theatre, the director must constantly bring *what he feels and thinks to the surface* so that it can be communicated readily to others. The director must perceive, evaluate, make a diagnosis, and devise remedies. The director's effectiveness in all these actions will lie precisely in his outside-inside responses, in finding an objective-subjective balance. To accomplish this balance, the learning director must become intensively aware of the structures of plays, the prevailing theories and the training processes of acting, the physical use of the stage, and the visual capabilities of design, for at the base, the director is the total designer of a production—the principal "idea person" who matches concrete form with imagined ideas.

As all artists must, the director must first be an adventurous spirit eager to cut new paths and be capable of "soaring" on the level of the dramatic poet. Too often, the director is regarded as only an interpreter of the creative works of others; yet if the director cannot reach some of the same heights as those achieved by the poet he is attempting to reveal on the stage, he is not fulfilling his function. At his best, the director will soar with the angels; but at the same time, he must be an engineer-pilot, a professional who is forever landing and taking off. He knows his plane, his instruments, and his flight plan—the limitations that bind his flight yet simultaneously make it possible. The stage is a flying machine that must be manipulated with the greatest skill. By knowing the limitations of his art form, he will know which way freedom lies and thus be able to lead others to it. Flight-in-restriction is the goal.

Turning On Audiences

Despite all this high-minded talk, you must never forget that the director's leading purpose is to entertain—"Make them feel! Make them laugh!" But this can mean dozens of things. Here's the rub: A good director does not make "entertainment" the primary goal, for it is *how* the director entertains that matters. A much better phrase than the word *entertain* is *turning on* audiences by getting their *involuntary* attention. This is the sort of attention audiences give despite themselves. It is what you as a director do to members of an audience that makes them sit on the edge of their seats despite the hold-offs and hang-ups. Never forget that "I've got 'em" is the goal.

Because of the direction taken in many movies and television shows today, we seem obsessed with violence as entertainment in itself. What makes good plays, however, is not how people are killed, but why. A shootout with the evil ones destroyed and the virtuous surviving, as we can see any night on television, tells us very little; it merely arouses fears and prejudices and sometimes violence like that portrayed. Remember, good plays—and there are many more that are bad than good—are made of different stuff. You will discover early on how easy it is to entertain, but how difficult it is to make good theatre.

Learning directing, as with any craft, is a process of personal discovery—doing basic things over and over until they become second nature. How long the learning process will take is a matter of your capability in perceiving concepts, in getting the message in a very personal way. A book of this sort cannot make you into a director, for no one can actually teach you how to direct any more than someone can teach you how to act. What can be done is to put you, as a dedicated learner, on the tracks that can lead to self-discovery. The artist in you will do the rest. The old saying "Life is short and art is long" is true only because artists have been challenged greatly by the demands of their jobs, and then have gone beyond themselves in making art that survives. If you want to be a director—the artistic leader of others in the theatre—you must learn it all.

EXERCISES

1. Did you notice how *theatre* is spelled here? Back in the nineteenth century, dictionary-maker Noah Webster dumped the word into a general category and gave it an *-er* ending, the ending most U.S. publishers have used ever since. But despite this, those who make theatre, especially in New York, have retained the old spelling because of all its special meanings and historical attachments. *Theatre* is a name that connotes heritage, traditions, conventions, public and private communications, mirror images—both visual and aural—great ideas, memorable characters, perceptive sentiments, live audiences, live actors, and much more.
2. How does live theatre, then, differ from the electronic media of television and motion pictures beyond the simple fact that it is live?
3. Compare the experience of a theatre performance with that of a religious ceremony. Can you envision the stage director as a "maker of ceremonies" rather than the customary designation of "coordinator" of entertainment? Explain your answer.
4. Why can a director be described as a ritualist who makes rituals?
5. Why is live theatre more of a "belonging" experience than watching television or a movie?
6. Is theatre a social institution?
7. Why do you want to direct plays? You may be aware of the decreased position given to the theatre today because of motion pictures and television, but are you fully informed on how the theatre has changed under their strong influences? The shift of professional theatre away from the commercialism of New York City's Broadway to the regional non-profit theatres, supported strongly by state and federal taxes together with private monies, must be taken into any critical evaluation. New York is still of top importance because of its many competing theatres, but decentralization has made a new-old context across the United States that is not unlike the city stock company theatres of the nineteenth century. With decentralization has come a divergence of theatre centers of quality and many more jobs for actors and playwrights in a rapidly declining medium. It has also encouraged and even fostered a widespread network of amateur-professional groups throughout the country.

2

What Is a Play?

Analysis and Improvisation

The playscript is the director's primary tool. If you don't know what it is in all of its parts, you will be lost. Treating it with respect is knowing your job at its base.

Do you know how to read a play? Most people don't, but go at it by reading the words, as in any other kind of reading, and being caught up in the story. A director, however, reads a play in a quite different way, paying attention to all the starts and stops, the gaps, the silences, and the bare minimum of description. Furthermore, the director is aware that it is all dramatic action. As a potential director, you must imagine all of those by supplying in your mind's eye what the actors and the staging are doing. If you don't know what written dialogue is and how it works, you will be lost or be confused or, even worse, take it all for granted as if it is as plain as the nose on your face. Shakespeare said it all 400 years ago, and it's hard to improve on his images:

> *The poet's eye, in a fine frenzy rolling,*
> *Doth glance from heaven to earth, from earth to heaven;*
> *And, as imagination bodies forth*
> *The forms of things unknown, the poet's pen*
> *Turns them to shapes, and gives to airy nothing*
> *A local habitation and a name.*
>
> —*Theseus in* A Midsummer Night's Dream

A play is like a tropical bird—at once exotic in its song and plumage, half-seen and mystical in its darting flight, and elusive and difficult to capture. Our forebears called the makers of these special stories play*wrights* on the assumption that a play could be made, just as other craftsmen could make ships (shipwright) or wheels (wheelwright). The product of the playwright, to be sure, is not nearly so concrete, for he is a conscious dreammaker, as Shakespeare says, who can, with the appropriate use of basic tools, stir up minds and create imaginative flights in others—the audience.

The peculiar characteristic of the playwright's making, the thing that differentiates it from other writing, is that the playwright's "dream-flight," his *improvisation,* has to take into account not only vocal and visual instruments (the actors) but also the peculiar place around which or in front of which he can gather his audience to hear and watch the story (the stage). The playwright is a rare artist because what he puts down on paper, at its most demanding level, is not really writing in the usual literary sense—that is, writing intended for consumption in solitude by one person at a time—but is the making of a thing that involves live *actors* and *objects* set out in a specific way for seeing and hearing *by a group* meeting together in a group belonging (the audience). What the playmaker leaves out—the gap for the actors to fill in—is usually as important as what he puts in. French actor-director Jean-Louis Barrault described a play as "interrupted silence." This concept moves us entirely away from thinking about a play as a literary product, *as merely conversation written down,* for we see it is far more difficult to leave out than to put in. Many celebrated novelists and poets have tried unsuccessfully to make "interrupted silences," but they abandoned their efforts, or audiences forced them to, when they discovered that they didn't have the know-how to devise this sort of skeletal improvisation. Nor did they know what to do with a live audience.

You should not be at all surprised to learn that such famous playwrights as Aeschylus, Shakespeare, and Molière acted in and often directed their own plays. After all, they knew, or assumed that they knew, as everybody else did, what their plays were all about. Today, a playwright also hears his words in his mind's ear and sees the actions in his mind's eye when he composes a play. The total thing is the dramatic poem—what the play does to an audience by arousing its emotions directly. *The process is physical and disturbing,* and it is only *secondarily intellectual,* though the experience requires a perceptive intelligence—which is not quite the same thing. When it works, it reaches out to grab and thrill; it can cause tears and laughter, chills and anger; it can also exhaust members of an audience as well as exalt them. Its powers are mystical and godlike. We can retain a well-performed play in our minds for years in the same way that we hold onto an intensively felt personal experience, because characters in plays can seem like friends of many years' acquaintance.

Perception: Play-Analysis

Many people in the theatre shy away from the phrase *play-analysis* because they think it has a dry, academic ring that implies cold, factual, scientific examination of a playscript, a process that will kill their gut (subjective) feelings about it. They assume that good theatre can be made if one *feels* strongly enough about a playscript; good sense and some general background in theatre will carry one the rest of the way. This book does not agree at all with that point of view. Certainly, there are aspects of many plays that cannot be described easily in words, but this difficulty does not suggest that a play exists in a mystical world, defying logical, mind-oriented examination. Having the right attitude about play-analysis at the beginning is very important.

The word *perception* has specific meanings here because it can imply both strong feelings (the subjective flight and freedom in a director) and a basic objective awareness of how a play is made. It implies much more than a felt reaction on a first reading: "I like that play. It moves me strongly." Perception implies that a penetrating search into a play—play-analysis—is absolutely necessary if one is to understand how a play works.

What a director finds in play-analysis will depend on how thoroughly he can take a play apart in his own mind and then put it back together again, thoroughly comprehended. Perception is the director's total view of a playscript after he has "felt" it and then "examined" its structure in detail. If his feelings are strong on the first reading, and he knows the job of play-analysis, he cannot help but have much greater respect and admiration for a play after analysis than he had before. At the very least, he will at least not be ambivalent about it.

Play-analysis, then, is the director's objective support *for his feelings* about a playscript *and his imaginative responses to it*. As a technique, it is tied to the primary thesis that directing is not a totally intuitive process but is also an art-creating process in which the director brings the materials (the playscript) of the form to the conscious surface. In other words, the director becomes *consciously* aware of the materials in the interest of finding their strengths and weaknesses, their peaks and valleys, and their rhythms, all of which will serve as a basis for theatricalizing the playscript in the best possible way. Adequate play-analysis is no guarantee of success, but it does ensure that the director is at least familiar with his materials.

Overview of Play-Analysis

Study the following drawing very carefully. It is a summary of what you will be investigating not only in Part I on play-analysis but also in Parts II and III as you work at putting a play on stage.

You should note in the drawing the five major areas to examine in taking a play apart: (1) given circumstances, (2) dialogue, (3) dramatic action, (4) characters, and (5) idea. Not seen in the drawing are rhythmic beats: (6) tempos and (7) moods. Although this breakdown is arbitrary for the purpose of explicit discussion, you should recognize at the outset that these areas overlap, as the drawing illustrates, and that some of these areas are so thoroughly dependent on others that they do not take shape until the force of the others has been determined. Other words might be used to define the same concepts, but this set, when fully delineated, answers the purpose very well. Basic communication in textbooks rests on clear definition of the terms used. Therefore, you must recognize at this point that play-analysis in this book is based on the meanings given to the terms here and in the following chapters. For the purpose of discussion, the seven areas are treated in three chapters: Chapter 3, "The Foundation and Facade of the Playscript: Given Circumstances and Dialogue"; Chapter 4, "The Core of the Playscript: Dramatic Action and Characters"; and Chapter 5, "Idea and Rhythmic Beats."

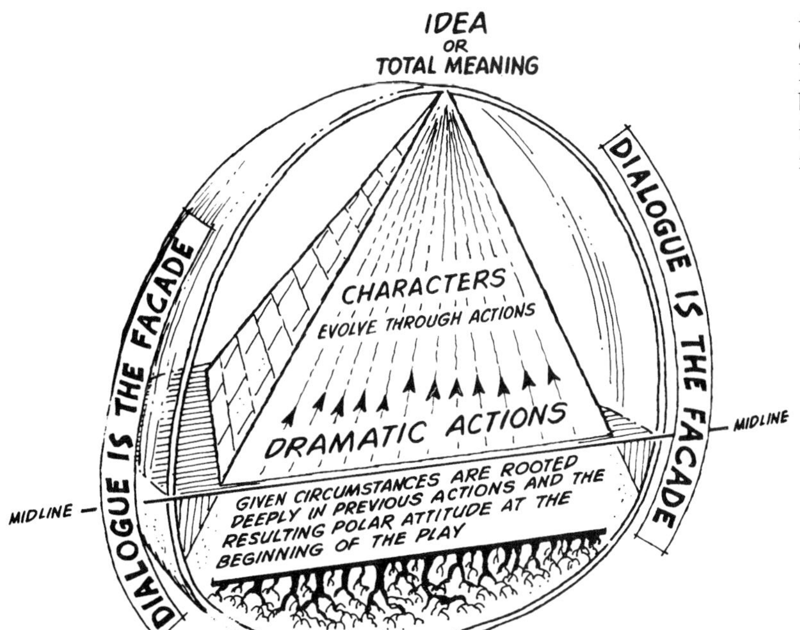

A graphic representation of dramatic structure. Note the midline: A play begins here, recapturing the past and moving forward to the present.

You must also be alerted at this point to a matter of great importance: Each of these words (for example, *dialogue*) or two-word phrases (for example, *given circumstances*) stands for a concept. Merely to define them is not to understand them. As in acting, *doing* in directing will lie not in defining terms or in debating concepts but in absorbing them so thoroughly that they are immediately recognizable in all contexts. You must discover for yourself the breadth and depth of these concepts so that they become an intuitive part of your thinking about a play.

In the discussions of the seven areas, the terms are first defined and then developed as concepts. Some examples are given to illustrate each step in this technique, but your comprehension will come about only through application of the approach to specific plays. There is no skipping around in this procedure. Try to understand and apply the concept of one term before you go on to the next. The series of seven is developed in an intentional order to show how each draws on what precedes it.

At first, you will be tempted to push aside the in-depth examination of these concepts. After all, simple impression—"I *feel* it this way"—is much easier. But if you proceed in this fashion, you will soon discover that you really do not know much about the inside workings of a play and that you do not really know *how to get through to actors.* Once you have mastered the techniques outlined here, you will feel a security you have not known previously, for you will know something very specific about your primary tool—the playscript.

Story versus Play-Analysis

Another problem usually confronting students in their first contacts with play-analysis is the difference between the playscript as mere story and the structure of that story. The story of a play is made up of so many things so well blended together that an unoriented reader merely experiences its final effect: its moods and its feelings. But through play-analysis, the director can get at what makes those moods and feelings. Thus, he can have greater assurance of getting the most out of his actors and in moving the audiences. In comparison with live theatre, the motion picture, as a form, is fixed because each scene has been perfected through several takes and is impervious to change. In the theatre, however, a playscript is made up of a series of scenes that must be played continuously without interruption, and then repeated at subsequent performances. This living quality is its individuality and its rarity. Your awareness of play structure, then, will give you the seeds for all that can happen later when you put a play into production.

EXERCISES

1. Discuss all the parts of the following premises of this book:
   a. A play is a symbolic device using live actors on a stage and a live audience for showing human beings caught in reciprocal tension and conflict.
   b. Directing is the process of revealing the conflict by coordinating and enhancing the work of live actors with that of designers in order to communicate a single vision of a play to a live audience.
2. What is a dramatic poet? Why is a modern writer of drama in prose also a dramatic poet? How does a play differ from a novel or a history?
3. Without getting involved in the complexities of the differences between serious drama and comedy, why is the writer of comedy also a dramatic poet?
4. The director is an image-maker. What is an image? Cite images of each of the five senses.
5. From your knowledge of acting and designing, can you see how an audience perceives a play through images? What is the process of transfer?

A Suggested Study Plan for Parts I and II

To coordinate all the new words and phrases you will be introduced to in the following chapters, and to learn more about play-analysis, two work tools are suggested at this point: a class study play and the process of improvisation. Both are ways of helping you discover what goes on in plays.

A. The Play Choice as a Tool

A one-act play of high quality should be selected by your class, or the instructor, as a common device for ensuing discussions. One suggestion might be J. M. Synge's familiar classic *Riders to the Sea.* (STOP: *Riders* is a Realistic play with a style many recent students of theatre turn off as old-fashioned and no longer effective. Realism is far from dead. It has been a dominant style in the theatre since Ibsen's day and is still the dominant style you see in motion pictures and television drama. Those of you who would neglect the study of Realism and long to make theatre stand on its own as distinct from the electronic media fail to see how the "new" is always tied to the old in an ever-changing form.) *Riders* is so well put together, so well constructed, that it has withstood nearly a century of picking apart while still retaining things to wonder about. It has survived because it is a dramatic poem of true stature and intensive meaning. At first, it may seem simple to you, but you will be looking at the outside, not the inside. If you are to understand much about the changes playwrights made in the twentieth century, you must take apart a Realistic play—a play that looks like life around you—and reassemble it fully understood; otherwise, you will get lost in disassembling those that are not realistic. Save those until later.

To offset what may seem old-fashioned about *Riders,* your class may want to look regularly at one or two other plays, chosen from later periods, to act as "control" plays. One of those might be a one-act play by Tennessee Williams, written during the 1940s or 1950s, and the other a one-act play by Edward Albee or Sam Shepard. Can you see how they differ from *Riders*? Don't let your enthusiasm to direct recent plays kill off what what you must learn now about the structure of all plays. Once you understand the principles of play-analysis, and something about Realism, you will be able to disassemble all kinds of plays, including musicals and operas, and make them work for you on the stage. The theatre will wait for you, but it will not want you if you don't know what is going on there.

B. Improvisation as a Tool

In this book, the technique of *improvisation* is suggested throughout as a classroom work method. In its early uses, improvisation was thought of primarily as Stanislavskian training for the actor, but as its values and possibilities became more apparent, it was used not only in the relationship between director and actor but also as a basis for playmaking. Consequently, not only were a number of experimental motion pictures made by using this approach, but the live productions of the Open Theatre and the Living Theatre in the 1960s showed us that unusual productions could also be developed through this technique. The improvisational approach as a method of freeing both actors and directors in training is still quite valid.

A play's written text is the form that has resulted from a series of improvisations that have been played out, developed, and refined as part of the imaginative, creative process in the playwright's mind. Subsequent interpreters of the play, including directors, designers, and actors, must be able to perceive and then release that master improvisation captured in the play's text—release it to new life in a theatrical production. To do this, it is important for directors and all the creative collaborators to develop their skills in improvisation and to perceive how form ultimately arises from this fertile aspect of the creative process. Each member of the collaborative creative team goes through a series of improvisations in the development of the production, whether in the give and take of director-designer collaboration or the interplay of directors and actors in rehearsal.

The director is therefore an improvisor of the first order. In this sense, he is very close to the playwright, who turns his dreams into forms—all controlled improvisations. The director is forever a game-player, always improvising, always making up spontaneously what seems appropriate and believable in a given circumstance.

You will note as you work through this book that many of the exercises require improvisation—spontaneous storytelling in declared or undeclared circumstances. If you have participated in such game playing, you will already know that improvising can make something very much like a play, but it is not a play at all, only an exercise in releasing imagination. The overall intention is to free those persons who play the game—to let them "fly." But in order to do so, several conditions are necessary. Here are a few that must guide you and your classmates when doing improvisations:

1. The participants are not actors; that is, they are neither acting out a portion of a playscript nor are they performing for an audience. Their intention is to *release each other* through full concentration on each other and the situation. Although some given circumstances may be set before an improvisation begins, the participants "work off" one another, with their imaginations dictating what to do in a certain context. There is no preplan of action. What happens will happen only as participants let their behavior, in reaction to other forces (other people in the same improvisation), be the result of their responses.
2. The watchers are not the audience. They are privileged to be there when the improvisation takes place. Therefore, they must not participate like an audience, but should watch silently and quietly with no verbal reactions whatsoever, because this would break the "happening" by distracting the participants, thus making them self-conscious. Once the participants become self-aware, the improvisation is lost because they have become themselves and not participants in an imagined circumstance.
3. The place to develop an improvisation is not a stage nor any location that would resemble it, because the artificial nature of this kind of setting would cause the improvisers to feel self-conscious. For this reason, this game should be played in a room, with the space defined only by what the improvisers find necessary.
4. Only the beginning of an improvisation should be suggested and only in a barely minimal way. What happens afterward is the improvisation.

It is obvious that a good deal that is playlike can happen in improvisations if the participants and watchers observe the conditions. You can see characters in action, with different moods and tempos, and, as a watcher, you can be moved by the truth telling and believability of such moments. But you must also realize that "achieving" a complex improvisation is not easily accomplished unless you have participants with experience in playing this game, because learning to release fully takes practice. In working through the exercises in this book, you must always give yourself seriously and with full concentration to improvisational exercises. If you do, you will find them most rewarding.

EXERCISES

1. Illustrate the difference between *restriction* and *flight* by doing the following improvisation: With the use of chairs, tables, or other essentially neutral forms in the classroom, compose a four-sided place. The class then tries to guess the *literal* place suggested by the forms and their arrangement by identifying the literal meaning of each form—such as a chair, a bed, a sofa—in the context of other forms. When a consensus has been reached on the literal meaning, the class suggests *alternate meanings* for the forms, with the intention of arriving at more exceptional locations and contexts. Thus, what might at first seem to be a normal suburban living room could be turned into the mountain hideout of a gangster or the primitive hut of a peasant. Repeat this game with several improvised places. The "flight" takes place as class members move away from accepted literal meanings of forms in their easily recognizable contexts—their own everyday realities—and begin to let the forms take on imagined places. Thus, *forms become the stimulators of flight,* not hard realities. (*Note:* This exercise is not that of making a groundplan for a stage, so do not set up the places with a stage in mind but only as places that could exist in real life anywhere.)
2. Continue Improvisation Exercise 1, arranging a place and then setting in it two people who have a specific relationship to each other, such as mother/son, boss/secretary, boy/girl. The class tries first to declare the literal place and its context; it then tries to identify possible "flights" by suggesting more exceptional places and relationships of the people.
3. Continue Improvisation Exercise 2 by having the students in the improvisation *develop a conflict* by using numbers, not words, as dialogue. Example: *A* says: 1, 2, 3, 4; *B* says: 9, 10, 20; *A* says: 2, 3, 6, 7; *B* says: 4, 7, 9, 10. In this substitute for dialogue, the numbers do not mean anything in themselves, but the attitude behind each group of numbers is the basic meaning behind the line. (The use of actual words in improvisations is very difficult for participants because they must think in terms of word choice. Number dialogue is much easier because participants need think only of their attitudes toward other people in the improvisation.) When the improvisers reach an intensity of interresponse, the improvisation can be stopped and the following points discussed:
   a. What is improvisation?
   b. What are the free circumstances of an improvisation?
   c. How was this improvisation like a play and yet not a play?
   d. What is a play? (Try defining it as an expert and highly developed improvisation.)
   e. What did the participants add to the suggested beginning of the improvisation?
   f. What are the limitations in the use of number dialogue?

Part I

Taking a Play Apart

Play-Analysis: The Director's Primary Study

[Alfred Hitchcock] is a magnificently prepared director. There is nothing that he does not know about the picture he is going to do. Every angle and every set-up he has prepared at home. . . . He does not even look into the camera, for he says, "I know what it looks like."

—Ingrid Bergman, *My Story*

3

The Foundation and Façade of the Playscript

Given Circumstances and Dialogue

After you have read the following pages, you will understand why the title of this chapter is "The Foundation and Façade of the Playscript." All you need to understand at this point, however, is that given circumstances and dialogue *frame* the play, just as deeply rooted pilings and a covering of glass and steel frame a modern skyscraper. The given circumstances resemble the deeply rooted base of a building—the substructure and foundation on which it is built; and dialogue is the outer shell, the façade, the transparent encasement covering the activities that will go on inside. If you keep these images in mind, you will be able to see why the real guts of the play (its core) reside in dramatic action and characters, but that they cannot be built into the structure without the foundation of given circumstances and the façade of dialogue.

Given Circumstances (Playwright's Setting): The Foundation

Definition

The term *given circumstances* (the playwright's setting) concerns all material in a playscript that delineates the environment—or the special "world" of the play—in which the action takes place. This material includes (1) environmental facts (the specific conditions, place, and time); (2) previous action (all that has happened before the action begins); and (3) polar attitudes (points of view toward their environment held by the principal characters).

Given Circumstances versus Playwright's Setting

Although Russian actor-director-producer Konstantin Stanislavski's phrase *given circumstances* will be used throughout this text after this initial explanation, the parenthetical phrase *playwright's setting* is also used because you are probably more familiar with it. However, as a term, it is so frequently confused with what a designer makes—the actual stage construction—that you should avoid using it altogether. Many readers of plays, including students of the theatre early in their training, commonly assume that the explicit directions describing a room or other location that usually appear in the printed editions of modern plays have been set down by their authors. However, more often than not, they depict the settings used in the first production and thus represent the conception of the designers as recorded by a stage manager or an editor. Even when such a description comes from an author's own manuscript, a further danger exists because the author may try to play the role of stage designer, a role about which he may know little or nothing at all. If you, as a reader-director, are not aware of this pitfall, you may find it very difficult to free yourself from these initial suggestions because the printed word may seduce you. There is much less harm in reading these directions after you have studied the play, for then you will have a strong conception of the inherent setting, and you can separate what the author considers significant about an environment from a designer's interpretation of it.

Dialogue is the only reliable source of given circumstances. As you study plays, you will quickly become aware that all authors write their settings directly into their dialogue, either overtly or subconsciously. Given circumstances are a matter of feeling about objects and places, about time and what has happened before the play begins, and about the feelings of the characters for the special world of the play. The totality is what a playwright must communicate to the audience as deftly and as accurately as possible, for what happens in a play will be based on these given circumstances.

Analyzing the Given Circumstances

You will note in the following discussion that the first two topics—Environmental Facts and Previous Action—are far more factual than the third—Polar Attitudes. Yet, it is this last area that will actually set up the beginning point of a play, because it is the most important aspect of the given circumstances. Look for the facts, yes; but the attitudes of characters toward those facts are extremely important.

Environmental facts. All plays establish some delineation of the exact place and time of the action as well as give specific information about the environment. These elements are called the *facts of the play,* regardless of whether the playwright has been historically accurate, because they remain fixed throughout the play. The director should isolate these facts by systematically noting them under the following categories:

1. *Geographical location.* The geographical location refers to the exact place. This category should also include climate, because weather often defines specific location and can affect dramatic action.
2. *Date.* The date includes the year, season, and time of day. Ask yourself: What is significant about the date?
3. *Economic environment.* The economic environment is the class level and the state of wealth or poverty. If two or more economic levels are used in a play, be certain to record the facts of each level. (In telling the story of the play and in communicating with actors, it is often important to understand who controls money in the world of the play, because this affects the choices characters make in the struggle of the dramatic action.)
4. *Political environment.* The political environment refers to the specific relationships of the characters to the form of government under which they live. Many plays have definite political settings that will strongly affect the behavior of the characters. Many other plays tacitly accept a form of government that has established basic restrictions on the characters. Do not take what you may think is direct omission to mean that it is unimportant. Look carefully for clues throughout the script, because the author may be taking this given circumstance for granted on the assumption that those who read the play will understand the context. But *you* cannot make such an assumption. The author will leave a trail of implications behind, and you must dig these out.
5. *Social environment.* The social environment is the mores and social institutions under which the characters live. These facts are extremely important because they may be manifested through their restrictions on the outward behavioral patterns of the characters; consequently, they may set up basic conflicts in the action of the play.
6. *Religious environment.* The religious environment consists of formal and informal psychological controls. Much that applies to item 4 also applies here.

When you study the given circumstances of a play, you must strictly avoid reading anything into the play; all facts must be explicitly stated or implied, as suggested in item 4 of the list. Do not assume anything. Some plays will involve all of these categories; others will involve only some of them. Above all, *do not try to reconstruct your own idea of historical fact* surrounding a play; *if it is not in the play, it does not exist.* A playwright is not writing a history but telling a story; he may not know his history well at all, or he may be deliberately shifting the facts to suit his own purposes. Do not try to correct him; rather, you should record his facts exactly as he prescribes them.

Previous action. It is necessary to make a sharp distinction between *present action* (what an audience actually sees *happening* immediately in front of it) and *previous action* (what an audience is *told happened before the present action begins*). All plays begin somewhere in the middle or toward the end of things; thus, given circumstances usually include some *narration* of past action so that the present action has a base from which to move forward. More recent plays, those written since the early 1960s, depend very little on past action, whereas others (those of Ibsen, for instance) require much retelling of past events. Both kinds of action—previous and present—are included in what is loosely defined as a story. But the director always works specifically with *present action,* although one of the major problems is to decide how to make the necessary narrations about the past as active as possible. In modern plays based on psychological revelation, the past plays an enormous part in the explanation, as it does in a Freudian psychoanalysis; yet, the vital play for audiences lies only in what is actively happening immediately before its eyes.

You must learn to separate these two kinds of action. The previous action, though it may take all of the first act and sometimes longer to narrate fully, establishes the point where the present action actually begins. Once you learn how to make this distinction, you will know how to make a narration of the past interesting on the stage, for narration in itself is very dull compared to present action. A good playwright will make narration exciting by giving the character a present action in the process of recalling it; that is, he will arrange for the recounting to do something to a character we are watching. Thus, to the director, there is never a dull exposition but only *a recalling of the past under the excitement and tension of active engagement with other characters in the present.* A director who does not know this point of structure will lose control of his audience very quickly. He will lose the key to handling the plays of Ibsen and Chekhov as well as a great deal of Realistic drama.

Because you will likely be dealing with plays that span the entire range of what may be broadly termed Realist drama, works from the mid- to late nineteenth century on down to the present, it is important to understand that previous action is one of the structural components to have undergone change in the way dramatists have deployed it in their playwriting. As Realism developed as a style in the twentieth century, certain dramatists began to use previous action in subtly different ways from how earlier Realist playwrights such as Ibsen, Shaw, and Chekhov had used it. Pirandello, for example, in such seminal plays as *Right You Are, If You Think You Are,* and *Six Characters in Search of an Author,* showed that a group of characters (not unlike people in real life) may have different memories or interpretations of what happened in the past with these differences feeding the present conflict and thus the dramatic action in a profound way. In some ways Pirandello, a key figure in the evolution of dramatic style, seems to use previous action to demonstrate that the past may not always be entirely knowable. Later in the century, dramatists such as Harold Pinter and Sam Shepard developed previous action even further as a structural component of story. In plays such as Pinter's *The Birthday Party* or Shepard's *Buried Child,* explicit explication of the previous action may be minimal on certain key points, lending a certain mystery to the basic situation the characters find themselves in, much as sometimes happens in life, wherein the past is not always evident, especially to participants in the story who may not have been present. But whether the previous action is as explicitly delineated as in Ibsen or as partially revealed (and mysterious) as in some Pinter plays, mastery of the previous action in terms of finding how it relates to the present dramatic action is one of the director's most important duties. And, like getting into the inner workings of a good detective story, this can be deeply satisfying and even fun for both director and actors.

A technique for separating these two areas of action is the simple one of underlining in the text all lines that *recall* the past. A text by Ibsen contains many such lines, particularly in the first act; and often there are important revelations later in the play, especially when new characters are introduced. If you list these previous actions on one-half of a sheet of paper as they are introduced and then write down the present actions, you will see their direct relationship.

A director can obscure a production by careless inattention to previous action, for some playwrights handle the necessary recalling in such subtle ways that an audience will miss important points unless the director carefully sets them out. Plays do not "talk" themselves; they are communicated by actors and directors who know what they are "talking" about. Congreve's *The Way of the World* is one of the greatest plays in the English language. However, if an audience misses the point—made very briefly in one line, that Mirabell was once a lover to Mrs. Fainall, that he left her pregnant, and that he arranged for her marriage to Fainall—the import of most of the action that follows involving Mirabell as well as Fainall will be misunderstood and its significance lost. This example is extreme, but in kind it is forever recurring. Learn what previous action is and then you will know what to do with it in production.

Polar attitudes. All characters in a play, as in real life, are conditioned by the special world they are caught in, the world of their own prejudices, tolerances and intolerances, and assumptions when they are forced to have relationships with others and must take actions affecting themselves and others. The special world of a character is conditioned, of course, by environmental facts and by previous action. Although it depends on these concrete details, it differs explicitly in that it is the "emotional environment" of a character, the stresses and strains under which that character lives. Modern slang would call them "hang-ups." The special world of the principal character is always declared *at the beginning of a play* because it declares his position vis-à-vis the other characters. This is the *inner environment* of a play that sets up the conflicts and the problems: the environment of love relationships in and out of marriage; the environment of family pressures that cause love and hate between mothers and sons, fathers and sons, and mothers and daughters; the environment of political, religious, and social pressures that force people to behave in ways that may destroy their families and their relationships to these families; the environments of fear of power, disregard of others, indifference to wealth or love of wealth, and indifference to religion or its opposite. *A character is caught in this special world, and the play is about how he is destroyed by it or escapes from it.*

Here is an important fact about plays: In the course of a play, a principal character *does not change in character, but his attitudes change* under pressures from forces outside his control. The other characters serve as specific instruments to these changes. As the principal character meets these forces, he must adjust to them, and, as he does so, certain capabilities dormant within him (his true character) come to the surface and force him to act. These capabilities have been present all the time, but they have never been called on and thus recognized as points of character. The development in a play's action, therefore, is composed of the changing attitudes in the principal character toward his *inner* environment, toward *his special world* as it was declared at the beginning of the play.

It is also important to point out that all of the characters in a play do not change their attitudes, but only the principal characters, a fact that makes them principal. Secondary characters thus act as instruments in these changes. In a play-analysis, it is always the primary characters that concern us most, for then we can determine the exact force and functions of the secondary characters.

Most plays show radical shifts in the attitudes of their principal characters from the *positions they held at the beginning* to those they hold at the end. A philosophical way of expressing this shift is to say that a character moves from ignorance to knowledge. He sees the world in which he lives more and more clearly *after* the actions he has been forced to take during the course of the play than he did before. Thus, it is necessary to pin down the attitudes toward the inner environment (special world) held at the beginning of a play by a principal character so that a director can clearly see the final pole of his character and can later help the actor find both poles, as well as help the other characters see their functions in the change. What happens in between these poles is the dramatic action.

By setting out the polar attitudes of each principal character, the director can see the scope of what happens in between the poles—the stretch of the characters—and the explicit effects that given circumstances have on the characters. Thus, the shape of the play is explicitly declared in the polarities of the principal character.

What is meant by the beginning of a play, then, is the defined positions of the attitudes held by the principal character of the play toward the special world he is caught in and within which he takes action. These positions declare explicitly where the *present action* begins. The characters in most plays (Ionesco's antihero is an exception) will have strong feelings of either like or dislike for the present inner environment in which they find themselves. The plot that follows (present action) will either shake them loose from their liking or bring their dislike to liking (or at least to acceptance). If a character does not finally accept what he dislikes at the beginning of a play, he will probably die or exile himself in the process of resisting the forced change that others bring on him and become what is called a *tragic hero*. In comedy, if a character strongly resists being pried loose from what he already likes intensely at the beginning, he will survive, but he will be ridiculed and become what is called a *comic fool*. But whatever happens to him, the attitudes he has at the beginning will certainly be radically changed by the end, or if he is a certain kind of comic fool, he may go on blissfully, never realizing that anyone has tried to change him.

An attitude toward the special world at the beginning of a play is usually more general than specific. It is usually something the character has taken for granted as the natural state of affairs, and he is therefore not consciously aware of it, although it most certainly will be pointed out to the audience in one way or another. The action of the play will make him aware of his special world because it will subject him to a test of his attitudes through direct conflict with others. The initial action in a play will usually point out to him where he stands in contrast to others, although he may be very blind about why he stands where he does. The attitudes of characters, then, should be general statements and not tied specifically to the present action that will follow. Here are some examples of initial attitudes:

> Men are foolish and romantic and can be manipulated rather easily. (Hedda in *Hedda Gabler.* What is her final attitude?)
>
> The only thing that really matters is money. (Regina in *The Little Foxes.* What is her final attitude?)
>
> "Good" women are dull, embarrassing, and impossible to talk to. (Marlowe in *She Stoops to Conquer.* What is his final attitude?)
>
> A king is sacred and no one can challenge his God-given right to dictate. (Oedipus in *Oedipus Rex.* What is his final attitude?)
>
> Love of women is all romantic adoration and worship. (Marchbanks in *Candida.* What is his final attitude?)

When you have learned to pinpoint the special world of a play, you will understand the secret of its inner workings because you will know what the environmental forces are that hold the principal characters in check at the beginning. This knowledge will show you what they must fight against to overcome those forces in order to arrive at the final pole.

In the actual practice of trying to determine polar attitudes, it is usually easier to find the initial pole for each character by noting what has happened to each character at the end. Remember that the interest of an audience will be focused on what happens between the poles, for this is the dramatic action, the specifics that bring about the change in the principal characters. This is what holds the audience so riveted to the play and what makes the change so climactic, so theatrical, and so emotionally disturbing.

EXERCISES

1. Using any Realistic play (*Riders to the Sea, Ghosts, Hedda Gabler, American Buffalo,* etc.), list the environmental facts in the specific categories suggested in this chapter. What do these facts suggest about a possible stage setting? Can you "see" the setting? Can you visualize some possible costumes? What do they tell you about body movement? About decorum? Do they suggest what the characters think about and what they feel? What does physical circumstance (environmental fact) have to do with human behavior?
2. Delineate the previous action in the same play you have studied in Exercise 1 by underlining all the parts of the speeches in the first act that literally refer to actions that have happened *before* the here-and-now of the act begins. If you are looking at *Hedda Gabler* or another play by Ibsen, how many lines by actual count contain references to

previous actions? (Be very careful not to include those recountings of actions that the audience has already witnessed as present actions; those narrations are present actions because the playwright intends the audience to weigh and evaluate a character in terms of that character's judgments of what has happened.) In your own judgment, what is the effect of this accumulation of knowledge about the past? Does it have any effect on what is happening in the present? Does it tell us anything about the characters? Can you see why it is unimportant in itself, but only as it affects a character's present action?

3. *Very important:* As an alternate exercise, study several opening pages of a play by listing the previous action on one side of a sheet and the present action on the other. In this way, you have a ready comparison of what the playwright is actually doing.
4. In working with the same play used in Exercises 1 through 3, delineate the attitude of each major character toward the special world or the inner emotional environment of the play—that is, what each major character thinks and feels about life around him. Whether he likes it or not is unimportant; what he likes about it or does not like about it is very important. Look for such hidden attitudes as love for others, fear of power, disregard of others, indifference to wealth, and indifference to religious feeling. Does he admire monarchy? Does he love freedom? Let the emotional environment tell you exactly how each major character reacts to the given world at the beginning of the play.

Dialogue: The Façade of the Playscript

Now that you understand the roots of a play—where, when, and how it derives from the immediate past (the given circumstances)—you are ready to examine its façade: the clothes on the package. What is inside will be given special attention in Chapter 4 when you study dramatic action and characters. But for now, you need to become aware that dialogue is not just the things people say but also, far more importantly, *what they do.*

Definition

Although dialogue is obviously the conversation between two or more characters in a play, it is not so obvious that its primary function is *to "contain" the dramatic action,* to be its primary vehicle. In addition, although dialogue may appear as a written line on a printed page, its primary intention is to be *heard* rather than read. It is talk and not writing.

Dialogue Is Action

Dialogue is not merely a verbal interchange between characters; rather, it is an artificial, highly economical, and symbolic intercommunication of *actions* between characters in which each forces his wants and needs on the other. *Dialogue always exists in the present tense* because it comes out of the mouths of speakers who think, as in life, only in the present and who say things to one another to get what they want.

Dialogue Is a Building Process

A says something to *B*, and *B* replies; this talk causes *A* to reply to *B* and *B* to *A* in a continuing cycle. But no matter how refined a line of dialogue may be, no matter how elaborate the choice of words, the purpose is always the same: to seek response out of another person, just as we do in real life.

Thus, the nature of dialogue is its built-in characteristic of *forcing*. The words used on the outside may try to conceal this forcing in a very elaborate way, or they may be very direct and not conceal it at all. From a casual reader's view, dialogue looks like it is only the printed text of the play, but its basic function is to contain the heart and soul, the blood and guts of the play—the *subtext* or dramatic action.

Dialogue Is in Verse or Prose

Plays vary greatly in the choice of language used by characters. This choice is dictated by the given circumstances, because they specifically delineate the decorum or outward show—that is, how the characters behave (their manners or lack of manners). Most modern plays have prose dialogue because of its likeness to the reality of everyday life, but a few are written in verse forms, as were many plays of the past. Verse forms are obviously more artificial in their use of language than is prose, but the basic intent is always the same: the containment of the dramatic action. More will be said about verse later in Chapter 29 in the discussion of plays of past ages, but it is sufficient to point out here that verse form is not merely a decorative exterior but a heightened, more compact, exalting language for conveying intense feelings and high actions. The effect of verse is often as potent as physical body movements, simply because verse conveys intensive inner feelings at the highest pitch. It thus has the capability of direct contact with an audience. This is why many playwrights who write dialogue in prose often try to find a language somewhat more elevated than what is used in everyday life, as Arthur Miller did in *The Crucible.*

Dialogue Is Inner Language

Dialogue should be analyzed in detail to discover its peculiar characteristics in addition to its function as a cover for dramatic action and its direct reflection of given circumstances. Even within the narrow range of the given circumstances for a particular play, an author has a large scope in his choice of words and their arrangement and in the images he may devise. Dialogue is thus said to be *connotative* rather than denotative—much more weighted with feeling and meaning than dictionary usage or definitive meaning. In the human context of plays, characters feel or sense one another (as people who live closely together do in everyday life) and consequently do not talk *at* one another but *with* one another. Thus, the language of drama is highly subjective, inner language. Realism has used a wide variety of folk-speech patterns—dialects—in the interest of showing how people talk from their "guts" and not from their minds. Motion pictures have fully exploited this aspect of dialogue, particularly in reproducing low-level environments.

Dialogue Is Heard Language

Any study of a play written in dialect requires penetration beyond the choice of words and the modification of vowels, for an author who has really heard the speech he uses for a certain character will reproduce all sorts of cultural overtones buried in the outer form, a subtle delineation of given circumstances. Thus, the speech sounds of Brooklyn or Dublin or London reflect the hardness of city life, just as southern (U.S.) speech reflects the slower rhythm of the rural South. Most recent plays that intend reproduction of local idiom (August Wilson's plays, for instance) do not set down the modifications of sound in spelling as playwrights once did, but rely on the specific choice of words or lack of them to convey the inarticulate aspects of the characters. The dialect (sound quality) is thus left to the actor to supply.

Directors must therefore learn to hear dialogue in the mind's ear—not only the literal reproductions of sound as they hear it in everyday life but also the reproduction of word-feeling as playwrights set them out in characters. You must learn the craft of matching speech decorum, as perceived in a play's text from the given circumstances, to character decorum. More will be said about this technique later in connection with acting and actors. (See Exercise 2 that follows in this chapter.)

Dialogue Is Structured of Lines and Speeches

As has already been pointed out, dialogue is artificially contrived. A close examination of any good play will show that the author has usually arranged his sentence structure to throw the important phrase—the actual point of each line—to the end of the line. This placement makes it climactic. Speeches made up of several sentences are carefully constructed in the same way. When a director is aware of this technique, he can be more certain of getting good line readings from his actors, and he will be more able to accomplish the desirable emphasis that he knows the play requires throughout.

The director's knowledge of line and speech structure can be aided greatly by the study of what is labeled "Interpretation" or "Interpretive Reading" in university curricula. In that study, the attention is concentrated on word and line values. At its base is the study of grammar, for grammar is the basis of effective speech, although no one actually thinks of grammar in carrying on a conversation. No director can go very far with actors, however, without a full awareness of word forms and punctuation, and their distinctive uses in the interlocking arrangements that comprise sentence structure. Many directors and actors trained in Stanislavskian approaches assume that if the subtext of a line is fully comprehended, the technical delivery of that line is assured. This assumption is simply not true, for the subtext and the text must both be communicated. This double value will be discussed in detail in Chapter 15 on the oral delivery of the text, but the important thing to understand here is that the *basis* for all dramatic meaning is the subtext—the inner quality of the line. This will be discussed in detail under Characteristics of Dramatic Action in the next chapter.

EXERCISES

1. Read aloud some dialogue from *Riders to the Sea* or another study play, and attempt to reproduce the lines according to the word order and other speech modifications. What does it sound like? Can you get in the swing of it? Now play a recording of an actor speaking in a dialect. Why does it sound more genuine than your attempts? Can you pick out any national characteristics in the sound alone? Can you hear social and economic circumstances? Can you hear the specific character traits in the sound?
2. Apply the same test to reruns of a television sitcom such as *Friends.* Can you visualize a "plain" script without the detailed inflections used by the actors? Why are the inflections so important to the dramatic action?
3. Examine some prose dialogue from a play by Eugene O'Neill. Point out the specific characteristics in the choice of words, the length of sentences and speeches, and the climactic build in each speech. Is the important word or phrase at the end? Does O'Neill seem to repeat any particular group of "sense" words? What does his dialogue sound like when spoken? Try it.
4. Watch and listen to two actors read aloud from a play by Harold Pinter. Examine in detail Pinter's development of a particular line, and then examine a group of lines. Do you hear given circumstances in the lines? What do you sense about the characters, about how inarticulate they are? What sort of dialects does Pinter intend?
5. Read aloud a passage from *La Bête* by David Hirson. Can you hear his regular beat, his verse form? What does the verse form do that prose would not do? Repeat the same experiment with T. S. Eliot's *Murder in the Cathedral.* Can you hear his different verse forms? Can you identify their beats (number of stresses in each line)? What does his word choice and verse form add that prose could not accomplish? For contrast, read aloud a passage from Eliot's *The Cocktail Party,* which he wrote in a verse form, although he declared that it ought to sound like prose.

Note: Exercise in the dramatic-action characteristics of dialogue is delayed until after the explanation of dramatic action in the next chapter.

4

The Core of the Playscript

Dramatic Action and Characters

Dramatic action is the clash of forces in a play—the continuous conflict between characters. Here lies the emotional content that moves audiences, for understanding the action will unlock the play. The hard core of all plays is thus action and characters—the instruments that *affect the action* or are affected by it and *forced to take action of their own.*

Dramatic action and the characters are thus inextricably tied together, a fact of dramatic form that you will understand better as you work through the contents of this chapter. The word *plot* is used here in the way playwrights or literary critics use it to describe the sequential arrangement of the conflict incidents that compose the action. For the purposes of detailed discussion in this chapter, dramatic action and characters are treated separately so that you can see their individual characteristics more clearly in isolation.

Understanding the nature and mechanics of dramatic action is a primary study of the director, because action is the life force of a play and because it is the living blood and viscera out of which all other forces grow. Unless the director comprehends its workings, he cannot possibly help the actors or effect the physical production. He will always be guessing. Again, what happens in a play is the action; it is what holds an audience, thrills them, or makes them laugh. As has already been pointed out, plays are not realities but artificial devices—contrivances, if you will—that may be likened, through analogy, to a human body. Just as the heart and other vital organs make possible living and breathing in the human being, so dramatic action provides the same life-giving force to the play.

Characteristics of Dramatic Action

Present Tense

Earlier, you learned that dramatic action exists only in the present tense. Thus, the participants in the action—the characters—are always in a state of "I do," not "I did." This is what gives the living quality to a play and what makes us aware that it is occurring here and now. Whenever two people meet in a play, as in real life, they start "doing" to each other, and this is what we watch through a time sequence. A play turns on life, and we watch and hear it being lived in front of us. There is never any past tense during a play's life; everything that happens, even the ways the previous action is conveyed, occurs in the present.

Dramatic Action Is Not Activity

It is important at the outset of this discussion to understand the difference between dramatic action and an actor's activity. The latter is the *illustration* of the action: what one actor or one director may have decided best shows the action. Such illustrations or pieces of business—sitting in a chair, crossing the stage, gesturing with the hand, and so on—can be infinite, but the basic dramatic action is fixed within a narrow range. *Acting is the process of illustrating the dramatic action—through activity. Activity is the how; action is the what.*

It is necessary to point out these distinctions, because the nineteenth-century common stage tradition usually accepted by actors and stage managers held that illustrations or pieces of business performed by actors were the actions themselves. This misconception of action has unfortunately been carried over into some theatre training with the result of placing a director's attention on superficialities rather than on basic drives and forces in a play. Understanding Realistic plays as well as knowing how to exploit the methods of the modern actor both require uncovering the dramatic action, for only then can the search for appropriate illustrations to externalize it take place. *Activities are thus the externalization of dramatic action.*

All Action Is Reciprocal

As defined previously, action is the clash of forces, the forces being the characters. All action, then, forces counteraction, or action in two directions with adjustments in between. The cycle goes this way: (1) *A* does to *B;* (2) *B* feels the force of *A*'s action (adjustment) and decides what action to take; (3) *B* does to *A;* (4) *A* feels the force of *B*'s action (adjustment) and decides what action to take. This cycle is then ready to begin again, but this time on a new and different level. This reciprocal process is carried on until either (1) *A* or *B* is destroyed; or (2) some outside force interrupts the progression (another character enters); or (3) the playwright arbitrarily concludes the action (end of scene).

Thus, all dramatic action is also *reciprocal;* there is no one-way road but always a *returned* action. Forcing goes on in both directions. Note that a very important part of this cycle lies in the *adjustment* that each character must make before taking a new action. As a result, much of the acting an actor does lies in receiving the force of the other character's action and in deciding what action to take himself. This not only excites the audience but it also moves the scene continuously forward.

The forcing or the doing, however, can take place in so many gradations that it frequently *looks* as though one character dominates the other so strongly that the scene gives the appearance of one-way action. This appearance is all a matter of quiet, low-key adjustment, however, as is the timing of the adjustment; the action will shift in the other direction before long, and the dominated becomes the dominator. Scenes in plays are composed of *A*'s dominance with *B* taking retreating actions; then *B* takes over and dominates *A*, who takes retreating action. The climax of the scene is reached when either *A* or *B* successfully dominates the other completely. But there is always another possible encounter, for a play is made up of delayed adjustments and the new actions they foment. Sooner or later, the dominated one will have another chance, with the possibility that he will emerge as the dominant force. A play moves forward, and the audience continues to be interested, just as long as *A* and *B* are in conflict over who will dominate. Once this question has been answered satisfactorily, a state of relative calm prevails, and the play is concluded.

Unless both characters (forces) are destroyed, the end of one play may only set up the given circumstances for the beginning of another one. It is possible, then, if characters are of sufficient interest, for a playwright to write more than one play about their conflicts, as did the Greeks and a few modern playwrights, such as Eugene O'Neill in *Mourning Becomes Electra* or Sam Shepard in certain of his family dramas, in which character names change, but the basic characters and conflicts emerge again and again. All endings of plays are contrived, and some rather unsatisfactorily. Rather than to say the dramatic action ends, it would be better to say that it is in a state of relative quiet, a dormant state awaiting new forces and pressures.

The Divisions of Action: Units

The total action of a play is divided into major sections. Because they intended their plays to be staged without interruption, the Greeks punctuated their major sections of action with choral songs, commenting on the action just seen or forecasting what is to come. Shakespeare ended his scenes with rhymed couplets and may have followed them with brief musical interludes. Today, we lower a curtain or the stage lights and give the audience a rest—an intermission—with the audience actually leaving their seats and moving about for 10 to 15 minutes. But whether we play the action continuously or take intermissions, we know that all plays are artificially constructed, that they are broken—plotted—into parts. The plot of a play, then, is the arrangement of the action: what a playwright thinks, out of a total possible story, must be shown to an audience. Thus, the play may be divided not only into acts but also into formal scenes—for example, Act I, Scene 2—each with arbitrary limits. The plays of the 1970s, 1980s, and 1990s may have multiple scenes to reveal prismatically several aspects of the action. Sometimes lighting is used to separate scenes, or a play may follow the Shakespearean mode of starting scenes in different places on the stage.

Printed playscripts in the French theatre, although they follow divisions into acts, further separate the action in a formal way that tells us much about all play construction. Whenever a character enters or exits, a new scene is declared and so marked in the text. This French method of marking scripts shows us that the major sections of action (the acts) in all plays are broken arbitrarily into many sections of action. These are delineated not only when a new character enters but also whenever characters in concert shift the line of talk (action) in a new direction or shift the dominant focus from one character to another. *A new unit is thus delineated.* The word *unit* is Stanislavski's word for divisions into dramatic action, his word for delineating all the segments of the plotting, even the very smallest ones. This definition provides a far better way for a director to see a play's action than by using the traditional act-scene concept or the division into French scenes, for he can then visualize the total action as one major unit broken into dozens of subunits, all interrelated and all pointing in one concerted direction. The large units are easily perceived, but the small units are much more difficult to delineate because they vary in size from two or three lines to a dozen or more, or sometimes they may consist of a single line followed by a significant pantomime (silent activity). Every experienced director knows that *audiences can be aroused to excitement only by the clear and explicit acting of these small units,* for a good play is packed with these detailed, revealing moments. The director's mastery of the unit concept is an absolute necessity if he is to understand at all the nature of dramatic action.

The smallest designation of dramatic action is, of course, the line (a speech). Every speech of every character throughout the play contains a dramatic action. If a speech is of more than three or four sentences in length, it may contain additional actions. Do not worry about long speeches until you have mastered the technique of extracting the action from short ones. Then you will be far more sensitive to shifts in action in major speeches.

Each speech, then, contains a forcing—an action—and it is directed toward another character: *A* does to *B* (Speech 1); *B* receives the forcing and adjusts to it; and *B* does to *A* (Speech 2); *A* receives the forcing and adjusts to it; and *A* does to *B* (Speech 3), with the process repeated until that series is stopped suddenly by interruption, pushed aside to be taken up later, or climaxed by a joining of the two characters on one side of the separation (love) or by a further dividing of the characters (hate). Thus, the actions (speeches) lead to the climax of the unit, which then ends, and another unit begins, repeating the process all over again.

Each unit has its own *objective.* It is the progressive (always moving ahead) building of these small unit objectives that accumulate into the large unit objectives, which, in turn, finally make the objective for the entire play.

The work of the director is primarily that of *helping the actors find not only the speech-by-speech dramatic action in a play but also the objectives of the units throughout the play.* At the base of this concept is the hypothesis that all actions are reciprocal (*A* does to *B* and *B* does to *A*), and that the director's function is to see that the appropriate reciprocation actually takes place with the actors. The process of acting is not just doing individual actions but, even more important, *reciprocating* all actions. Unless *A* does to *B* and *B* does to *A,* nothing will happen for the audience. Emotion can emerge and the audience be moved *only when the reciprocation takes place,* for emotion is a by-product of dramatic action. *Emotion cannot be made directly in itself but is brought about by the forcing of one character by another.* More will be said about this process later in the discussion on acting and the director's relationship to the actor. It is sufficient here to state that the actor who acts alone (without reciprocation) and is permitted to do so by the director cannot possibly produce emotion, for he is not acting but only performing like an individual entertainer in a nightclub who plays directly to an audience without help from others (except the audience).

A play is always a dialogue—action between two or more characters—and never a monologue. A soliloquy or interior speech, such as that used in *Hamlet,* is not a monologue but an argument carried on between two warring sides within the same character, frequently between the character's outside self (what others force him to be) and the character's inside self (what he knows he must be).

Finding and Labeling the Action

Because each speech in a play is intended "to do," to force, each speech can be reduced to a verb in the present tense, because verbs are the symbol-words for action. The subtext in a sequence of speeches, for example, could be recorded in this way:

A shames

B ignores

A pleads

B berates

A begs

B storms

and so on

Notice how each of these actions is expressed in the present tense and how each successive verb seems to grow out of the preceding verb and is more climactic and dramatic. Reciprocation thus takes place as in real life. Also notice that *no other qualifying words are used.*

Your problems in using this method will not derive from what you may think is a deficiency in your vocabulary but in *discovering what is going on* in a line and in a unit. Director-actor language must be simple or it will not work at all. Thus, the problem is one of perception: *If you can sense the action, the verb will come easily to you.* Don't work too self-consciously, too intellectually, but let your feelings and responses tell you what is going on in a series of speeches, just as a good actor does. Once you catch on to this game, the technique of playing it is not difficult at all. But a very real problem will always be there: *What is going on in the line?* What is the *subtext*? This question can sometimes be quite baffling. No matter how many years of experience a director or actor may have, or how mature he may be, this problem will always exist. As pointed out previously, directors and actors should think of playscripts as the improvisations of playwrights. As such, the inner recesses of their plays may be very difficult to rediscover simply because what goes on may lie outside of the personal experiences of both actors and directors.

But once you, as a director, are aware of this technique of *looking for the subtext* and setting it down in verbal form, you will have at your command the most important key available to the director in communicating with actors, for you can both talk the same language: *the verb-motivations that the actor can act.* Anything less lies in the cloudy, fuzzy realm of "how I *feel* it should go," instead of in "what I (the character) *am doing*"—the only way a director can get through to an actor. Leave it to the actor, if you will, but be certain the actor accomplishes the action.

Verbs that are too general, such as those that apply to the nature of dialogue itself, do not "do" to others but merely assert that dialogue is a form of communication. Therefore, do not use such verbs as *ask, tell, say, question, interrogate, explain, show, see, perceive, illustrate, examine, reflect,* and all others that are similar, because *they cannot be acted.* The question you must always ask is: *Can the verb be acted?* Can it force another character to "do" something? The search is for *specific* and not for general verbs, for acting is a specific, never a general, thing.

Another class of verbs to avoid are those that overtly and directly call up specific illustrations: *run, jump, walk, bounce, laugh, smile,* and so on. Only occasionally do these verbs work as dramatic action. They are surface illustrations and not the deep-lying, motivating actions you must look for. The clearest verbs are those full of direct, though not overtly stated, *doing,* for they contain the basic passions and emotions.

Again, if the verbs are too general—for example, *I love, I hate*—they will not stimulate the actor to specifics and will not work. Each of these verbs stands for a whole category of gradations, and as such they are too gross when they stand alone. Because the full intention of verbal delineation is to energize the actor, only a specific verb—a verb that delineates the exact gradation—can accomplish that end.

Finally, note that the word used is a verb. Let an initial stand for the character, and *do not use any other qualifying words.* Again, look only for transitive verbs, for in them you will find the action words.

Recording the Action

During the training period, the student director should practice the verb technique by explicitly writing down an analysis of the action. The following procedure is suggested:

1. Divide a short segment of a play (10 minutes with two characters only) into units (usually three to six).
2. Write down in verbal form (as indicated in the example given on page 32) all the action in each of these units.
3. Now make a summary for each unit by finding a single verb that summarizes the action of each character in the unit. Use this form of expression: *A* does to *B*, and *B* does to *A*. (A more specific example: *Mary pleads and George berates.*) The preceding statement is now a summary for the whole unit; it is reciprocal because both forces are shown. It is reciprocal also because the use of the coordinating conjunction *and* ties the two characters inextricably together as if they were on either end of an elastic rope.
4. Record the summaries of all the units that make up the segment of the play selected. These summaries are what you, as the director, can retain in your mind

as the unit objectives to be accomplished. The actors may get lost in the details of the action and thus lose sight of the objectives. But if you also lose your way, all is lost. If the summary is well done—if the verbs are well chosen—the structure of the play can be readily seen. The total play will be only as good as the unit perception, *made by you and the actors working together,* for you can communicate only what you understand; and if you don't "see" very well, neither will the actors or the audience. Again, don't force actors with verbs, but help them find the action as indirectly as you can.

5. One further device is of specific use: the titling of units with a nominative phrase. Although not a very accurate way of describing what goes on in a unit, it is still quite useful because it gives you another handle for understanding a scene and holding it in your memory. The phrase must be a simple one: *The Arrival; The Close Attachment; The Announcement of the New Plan; The Announcement of the Other Plan; The Head-On Struggle; Left Alone;* and so on. Such phrases are a good supplement to the reciprocal sentences of the summary (as in item 3) and can help you find the verbal statements. They are also good phrases to use for conveying the objective of each unit when you are talking to actors. Although they are helpful devices for communication, they are not actable in themselves.

Types of Action

The types of action—tragic, comic, melodramatic, farcical—are not treated at this point because they are so complex in theory that they will tend to confuse you as a beginning director during the period when you should be concerned with getting a grasp of techniques for play-analysis. It is sufficient to be aware that there is another level of analysis that you will learn later when you have mastered the basic concepts of play-analysis. From a practical point of view, it is suggested that in choosing plays for projects, you select serious ones because of their usual straightforward directness. Dramatic action in comedy is usually not only more difficult to perceive but it also presents many more problems for young actors, and thus for yourself.

Action in a Whole Play

In working out the procedures outlined in this chapter for delineating units of action, the beginning director may think he has become lost in detail and will be unable to see the forest for the trees. But remember that once you understand the nature of action and how to find it in a play, you will proceed quickly and spontaneously. The process here is similar to learning to read and play music: reading the notes, observing the bars, practicing the phrases, and eventually attaining the speed that will make a tune. Your desire to want to work with full plays is quite understandable, but you must first learn how to play the notes and join them into units.

Later on, when you do tackle full plays, all you will be doing is expanding the concept of unit structure outlined here to cover the whole play. The following Exercise 1 will give you that opportunity. Try it for size just to see the relationships, but then return to work on the *parts* of plays as the best way of comprehending the whole. Learn to crawl before you walk and run.

EXERCISES

The best way to work with dramatic action is to study a one-act play or, better, a 10-minute section of a long play. The instructor could select such an example for class use. Later, each student should work out an action-analysis from a play of his own choice. The following exercises should be done in the order indicated:

1. What are the major divisions of the action of the whole play? Can you find a summary statement for the whole play?
2. Distinguish between an arbitrary division (Act II, Scene 2) and a French scene.
3. Pick out several French scenes.
4. Select a segment of a play (10 consecutive minutes) and do the following:
   a. Isolate the units in the text by drawing a line separating one unit from another in the text. Note their beginnings and endings; try to find specific speeches on which they occur. Now number the units.
   b. Write a noun-phrase title for each unit.
   c. Now write the dramatic action verbs for each speech, being careful to follow the procedure for each recording. If you do not do this exercise *at least once,* you will not see the power contained in each line. Don't leave it for the actor to do—that's shirking; beat him to it. You will discover how condensed and concentrated good dialogue really is. Poor dialogue will have reduced action; nothing happens for an audience. Remember: This analysis is for your imagination—what you will draw from for communication with an actor. This look inside the dialogue can give you real freedom in communication by knowing what is there.
   d. Write out the reciprocal action, summary sentences for each unit.
   e. The class should discuss in detail each of these steps.
5. Discuss the playwriting in a television soap opera by citing aspects of unit structure (action, goal, length, etc.). Does the camera watch the adjustments as much as or more than the actions? Why? How does each segment build climactically?
6. Illustrate dramatic action "backwards" by setting up a live story improvisation with given circumstances and a brief plot line. (It is described as "backwards" because the class will see an action happening, one that it has not had to analyze from a playscript in advance of the playing.) Be certain that the improvisers know why they are in conflict. Use number dialogue so that the improvisers can concentrate on actions and will not have to think of specific words. They will also be much clearer in their intentions than if they had to improvise both actions and words. Help shape the improvisation through off-stage suggestions (low-volume directions to the participants) while it is in progress. The participants then begin the improvisation. The class instructor lets it run for a few units and then stops it. Immediately he opens up the following discussion:
   a. Designate the units.
   b. Why did the improvisers make units automatically?
   c. Why did some units (name one) not work well? (Did the improvisers know what they were "doing"?)

   d. Why is it very easy to delineate the actions behind each speech? (Relate illustration/activity to dramatic action.)
   e. Specifically designate some actions behind speeches.
   f. How would real dialogue have helped delineate and intensify the actions behind speeches?
7. Repeat Exercise 6 two or three times until the class can answer all the questions with perception.

Characters: The Second Core Element in Play-Analysis

Definition

A character is made up of all the dramatic actions taken by an individual in the course of a play. Therefore, *character is a summary statement of specific actions.* (*Note:* The word *character* is used here to describe what a playwright makes, which reserves the word *characterization* for use later in this book to define what an actor makes.)

Character Is Action

In the *Poetics,* Aristotle places dramatic action first and character second, with the second flowing out of the first. Although playwrights may not actually write plays in that order, because plays can be conceived and evolve from many stimulations, they must achieve this ordered association in the final draft or the character will not have a life of his own. A character does not exist, except in a superficial, external way, through what he says he is or through what others say about him, although these clues help us to see him more clearly. Instead, he exists in what his actions, particularly those under pressing circumstances, tell us he is. Consequently, character is wrapped up in action, and it is for this reason that *a character is a summary statement.*

Mere impressions of a character—what one *feels* he is—are no substitutes for a director's close analysis of the action. An actor, on the other hand, can discover character, piece by piece, in the process of trying to put him together by *doing*—by acting the various incidents in which the character is involved. For this very important reason, during the rehearsal period, directors should encourage actors to play the scenes over and over, with new suggestions of action for each playing, rather than discuss the characters in an intellectual way. (*Note:* Professional directors proceed here with great caution because this is a major part of the professional actor's job. Regardless of how he handles actors, a good director will see this as a crucial point in his directing of a play.)

Simple and Complex Characters

The density of a character—how simple or complex he may be—is determined from how much he participates in the action of a play and from the quality of his participation and what kind it is. It is the density that separates the primary characters from the secondary or supporting characters who act as instruments for revealing the principals. We know much less about these secondary characters than about the principals—we know only a few traits—because they have little opportunity in the action to tell us who they are, because most of the attention is focused on the principals. A third level—house servants, aides, and so on—we know scarcely at all, although good actors may seem to give them more body (personality) than the playwright actually has. A fourth level—a group or a chorus, a collective body with a collective trait—is obscure to us as individuals because we see only a group mind and a group feeling.

Although a play focuses on all the principal characters, one character usually dominates the action. Because conflicts cannot exist without two forces, a protagonist and an antagonist, the play's action revolves around these two (or possibly three, if there is more than one antagonist). The director must determine during his analysis who the principal character is (*whose* play it is), along with the primary antagonist(s). Thus, another polarity (other than the polarity already discussed in the section on polar attitudes in given circumstances) can be specified if the director understands the nature of character and how characters are used in plays.

A beginning director is sometimes confused by studies of plays (dramatic criticisms) that point out that certain principal characters are very poorly drawn or that characters are very thin, such as in Greek plays. Greek plays have very few incidents to reveal character so they incline to greater simplicity in this respect; but this simplicity does not mean that they will be any less effective. Simple characters in certain contexts can have great power over an audience. One of the characteristics of modern drama, one aspect that delineates the Realistic style beyond the minutiae that make up the given circumstances, is the complexity of character development brought about through a large number of incidents in a play. Many character traits are thus demonstrated to an audience, and what we can say about a character is that we know the complexity of his "psychological self." But we can often become confused because there is so much to assimilate. Good direction is the ordering of this complexity with such clarity and emphasis that an audience can readily assimilate the main points, with the secondary points relegated to their proper places.

When a director understands how action reveals a character, he can understand more fully how to direct plays with simple characters (musicals) as well as those with complex characters (*A Streetcar Named Desire*) and to recognize the different values developed in each. Without this comprehension, he may try to impose the values of the complex on the simple, or vice versa, and may be confused about why a play does not work.

Character Is Revelation: The Principal Characters

From the preceding discussion, it follows that an actor cannot play his entire character at once. Certainly before a rehearsal period has ended, an actor must be fully aware of the complete body of the character he is acting, just as a playwright must be aware of his whole play; but if he tries to play the full character at the beginning or even in the middle of a playscript, he will find himself confused and lost. *A character takes shape and is revealed in the course of the action.* Thus, characters do not change; they *unfold.* The stuff a character is made of has always been laying dormant, and only under the impact of conflict—of the forcing of both himself and others—will the buried qualities come to the surface and stand revealed.

As already noted in the previous section, dramatic action is a progression of incidents with one incident leading to another. Acting is therefore self-revealing with a sort of inevitability guiding it: "This must be told, this must come out!" As a result, a play is made up of discoveries and surprises. Some are minor; a few are major; and one is exceptional. These are the climaxes. As a character meets each of these moments in a play, something in him comes forward to meet the circumstances—a character trait.

In this way, aspects of character are fully illustrated in a series of climactic moments. An audience can keep these traits in mind because, if the author is a good one, the traits will have a logical relationship and a close association with those still to be revealed in the following climaxes. Thus, the actual progression for the audience—what interests each spectator in the play—is the progressive unfolding of character traits in the protagonist and the antagonists, traits that finally accumulate with clarity and force at the major climax when all the previous character revelations come together. This major clash is of such force that the principal character stands fully revealed, and the audience can see what really makes him work. What follows this climax is usually very brief, for all we need to know is what the principal character is like after his head-on collision with the forces he has tried to overcome.

For the director, analysis of the action is paramount if he is to understand the growth in a character, whether he be secondary or principal, and thus bring about this growing in the actor he will direct. *Progressive unfolding* is the concept he must understand. It will tell him where the climaxes of the play are, what they are about, how important each one is, and what to do with them in getting the play acted. This concept has the most personal significance to a director because he can work intelligently and perceptively with the actors only when he understands these points. Progressive unfolding is at the core of director-actor communication.

Techniques of Character Description

Describing a character by writing it down in your own words is the best way to assure yourself that a character analysis is fully developed and nothing has been missed. But you must be absolutely certain that you determine what a character is by giving the principal attention to an analysis of the action, as has been previously emphasized, for you will be strongly tempted to read the description authors sometimes insert in their plays. If you do the latter, you must keep in mind that the author is providing these suggestions for a casual reading and not for a director or a tip-off to the reader of what to expect. You must remember that a character is determined *only after* his actions, not before. Thus, a playwright's advance suggestions may certainly give you a hint about character, but such suggestions can be quite misleading in the overview and can cause you to miss the dominant traits. (See Exercise 8 at the end of this chapter.) Consequently, you must treat author descriptions with great caution and perhaps avoid them altogether.

The technique suggested here bases your analysis of a character on your own perception of the dramatic action. Give each of the following areas primary attention and *record your assessment in writing.*

Desire. Desire is a statement of what a character wants most. He may appear to want a material possession, but this is superficial; what he wants is usually something far less tangible, such as power or dominance over others. It may also be love for another, self-integrity, dominance over fear, or something similar.

Will. Will is a character's relative strength in attaining his desires. How strong or weak is his inner strength? Is it strong enough to push him the full limit, or will he compromise? We take actions in everyday life out of our willpower, and in plays we see this clearly and dynamically illustrated. This needs much discussion to clarify.

Moral stance. A character's moral stance—the stance that will strongly affect the attainment of his desires—consists of his values. How honest is he with others and with himself? Does he have any sense of moral responsibility to others? What is the moral code that governs his inner behavior? What is his sense of integrity? "Evil" characters are usually given low values because, in their view, the end justifies the means. "Good" characters are given higher than average values, a rating we admire in heroes.

Decorum. Decorum describes a character's physical appearance—what he looks like, his manners, and his poise. Such a projection of the outward appearance of a character is superficial because what a person looks like is not a prediction of what he is. Nevertheless, it can be of some value if only to help project the character into the society in which he lives. It is also possible that his physical makeup may be closely related to his mental and emotional temperaments. It can be helpful to make an actual list of a character's physical characteristics seemingly required by the given circumstances, although you may go in the opposite direction when it comes to the point of casting the play. How does he behave in the varying contexts of the play: How does he walk? How does he stand? How does he speak? What is the quality of his voice? and so forth. Is his outward manner affected by his occupation or by the social mores under which he lives? (All of this is a primary consideration in casting a play, *but unless a director thinks an actor is capable of getting out the dramatic action, "looking like the part" will accomplish little.*)

Summary adjectives. Summarize all four of the preceding categories by using adjectives only. Do not set down a character's dramatic actions but *only the traits of character the actions reveal.*

Character-mood-intensity. Character-mood-intensity is *the physical or body-state of the character*—his nervosity—at the *beginning* of the play and at the beginning of each group of associated units. By describing a character's initial physical state, the director has a point of departure for all the ups and downs in the character that follow. In playing a character, if an actor can start at the appropriate level of intensity, assuming good concentration and awareness of the action, he will continue to build from that level. This communication device is very important for the director, for with it he can directly help an actor find the appropriate levels of a character at all times.

Character-mood-intensity thus means the actual physical state of the character: his heartbeat, his breathing, his state of perspiration, his muscle tension or lack of it, the state his stomach is in (queasy, jumpy, calm, etc.), and the like. *Nervosity* means all of these—his total nerve vibration, his sensory awareness. Because these states are points of departure, the actual shape of the play can be understood and made evident in the acting.

You should also be aware that each character in a play begins at a different character-mood-intensity because each character is independent by definition. Thus, one character will feel different from another character who will be in a different state of nervosity about the same situation. A director's job is often to point out to the actors the difference in these points of departure—*the different beats of the characters.* Defining a character-mood-intensity for an actor is like backing him into a scene: He feels the level of physicality first; then when he plays the dramatic action, he can sense its validity as a beginning point. Because all that follows will be based on this beginning point, he will become aware of the necessity for appropriate departures. The *pitch* of the action can thus be assured.

You must remember that when an actor initially faces a new character, that character will seem strange and odd to him because it is so different from the actor's self. Therefore, for an actor, approaching a new character is like trying on someone else's coat: It hangs too long or pinches or smells; it simply does not fit or feel right. In this sense, the character-mood-intensity is the new coat defined, for the actor will know why it does not fit and what he must do to make it fit. The director can assist the actor by helping him delineate the feeling of the character he is trying to play through character-mood-intensity.

EXERCISES

1. Compare Sophocles' *Oedipus Rex* with Ibsen's *Hedda Gabler* in the density of character development. What do you note about each?
2. Compare character density in Shaw's *Candida,* or in another modern Realistic comedy, with Ionesco's *The Bald Soprano.* Try it again with the early scenes in Elmer Rice's *The Adding Machine.* Are the plays by Ionesco and Rice more nearly alike in their development of characters? Why?
3. Read a brief, early scene—one that concerns the principal character from a class study play (for example, *Hedda Gabler* or *Ghosts*). How does the action in the scene

reveal a character trait? What trait is revealed? Study another scene later in the play and answer the same questions.

4. Continue Exercise 3 with the same character by selecting the climactic scene. What character trait is now revealed?
5. Study the first act of a long play (the same one used in Exercises 3 and 4) and note each incident. What are the character traits revealed in this act? Make a list of what you know by the end of this first act. Be very careful not to include any traits revealed in the previous action. Now study the last act of the same play. How much more do you know?
6. Analyze the principal characters in a study play by applying the technique that has been suggested: desire, will, moral stance, decorum, summary adjectives, and character-mood-intensity.
7. Compare the character-mood-intensity of two characters in the analysis made in Exercise 6 at the point where they introduce a formal division of the play together or very closely together. How different are these character-mood-intensities? A scene can mature only through this difference.
8. Using a study play, list any character traits an author may have inserted in his text as description. Now carefully assess these traits against the action in the play in the interest of discerning their relevance. Note the important traits the author does not mention and whether those he does mention are relevant to the main line of the play. This exercise should convince you that it is necessary to use action instead of an author's description as the primary source of character traits.

5

Idea and Rhythmic Beats

You have now reached the breathing heart of a play and it will challenge all your sensibilities, all your feelings. These emotions are difficult to pinpoint because you must bring to the surface, and *actually describe in words,* what you both feel and think about a play. It is turning the insides out, showing the viscera, the nerve system of the living organism. You will have to work hard at seeing each element's separateness and individuality. As in the two previous chapters, idea and rhythmic beats (moods and tempos) are treated separately here so that you can more readily distinguish their differences and know the force each exerts on the structure of the play.

Idea

Definition

The *idea* of a play is the core meaning of what it has to say. It is derived from an assessment of *characters in action* and is therefore a summary statement of such action. Consequently, *the idea is the sum total of the playscript.*

Formal Ideas or Creative Playwriting?

All plays have "ideas" but they vary greatly in their choice, their quality, and their declaration. In poor ones, ideas may be trite, overused, or simply blurred and unclear.

Because all good plays appear to be well ordered, and because some plays seem to "sell" certain ideas very specifically, the unoriented reader might well assume that a playwright begins with a formal idea and then develops it in incidents and characters. However, what is meant by creative playwriting is letting things happen. Consequently, a playwright may begin his improvision in any way—for example, with an imaginary character involved with another character; at a particular moment in the action; with a given circumstance; or with a patch of dialogue. But as he works with his characters, letting them be themselves, they will determine the flow of the action and, eventually, the idea.

No matter how he goes about putting a play together, sooner or later a playwright must decide what his characters are doing *consistently* and what they are trying to discover. In other words, he begins to make *unity in the action,* action that is all about one thing, one idea. He may never actually state his idea of the unity directly in words in the play because he believes that creative drama is subliminal—that is, the audience must experience an idea through *feeling* the action and not be told overtly what it is about. Pinpointing a play may therefore be relatively difficult. But an idea is surely there and the director must find it, for it will declare his comprehension of the unity of the playscript and, subsequently, the unity he will bring to his production.

Idea Is Action

To understand the relationship of *idea* to the other elements in play structure, look again at the drawing in Chapter 2. *Given circumstances* provide the underground foundation. *Dramatic action* is at the ground level and moves upward with each incident to unfold characters until the summit—the idea—is reached. The whole structure is covered with a façade of *dialogue.* Thus, *the idea is the result of characters acting out the incidents in the action.* Not until the action, and consequently the characters, is complete, can we assess the idea, for the major climax and the ending will tell us more explicitly than any other portions of the play what the play is about. (A well-directed play is always delineated from second-rate work by its relentless pursuit in a straight line to the idea.)

Finding the Idea

Although there is no question that the idea of a play will lie in the development of action and characters, two other sources of information are sometimes useful guides: (1) a play's title and (2) a philosophical statement in the dialogue.

A play's title is frequently a symbolic or a metaphorical representation of the inner meaning—a playwright's image of the poetic statement he is trying to make. Some titles are fairly obvious: *The Little Foxes, The Hairy Ape, Death of a Salesman, Cat on a Hot Tin Roof,* and *Riders to the Sea.* The essence of each of these plays has been stated in the titles given them. But other titles may lead the director into confusion, such as *The Bald Soprano, The Birthday Party,* and *Happy Days.* Others tell us very little: *Hedda Gabler, The Lark, Luther, The Homecoming,* and *Lost in Yonkers;* although each says something. But when a title is supported by an analysis of the action, the director has a guiding metaphor that will bring the playwright's idea closer.

Philosophical statements, although occasionally pinpointed in specific speeches, are not very common in plays because most playwrights, in their desire to remain on the poetic level, shun obvious statements of meaning. They are poets, and they want to reach audiences directly on the most primitive level of understanding: emotional understanding. Intellectual statement is too obvious, too self-conscious.

The principal means of uncovering the idea, then, is to search within the dramatic action of the principal character or characters: Where is the emphasis in the action leading? Why does the principal character take the climactic action that he does? What is the result of that action? There must have been other courses of action he could have taken, so why did he take this one? At the high point of his agony, what seems most important to him? After the climax, what is the effect of the discovery on him and on others? There are many questions a director can ask himself about the action that will lead to the idea. *Once he thinks he grasps the idea, he should set it down in words as briefly as possible, and then test his strength backwards against the action.*

One of the easier ways to see an idea is to place it in a simple sentence combining characters and action. This sentence will be the idea *stated in action*—for example: *This play is about a childlike woman who. . . .* By completing the statement of action, the director will still keep the idea submerged up to a point, but bringing it to the surface will be easier because of the emphasis thrown on one character and on the principal action.

You can often find the idea by recording the action in a play, taking great care in setting it down as accurately as you can in the order it occurs. A director should be able to record the action of each act in three or four sentences. This record is a précis, or a summary, and it is the easiest way to find the focus in an action. You must learn to "tell" an action to others briefly and to the point without getting lost in details.

EXERCISES

1. Test the validity of the title of a study play by pinning it down in terms of consistency with the play's action. Do the title and the action say the same thing? Support your answer. Try *A View from the Bridge.*
2. Compare the title of a serious play with the title of a comedy. Do you find the latter essentially different? Could it be taken seriously and could a serious action be construed from it?
3. What do you think might be the actions in the plays with the following titles? *Luv; You Can't Take It With You; The Importance of Being Earnest; Ah, Wilderness!; Who's Afraid of Virginia Woolf?; Conversations with My Father.* Play this exercise as a game with people who have read a play; listen to the comments of the "guessers."
4. Discuss the relationship of the titles to the actions in four or five plays all the members of the group have read.
5. Examine *Riders to the Sea* for a philosophical statement. Do you find one? If certain lines seem to be immediately obvious, are they completely verified in the action? Are they misleading? Remember that *Riders* is also about Nora and Cathleen and not just about Maurya (young women versus old ones).
6. Arrive at the idea of a play by analyzing the action—that is, by drawing the logical conclusion from the actions. Express the idea in one short sentence. Do this exercise

alone, and then compare your results with that of other students. Is there any agreement on the idea? Why may there be differences of opinion? (*Note:* If there is wide divergence, the action of the play should be reexamined by the group in order to be certain that each member understands exactly what is going on and sees the significance of what is transpiring. Understanding the action in some plays may require more maturity than you presently have; but don't let this bother you, because even great actors have confessed to being puzzled over a playwright's meaning.)

Rhythmic Beats

Definition

The *rhythmic beats* comprise the playwright's "music" in a play—its *moods* and *tempos.* All plays have them; audiences vibrate to these rhythmic beats. They derive from (1) the qualities of the dramatic action in each unit and (2) the juxtaposition of these actions. Thus, the rhythmic beats give a play its emotional power, its poetic qualities, and part of its mystery. *Directing is the process of recovering these beats.*

Moods

Moods are the feelings or emotions generated from the clash of forces in the dramatic action—the result of the action. When taken together in their accumulative effect, moods declare the *tone* of a play; thus, they are the *tonal feelings* of a play.

Effect on the Audience

The concept of moods can be understood better by going backward from the play's *effect on the audience* to the playscript itself as the generator of the reception. Of course, there is no question that a director is aware of the moods in a play when he first reads it; but, like tempo, moods are difficult to understand as a concept and particularly elusive to put into words. However, once you understand the nature of mood values and their relationship to the other elements in play-analysis, you can see how to put mood values to work for you.

Moods are not mysterious; it is only explaining them that makes them seem elusive. *Moods are basic feelings; they are the disturbances and the excitements we are moved by as we watch a play.* When you are a member of an audience, you *experience* the play; that is, if the play is well acted, even you, who may be studying directing and are therefore more conscious of what is being done on the stage, will lose your objectivity and become immersed in the play—you will feel it and be moved by it. You are moved by the mood values. This arousal of feelings in the audience can begin early in a performance and accumulate in force throughout, rising to a peak at the major climax of the action and then gradually calming as the play closes.

We all know this arousal to be the "fun" of watching a play—the vicarious experience. Experiencing the shifts in the moods not only holds our attention in a performance but, at the end, it also leaves us tired, or even exhausted or happy or ecstatic. We are so busy feeling the emotions generated by the characters in action—empathizing—that we expend almost as much physical energy on the play experience as we might on a real-life happening, even though we know that a play is not real life but only a semblance of it. It has been a vicarious experience, to be sure, but it has involved our feelings—our entire nervous system. We go to plays because we like the sensation of being aroused, of feeling intensely without the traumas that real-life experiences hold for us.

Dramatic Action and Moods

Again, before discussing the director's work with the printed script, we can get a clearer idea of moods by noting their relationship to dramatic action. Because we think of action in units, we must also think of moods in the same terms. A play is thus composed of many shifts in moods, with every unit of action having its own specific mood.

As you have already learned in Chapter 4, the phrase *character-mood-intensity* means that a character enters a unit of a play at a certain physical (nervous) pitch—the nervosity of the character at that point. As he participates in the action of the unit, his mood-intensity will shift; if he begins at the right pitch, what he does to another character and what that character does to him will modify his mood-intensity, making it either more relaxed or more tense.

As members of the audience, we experience these specific changes in moods, for *a play always moves forward* in a cause-effect progression. The goal of a unit of action, then, is a mood-goal. Several of these mood-goals put together cause the surge in a play, and as an audience, we surge with it. The dramatic action, then, is the source of moods; and the characters with their changing mood-intensities are the instruments. (How the actor makes moods through his technique of acting will be discussed in a later chapter.)

Tone-Goal

The *tone* of a production is the *achievement of the appropriate moods* in a playscript. Tone is what the director is striving for, because it is what the playwright felt when he improvised his play. Tone is the maximal state of feeling, the actual purpose of the play. Unless the director achieves this state, he achieves nothing. All of his preparations, all of his production designs are for naught unless he can move his audience in the way the play demands.

Finding the tone of a play and achieving it in production is thus the goal of the director. Note that it is not *a* tone but *the* tone, for the mood-goal will contain the ultimate meaning of a play because the audience receives the meaning subjectively (with only a relative few ever consciously bringing that meaning to the surface). An audience's experience with a play, for the most part, will depend on the director's perception of the mood-goal and how well he is able to achieve this with his actors.

Although the audience's perception may be subjective, it does not follow that the director can achieve the mood-goal by being subjective himself. He must not only keenly feel the tone of a play on the first or second reading but he must also be able to achieve this tone after weeks of "getting lost" in the details of rehearsals and production.

The Director's Analysis of Mood Values

When most people read a play, they sense the shifts in mood; they are impressed by or get the impression of mood shift. This response is expected and natural. But the director must be much more aware of and more consciously perceptive to these mood shifts, as well as to the overall tone. Many readings of a playscript, together with the disassembling and detailing that goes on during a rehearsal and production period, can often obliterate the first feelings a director may have had about a playscript. *Because a major job of the director is working with actors, if he knows the unit mood-goals and the overall tone he wants to achieve, he will not only be able to help the actors find these goals but he will also bring them into a unity within the play.*

How to record your initial feelings about a play may at first seem elusive to you because it involves trying to record your personal and very subjective reactions. But once you have worked at this sort of conscious reproduction of your feelings, you will find it of enormous value in communicating with actors.

Moods can be recorded in words in two different ways: (1) through mood adjectives and (2) through mood metaphors.

Mood adjectives. Because moods are emotions or feelings—not actions, but the result of actions—they can be recorded in the way an actor works because the result of acting is showing others through visual and aural means what a character is feeling. Though the actual process for the actor lies in the execution of the action, out of that execution flows the feeling—the goal. In real life, a person can be undergoing a tremendous emotional response to some happening but show very little on the outside. On the stage, however, the actor must demonstrate what is happening. His language of transference is through the physical senses: touching, tasting, smelling, hearing, seeing—all sensations. Therefore, the words that can best describe moods are the adjectives that fall into "sensations" categories. Here are some examples:

touching:	rough, smooth, hard, soft, sandy, cool, hot
tasting:	tart, sweet, puckering, cool, hot, smooth, rubbery
smelling:	pungent, perfumy, stinky, sweet, sour
hearing:	loud, soft, raucous, blaring, piercing
seeing:	red, blue, all words of size and shape, all varying words of lightness and darkness

A number of these adjectives strung together will help you recall unit moods and talk about them directly—for example: *This unit is rough, tart, pungent, red, big, and loud.*

Mood metaphors. A *metaphor* is a figure of speech in which a word or phrase literally denoting one kind of object or idea is used in place of another to suggest a likeness, or analogy, between them. The mood adjectives are highly useful, but they are more limiting than metaphors. The latter allow your imagination to play freely and creatively on a play because you are trying to find images that *resemble* the sensations you have about the units. You therefore say to yourself: *The mood in this unit is like a* ________, and you fill in an image. Do not try to think in the "sense" categories suggested for mood adjectives, but let yourself go free. Here are some examples:

> The mood in this unit is like:
>
> *a moth fluttering around a lamp* (the unit mood-goal is nervous, fluttering, indecisive, trembling, etc.);
>
> *an air compressor riveting machine* (the unit mood-goal is noisy, hammering, erratic, jolting, etc.);
>
> *lemon juice* (the unit mood-goal is sour, flows like liquid, smells fragrant but would pucker the mouth, etc.).

Learn, through continuous practice, to use metaphors; they are how a director brings his subjective sensations to the surface. Inherent in metaphors are ways of talking to actors and designers in order to convey something that can really exist only in the doing.

Rhythm in Moods

It should now be obvious that the mood structure of a play can declare its basic rhythm. Rhythm has a far wider application than tempos alone, for tempos, like heartbeats, are tied inextricably to the shifts and changes in mood. Further discussion of rhythm at this point may only confuse you, but you must always think of a play as having a rhythmic structure in its moods, like music, which rise and fall with increasing intensity as the play progresses.

Atmosphere

The *atmosphere* of a play is the meaning of the mood of the given circumstances. If the circumstances are perceived well, the atmosphere will automatically be evident in the reader's mind and feeling. A director who is thoroughly aware of the atmosphere or aura in a playscript, and can state it in a particular way, will be able to exert a strong command over the design of his production. A director must thus be able both *to see and to hear the given circumstances* of a playscript, and then be able to translate these feelings into the concrete terms of stage production.

EXERCISES

1. Discuss in class how you receive a play. Try not to let self-conscious attitudes, which may likely be developing in your training, interfere with an honest appraisal of your ex-

perience as a spectator. This exercise can be done best after your class has watched the performance of a scene or a play.
2. Examine the nature of *empathy* (feeling out the lines of an object). How does it work in the other arts? Apply empathy specifically to a theatre experience.
3. Examine the difference between a real-life experience you have witnessed and what it would look like as a unit in a play. Be certain it is limited and specific enough for you to make the comparison.
4. Record some mood adjectives for a unit of a study play.
5. Record some mood metaphors for a unit of a study play.
6. Record some mood-goals for a unit of a study play.

Tempos

Tempos are the changing rates or beats of the dramatic action in a play, like a drum beating fast or slow. When a sequential arrangement of tempos is combined—that is, when the varying beats of several consecutive units are strongly felt—you have identified the *rhythm,* or the pulsations of a play. Unless a director comprehends the rhythmic markings in a play, he will be powerless in making it work on the stage. *The director is a musician in every respect.* (The only thing that professional play reviewers seem to recognize as a director's sole responsibility is his *pacing* of a play. His expert "musicianship" is thus a major point of evaluation.)

Unit Beats

Because all plays are made in units of action that, though related, are different in content and purpose, each unit has its own particular tempo or, to use a term employed in music, its own *beat.* A play is made up of varying tempos, or *unit beats.* The director must become very much aware of this built-in musical characteristic because it not only strongly determines a play's individuality but *it is also a primary way the play holds an audience's attention.* Directing is thus the stringing together of the emotional beats of the units. This is what entertains an audience.

A musical sense is one of the marks of talent in the director, one of his best natural tools. If this sense is poorly developed, if he cannot readily discern the difference in beats or have the exact sense of time that an orchestra conductor has, he will not be sensitive enough to the up and down swings of a play. Unlike music scores, where tempos are marked and where rates of speed of the various passages are indicated by a series of directions such as *largo* and *molto allegro,* and often by exact metronomic markings, plays have no such textual warnings. *The director and the actors are expected to sense the beats.* If a play reader has a strongly developed dramatic imagination, he will also sense them automatically: He will feel the flow. But even the talented director must search each playscript for the unit beats in order to verify and *bring to consciousness* his perceptions of tempo. If your sense of tempo is poorly developed, you must set out to improvise it through the rhythm exercises provided by dance or music training. Your dramatic imagination will do the rest.

Surges

A play is like the waves on a seashore. The small waves accumulate and finally climax in a major breaker that hurls itself toward the beach to dash its force on the sand; then it disintegrates, loses its force, and draws back toward the sea again. When a storm (the major conflict in a play) is coming, the waves increase in size and their pattern becomes less regular than before. A play is made up of such surges, retreats, and new surges, all with accumulating force that finally culminates in a climax (the storm). The director, then, must not only see small unit tempos but the cumulative, large ones as well. His primitive sense of the large surges will tell him, in one way, what the play is about, for a play has these surges built into it; without delineation of these elements of tempo, a play's "music" will be hidden.

One problem with the "ocean" metaphor used here is the danger of assuming that plays have regular surges that grow only in size and intensity. This assumption is quite misleading. Although some plays have this regularity, many are as erratic in their tempos as are some examples of modern music. One of the ways of sensing a play's tempos is to compare beats. This paralleling of form has the distinct advantage of making you aware of the beats without making you too intellectually conscious of them. "Beating a play" (or parts of a play) on a drum—that is, finding different beats for each unit—also helps bring about a partially conscious awareness of the inherent tempos.

Rhythm

Rhythm, which refers, in part, to the accumulative effect of the unit beats, is perhaps another way of describing surges. Webster's definition is useful as a starter: "The effect created by the elements in a play . . . that relate to the temporal development of the action." From this definition, we can see that rhythm is the *effect* of accumulating tempos and that it is a way of describing *multiple tempos* brought together. But this is only a partial definition of rhythm, for the moods in a play exercise an important effect on rhythm and must be considered in defining it. Because of the elusive nature of the word *rhythm* and because of its double nature when being applied to a play, it is not used much in this discussion. The emphasis has been placed on tempos and moods (note the plural forms of the words) as the keys to discovering rhythm. If you can master these concepts and put them to work for you, you will have a very good understanding of how to find rhythm in a play. Again, a *sense of rhythm* is largely an inherent talent, but it can be developed to an extent through training in music and dance.

Sound and Silence

Do you remember the quotation from Jean-Louis Barrault referred to in the second chapter: "A play is interrupted silence"? Note carefully the idea in that definition. Barrault did not say, "A play is sound interrupted by silence," the way we usually think of it, but he said it the other way around—silence interrupted by sound. This is an extreme view, to be sure, but it is a good way of understanding the concept of drama. In one sense, it can be said that a playwright starts with a silent void and then fills it with sound—the cover of his dramatic action. But if he is a good playwright, he will never completely fill the silence; he will only punctuate it.

What Barrault leaves in the way of silence is the pause—an element of tempo. *Pause* is a silence gap, created first by the playwright, then reproduced by the actor, that has theatrical effect on the stage because its tempo values can be very moving. What is not said is often just as important as what is said. The duration of the pause tells us much. The director should study and mark the pauses in a playscript; again, if he does so, he will have a half-buried device that will tell him much about a play's structure.

The silent moments are also the moments for the actor's pantomimes. Nineteenth-century acting was frequently made up of an alternation of speaking and illustration. Today, because of the demands of Realism, actors are much more motivated to do these two things simultaneously. But in this process, it is easy to forget the extreme importance of the silent moments—the erratic gaps of tempo. The director's imagination should lead him to a careful examination of a playwright's suggested illustrations for the silent moments, particularly at the ends of scenes or acts.

Whether he follows them explicitly or not is a matter of personal decision—but at least he knows that the gaps are there, that they form part of the tempo structure of the play, and that they cannot be ignored without causing much damage to the rhythmic structure.

Ostensibly, a play is very much like a dance-drama set to music. Without hearing the music—the sound and silence—the play's form is almost entirely lost. If the director has a musical ear, he will *hear* the written play.

Recording Tempos

Tempos can be readily noted, whether for an entire play or for a succession of units in that play, in two specific ways:

1. Tempo can be demonstrated by the use of rate words—such as *fast, medium, slow*—and their variations.
2. Tempo can be demonstrated by the use of a horizontal graph that shows the relationship of tempos to the horizontal line of the play. In this way, the peaks and valleys of the action are visually revealed. Again, as with the use of the rate words cited in item 1, this can be done with any unit division desired: the three acts of a play, the major scenes of a play, or the units of a specific scene.

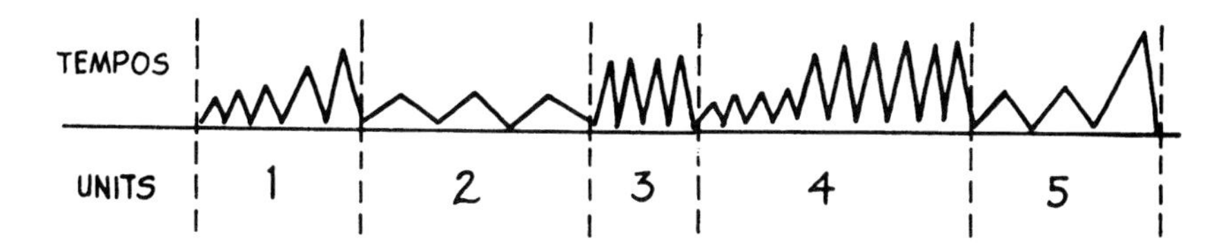

EXERCISES

1. With you acting as the leader, tell the class the category you are illustrating. Have one student beat a drum at different, improvised speeds. The rest of the class imagines the following for the rhythms:
   a. Different character types that each beat prescribes
   b. Different character-mood-intensities for each beat
   c. A unit improvisation (one unit only of reciprocal action)
2. One student beats a drum at three different speeds. Try to improvise a story for the three units indicated.
3. One student beats a drum at the speed that he feels expresses a unit from a specific play. The class describes what they feel about the tempo he has played on the drum. They compare their feelings by reading the unit from the playscript.
4. Play some music. What visual images are suggested by the beat of the music? Take care in this exercise not to confuse *tempo* with *moods.*
5. Each student finds some music that expresses his feelings for the rhythm of a study play. Compare the findings.
6. Examine a study play for sound and silence. Identify the silent moments. What will specifically punctuate them?
7. Suggest improvised activity for the opening and closing of a certain section of a study play. How does the visual, as imagined, emphasize the action of this section? What is the tempo of such visual activity?

6

The Director's Preparation

A director's preparation is a *written* analysis of given circumstances, dialogue, dramatic action, characters, idea, and rhythmic beats (moods and tempos). It must be written because this method is the only way a learning director can be certain that he has covered all the points in the improvisation provided by the playwright and has not substituted his own for the original. Don't eliminate this step until you can do it well.

Homework

No matter how skilled a director may be, no matter if he has been directing for many years, he will always have to do intensive homework—the study of the playscript. After you have done several written analyses, you may not actually record in written detail all of the structural facts about a play, but you will record some of them in your head and some of them on paper—always in the interest of clarifying your ideas and of developing specific communication that will be necessary between you and your actors and designers. Beginning directors, however, must work hard at written analysis, if only to be certain that all its aspects have been covered thoroughly.

The basic function of homework, then, is not only to help you ferret out and understand a playscript but also to put you in a position of extensive and sensitive communication. *Homework will make you articulate in the right way.* Good directing is not a gabfest of talk, talk, talk; it is made up of economical and appropriate suggestions made at the right moments. The job of the actor is to act, to physicalize; it is not the job of a student in a seminar where talking prevails. The director who thoroughly comprehends his primary tool—the playscript—will not only be able to let an actor proceed on his own but he will also have a dozen ways of communicating a difficult point to an actor, not just one or two that may emerge after the director has stumbled around in a maze of language. A director's suggestions to an actor must be simple, direct, honest, economical, and pointed. At the same time, the suggestions are imaginative—*imaginal* (full of images) is a better word—not coolly denotative but existing in the half-sublimated language that actors can understand and use.

Directions are also personal because they are directed to a particular actor and not to a puppet or a robot or a bit of pasteboard. Actors are not modeling clay. The director who knows his business will be prepared to make the appropriate suggestion. Plays in rehearsal are built in a ladderlike construction with *the director building on what the actor contributes and the actor building on what the director contributes,* with this reciprocal process repeated over and over. The prepared director can make it work, but the unprepared director will be forever working out of his own subjectivity, and instead of being able to answer questions, he will forever be posing them to his confused actors, just passing the buck.

The purpose of a director's homework, then, is to place the director in the best possible position for communication to actors. The well-prepared director will know not merely a play's skin but its guts, bones, muscles, and blood.

Why a Written Preparation?

There is something about writing notes on observations about a playscript that particularizes and pinpoints them. At first, you might think that this procedure is dangerous in an artistic process such as play production—that it could inhibit, or at least restrict, your flight as a director. This fear is nonsense. After you have done an analysis or two and have seen them work, you will know that analysis does just the opposite: *Preparation acts as a freeing device.* By writing down your ideas, you see many more possibilities open up. After all, the playwright had to record his improvisations in a written playscript. Why shouldn't the director pin down his own understanding of the playwright's work in the same way? If a scene designer went directly into a shop and began building with only an idea in his head and nothing recorded in detail on drawing paper, the operation of building a set would be haphazard and ineffective. Without adequate formal preparation, a young director's work with actors not only will be haphazard but it also will follow a line of general directing and not of specific directing. A general development is dull and boring; only the specific can hold the attention of an audience. Do not think of a written preparation as an albatross around your neck but as the best possible tool you can give yourself.

A Sample Outline for Play-Analysis

Although you can plunge into an analysis at any point, a better technique is to approach it systematically. Thus, you should begin with given circumstances and then proceed to dialogue, dramatic action, characters, and idea, and wind up with moods and tempos. This procedure works well because the analysis of given circumstances tends to flow into dialogue, and dialogue into dramatic action, and so on. Also, when a fresh idea comes, you can check it with what you have already recorded: If it is logical, it will tie in easily, and the freeing process can begin to work.

Following is a suggested plan for play-analysis. Although this plan is shown here in outline form, an analysis of a scene taken from a long play (10 minutes, with three to five units) or a short one-act play would easily fill several pages; in other words, you must not complete the outline in an abbreviated way as you do in answering a true-or-false question, but develop your answers in detailed exposition.

Worksheet for Play-Analysis

I. *Given Circumstances*
   A. Environmental facts. Discuss under the following numbered headings. And how does each affect the action of the play?
      1. Geographical location, including climate
      2. Date: year, season, time of day
      3. Economic environment
      4. Political environment
      5. Social environment
      6. Religious environment
   B. Previous action
   C. Polar attitudes of the principal characters, both in the beginning and at the ending
   D. Significance of the facts in the total meaning of the play

II. *Dialogue*
   A. Choice of words
   B. Choice of phrases and sentence structures
   C. Choice of images
   D. Choice of peculiar characteristics (for example, dialect)
   E. The sound of the dialogue
   F. Structure of lines and speeches

III. *Dramatic Action*
   A. *Titles of the units.* Number the units in the scene or play and give a nominative phrase as a title for each unit.
   B. *Detailed breakdown of the action.* Do this before going on to (C) because the verbs will help you do the summarizing of the units. Separate the action into numbered units. Express the action in each line (speech) by using the initial of each character followed by a present-tense verb (for example, *N pleads*).
   C. *Summary of the action.* Summarize the action of each unit by following the number of the unit with a compound sentence expressing reciprocal action (for example, *A* [present-tense verb] to *B* and *B* [present-tense verb] to *A*).

IV. *Characters*
   Treat *each* character under the following headings:
   A. Desire
   B. Will
   C. Moral stance
   D. Decorum
   E. Summary list of adjectives

F. Initial character-mood-intensity at the scene opening expressed as:
1. Heartbeat: rate
2. Perspiration: heavy, light, etc.
3. Stomach condition
4. Muscle tension
5. Breathing: rate, depth

V. *Idea*
A. Meaning of the title
B. Philosophical statements in the play: Cite actual quotations
C. How does the action lead directly to the idea (meaning)?
D. For the scene in preparation: Cite its purpose and use in the play

VI. *Moods*
After the number of each unit, express the mood for that unit in two categories:
A. A list of mood adjectives with one for each of the senses
B. A mood image

VII. *Tempos*
After the number of each unit, designate the rate of speed for that unit by using a rate word (for example, *fast, medium-slow, largo*). Also make a horizontal graph of the tempo relationships by inserting connecting perpendicular lines to a horizontal line in order to show the peaks and valleys of tempo change.

VIII. *Tone*
Summarize the analysis by finding a word or phrase to declare the play as a whole.

EXERCISES

1. Review the outline in detail in class discussion. Be certain you understand all the parts before attempting a complete analysis. (Your instructor might wish to provide numbered forms for all sections.)
2. The instructor will select for group study a one-act play or a 5- to 10-minute scene from a long play. Each student does his own analysis. The group then examines the play or scene in detail by comparative reporting from the prepared analyses. (*Note:* This exercise can be an accumulative one if you write an analysis of each part as it is studied. In this way, a full play-analysis is prepared during the course of the study of Chapters 3, 4, and 5, and the total analysis will be on hand for discussion at this point.)
3. Select a 10-minute scene (four to six units) from a long play and analyze it.
4. Do a play-reading of the study play chosen for Exercise 2, *sitting at a table,* and use members of the class for the different roles. Pass the roles around, disregarding gender difference, and read several times. A participative discussion should follow each reading. (In actual practice, many directors use the first rehearsals of a play for this process, because the emphasis can be placed on fully understanding the dynamics outlined in Chapters 3, 4, and 5.)

Part II

Communication

One of the marvelous things that happens with people who are good is that they talk very little. That's the truth of it—one word, two words.

—Director John Hirsch, quoted in Arthur Bartow's *The Director's Voice: Twenty-One Interviews*

7 The Director-Actor Relationship and Stage Blocking

Directing Is Working with Actors—1

In the previous chapters on play-analysis, you learned how the playscript, when intensively studied and taken apart, can give you all sorts of ways to reach actors through special "languages" in the play structure. Now you are cast adrift on your own and are going to explore directly a new group of "languages" that will help you communicate with actors beyond their own creativity. At the same time that you will be encouraging actor-ownership in approaching a role, you will be looking for ways to bring about an ensemble, a group harmony of a play as you see it.

Communicating: The Director's Primary Job

As has been pointed out, *the director's field of action is communication.* However, you must make a very important distinction. Although the director's ultimate responsibility is to touch and move audiences with a play, he cannot do so by himself; rather, he must communicate to audiences how he thinks and feels through actors and designers—his collaborators. Consequently, what the director manages to bring about will depend entirely on his talent for, and his capabilities in, communicating with these collaborators. The director will be successful only if he has a strong faith in their creative abilities and can see his own job as one of encouraging and stimulating them to their highest expression.

But here is the rub! Because he is so devoted to helping others, the director can easily be called a leech, a bloodsucker, a hanger-on, and a bully. Yet, at his best, he is also a friend and a confidant. Once the learning director recognizes that communication is his core work, he will concentrate on using every device he knows to *get through.* At the same time, because he expects people to pay attention to him, he must go out of his way to pay the closest attention to them. Actors and designers are tender people, and their creativity simply does not flourish in an aura of confusion and tension. A successful director communicates that he is a natural leader who knows how to work *with,* and not *at,* other human beings. Because he loves the artist in himself, he can love the artist in others.

How well you, as a director, do this will depend on the sort of person you are, because touching other people with theatrical ideas is a vastly intricate process largely outside the purely intellectual. A director who thinks that all he need do is talk with actors on a logical, intellectual, expositional level fails to understand the type of creative people with whom he is working. Acting problems are not solved *in discussion* but *in doing,* and the director is the freewheeling agent who can find the images or the circumstances that will make doing more likely to succeed.

Communication with actors, then, is a matter of a director's interest in and understanding of human beings, and not just an interest in their acting capabilities. Getting through is not a mysterious process; it is based on a director's meticulous homework with the playscript as well as his recognition that there are no actors in the abstract but only individual "people" who must be reached on a level of personal feeling. If he understands something about how the creative imagination works, and if he understands the process of acting—the using of the human instrument to effect communication—he will be able to achieve his basic goal of energizing actors in the right way and of inspiring them beyond their usual capabilities. Both actors and directors are working for the same goal—communication of a play to an audience—but only the actors will carry it onstage and bring about the actual contact.

The Director's Training in Acting

Because the director's primary function is "bringing out" the actor, his background must include intensive and specific training in the acting process, including a thorough understanding of actor-ownership and all of its projections. He can learn much in the classroom with other actors, but he can expand that learning with close reading in the field of actor instruction. (See the Bibliography for books that will tell you about how acting is presently being taught.) No matter what your knowledge of acting may be, however, as a director, you must be highly sensitive to how actors think, feel, and work, and what their central drive toward creativity is about. You must also understand the actor's use of his voice and how he speaks on the stage. Directing is not the simple manipulation of other people by someone with a dominating ego; rather, it is a mature awareness of how to work skillfully with others who offer their own creativity to bring out the life force of a breathing and pulsating story on the stage.

Image-Makers

All the people who work on a play—the playwright, the actors, the designer, the director—are image-makers. Because a play is an artificial device, an imitation of life and not life itself, its poetic power resides in its capacity to arouse the imaginations of the watcher-hearers. This response from an audience is *empathy*—an automatic response, if conditions are right, to what is seen and heard. All aspects of the produced play are more symbolic, more typical than they would be in everyday life because they have been painstakingly selected and simplified, meticulously arranged, and carefully unified. And because of this treatment, they possess the inherent capacity of arousing images in members of the audience, each of whom can then connect those images with his own personal experiences and view of life.

Thus, *the produced play actually hovers in the air between the actors on the stage and the audience in the house; it is a froth of images waiting to be rescued and assimilated by the audience.* Consequently, the playgoing experience does not stop with what is literally set out in these images from the stage but continues in a very personal way in the minds and feelings of the viewers. *Everything a viewer sees and hears is converted automatically into his own images.* This conversion is his work on the play, and it is obvious that the process of play production cannot be completed without him. Thus, the *kind* of images made by the director through the actors is very important in the theatre.

As you can now readily see, if a director is to justify his place in the theatre as a theatrical artist, he will have to be not only someone who can help actors enhance their own capacities for image-making but also someone who can discover *appropriate* images for certain passages of a play and can see that they are set in motion. As a director in training, you must become highly aware that the theatre experience is primarily a sensuous experience, and that image-making involves the visual and oral deployment of the senses—seeing, hearing, touching, smelling, and tasting. The sense arousal of the theatre can be readily seen in a performance of a play when the audience responds warmly to the color and texture of a costume, to the line of a piece of scenery, or to the sound of something mechanical, such as a clock bell or an offstage airplane engine.

What the audience is usually not so aware of is how actors continually assault all the senses by making the viewers constantly taste, smell, and touch, as well as see and hear, in very special ways. There is an inclination to take actors for granted because much of what good actors do is usually so deftly and subtly done, and is so right and truthful, that one is rarely conscious of the process. Yet, this is the process of acting, for *acting is reaching audience imagination through the direct transfer of sensuous imagery.* What an actor touches, we, as audience, touch in our imaginations; what he smells, we smell; and so on.

The young director, then, cannot be fully responsive to his communication possibilities until he comprehends the sensory-arousing aspects of acting. He will know that he can get through to an audience only when he can bring about in his actors the images with which he wants to assault the audience.

The final goal is, of course, to bring about a high state of *involuntary* attention (unaware or unself-conscious attention) in the audience. How well a director can achieve this goal depends on the sensory inspiration he can bring about in his collaborators. *A director must first be an image-maker for his actors* if he is to be an image-maker for an audience.

Techniques of Communication

Intellectual Talk

You should now be aware that there is a good deal more to the communication process between director and actor than exchanging ideas about a playscript on an intellectual level. Of course, a certain amount of useful information can be conveyed in this way, for an actor must understand the intellectual argument in a play, and the part his character plays in it. But when it comes to the hard core of dramatic action and character, such a self-conscious, objective method usually fails. Young directors are often baffled about why they are not getting through to actors because they are unaware that they are trying to reach them largely through objective discussion. Consequently, you must learn to work in many different ways, realizing that *your intention is to free,* rather than to tie up, *the imaginations of actors.* You must remember: An actor who thinks too much cannot act. A character is the embodiment of his thought, and he acts accordingly. Consequently, actors must move spontaneously out of natural responses (as we do for the most part in everyday life), relying on their senses and not on conscious thought.

You must therefore learn to restrict intellectual discussion to those matters that do not strongly affect the senses of the actor; and you must learn how you can free his imagination, how you can give him flight in as many ways as possible. Objective talk will take your actor only a short way. Image-inducing direction will comprise your major communication with the actor. Talk little; do much.

Improvisation: The Inside-to-Outside Process

From your experience as a student of acting, when you started doing improvisations you likely began to see what acting is all about—that it is not a laid-on process of one's exterior self on show but that it starts from inside yourself and is all tied up with relating intensively to other actors. At first, your improvisations were probably arranged to reveal to you how relaxation and concentration could let you show something with honesty and believability, through yourself and without self-consciousness. You probably did brief sense exercises with imaginary objects and sometimes with real objects. Later, you likely worked with dramatic actions, and eventually you may have tried complex exercises that involved other participants—improvisations that worked only when you learned to play *off* the other improvisor. You learned that improvising requires the utmost attention to what the other improvisor does to you, because you have to adjust to him before you know what to do yourself. Do you remember how free you felt without a scenario or an established line of development such as a pantomime would prescribe? You could let the improvisation take form and develop out of that freedom. Did you feel the exaltation and power that freedom gave you?

This is the sort of feeling you must induce in your actors when you use improvisation as a technique of communication. *The goal is discovery in the most per-*

sonal way possible, for that is what moves from the inside of the actor outward. Improvisation becomes a device enabling an actor to discover his relationship to another actor on an intimate level (reciprocation); to establish a relationship to another character; to feel the sensation of the dramatic action being expressed; to discover dramatic action; to discover an illustration of dramatic action; to feel the special quality of a given place and its climate; to feel the decorum of a character in a given circumstance; to hear what the voice is like at high volumes and low volumes under forced conditions; and to find the extent of movement and body behavior under specifically delineated circumstances.

These are only a few of the enormous number of things that can be accomplished with improvisation, for it is literally imaginative game playing that can open up a play's mysterious moments. The director, of course, is the leader, and as such he can use improvisation for any purpose he wishes. Some directors, for example, use it extensively throughout the rehearsal period and do not actually shape a performance until the later rehearsals.

There are many problems, however, in using only the improvisational approach as the means of releasing actors. Beginning actors will have a particularly difficult time with it simply because improvisation requires experience, and it may not have been part of their training. Advanced actors may do somewhat better, and some will be very good at it. Nevertheless, the primary problem with improvisation is that it has no performance status of its own; that is, although it can lead to very sensitive moments of discovery, they are still only moments, and a performance is made up of many moments joined together. What happens in between making improvisations and making a performance is of primary concern. Some directors try to show the improvisations they have made in rehearsals to audiences without any modifications whatsoever, and then wonder why they do not work. You will keep out of trouble if you remember that *improvisations are highly valuable as devices for discovery,* but they are not intended for performance because they inherently lack the essential power of projection (selection and emphasis), and without that, an audience cannot gather the play together.

If you can see improvisation primarily as a rehearsal technique, it may become a valuable tool for you. Used for its proper purposes, it can help you reach many actors on very primitive levels and make your play that much more sensitive. But recognize at the outset that it is largely a rehearsal and not a performance technique and that it requires experience and talent in the participants to accomplish successfully. After you study the chapters on *organic blocking,* you will be in a better position to know what to do with improvisation.

Organic Blocking: The Outside-to-Inside Process

Organic blocking is the process of stimulating actors to image-making through the use of six visual tools: (1) groundplan, (2) composition, (3) gesture, (4) improvisation with properties, (5) picturization, and (6) movement (discussed thoroughly in Chapters 9 through 13, respectively). Its function is to help actors discover dramatic action by "feeling" its inherent illustration. This outside-to-inside process contains rehearsal and discovery techniques, as well as techniques used in performance. (*Note:* Don't be put off by the word *blocking,* a word professional directors and actors often think is old-fashioned. Once you understand how organic it can be, its seemingly mechanical aspect will be absorbed in the game of using this device.)

In line with the previous discussion of improvisation, you must first understand that these six tools for director-actor communication are used *for the purpose of communicating directly with the actor, who will, in turn, communicate with the audience.* You must therefore view these tools as *actor stimulators:* By using them as *external suggestions,* a director can ignite all kinds of chain reactions within an actor. The word *organic* is used to denote that *such blocking is in no way superimposed on a play or forced on an actor,* but it implies that such blocking suggestions derive from the play itself (the organism) and are therefore inherent in it. Organic blocking, then, is not a pictorial process, not a way of making a performance more beautiful through stage arrangements, but *an inherent activation of a playscript through a body of physical suggestions that can arouse imagination in actors.*

At first, this technique may be difficult for you to comprehend, especially if your actor training has been dominantly improvisational with the emphasis always on the inside-to-outside process. However, skillfully used, the outside-to-inside approach to actors can work very well indeed and will not be at all in conflict with the other approach. As a matter of fact, both can be used, and are used, simultaneously. Indeed, many actors like the assurance of the outside-to-inside approach because it is tangible and physical: They know in a physical way where they are going.

The question raised here is what seems to be, in the view of some directors, a strong conflict between using improvisation and blocking at the same time. These directors argue that blocking freezes the actor and that improvisation is the only avenue to his release. The answer to this argument is that *there is no single way to release actors.* Either of these approaches can be used effectively; and often they can be used in combination, paradoxical though that may seem, because blocking is self-conscious and objective, whereas improvisation is largely intuitive and subjective. However, if both are used with care, they do not battle with each other but tend to support and intensify each other. You will need to learn how to do both if you are to take full advantage of available director-actor techniques of communication. Shutting yourself off only with improvisational techniques is to limit greatly what you can do with actors, especially if your actors have been trained in body-release or other physical approaches to acting. In addition, if you should decide to work in the professional theatre, you will find that actors use a wide range of techniques but seldom employ improvisation as a process.

Actors frequently feel quite uncomfortable when they participate in first readings because a play—an ensemble effort—can be very confusing until it has been given some outward form. A director can be of great assistance in helping actors get over this initial discomfort by placing them physically in specific relationships to one another in conformity with the dramatic action. This process will not only give an actor time to locate himself but it will also allow him to know who his adversaries in the play are, something he may already know intellectually but not in a physical sense. Anyone who has acted in a play knows the discomfort described here; yet, directors who are busy looking elsewhere too easily forget the strangeness and disorientation of first contacts.

When the refinement of illustrations begins later in rehearsal, the concept of aiding the actor with visual suggestions can be stepped up in full force, always with the intention of communicating ideas to the actors—ideas about emphasis, intentions, or shadings in the action. If you keep in mind that transfer to the audience is a transfer of the sensory images of the actor, you will begin to appreciate the full value of this sort of direction. A good actor will, of course, provide much of this illustration on his own, but illustration is infinite, and the best selection must be made. The director's function is to assist with selection, by constantly working toward what he believes to be refinement and improvement. Where an actor stands on a stage in relation to other characters or other objects, how and why he moves and the nature of that movement, and how he handles an object are all of primary concern to a director, for all of these considerations will convey images. The important question is: *Do the actors convey the images the director has imagined and selected?*

You will have more control over some of these visual tools than you have over others, but they are all tools that you can put to work. Learn to tell the truth with them by finding appropriate images, because the tools have great capacity for telling lies; the actor can *speak* one thing and *do* another. "Suit the action [illustration] to the word, the word to the action," says Shakespeare. This principle is what the actor is learning to apply. If you can exploit the actor's own training to the fullest, you will find yourself in ready communication with him.

Actors are also great experimenters. Always remember that the process of rehearsing a play is not talking about it but doing it. One thing you must learn is that you should not freeze actor illustrations until late in a rehearsal period when you must consistently use the best ones you have discovered. Some students think that by learning techniques, their imaginations will be dried up, that they will become more rigid. Just the opposite actually happens. You will certainly be self-conscious when you are learning how to "see" these tools and how to use them, but later they will become second nature to you, and you will know how to utilize them to the fullest possible advantage. Scene discovery or opening up the action will usually depend on experimentation with these visual tools. Gamble on shifting and changing their values as part of the process of actor-discovery in rehearsals.

Organic blocking is developed rather extensively in the following chapters not only because it must be understood in some detail to make it work as a technique of director-actor communication but also because it provides the process for the projection of a play in performance. As you work through these chapters, you will see how to use these tools to make clear and forceful statements of dramatic action as well as character statements that may take shape in spontaneous ways during the rehearsal period but that can be sharpened and focused during the polishing period.

EXERCISES

1. Discuss in a group the approaches used in *your* acting training. Try to isolate the different approaches cited. When did you first think you were really acting, as distinct from merely using your exterior personality? What was the experience like?
2. What kinds of communication reach you as an actor? Examine the various approaches directors have used to bring you out as an actor. What worked best? What was least effective?
3. What is an image? Read some short poems and analyze each for its imagery. Look particularly at some five-line Japanese poems and their imagery. Why is poetry so compact? Compare this to the compactness of a play.
4. "Talk" to another student in images, using as few words as possible. You will be surprised at how few words are actually needed to convey ideas and human feelings.
5. How does *organic blocking* differ from merely blocking a play? Can you see how the first is deeply rooted in both dramatic action and actor training, and the second tends toward the pictorial only? Discuss.
6. Discuss the good and bad points in using improvisation as a director's method of communication.
7. Define the proscenium stage. What is the use of the proscenium wall? How does the "wall" concept differ from the "arch" concept? Does Realism as a style require the proscenium stage? What is the audience's relationship to the actor on a proscenium stage? What rules do you think should be observed by actors performing on the proscenium stage? In discussing the proscenium stage, the tendency is to think of it only in terms of set design. How is it also a playwright's stage? An actor's stage? What are its merits? What are its limitations? (The proscenium stage will be discussed in detail later, but it is important at this point that you understand it in a minimal way.)

8

Learning to See

The Games of Visual Perception

The text pauses here to consider one of the most important aspects of stage direction and the capabilities of the director: How well do you see? Learning to see—learning to observe meticulously and perceptively—is a skill the young director must acquire early in order to help him make images that can excite and move audiences. It is not enough to give casual attention to what an actor wears, or the place he tells his story, or how he moves around the stage in relation to other actors. Instead, *the director in training must learn to see so incisively that after a quick viewing of a few seconds, he can recall explicitly every object, every move, the quality of light in the specific place, the color of the upholstery in relation to the color in a costume, and much, much more.* What follows is a rundown on making you aware of this problem of "seeing."

The line drawings used in Chapter 9 will get you started on the Games of Visual Perception by asking you to look carefully at stage space, first looking down from above (a groundplan) and then from an elevated angle out front. Later in the book, as you become more accustomed to looking at groundplans and have learned how to translate them into stage space, photographs of live productions are added so that the Games of Visual Perception can be practiced with specific examples.

If you will deliberately play this game with the drawings and photographs that follow, you will learn how to examine *meticulously* the captured moments in the work of others and how to increase your instant recognition of visual illustration.

In addition to the few specific questions suggested with each set of photographs, you should ask yourself: *What did the director do? What would I do? How much can I see?* Don't think of these productions as ideal in any way but as challenges to your own work.

The Games of Visual Perception run throughout the text, with each set of photos assigned to groups, as follows:

1. Composition: 1–4
2. Picturization: 15–26

3. Choice of Stage: 27–34
4. Scenery: 35–40
5. Properties: 41–44
6. Lighting: 45–50
7. Costume: 51–54
8. Makeup: 55–58
9. Style in Modern Plays: 59–72
10. Style in Plays of Other Ages: 73–80

The photographs used in this book were selected as useful, practical, examples of work being done at different levels of directing: some the work of student directors and others the work of faculty directors or regional theatre directors, with the latter classification covering the wide range of directing in semiprofessional and professional theatres outside training programs in the schools. A full identification for each photograph can be found in the Dedication and Credits for Photographs at the front of this book. They have been loaned by directors to help make explicit the points of visual perception, and their use as examples may supercede their quality as photos in some instances.

9

Helping Actors Communicate through Groundplans

Chapter 7 was primarily concerned with discussing the nature and process of acting and how directors work with actors. This chapter and Chapters 10 through 13 discuss stage values and how they can help actors communicate *with each other* and thus to an audience. Some of what is discussed here, particularly as it applies to the single actor, may be taught in your acting classes, but stage values, as a whole, fall into the director's province of helping two or more actors communicate. Awareness of stage values is an important part of your job.

A *groundplan* is both a representation of the given circumstances and a tension device for discovering and illustrating the dramatic action of a play *in specific terms of space and of the necessary obstacles that break up that space.* No matter what sort of stage you may be working on—proscenium, arena, thrust—a groundplan is still the basic tool in director-actor communication because all the other tools are dependent on it and flow naturally out of it. If you can master the concept of the groundplan as a machine tool for communication, you will be able to see how the other tools can also work for you.

Although a groundplan is usually represented in a two-dimensional drawing, like an architect's floor plan, it is actually three dimensional in concept, for the drawing represents physical objects occupying vertical space (from the floor upward) as well as space on the plane of the stage floor. A director, then, must always think in three-dimensional terms: Stage space is a cube, not a flat rectangle (floor). Using this point of view, the director will see the vertical as well as the horizontal aspects of the design, and he can thus better visualize how he can suggest to actors the feelings and facts about the given circumstances.

For this reason, in devising groundplans for the proscenium stage—the basic stage in which the audience sits directly in front of the stage platform—a director should also include walls, platforms, steps, furniture, and anything else that has height. Only by doing so can he define the cube he and his actors will exploit and his audience will see and feel. Always try to see a groundplan in your mind's eye, just as you would if you were looking at a perspective sketch of it with your eyeline slightly above the stage floor.

In composing a play, a dramatist will choose a symbolic place for the dramatic action because he feels that it exerts some particular force on the action itself; that is, he feels the pressure of the place. A director must reconstruct this feeling from the dramatic action (not from a physical description the author may have inserted) as nearly as he can, for what he must find is the *appropriate obstacle course for that action.*

Obstacle course is used here because an actor, until he is much advanced, can sense actions much more quickly and keenly with a physical obstacle between him and the opposing force represented in another character than he can when there is no obstacle. A table, sofa, or chair between two actors gives them both something to struggle over, something that prevents them from getting together. This technique is based on the premise that plays are mostly about clashes rather than harmonies. Differences in levels—steps, platforms, and so on—do much the same thing, because one character can feel from such juxtapositions his dominance or lack of dominance over another character. The purpose of a groundplan, therefore, is to give actors strong sensations of tension by placing in their way physical obstacles that must be overcome if they are to reach other characters.

From this discussion, it should be obvious that a director must search for the *appropriate space* for the play he is producing. What he finds will be a specific place, not a general place. The given circumstances will tell him whether that space is large or small; frequently interrupted by objects or only occasionally so; whether it has strong vertical possibilities (everything from platforms to balconies) or primarily horizontal possibilities (low-ceilinged, hugging the floor); and so on. Good designers also think in these terms, although they may not always think about a director's specific communication with actors. (For this reason, it is imperative that directors work intensively at developing their own sense of design for the groundplan. When they work with designers, they can then be certain that the major point of a groundplan—director-actor communication—is accomplished.) The detailing of the space and the objects can be done by a designer because he can greatly intensify the visual effect. But unless the architecture of a groundplan is well conceived in terms of the dramatic action, not only will the director have lost basic possibilities for communication with his actors but he will have also reduced the effectiveness of all the other visual tools for director-actor communication that depend on it.

EXERCISES

You may wish to do the improvisational approach to "thinking and feeling" about the groundplan outlined in the following exercise. This step-by-step "game" will enable you not only to grasp the difference between a groundplan and a room used in everyday life but it will also give you a much better understanding of the concepts that follow. *Doing* is far better than talking about it.

In order to understand thoroughly why the groundplan is an artistic device for presenting an illusion of reality and that it is not reality itself, do the following set of progressive exercises. Do the exercises carefully, step by step, and do not proceed to item 2 before you have mastered item 1, or move to item 3 before item 2 is fully understood. Remember that the whole exercise is a game that must be played in pieces.

1. Improvise a place with an inside measurement of 20 feet wide and 14 feet deep (an average-size living room) by lining up classroom chairs and having them face outward on four sides. In setting up this place, now is the time to practice the technique of rehearsal-room measurement, something you will do over and over again in setting up a rehearsal space, by using the three methods for determining approximate footage: (a) if you know the length of your pace (the distance between your feet—heel to heel—when extended in walking), you can make a fairly accurate measurement by counting the number of your paces walked off; (b) if you know the length of your shoe, you can mark out a desired measurement by placing one foot immediately in front of the other until you have covered the distance; or (c) if the rehearsal room floor is made up of square rubber tiles, you can find the exact measurement you want by counting the number of tiles (each tile will probably be 8 to 12 inches wide).
2. When the space is accurately determined, mark off two "entrance doors" to the room by removing chairs in appropriate places. Now arrange living room furniture (classroom materials) in a very similar fashion to that in a room you know in real life—your living room at home, for instance. Note that you will probably be making at least one conversational group, with a sofa placed against one wall and chairs placed in relationship to it. It will probably look something like Figure 1.
3. Improvise some dramatic action in this room. Here is a suggestion: A host receives three or four visitors, one at a time. After doing the improvisation, discuss where they sat down (probably in the easiest available spot, and undoubtedly in the conversational group). Also note that most living rooms this size probably have only one conversational group in order that everyone sitting in such a room can be easily included. Note how easy it is for people to carry on conversations in this physical relationship. Try some conversations using number dialogue. Try two or three other improvisations before going on to Exercise 4.

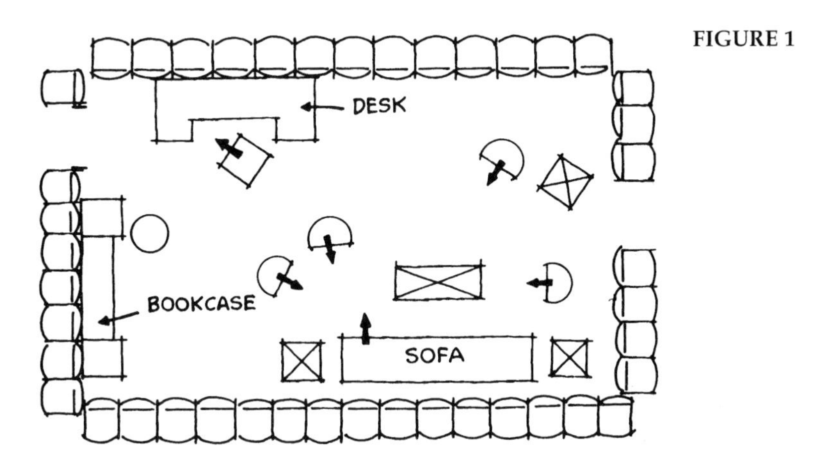

FIGURE 1

FIGURE 2

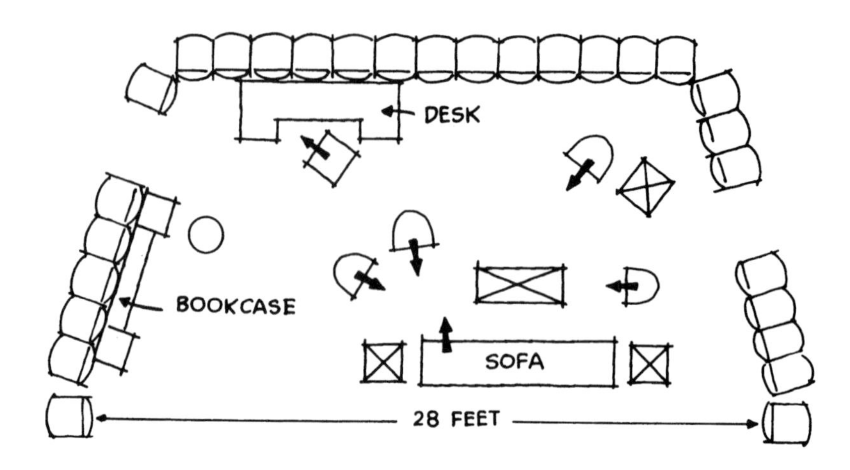

4. Now convert the room to a groundplan by doing the following:
   a. Place two chairs to represent a proscenium arch 28 feet apart on one long side of the room and center them in the middle of the room.
   b. Remove the chairs on the side and angle (rake) the side walls of the room along with any furniture placed against them to meet the proscenium chairs (the chairs mentioned in Exercise 4a). Note that the room will now look like Figure 2. Note also that the walls have been raked to allow good sightlines (so side audiences can see). Thus, it should now be clear to you that a groundplan is an artificial device that is not reality but only an illusion of reality.
5. Increase the departure from reality further by reversing the sofa and coffee table so that they face the audience. It will now look like Figure 3. The groundplan is improving but it still is not a good one because it is too simple to provide a continually varied illustration for a two-hour play. Rearrange the furniture even further by placing pieces in the downstage corners of the room (pinning down the corners) and by making a second conversational group on stage right. It should now look like Figure 4.

FIGURE 3

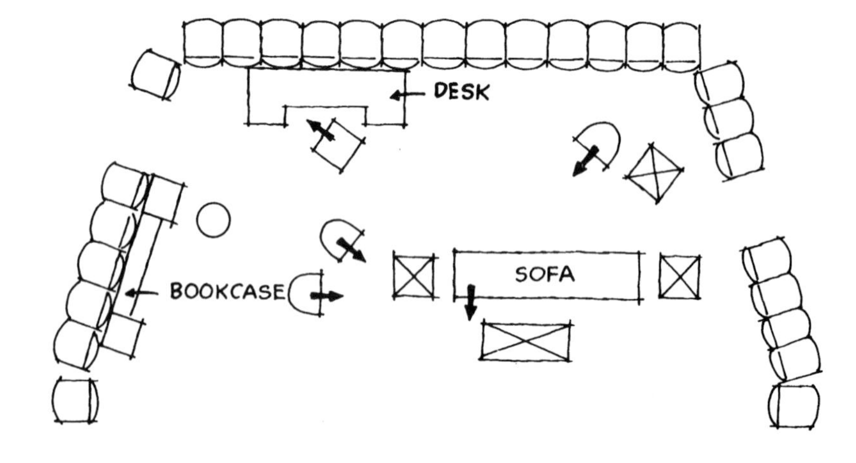

FIGURE 4

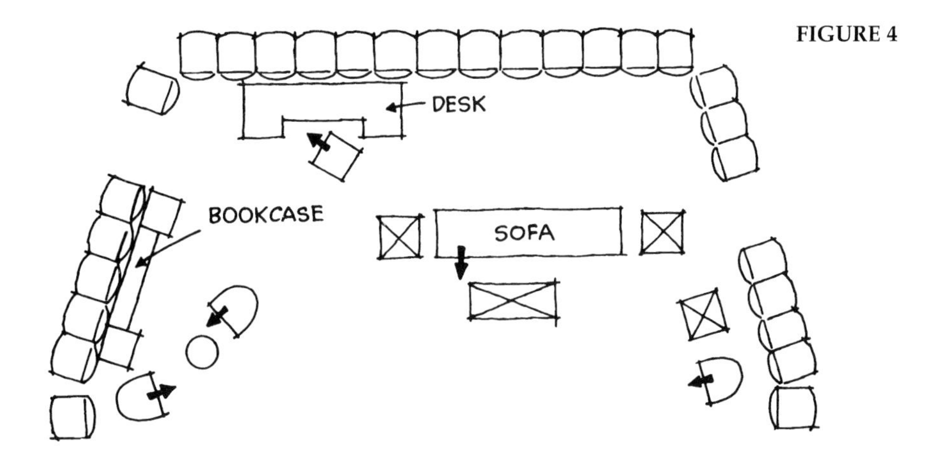

6. Now increase the architectural "strength" of the room by creating a jog in the upper left corner. Note that this modification makes the room more interesting architecturally because it reduces the obvious symmetry of the wall areas. Add chairs and furniture pieces to make it look something like Figure 5.
7. Now note the following:
   a. An *obstacle course* made of furniture has been established.
   b. Two conversational groups allow more flexibility in where people can sit to talk.
   c. The "acting" furniture for the most part occupies the middle planes of the stage—a clear departure from the real room with which you started.
   d. Multiple acting areas (see the next section) have been established, allowing very flexible use of the groundplan.
   e. The corners of the groundplan have been tied tightly to the rest of the plan, thus making the groundplan, as a whole, seem to hold the stage more solidly and to frame the actors.

FIGURE 5

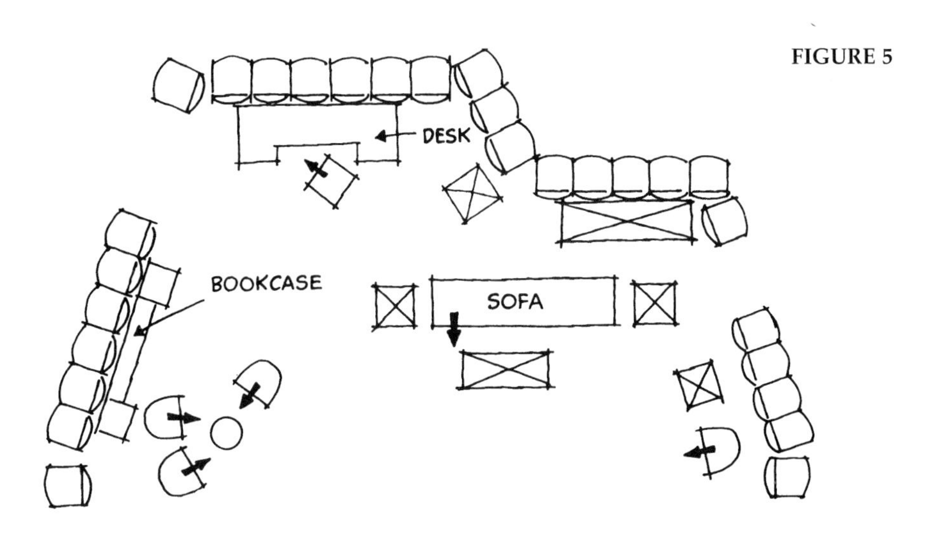

Acting Areas

Because Realistic plays involve dramatic actions in domestic environments—such as living rooms, bedrooms, kitchens, porches, backyards, and offices—they are "sit-down/stand-up plays" in a literal sense, in contrast to the stand-up nature of historical drama. *The groundplan's potential power to illustrate can be measured by defining all the acting areas.* A very handy way of doing this sort of advance forecast is the plan for sitting down, *an acting area consisting of two sit-down positions at least six feet or more apart*—that is, two chairs, or a sofa and chair, in different parts of a room. As you can see, this excludes *not only all standing positions but also those sitting positions, such as on a sofa, where two people are placed very close together.* When a groundplan is designed with *five acting areas* defined in this fashion, it can be really effective. As you can imagine, an inherent part of this rule is the concept of keeping characters apart while playing a scene, not close together as in television and motion pictures where close positions are required in making close-ups of two people.

Note in Figure 6 how each area is delineated by circling two sitting positions at least six feet apart, and how the merits of the groundplan as a whole can be tested by showing all of the available areas in one drawing (as in Figure 7). Six areas are delineated in Figure 7, but there are at least two or three more not shown because the lines would overlap too much and thus would obscure the drawing as an example.

Using the sitting-down plan to estimate the number of acting areas, and thus the flexibility of the groundplan, does not imply that standing positions are not constantly used in very effective ways. In fact, it implies quite the contrary. But standing positions will be all the more effective when enough obstacles have been placed in the room to keep the characters at some distance from one another. Each of the obstacles also acts as a physical support to any actor who stands near it, for it will emphasize the weight and mass of the actor's body. *If any groundplan has less than five acting areas, it means that the number of obstacles has been so reduced that the possibilities for tension are very limited.*

FIGURE 6

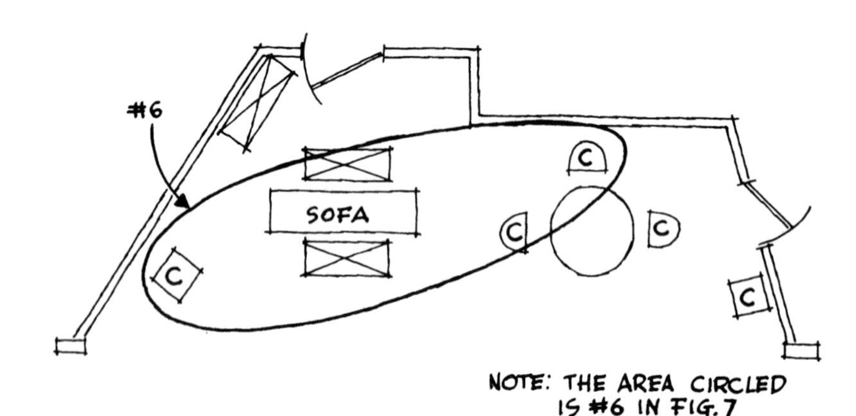

FIGURE 7

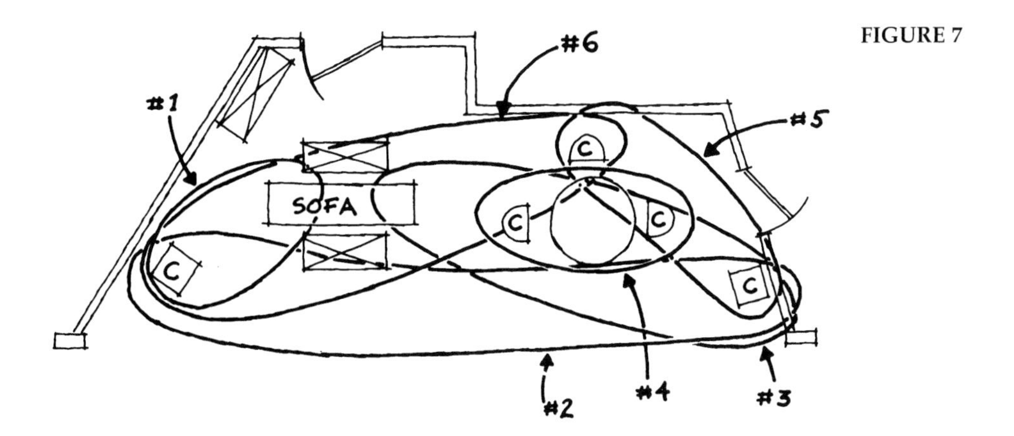

Learn this plan for sitting down because it is an effective safeguard in planning high-tension groundplans. A groundplan conceived on this principle of multiple acting areas will suggest all sorts of illustrative possibilities to actors because of its built-in tension, and you will find that it will become a quick and effective device for communication.

Tension Arrangements

A multiple-area groundplan always has high tension values because the possibilities for arranging furniture can be extensive. Your arrangements will need a certain amount of logic, of course, because rooms should more or less look like what they are intended for (likeness to real life). However, appearance is largely a secondary matter. Of much greater importance in a groundplan is its tension-creating possibilities, and if tensions are there, the appearance will probably be more interesting, even more exciting. Here are some specific suggestions for creating tension values:

1. Place your primary objects in space free of the walls so that actors can move easily around them (see Figure 8). *Objects placed against the walls merely create standing spaces with no obstacle course.* They will provide a certain amount of

FIGURE 8

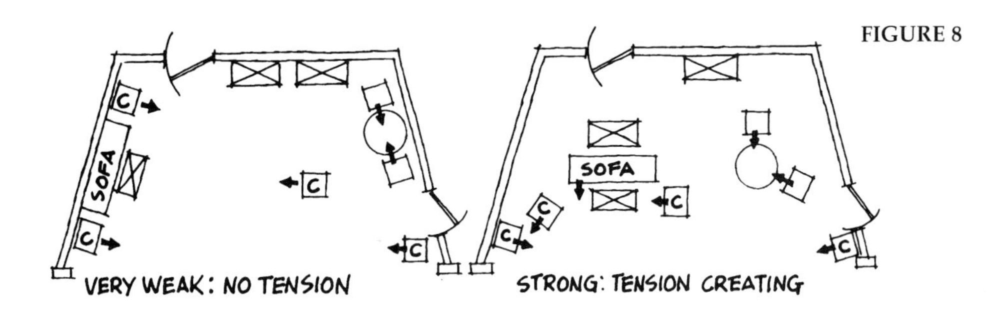

FIGURE 9

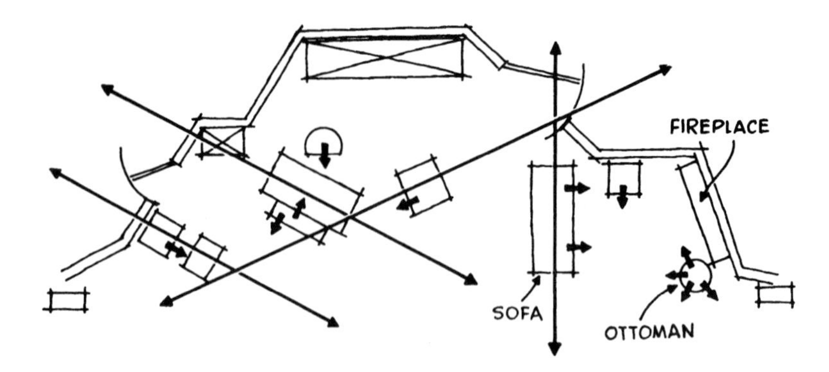

verisimilitude (likeness to real life), but they will not normally provide possibilities for conflict.

2. Work on the diagonal principle whenever possible because diagonals create more tension than objects parallel to the proscenium line. (Note the direction of the long arrows in Figure 9.)
3. Place objects in contrasting positions that can create tension by their oppositional force. (Note the short arrows in Figures 8 and 9 that show the directions the sitting positions face and consequently the oppositional forces they create.)
4. Note that walls create tension when they are broken up with jogs and diagonals (Figure 9) because they not only create architectural strength and interest but they also cut into and compress the action space.

The placement of furniture definitely takes these lines into account. Good tension-creating arrangements will arouse strong feelings in actors, thus motivating them to work against tensions as well as with them. You will be amazed at the strength of the compositions automatically created by the actors when there are strong lines of tension in a groundplan.

Groundplan on the Proscenium Stage

Although creating strong tension values is absolutely essential, you must also arrange the groundplan in accordance with the primary convention of the proscenium stage, the convention that places the audience in front of the stage within an arc of 60 to 70 degrees (see Figure 10). This arrangement implies that some arbitrary rules are automatically put into force in order to help the audience see and hear better. Normally, we are supposed to be looking in at a reproduction of real life, but the placement of the audience makes the use of the proscenium stage quite artificial and not like real life at all. The theory of the proscenium stage will be discussed in Chapter 19, but it is essential at this point that you understand that you are trying to overcome the effects of a one-sided view and are compensating for the loss of a true three-dimensional quality.

FIGURE 10

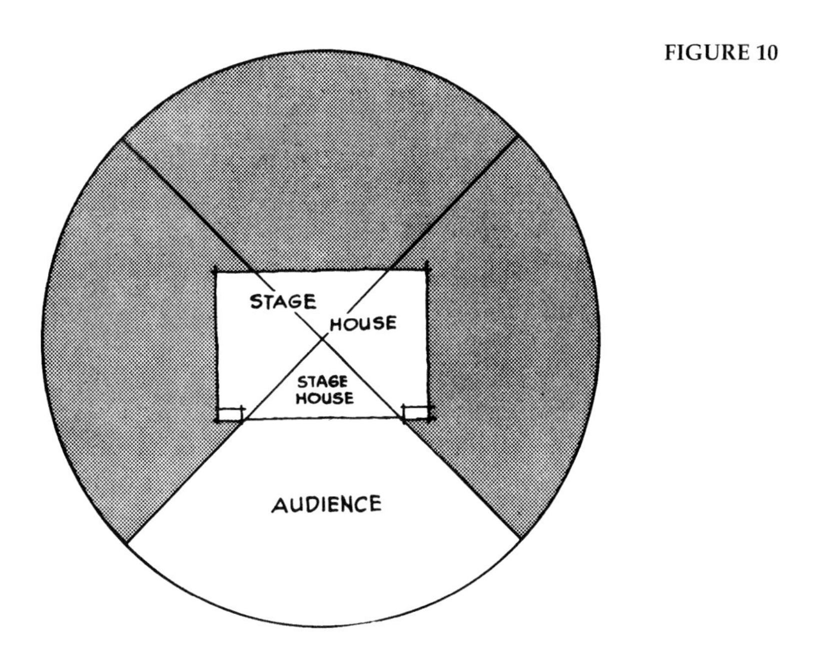

Here are a few rules you must follow if you are to overcome the flat qualities of the proscenium stage. They will also help your audience see and hear better.

- *Open the side walls to the audience.* Side walls are usually raked to open up the upstage corners of a setting (see Figures 11A and 11B), although walls perpendicular to the proscenium line (see Figure 11C) can work if the audience's seating angle to the stage is less than 70 degrees and if entrances are not placed in upstage corner positions. You must never think of the upstage corners as dead areas, for you will need every possible square inch of space to keep your compositions interesting,

FIGURE 11

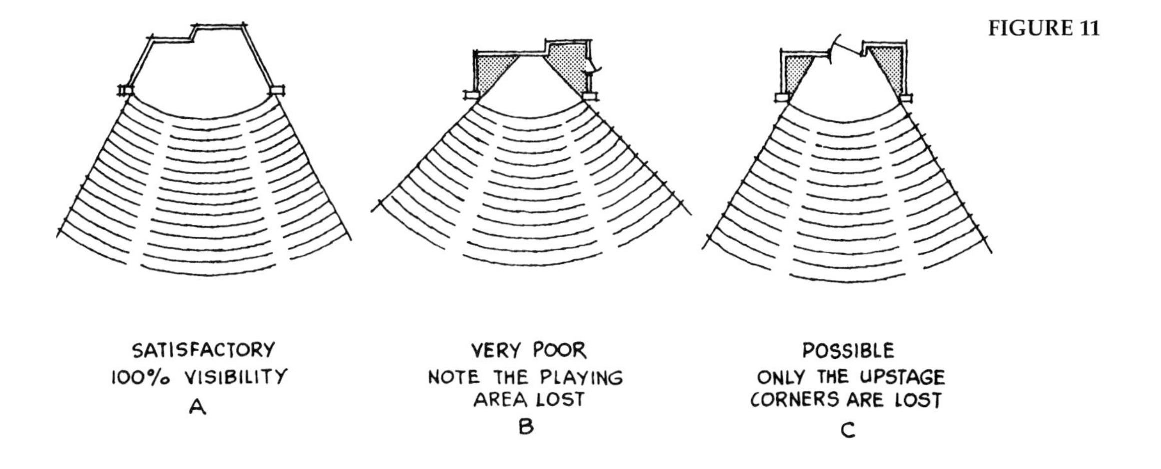

especially in one-set plays where action is carried on for two to three hours. Always consider the sight lines in composing a groundplan (see Figure 10).

- *Open the set properties (furniture) to the audience.* Throughout the seventeenth, eighteenth, and much of the nineteenth centuries, actors faced the audience when they were speaking, just as opera singers still do today. With the introduction of Realism toward the end of the nineteenth century, however, turning away from the audience, even showing the back of the actor—a very shocking behavior to turn-of-the-century theatregoers—replaced the old convention in the interest of creating a semblance of real life. Although a certain amount of psychological truth was revealed in this way, turning away from the audience resulted in obscuring both the actor's voice and face. Because there was much to be said for the old give-it-to-the-audience convention as opposed to the new concealment aesthetic, the new convention as it developed used both ideas, with the emphasis on playing to the house. The groundplan convention has developed in the same way, for the intention has been to help the actor deliver the play in every possible direction, but primarily to the frontal audience. As the furniture placement took on more and more aspects of an obstacle course by occupying the spaces where the actors had always stood, it became general practice to compensate by opening individual furniture pieces to the house. *The general rule thus requires that all much-used furniture pieces be placed prominently as far downstage and as near center stage as possible.* The *illusion* of reality is thus preserved, although the room is anything but real. Do not think, then, that you will help an actor by placing a chair on the curtain line facing upstage, for you will merely be blocking the audience's view of the stage and forcing the actor, if he sits in the chair, to talk upstage, thus cutting off the audience's hearing, as well (see Figure 12). Such placement does not in any way create more reality but instead

FIGURE 12

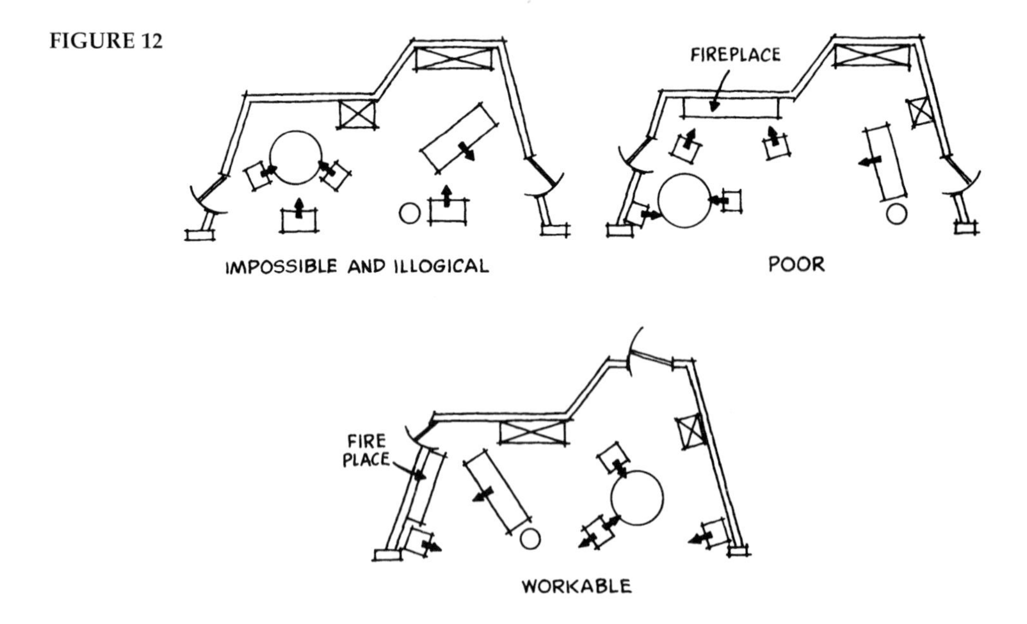

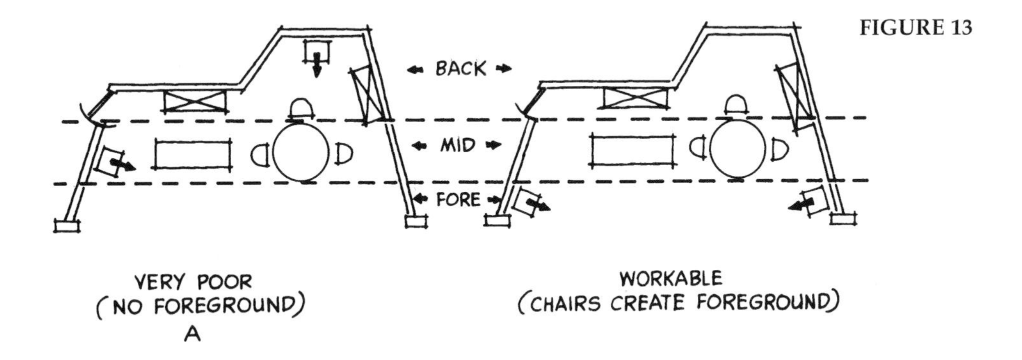

FIGURE 13

merely confuses an audience. Avoid such odd theatrics; instead, you should comply with the conventions of the proscenium stage.

- *Pin the downstage corners of the groundplan tightly to the rest of the plan.* Because the illusion created should be that of a walled room, you will not only help the effect of wall enclosure but also increase the illusion of depth to the room if you place pieces of furniture (chairs or other sitting pieces) at both of the downstage corners of the room and *encourage actors to use them. This arrangement will provide a downstage foreground to contrast with midground and background,* thus tying the groundplan together and intensifying the three-dimensional quality of the staging. This rule is very important because the furniture will help frame the actors in all the positions they take on the stage (see Figure 13). Moreover, without such sitting positions, actors will tend to avoid using the downstage corners, which will result in only a partial use of the total possible acting area.

Ingenuity in Groundplan Design

You must learn to be ingenious in arranging groundplans. Always avoid the dull and trite—what may be called the *no-room:* that bare, three-walled room without architectural jogs for relief; that room with a routine selection and placement of furniture; that room with doors placed in balanced positions in the walls. New ideas about illustrating the action will present themselves to both you and the actors if you think and feel freshly about what makes up a groundplan.

Flexibility, Testing, and Improvisation

You should make not just one groundplan, but several, and then remake them. Because the groundplan is the basis for all the other visual tools, it must be the best possible one you can devise. Therefore, your personal flexibility in this regard is absolutely essential; you must always be ready to discard the groundplan that does not work and start over again, rebuilding on what you have discovered. Making a good groundplan always involves improvisation, for you are trying to project its uses through your own imagination.

One way to approach making a groundplan is to have some specific ideas in mind, and then have the actors help you discover the best possible arrangement. They will enjoy this game of looking for fresh ways of illustrating, and such play will help them better understand the given circumstances. Remember: *A groundplan is only as good as its potential to arouse the imagination of the actors who will use it.* They must learn to live in it and to exploit its every possibility. If you are to help them fly, you must help them find the flying machine that will get them off the ground. Once again: make, test, remake, improvise; make, test, remake, improvise; and so on.

EXERCISES

1. On the basis of the given circumstances of a study play, design a groundplan. (Be absolutely certain to avoid any directions in the playscript that may prescribe a setting. Find all you need in the given circumstances buried in the dialogue, and then let your imagination go free.) Now answer the following questions about the groundplan: Do you have an obstacle course? Is it a no-room? How many acting areas does it contain? What is tension creating in the plan? How ingenious is it? Now compare your groundplan with those groundplans done by other members of the class. Evaluate the differences carefully. Who has been trite and who original? How many different kinds of furniture has the whole class used?
2. Design groundplans for two or three plays and measure their effectiveness with the same criteria as is used at the end of the improvisational exercise earlier in this chapter (pages 70–73).
3. Set up a groundplan on the classroom floor (be certain to measure the outside dimensions carefully) by using whatever classroom furniture is available. Discuss its effectiveness. After suggestions have been offered, alter the plan to produce a maximum of interest. Repeat this exercise several times, with different students setting up plans and others criticizing their effectiveness and doing the alterations. Work for ingenuity and freshness.
4. Do a group improvisation in one of these plans using number dialogue with three or four improvisers. What did the plan suggest to the improvisers? What can you, as a director, suggest to the improvisors to help their imaginations find different uses of the plan? After discussing the plan and after reviewing the possibilities of dramatic action in the improvisation, redo the improvisation with a different set of participants.

10

Composition

Helping Actors Discover and Project Basic Relationships

You are now ready to put organic blocking to work (see pages 63–65). The techniques discussed in this and the following chapters are devoted to two ways of looking at *activity* on the stage: (1) from the actor's view and (2) from the audience's view. The first is absolutely basic to an actor's understanding of the conflict his character is going through in a play, and the second is about the craft of showing that conflict fully and clearly to an audience. Your attention should be focused primarily on the first objective, but *the second objective,* if the first one works, *will probably be accomplished simultaneously.* Later, when you work with more accomplished actors, you will not need to position them so much, because the actors will know how to relate by themselves; they may actually insist on participating in working out their own blocking as they develop their intensive relationships with other characters on the stage. But now, you must learn "to see" in these two slightly different ways.

Definition

Composition is the physical arrangement of actor-characters in a groundplan for the purposes of discovering dramatic action and of illustrating it in the simplest possible way through emphasis and contrast. *If actors are made aware of basic physical relationships, they will perceive dramatic action in greater depth and be able to transfer this intensity to an audience.*

Compositions on the Proscenium Stage

Because the proscenium wall (the wall that separates the audience area from the stage) has a frame and the audience sits out front and looks through it, all the basic requirements of perspective drawing apply; that is, you must be able to see depth as well as width and height. The director's job, then, is to help arrange the actors in this three-dimensional cube of the stage in a *series of still shots*—a full play would require several hundred such still shots—so that an audience can sense and feel basic forces in a play.

Strictly defined, composition does not involve a movement (transit of the actor from one point on the stage to another). Instead, composition is static. *It is a caught moment. It is a primitive form on which will be superimposed the other elements that make illustration*—gesture, picturization, and movement (which have yet to be discussed). Without the primitive, architectural arrangement of composition, actors cannot convey the meaning of their basic relationship, and thus their feelings about a dramatic action.

Because a play is spoken—an enormously important fact in the theatre—*an actor's body must be relatively, if not entirely, quiet* during much of a play; otherwise, an audience simply will not be able to hear what the actor says. Animated illustrators (gestures and movement) are so alive and vigorous because of their living and breathing qualities that their meanings are conveyed first (the eye is quicker than the ear); therefore, they must not be allowed to dominate composition. Although you must keep the still-shot concept of composition in mind, you should understand that a play in performance is made up of a great many of these shots that are tied together by movements of the actors that place them on one or another part of the stage. In this sense, *a performed play is a continuous alternation of composition and movement.*

In the nineteenth century, when the laws of the proscenium stage were taking form, this rule of alternation was observed quite rigidly. With the passing of nineteenth-century poetic drama and with increased emphasis on visual representation in the twentieth-century theatre, the rule of alternation was modified by allowing actors to move during their own speeches as well as during the speeches of other actors. The easier-to-hear prose dialogue not only made it more feasible to break down the old rule but it also encouraged the desire for a more completely animated performance. Whatever that modification may be, *a large amount of movement is risky when significant speeches are being delivered.* Consequently, experienced directors and actors learn to stand still and to *hold composition* at important moments. Motion pictures always appear more animated than plays because they seem to be continuously moving; but when you watch the work of a good motion-picture director, you will see an enormous number of still shots (largely close-ups). We "hear" a film because we are forced to do so by the director's selection of shots and by the actors who learn not to move their heads because they find that moving their eyes and lips—a required motion-picture technique—is more effective. *An important principle in acting is learning to hold the body and head still,* so that when they do move, they will "say" something specific.

A composition on the stage, then, is a photographic still shot of great value. Once again, here is the point: The director must learn the importance of encouraging actors to evolve good compositions because they form the basis of all good illustrations by containing primitive meanings and mood values.

Characteristics of Composition

Compositions Have Basic Meanings

From the preceding discussion, you can see that a composition involves *two or more actors* taking specific places on the stage. Try to see composition as made up of bodies *without* moving arms or legs—neutral forms like mannequins—who stand on marked points on the stage floor but that have the capability of facing different directions and bending to kneeling or sitting positions. This neutrality of the body position is very important if you are to see the meanings that come from compositions alone and not confuse them with those that come from gestures and movements.

Now observe the relationships of the two bodies in Figure 14. The arrows on the heads represent the directions that the bodies are facing. What does each composition mean? Try to guess their meanings before looking at the suggestions in the following list:

1. *A* and *B* either like each other or are confronting each other in anger.
2. *A* is playing hard to get, with *B* the weaker.
3. The situation in item 2 is reversed, with *B* playing hard to get.
4. The relationship between *A* and *B* is disrupted completely with backs turned to each other.
5. Although *A* and *B* face each other, *A* is now much separated from *B*, indicating a coolness, though opposition is still present.

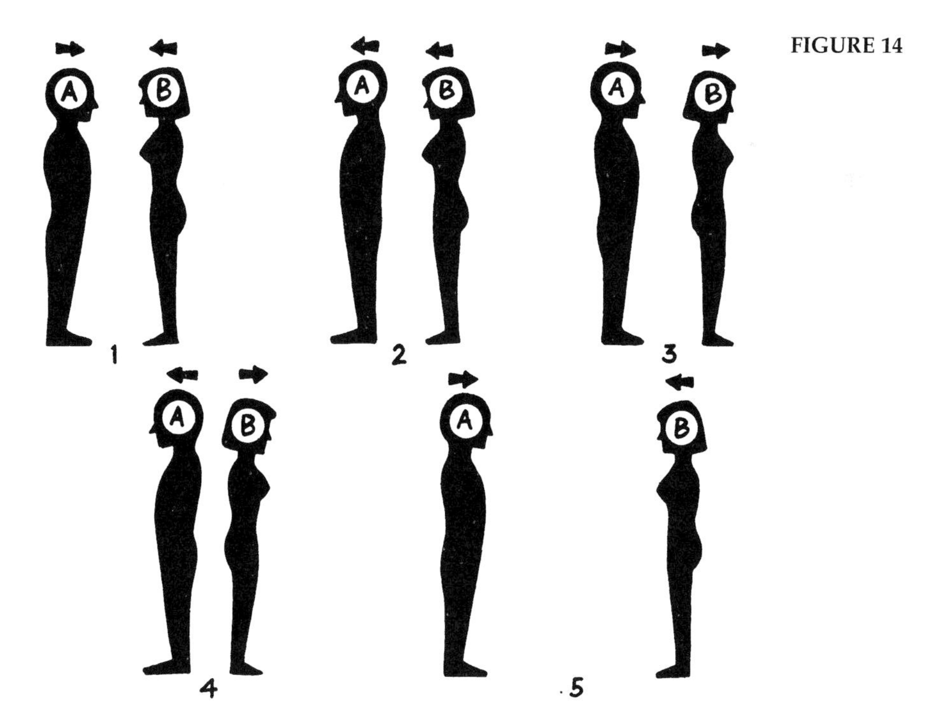

FIGURE 14

If you try these same exercises with one or both bodies seated, you will see that new meanings emerge.

Here is the point: All compositions are made of roughly these same juxtapositions. *Characters in a play are either together, apart, or conform to some gradation of these two basic situations.* Thus, composition illustrates in the simplest possible way the dramatic action—the conflicts—between two or more characters. Without good composition, there is no clear storytelling.

Composition as Director-Actor Communication

The communication inherent in composition is now evident. A director can suggest to his actors their basic relationships with other characters by merely placing them in stage arrangements: By keeping the actors apart, they can sense some level of their separation; by placing them close together, they can sense the intensity of their conflict (love is also conflict). Actors usually accept these hints quickly and are eager to experiment with them.

However, when doing improvisations, young actors, in the interest of developing an action (maintaining improvised dialogue), will forget that composition is a device for illustration. Though the action may be intense in the minds of the improvisers, it will appear to a viewer to be completely internal because it is not illustrated. In other words, the improvisers may understand the action completely, but without employing strong compositional values, they fail to illustrate it (or else they illustrate it very poorly); frequently, they will use the same two or three compositions over and over again. On the other hand, a well-trained actor sees compositions as one of his most valuable tools for illustrating his actions, and he will look for every possible variation to keep that illustration as fresh and as varied as possible.

Composition can be used most effectively as a device for communicating with actors when rehearsals are well advanced. It is then that a director can communicate his most subtle points about the action by helping the actors find fresh and meaningful compositions, particularly in accord with the set properties in the groundplan. These properties always play a part in composition by becoming animated when they are employed by the actors. *A director who is afraid to introduce new compositions late in a rehearsal period fails to recognize their value as communicative devices, for good illustration of dramatic action can only be found through constant experiment.* The director must learn to gamble with new compositions in the interest of stimulating in the actors new insights into dramatic action.

Composition, therefore, is not something arranged only for its pictorial value to an audience, but it is a *basic device for communicating to actors perceptions about their relationships with other characters.* If this arrangement is dynamically effected, even though a composition holds a set place on the stage floor, it will move an audience. There is certainly something pleasurable in the harmonic balance of a stage picture, but that matter is secondary. If the action is illustrated honestly and intensively, its beauty will emerge in all its truth.

Techniques of Composition

The actor, as well as the director, must learn all of the following basic techniques of composition in order to know as many ways as possible of bringing variety to stage illustration. Holding an audience for two to three hours requires much skill in finding variety, especially if only one setting is used.

The Individual Actor

When talking about composition, we mean the arrangement of two or more actors on the stage. However, *the director and actor must be fully aware of the compositional force of each individual on the stage before any arrangement of groups can take place.* The purpose here is to see the individual isolated in order to assess his potential force in a group arrangement.

Body positions. Stage right and stage left are the actor's right and left as he faces an audience. Now face the body to the major points of a circle, and you have the body positions (see Figure 15). Note the designations for these positions: full-front, one-quarter left, and so on.

The force of body positions is very great in any composition, for turning your back on another actor has one meaning, and facing him has another, as already suggested in Figure 14. Variations between these extremes give us the necessary nuances. Beginning actors either want to face the audience because they don't understand the concept of reciprocation in acting, or they want to face other actors continuously, thus losing the freshness and new illustrations brought about by varying the body's position.

FIGURE 15

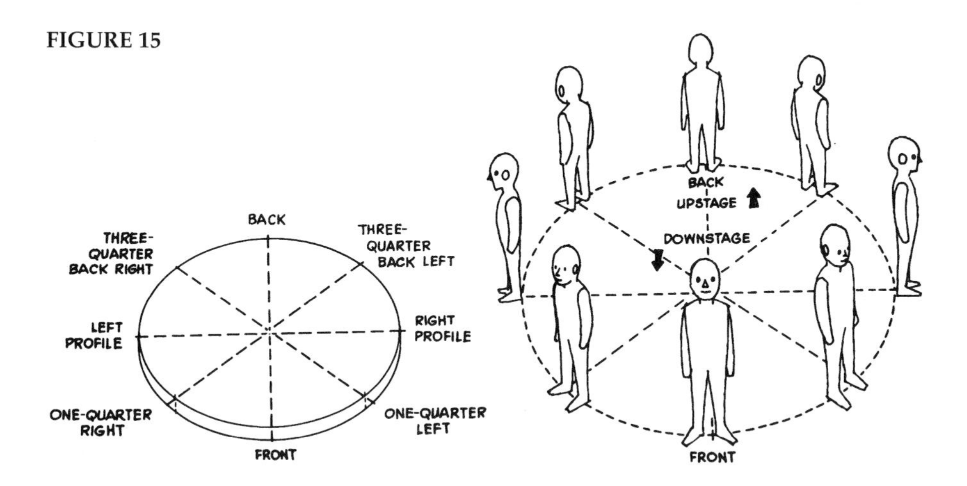

EXERCISES

1. You and five classmates assume different body positions, with the remaining members of the class identifying each. Be absolutely certain that each of you observes the neutral position—that is, arms at the sides, head facing the same direction as the body, and no facial expression.
2. At a signal from the instructor, each of you take a different body position, and the class identifies all the different positions. Repeat this exercise many times until the positions are thoroughly learned and can easily be identified in the stage terminology indicated in Figure 15.
3. What is the basic meaning of the full-back position? The full-front? Either profile?
4. Can one actor force another (dramatic action) through his use of body position?

Levels. Levels refer to the actual *head level* of the actor. He is at his highest level when standing, and any variation that takes his head toward the floor is a change in level (see Figure 16). When he uses an artificial level introduced in a set design, such as platforms or steps, the actor's level changes even more drastically (see Figure 17).

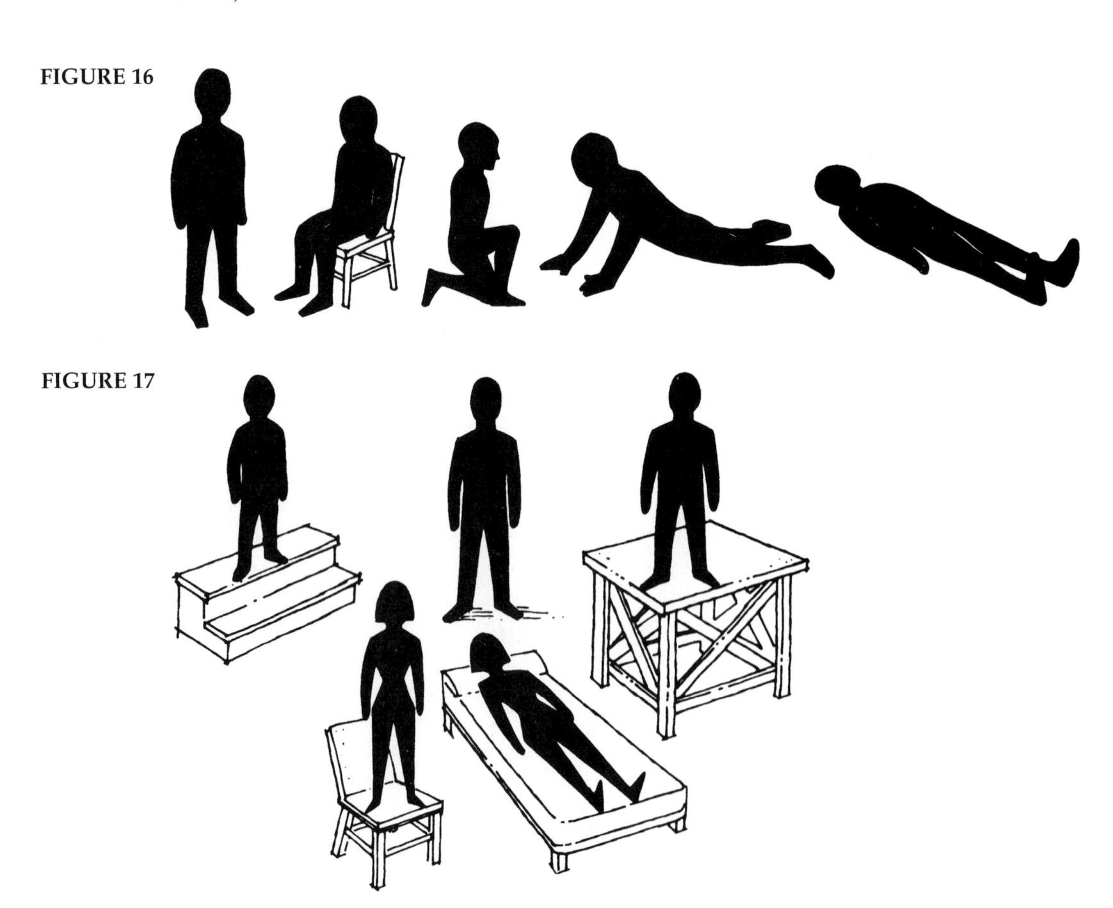

FIGURE 16

FIGURE 17

EXERCISES

1. Without using any artificial levels, you and two classmates (observing the rule for the neutral actor as far as possible) assume different body levels. Identify these levels. Now, at the instructor's signal, each of you assume a new level. Identify and repeat.
2. Repeat Exercise 1 with artificial levels (platforms, chairs, etc.), beginning first with fully erect bodies, then progressing to variations in body level. Identify and repeat several times. Be sure to observe neutrality as far as possible.
3. What are the meanings of the various levels? Compare the meanings of a standing actor with those of a sitting actor, then with those of a reclining actor. Do you see how each position conveys a general meaning? Keep in mind that until Realism came to the stage in the nineteenth century, actors seldom sat on chairs or other objects but performed plays in standing positions. As noted previously, Realism is sometimes called *sit-down drama* in contrast to the *stand-up drama* before the middle of the nineteenth century.
4. Contrast the meanings conveyed by an actor when he first stands on a high platform and then reclines on the floor. You must suggest the most basic meaning, not the storytelling or pictured meaning, such as making a speech or sleeping, because the actor could be doing a dozen different things in each position. How dominant would he be in the elevated position? How weak would he be in the reclining position?
5. Can one actor force another (dramatic action) through the use of levels?
6. Combine body positions and levels by placing yourself and two others in separate chairs. At the instructor's signal, each of you takes a different body position and different level. Note the variety and contrast that are possible.

Planes. The concept of stage *planes* applies only to the proscenium stage, where the term is used as a way of pointing out that the proscenium stage has depth as well as width. When talking about an actor "moving through the stage planes," we mean that he moves upstage or downstage. *Up* and *down* are terms that have been used by theatre people for nearly 300 years to indicate directions. In the past, stages were raked; that is, stage floors actually *inclined upward* toward the rear of the stage, some of them very steeply, as can still be seen in the famous Teatro Farnese, built in 1619 in Parma, Italy, where an actor quite literally walks *up*hill or *down*hill, depending on which way he goes on the incline. In modern times, stage floors are flat so that scenery can be erected with little difficulty anyplace on the stage. But the old stage terms are still used to specify depth, and therefore the concept of stage planes endures. To compensate for the loss of the incline, theatre architects have inclined the audience, and very steeply in some recently built theatres.

Although planes are purely imaginary, you would be able to see them easily in a physical way if you were to hang several drops on stage battens located two feet apart, and then were to look at them either from overhead or from the side (see Figure 18). Each drop would represent a plane. Now remove the drops but keep the idea of the positions they occupy by placing actors in each plane (see Figure 19).

A human being is about a foot thick. But because we cannot actually see much difference in planes if they are too close together, we think of each plane on the stage as being about two feet deep. More important, because the audience sits directly

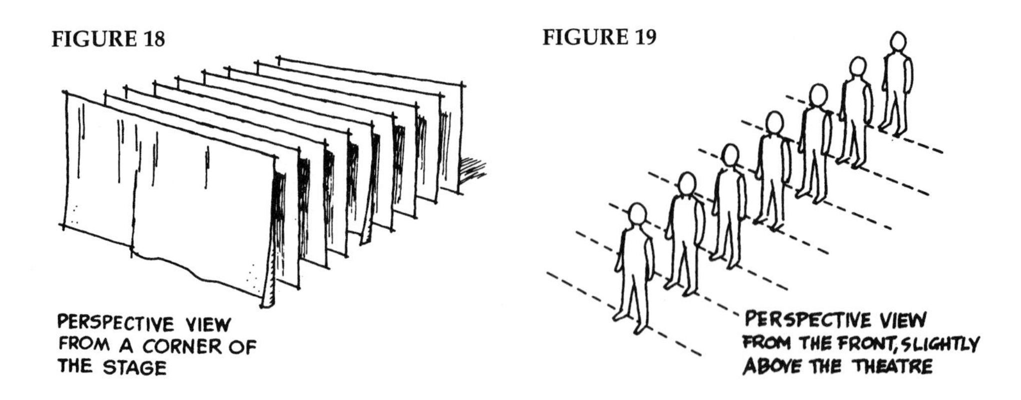

facing the stage in proscenium theatre, objects close to them seem much larger than those farther upstage. Thus, instead of seeing actors or objects as they are represented, we see them as they appear in Figure 20.

Understanding the concept of planes is valuable to an actor because then he can think in terms of moving from or toward an audience as well as crossing in front of it. Most beginning actors and directors think only in terms of the latter and do not see the strong dramatic ideas that can be conveyed by the graduated upstage and downstage positions.

EXERCISES

1. If your class is working on a stage, lower some battens and try to imagine drops hanging from them. Count the number of lines on your stage and note the space between each of them.

FIGURE 20

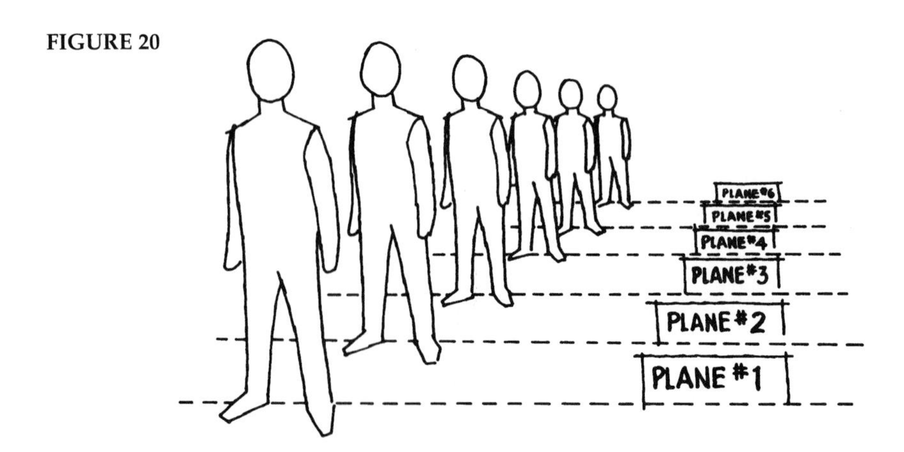

2. Place six of your classmates, all facing full-front, in six successive planes (two feet apart) in a slanting row upstage. Observe neutrality. Can you see the different planes? Can you see the difference in size? Squinting will help you see better.
3. Now place the six classmates, all facing full-front, in different planes but in various parts of the stage. Observe neutrality. Identify the planes.
4. Place one classmate in an extreme upstage plane and another in an extreme downstage plane, both in full-front positions. What is the meaning of each position? Why is the one nearer to you stronger?

Horizontal locations. Just as planes are the designations of depth on the proscenium stage, so horizontal locations declare the position of an actor on the width of the stage. Thus, we say *stage right (SR), stage left (SL),* and *center stage (CS).* Often, the width is divided into even more precise locations: *left center (LC)* and *right center (RC),* as in Figure 21. This concept of horizontal location implies that the stage has horizontal meaning as well as depth meaning. There are also differences in the actual location simply because in a proscenium theatre, where the audience sits in front, the center can be seen well by everyone. Thus, the center location is designated as the strongest and the two side extremes are considered less strong, much in the same way that differences are seen in the extremes of upstage and downstage.

EXERCISES

1. Place five classmates, facing full-front, in the five horizontal locations of stage right, stage left, center stage, left center, and right center. Observe neutrality. Identify each position.
2. What meaning does an actor have in the center location? What is the meaning at either the extreme right or extreme left location?

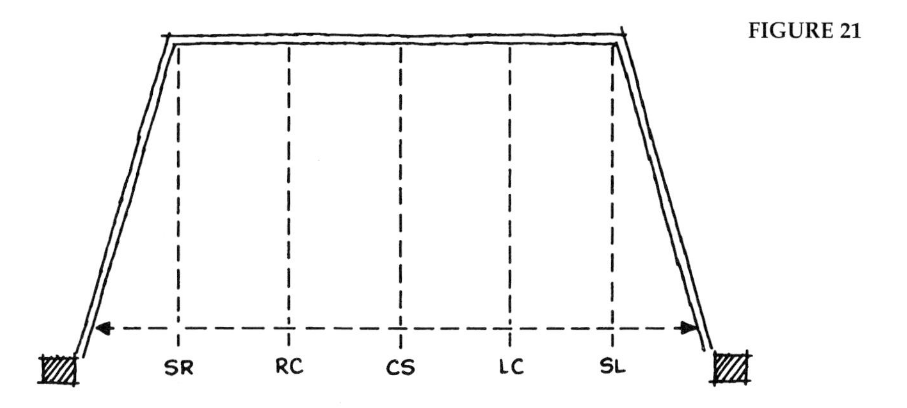

FIGURE 21

The Group: Creating Emphasis

Because all compositions are made up of two or more actors, a problem immediately arises over which actor (or character) will have the emphasis. If a director looks at a composition purely as a member of an audience, he realizes that *he must create that emphasis or the audience cannot follow the dramatic action simply and effortlessly;* that is, it will be difficult to tell who is talking or who is strongest in the action. But when the director looks at his possibilities for director-actor communication, he knows that his best hope of finding the appropriate emphasis is to convey to his actors what he thinks is important in the action and how important it is. Only out of this sort of suggestion will a natural emphasis flow. He thus encourages specific groupings in order to suggest not only literal meanings to the actors but sublimated ones, as well. He is working on the principle that sensitive and varied compositions will arouse appropriate tensions in the actors (organic blocking), who will then communicate directly and much more sensitively to an audience. An actor who is given a dominant position will certainly exploit it fully in his forcing of other actor-characters.

Emphasis, then, is a basic necessity in good composition. It is created by contrasting the four variables of composition—body position, levels, planes, and horizontal locations—in the following group arrangements: focuses, diagonals, triangles, space and mass, repetition or support, climactic compositions, stage areas, and compositions with furniture.

Focuses. There are two kinds of focuses: (1) *eye focus,* in which one actor looks directly at another actor (see Figure 22); and (2) *line focus,* in which one actor turns his body directly toward another actor and may emphasize it further by pointing with arms, legs, or torso, or all three simultaneously (see Figure 23). Both eye and line focuses are frequently used at the same time (see Figure 24). Both work on the principle of imaginary lines that run from one actor to another; the lines may be only partially suggested, but such is the nature of the imagination that it is able to complete the lines by seeing them in the mind's eye. (Note the dotted lines in Figures 22, 23, and 24.)

EXERCISES

1. Illustrate eye focus by placing two of your classmates in contrasting one-quarter positions with eyes straight ahead. Without moving his head, have *A* turn his eyes on *B.* What is the effect? Now have *A* turn his head and look full face at *B.* Is the effect even stronger? Now have him turn his body, as well. What is the effect? Repeat this exercise many times in all variations of eye contact and head positions. What do the actors feel?
2. Illustrate line focus by setting up many compositions like the examples given in Figures 23 and 24. *Be sure to be at a distance from the compositions so that you can actually see the lines.* What do the individuals feel? What do the compositions mean? You can actually see the lines in a literal way if you use a piece of cord attached to each actor. A large piece of rubberized material, such as an elastic band, works even better because the tension between the two actors can be literally illustrated.

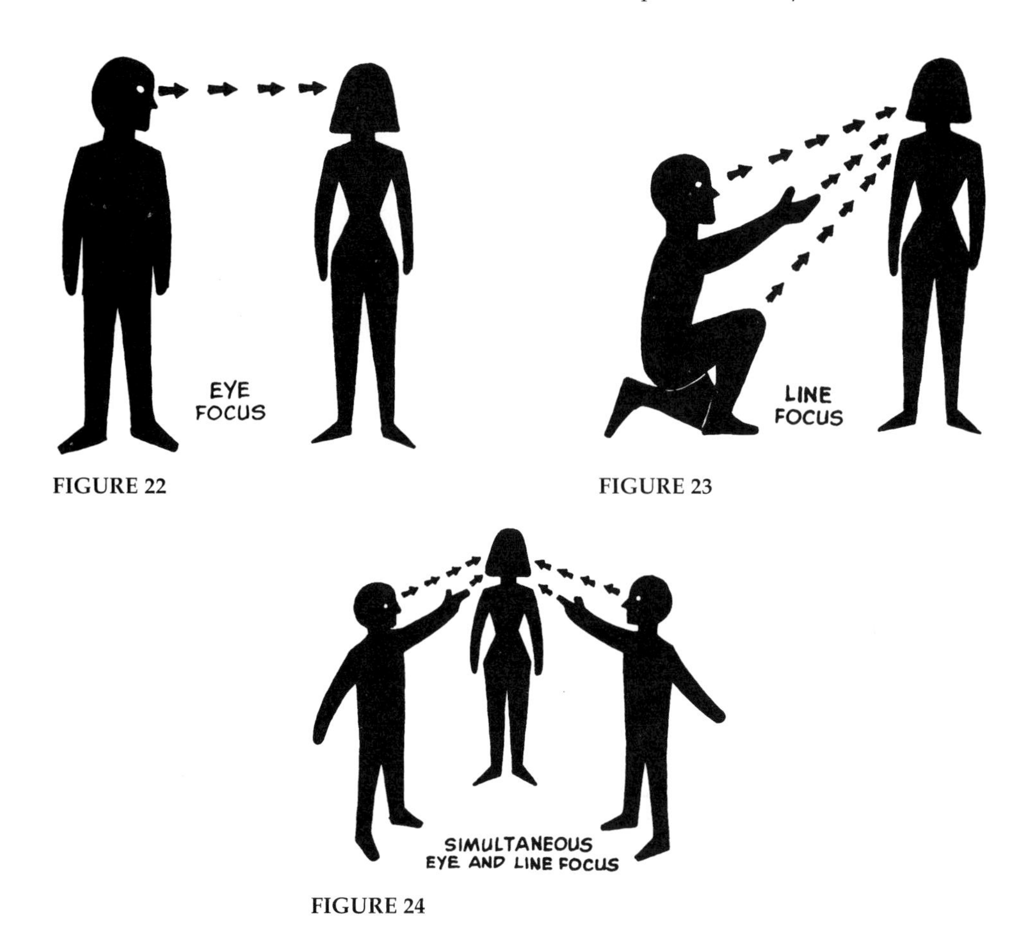

FIGURE 22

FIGURE 23

FIGURE 24

Diagonals. A composition of two actors may be made with the actors in the same plane. This is a *shared* composition because each actor has equal emphasis (if the level and body positions are similar), as in Figure 25. However, they will take on different meanings if the planes are contrasted, thus creating an imaginary diagonal line (see Figure 26). Note that the emphasis here is on the upstage figure. *The diagonal is more emphatic than a line parallel to the front line of the stage* because it moves both horizontally and vertically (upstage) in the imagination of the spectator. Directors learn to employ diagonal compositions because of the tension that they readily create.

EXERCISE

Illustrate the strength of diagonals by showing the contrast they make to those lines parallel to the front of the stage. What do the individuals feel?

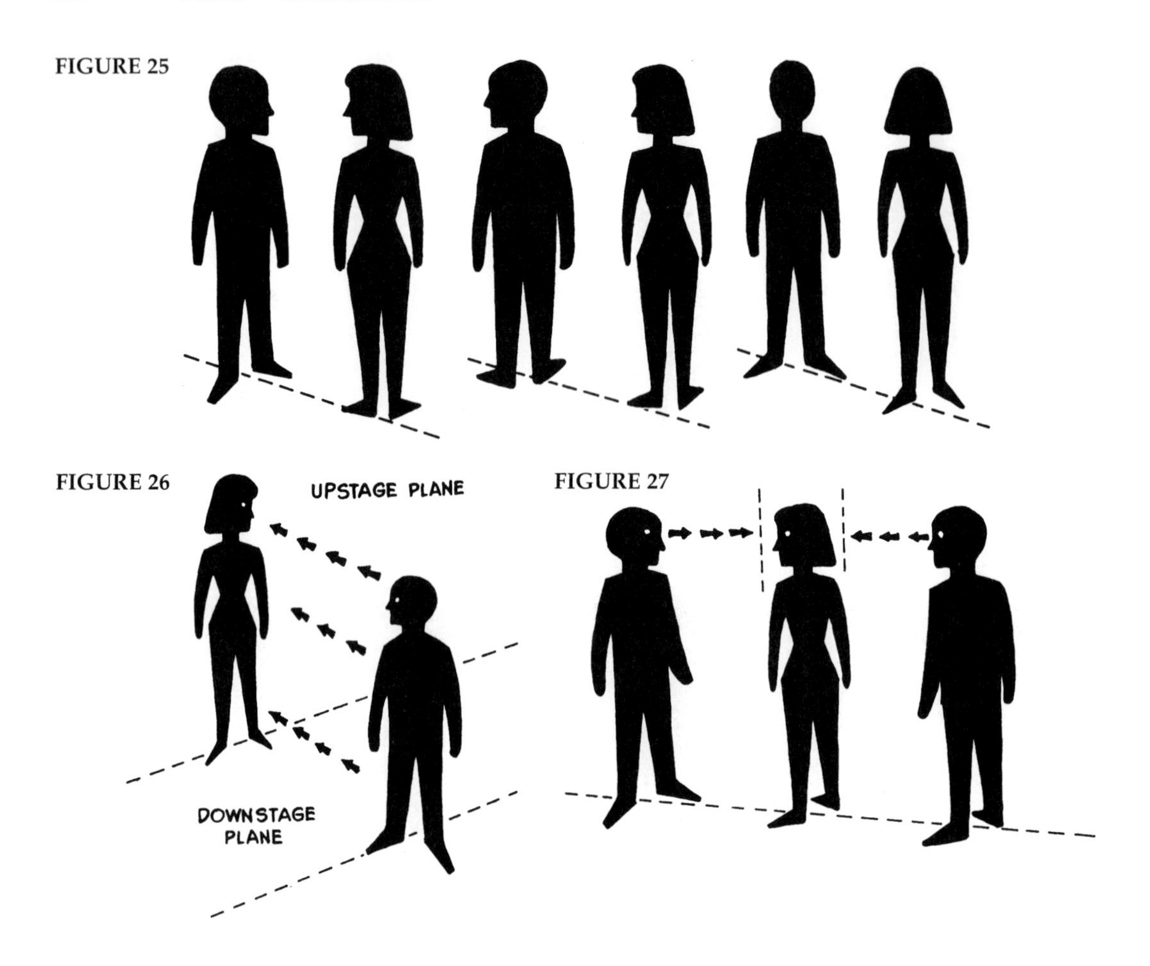

Triangles. Compositions of three or more actors are arranged in *triangles.* It is obvious that if three actors stood in the same plane, they could not easily see one another, for the actor in the center would block the vision of the other two (see Figure 27). In addition, triangles employ diagonals, the dynamic lines on the stage. By varying the four basics of composition (body positions, levels, planes, and horizontal locations) at the points of the triangle, a variety of meanings will emerge.

An endless variety of interesting compositions can also be made by varying the triangle in the following ways:

1. Shorten or lengthen the legs of the triangle (see Figure 28).
2. Increase or decrease the angles (see Figure 29).
3. Change the total area of the triangle (see Figure 30).
4. Change the position of the base leg from a line horizontal to the front stage line (see Figure 31) to a line that runs diagonally to it (see Figure 32).
5. Break the legs of triangles when there are more than three actors by inserting actors at points in the legs (see Figure 33).

FIGURE 28

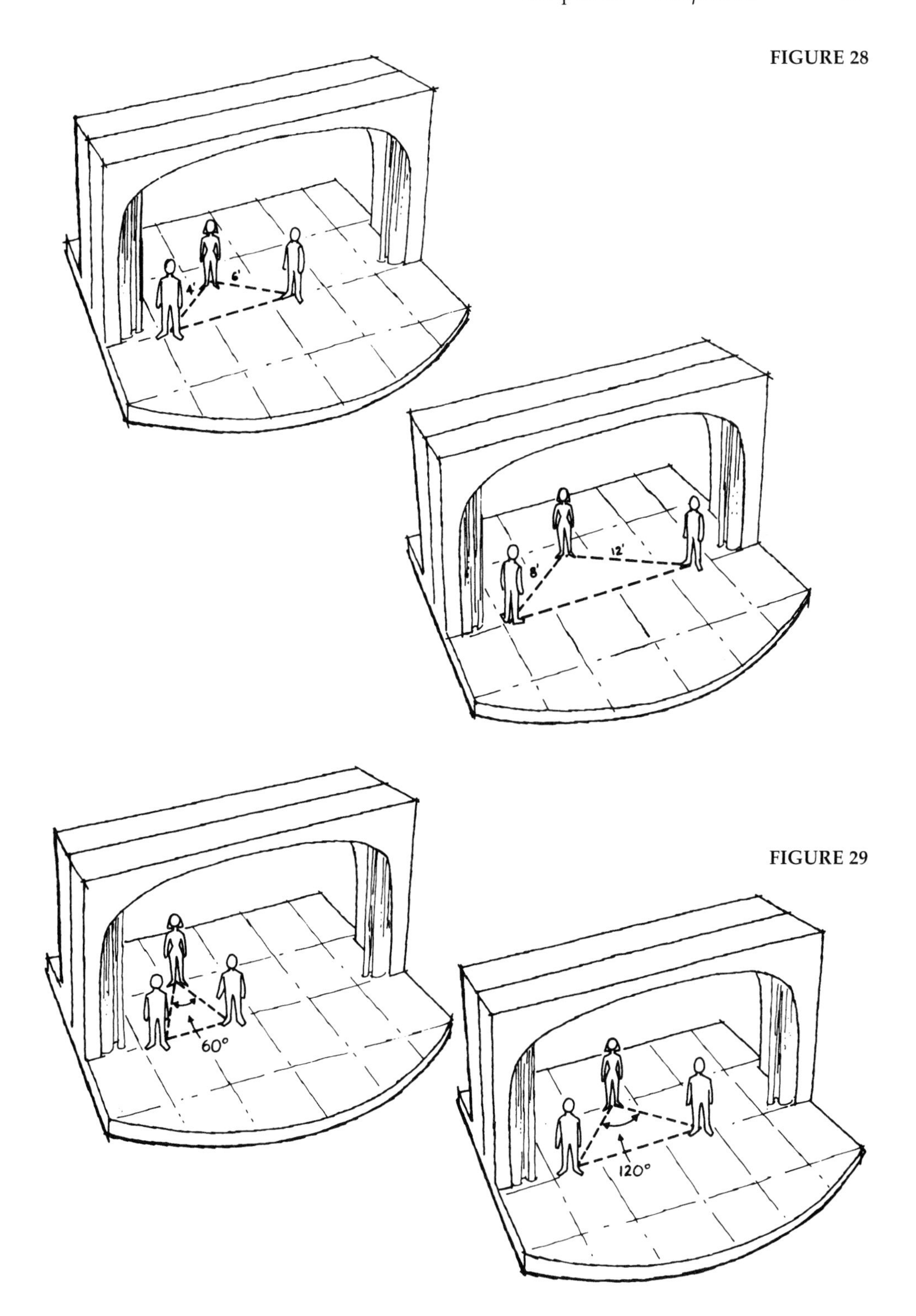

FIGURE 29

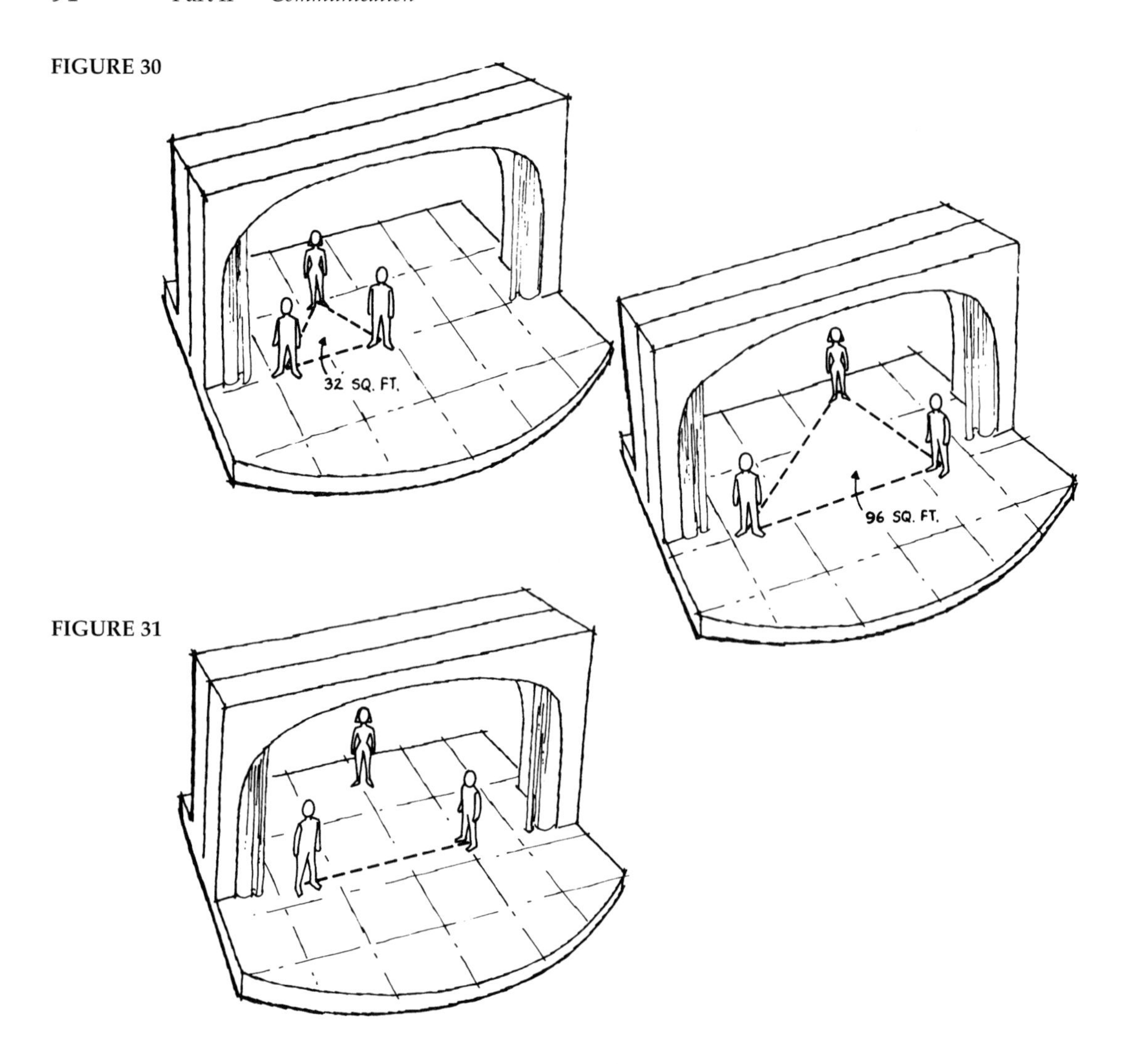

FIGURE 30

FIGURE 31

You must learn to avoid *flat* triangles (those having little depth) because they can neither be seen by an audience nor can they convey to actors much sense of character relationship. Make a rule for yourself not to allow triangles less than two or three planes in depth (see Figure 34).

EXERCISE

Illustrate the use of triangles by placing classmates *in all the examples described in this section.* Identify the location of the points of the triangles and the length of the lines. Make some flat triangles and illustrate their ineffectiveness in contrast to deep ones. What do the individuals feel? Do you see differences in meaning as the triangles change?

FIGURE 32

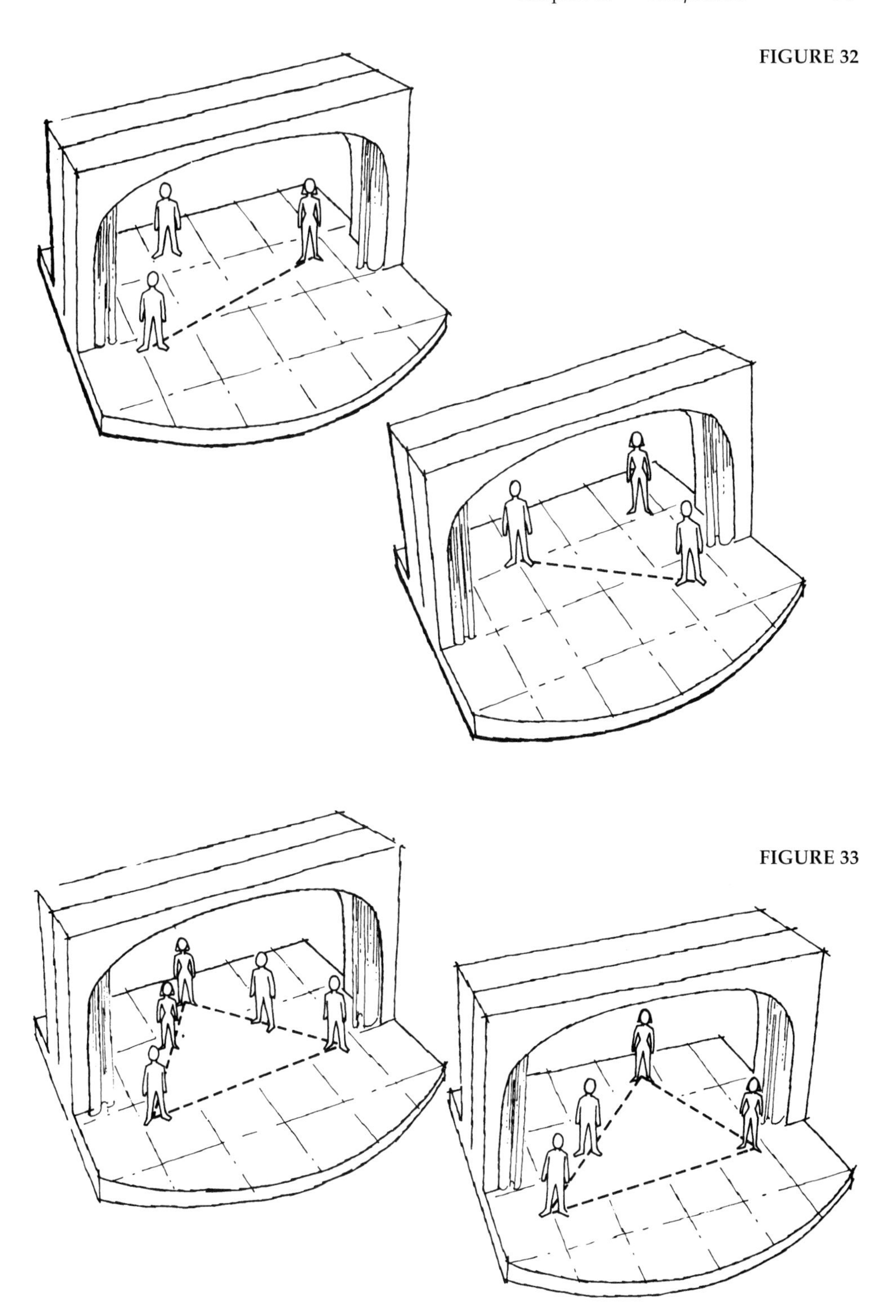

FIGURE 33

FIGURE 34

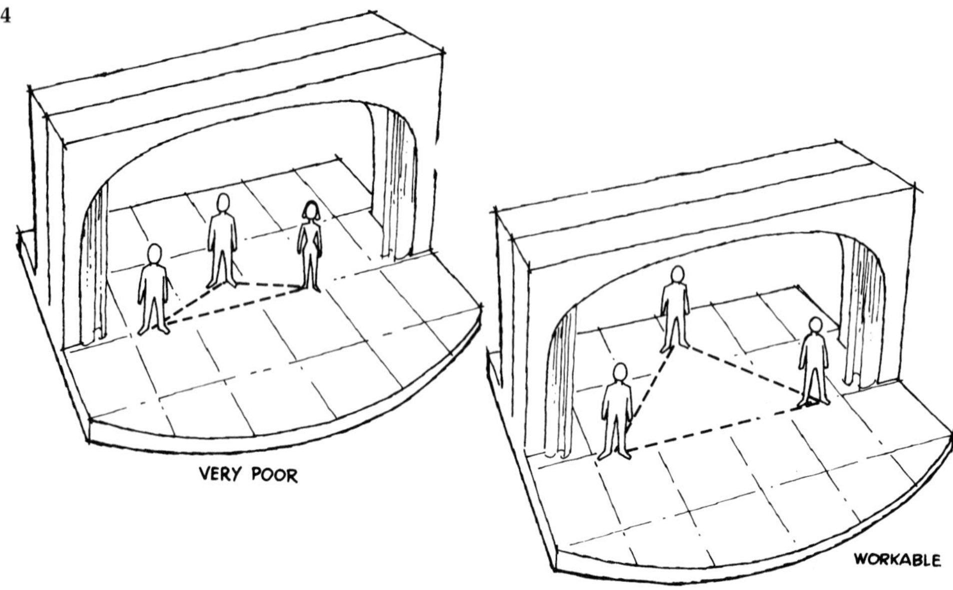

Space and mass. Effective compositions can be made by isolating one actor on one part of the stage and contrasting that isolation with a number of actors on the other side (see Figure 35). The single actor is thus surrounded by *space,* which gives him emphasis and individuality, and the others make a *mass* with only group identification.

EXERCISE

Do several illustrations of making emphasis through space and mass. Evaluate each of them.

Repetition or support. When four or more actors are used, the dramatic action frequently places them on two opposing sides. The supporting actors who stand behind the principal actors are said to *repeat* or *support* the principals, thus giving emphasis to the principals (see Figure 36).

EXERCISE

Do several illustrations of making emphasis through repetition or support. Evaluate each of them.

Climactic compositions. As previously noted, old compositions give way to new compositions continuously throughout a performance because they are the

FIGURE 35

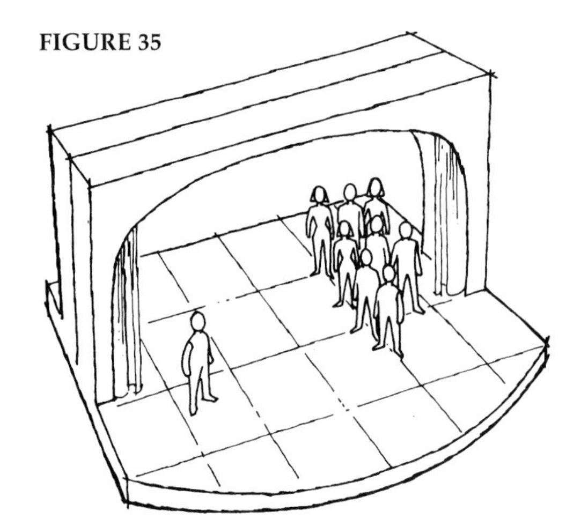

FIGURE 36

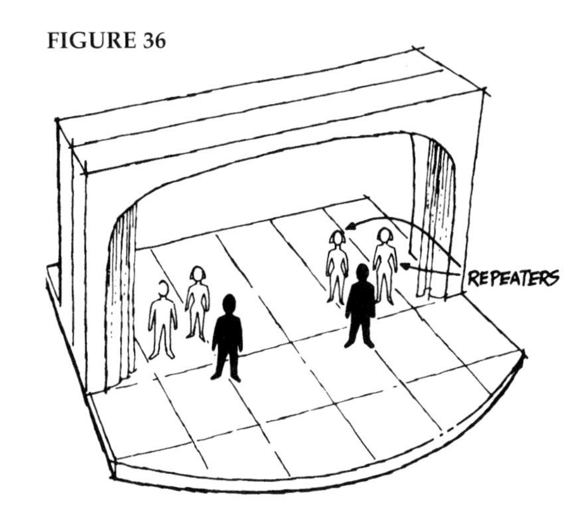

still shots that an audience can easily comprehend, simply because it knows who has emphasis (and thus who is speaking). *These changes consist of variations on the actual distance of separation between actors,* which depends on the illustration needed to show the forces between the actors. Thus, two actors may play at the extremes of the stage or very close together, with each composition having explicit meanings. *When they are close together (less than six feet) they are in a climactic composition.*

Climactic compositions should be used for only two actions, including all their variations: (1) extreme love, in which the actors are about to embrace; or (2) extreme hate, in which they are about to fight. *Climactic compositions must therefore be saved for the climactic moments* of a play. Young directors and actors tend to overuse climactic compositions on the stage as a matter of course because they see them so continuously used in motion pictures and television, where it is necessary to bring two people close together to get them on camera. But they forget the alternating use of multiple isolation shots (close-ups) that make the actors appear to be well separated. This technique of breaking long shots, however, cannot be used in the theatre, where the continuous long shot is the way of life. *A climactic composition has the force of a close-up and must therefore be used sparingly for this purpose or it will have no meaning at all.* Think of compositions as a succession of shots that show actors in successive stages of either making contact or breaking it (see Figure 37).

EXERCISE

Illustrate climactic compositions first by setting one up and then by dispersing your classmates to extreme positions. What do the individuals feel?

Stage areas. Compositions may occupy (1) the entire stage, (2) the left or right half of the stage, or (3) a quarter of the stage (see Figure 38). Compositions that

FIGURE 37

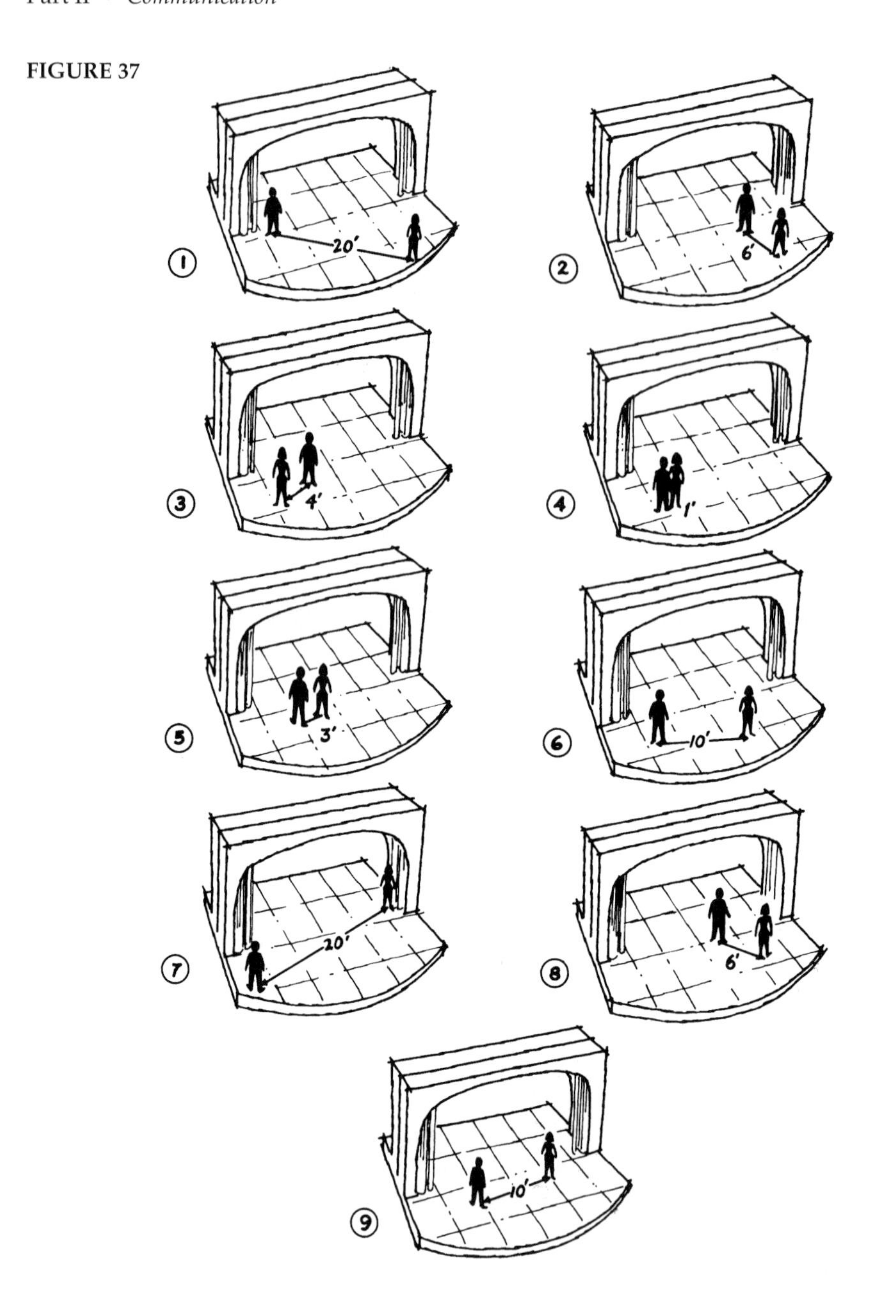

occupy less space are usually climactic and can be placed in any location on the stage. But because climactic compositions must be used sparingly, the director must learn to use a wide variety of larger compositions placed contrastingly in all the areas (see Figure 39).

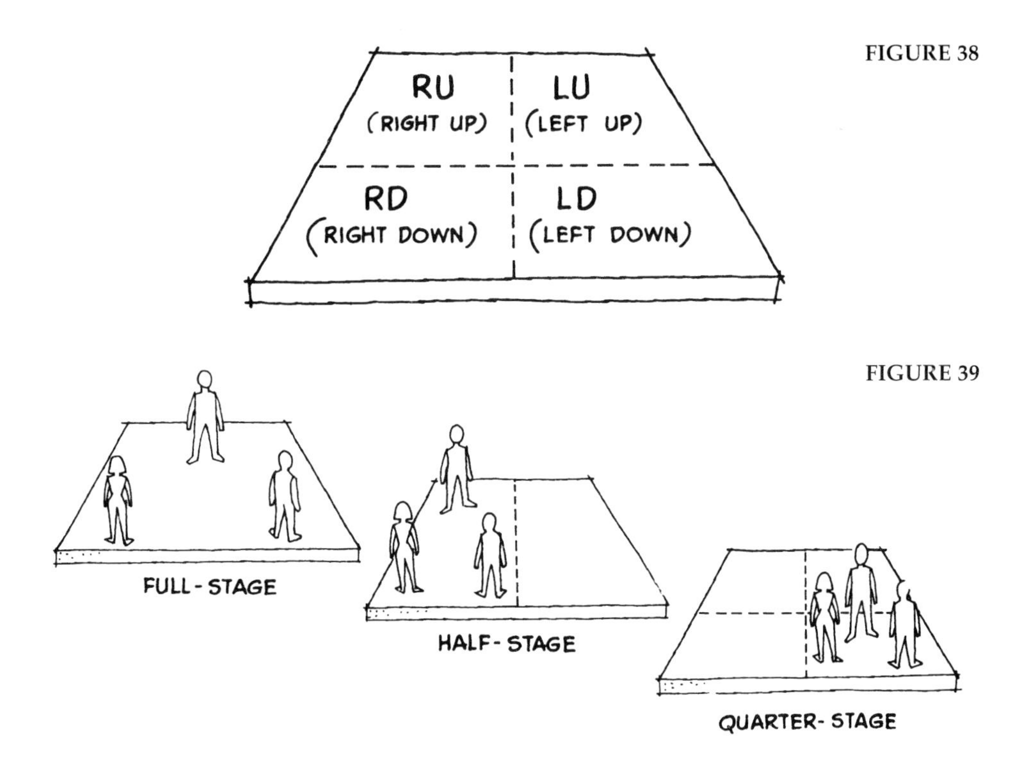

FIGURE 38

FIGURE 39

EXERCISE

Illustrate stage areas by setting up compositions on (1) the full-stage, (2) a half-stage, and (3) a quarter-stage. At the instructor's signal, shift the composition to different areas. Evaluate.

Compositions with furniture. Figures 28 through 39 have assumed a bare stage because the intention was to show the techniques of making good compositions; but the bare stage is, of course, a very exceptional circumstance in Realistic drama. The problem is to see compositions in the midst of furniture (properties) placement. If a workable groundplan has been devised, compositions will fall naturally into it, for actors will feel relationships on the basis of where they can sit or stand. *Groundplan designing thus always gives prime consideration to how composition can be exploited by the actors and the director.*

One important aspect is how furniture pieces participate with actors in compositions. Without actors, properties are dead objects; but when actors move around them and use them, they take on an animation resembling that of silent actors. Triangles, in all their variations, can be made in this way, with two actors and a piece of furniture as the third point. Again, if you and the actors think of a groundplan as an obstacle course, good compositions will mature of themselves. Remember: Using the stage compositionally does not imply clearing the space for

FIGURE 40

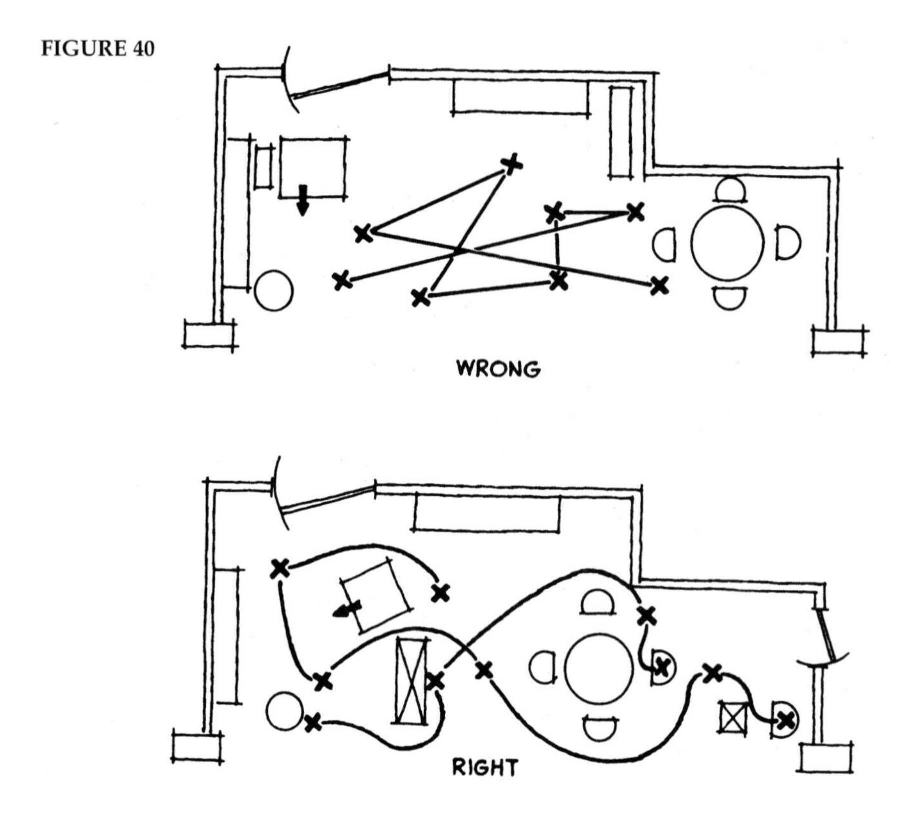

the actors to move in front of the furniture pieces, but it means allowing the pieces to interrupt space (obstacle-course concept) and thus to interrupt an actor's goal to reach and touch another actor (see Figure 40).

An obstacle course will automatically defeat the desire of actors to make climactic compositions, which can then be saved for the appropriate moments. An actor moves *in* a groundplan, not in front of it, for the basic concept declares that the only space available is that space falling between objects. Consequently, the more objects there are in a groundplan, the more difficult it will be for one actor to reach another. If your groundplan is skillfully devised, you can suggest compositions to actors that will impede them—that is, compositions that will keep actors from reaching one another easily, with the result that they will unknowingly intensify the illustrations of their dramatic actions.

Compositions as Actor Communication versus Pictorial Communication

It is not the purpose of this book to take up an extended discussion of composition in terms of pictorial design. Rather, the intent is to view composition from the standpoint of director-actor communication. This presupposes that the only aspect of theatre that really matters is to move an audience through dramatic action and characters; therefore, the principal function of directing is to arouse actors to assume the positions that will be most effective in communicating appropriate imagery to an audience. Furthermore, although it would be possible to delineate more rules of pictorial design, it is assumed that the young director can neither absorb them nor use them at this point.

However, as you grow more experienced, you will develop your own sense of the pictorial. At this point, you must learn all you can about the effect of the pictorial. The more you know about composition as the liaison between actor and audience, the better you will be able to communicate. Practice composition diligently from every point of view, for good direction is also good picture making.

EXERCISES

Summary Exercises for All Aspects of Composition

1. Coordinate all the exercises throughout this chapter by setting up a groundplan (with furniture pieces) on the classroom floor and by arranging compositions within it. When the instructor gives a signal, use three actors to change locations, thus making new compositions. Other students should identify all the elements in each composition and then evaluate the effectiveness of the elements in the groundplan.
2. Each student should compose at least three different groundplans and then set up multiple compositions on each. Intensive practice in this problem will prepare the director for all that is to follow, for without a basic understanding of the techniques and the uses of composition, he will not be able to bring about truthful illustrations in a play.

GAME OF VISUAL PERCEPTION: COMPOSITION (see Chapter 8)

1. Photos 1 through 6 illustrate full-stage compositions from a frontal position.
   a. Identify the following in each photograph: body position, planes, areas, eye focus, line focus.
   b. Can you see possible acting areas other than the ones being used? Explain your answer.
   c. Are obstacle courses provided? Describe them.
   d. Do you see the triangulation: size, length of legs, upstage apex, relation of the base line to the proscenium line if visible? Explain your answer.
2. Photos 7 through 14 show compositions in groups, not especially related to a front line. Answer some or all of the questions in Exercise 1. Additionally: What character has the focus in each photograph and why? Do you see how actors are tied to set properties? How is dramatic action conveyed through composition in each photograph?
3. Photo 12 is a type of *Performance Art*—an original work where the creator is also the performer. Why is a director useful in this form of dramatic production?

PHOTO 1 *The Crucible* (Miller)

PHOTO 2 *Idiot's Delight* (Sherwood)

PHOTO 3 *Hair* (Rado, Ragni, and McDermott)

PHOTO 4 *Oliver!* (Bart)

PHOTO 5 *Saint Joan* (Shaw)

PHOTO 6 *True Love* (Mee)

PHOTO 7 *Orestes 2.0* (Mee)

PHOTO 8 *Curse of the Starving Class* (Shepard)

PHOTO 9 *Look Back in Anger* (Osborne)

PHOTO 10 *The Resistible Rise of Arturo Ui* (Brecht)

PHOTO 11 *Rosmersholm* (Ibsen)

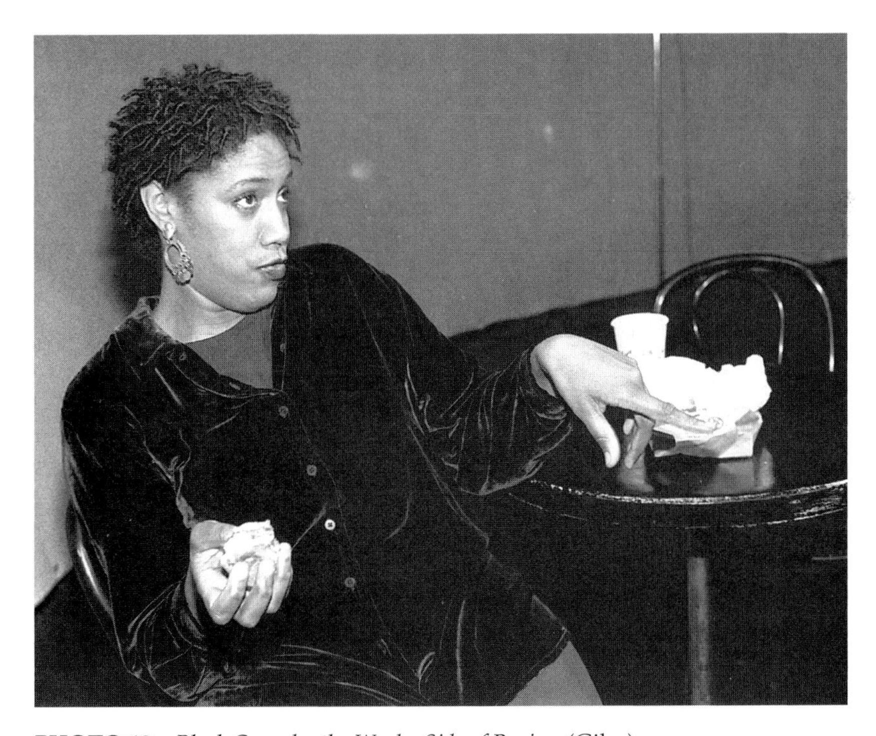

PHOTO 12 *Black Comedy, the Wacky Side of Racism* (Giles)

PHOTO 13 *School for Wives* (Molière)

PHOTO 14 *The House of Blue Leaves* (Guare)

11

Helping Each Actor Intensify

Gesture and Improvisation with Properties

Gesture and improvisation with properties are rightfully the province of each individual actor, but the director can use them as tools in helping actors discover the subtleties of dramatic action as well as learn to build character illustration with imagination and sensitivity. The two previous chapters have shown how the groundplan and composition can lead actors into discoveries about given circumstances and relationships in dramatic action, and thus to basic image-making. This chapter will show how you can lead actors into making highly detailed and refined visual illustrations.

Gesture

As noted in the preceding chapter, preserving body neutrality is absolutely necessary to see composition as a powerful force in itself. In this chapter, you will see neutrality abandoned and the body fully animated through gesture. Here are two dictionary meanings of *gesture:*

1. The use of motions of the limbs or body as a means of expression
2. A movement usually of the body or limbs that expresses or emphasizes an idea, sentiment, or attitude

Note that these definitions suggest three things: (1) that the body is set in one location—in other words, that gesture is not movement, an activity that takes the body from one point to another on the stage; (2) that *gesture is the animation of all the movable parts of the body;* and (3) that gesture is capable of expressing ideas, sentiments, or attitudes. Now go one step beyond these definitions by thinking of

FIGURE 41

this activity as taking place in the body's sphere—the sphere that stretches from tiptoe to the fullest extension of the arms in all directions. Figure 41 illustrates this concept.

Think of gesture as extending outward from the center of the body's sphere and occupying whatever space an actor's imagination wishes to give it. Frequently, only part of the space is used, as in the figure on the far right. Gesture can be as large or as small, as free or as restricted, as an actor desires in expressing character.

Again, in contrast to composition, which is architectural and abstract and always expressed in terms of the neutral body, gesture is the living quality of the body—the body's animation. Shakespeare's line "the hand is instrument to the mouth" is the very essence of gesture, for we always use the hand in the hope of amplifying the meanings of the language we use or, in the words of one of the definitions quoted earlier, "to emphasize an idea, sentiment, or attitude." *Words are one kind of symbolic expression and gestures are another, with each having specific uses in conveying ideas.*

Gesture, then, is a prime means of actor communication. The suppression or the controlling of gesture is what we usually designate as *poise,* the body behavior we usually associate with refinement and cultivation. We tend to designate levels of cultivation by the amount of gestures employed, with the inference that the more a person can suppress his gestures, the closer he is to being dominated by his mind. Thus, in plays and movies, we are apt to see lower-class characters illustrated with many gestures, and upper-class characters with relatively few; that is, there are few until the characters lose control of themselves and revert to the animalism that hovers in all human beings.

Gesture can convey ideas simply and clearly, as is illustrated by people who are deaf who "talk" in sign language with their hands and fingers as well as indicate attitudes with their whole bodies. Watch them closely and you will see how really animated they are in their own type of conversation—much more so than people with normal hearing. As an animated tool of illustration, gesture can thus rephrase and intensify the crude meanings of composition into highly refined and subtle ones. But the actor must learn some very important lessons early in his training, principally that indiscriminate use of gestures will convey very little meaning, that he must be highly selective, and that he must, above all, start from the neutral position of basic composition.

Gesture in Director-Actor Communication

So subjective is gesture that it is primarily an actor's, and not a director's, tool for communication. Yet, the director who is unaware of its force does not know how to reduce or increase its use. It is very important to note: *An actor who does not stand still or hold his head still cannot be heard by an audience or is heard poorly.* Repeat that over and over to yourself, as well as the saying, "The eye is quicker than the ear." The director must also know how to strip an actor of gestures and how to help him build new gestures that will reveal the character he is playing, not just himself as an actor (what we call *actor mannerisms*) or the gestures belonging to another character. Certain gestures, as well as their size or the state of their control, can also be suggested by the director and thus can become subtle ways of communicating dramatic action from the director to the actor. An actor, when learning to characterize, will discover that the appropriate use of gesture—always within the range of his character and always done economically—provides the subtle visual clues to a character's states and feelings.

Decorum

As was just suggested, an actor can declare some aspects of a character by the gestures he uses—gestures that can indicate not only a character's inner feelings but also his position in society. *Decorum* means specifically *the outward show of a character*—an appropriate reflection of the given circumstances in a play. A king moves like a king because he leads a life of ceremony and is as much symbol as person. Similarly, a ditchdigger moves like a person who uses his body continuously in physical labor. Decorum is simple symbology for what we expect from these occupations, which are nevertheless prototypes. In real life, we notice this relationship often enough to expect it, but the rules of decorum do not always hold, a fact that encourages actors to look for the exceptions that can be carried over to the stage as fresh observations.

Because decorum is the outward show of a character, a director and an actor must search for the appropriate decorum for a character. Without this, the outward show will lie about the character's given circumstances, and the audience will be left in confusion about what to expect. Occasionally, directors exploit this confusion with the full intention of misleading an audience into fresh thinking about a character.

In actor training, so much pressure is placed on developing the inside core of character—that is, of ensuring full comprehension of the dramatic action—that actors frequently give little attention to the force of the exterior look of a character. In contrast, good professional actors always look for the appropriate decorum of a character in order to convey given circumstances quickly to an audience, just as a designer does with his stage scenery. By imaginative suggestion to an actor about a character's decorum, a director can arouse fresh ideas about interior action because the actor can see more clearly the contrast and conflict between the outer and inner selves of a character. The director can also encourage an actor's sense of physical illustration and thus be able to convey many more specific and appropriate images to an audience.

EXERCISES

1. Demonstrate the "sphere concept" of gesture by assuming different positions that will occupy the full sphere. Repeat with the full class. Get the feeling of the sphere. Compare and contrast formal dance (full use of the sphere) with acting by illustrating the use of gesture in both forms and showing how they differ.
2. Repeat Exercise 1 by using several classmates who change positions at the instructor's signal. Try to keep the positions within the boundary of everyday human behavior. These illustrations will show not only the full opportunity an actor has in occupying the limits of the sphere but also how his movements stretch outward from the center point of the body.
3. Do a series of huddled gestures to show how head, arms, and legs can also be drawn inward toward the body.
4. Have one person sit on a chair in front of the class. At the instructor's signal, he changes his gestures to convey different inner feelings (dramatic action). Identify the meaning of each. How do the gestures help his face? Repeat with three actors, unrelated to each other.
5. Place two people in a composition in a groundplan and encourage them to add gestures after telling them, out of the class's hearing, of their relationship to each other (dramatic action). Have the class describe the gestures and their meanings.
6. Have two people illustrate decorum by sitting or standing in their spheres after they are secretly told different occupations to convey. Do not let them move from one place to another on the floor, but encourage them to take within their spheres any positions that they like. Have the class identify the occupations they suggest. Can other aspects of decorum be recognized?
7. Do Exercise 6 in the opposite direction by suggesting a decorum to an actor and letting him improvise dramatic action through that decorum. Repeat extensively with other actors.

Improvisation with Properties

Hand Properties

Definition. *Hand properties*—any objects that can be held in the hand and easily manipulated—*are extensions of gesture because they increase the variety of possible illustrations with the arms and hands, frequently with the legs and head.* Because the director, as part of his design function, can suggest the use of specific hand properties and how to use them, he can make them specific tools of director-actor communication.

Concept. Although a hand property has inherent meaning—for example, an umbrella is something to ward off rain or sun, a book is something to read, a cigar is something to smoke, a cup is something to drink from, and so on—*most of the hand properties used on the stage should be employed for reasons other than what their literal functions intend.* Only occasionally do we draw an audience's attention to a hand property in its functional use—perhaps a knife for cutting, a gun for shooting, or a weapon of any sort for murdering. Nor are hand properties used merely to provide the obvious exterior reality of everyday life. By and large, *audiences should notice hand properties* *only peripherally and should not be made to concentrate on them,* except in unusual circumstances when attention is obviously drawn to them. Hand properties have many more values than their functional qualities.

The principal use of hand properties is to help actors "talk" through gestures, for they can (1) extend the length of the arm (with a pointer), (2) increase the size of the hand (with a book), (3) make the hands and fingers active (with a cigarette), (4) produce sound (by closing a book), (5) show nervousness (with a handkerchief), and much more. *Everything an actor touches, if he uses it properly, can convey a sensory impression simply because an audience can actually feel the way the actor touches it and can empathize with him.*

The primary purpose of a hand property, then, is not its functional use but its potential for underlining dramatic ideas—the subtle aspects of characterization. In one sense, properties provide an additional pair of eyes for the actor. Because the members of an audience vary in their actual distance from the stage, with a large number actually unable to see the detailed eye movements of the actors, the skillful use of hand properties by the actor can actually tell even the farthest reaches of the audience what his eyes are doing, so closely is such amplified gesture allied with inner feeling. Movies and television, with their close-ups, have no such problem, but the stage must rely on significant illustrative tools such as properties to augment the eyes, particularly with Realistic drama.

Characteristics of hand properties. Actors and directors should be highly aware of the qualities and characteristics of hand properties. It is *how* an actor uses a property that will convey idea, and the *how* can be exploited only if the property is completely understood. As a director, you must develop a keen imagination with properties if you are to learn how to exploit them fully. Make a habit of looking carefully at a property: What are its peculiar and individual characteristics? If it is smooth, can it be rubbed against the face? What are its "sound" characteristics (does it snap, pop, etc.?) and how can they be exploited? Will its weight cause it to do certain things in the hands of an actor? Can it be stretched or rubbed against other materials? Can it be torn or pulled apart? All questions of this sort open up the imaginative, fresh use of properties. The trite use of a property by an actor implies that he does not actually *see* and *feel* the property; in other words, the actor does not actually know the property's nature and possibilities.

As you can see, then, all of the preceding questions are pursuing the same point: how a hand property is used effectively by an actor to illustrate dramatic action in a fresh, active, and sensitive way. *The purpose is to reveal a character's state of mind, not to show the property itself.* The audience's attention must be on the feelings of the characters, and not on the object, except in those rare instances when an object (for instance, a gun) becomes momentarily the dramatic action itself.

For these reasons, you can see that an action such as eating is not intended to improve the health of the character in front of the audience or to give a reason for sitting at a dining table. Instead, it gives an actor some hand and mouth tools for illustration. A book in an actor's hand might possibly be read to show the audience that the character is improving his mind or that he is the intellectual sort; but usually, it is used to illustrate nervousness, to emphasize a point by banging the book closed or slamming it on a table, or to show preoccupation and interior disturbance. Appropriately used hand properties have the ability to reveal detailed psychological states in characters in line with the structural core of modern prose drama; *they have distinctive capacities for revealing subtext.*

Improvisations with hand properties. The word *improvisation* is used here to denote what the actor and director must do in order to find the best illustrations. Only through constant experimentation can a property be fully exploited or another property substituted to make the necessary revelations. Actors should always work with real hand properties just as soon as their hands are free from carrying scripts, because properties will suggest buried dramatic action to the actor, as well as tell him how to show what he already understands. Only when the use of a property has been fully exploited in rehearsal does it become a set piece of business in the old sense. Even if a playwright requires specific use of a hand property, the actor must work with it improvisationally to maximize its highest potential. The old idea of set pieces of business handed down through tradition is irreconcilable with modern training in acting in which each actor must first decide whether a property is needed to illustrate a dramatic action, and then must discover for himself how to best make it meaningful.

EXERCISES

1. What is the difference between hand properties and set properties? Look ahead at the definition at the beginning of the following section if you do not know. The distinction is an important one.
2. Observe for 5 to 10 seconds. When the property is removed, look at one hand property placed on a table. Write a complete description of it: its size, shape, weight, color, and so on. Compare results with your classmates. Repeat.
3. Repeat Exercise 2 but instead of writing a description, define the characteristics of the property—what its special nature is, what its peculiar characteristics are, and so on.
4. Repeat Exercise 3, and add to it all your suggestions of how the property could be employed to illustrate dramatic action.
5. A dozen chairs are evenly distributed in a 15-foot circle facing away from the center. You and 11 classmates stand facing the center inside the circle of chairs. At a signal, each person places a hand property (something personal) on the chair behind him or her, being careful not to look at objects placed by other students. At the instructor's signal, you and the others start revolving around the circle, always facing center. At the instructor's signal, everyone stops, and one student is designated to pick up the property behind him and describe its characteristics to the group. Repeat several times.
6. Now repeat Exercise 5 in a spontaneous improvisation. The student who picks up the object examines it for a few seconds, then, employing the object as illustration, selects another student in the circle and does a dramatic action with the other student. The class then evaluates the use of the object. Was it used too literally or with imagination? Did the student really find the peculiar characteristics of the object? Repeat several times.

7. Each member of the class does improvisations, each with a different hand property. The intention is not to call attention to the property but to use it as a means of revealing dramatic action. (*Example:* The improvisor enters a store to buy a hat. A hat becomes a mere illustration for an intensive conflict with the saleswoman or manager.) This exercise is invaluable in pinning down the difference between using objects for their own sake and using their qualities for illustration. Therefore, it should be repeated several times to reinforce the concept.

Set Properties

Definition. *Set properties* are those large items, usually pieces of furniture, permanently placed in a groundplan. *They are specific tools of director-actor communication and not merely set decoration, for they amplify and intensify objects given life by actors.* On occasion, such as when an actor moves a chair, they can become hand properties.

Concept. Chapter 10 emphasized that pieces of furniture not only come to life when they are used by actors but they also participate directly in compositions because of their space-occupying characteristics. You will also remember that the groundplan was referred to several times as an obstacle course that must be navigated by actors in illustrating a Realistic play. Again, you must be *fully aware* of the dramatic storytelling strength of this use, because you must learn to exploit set properties in this way.

"Tie into the furniture," which you may have heard experienced directors say to actors, tells actors that their composition will be stronger if they stand near or touch a piece of furniture. Such a suggestion has significant validity because furniture pieces not only give mass to the actor by extending his stage values but they also help him discover subtleties in the dramatic action. Members of an audience will take for granted that an actor sits on a chair or sofa, but a great deal more is being done for them than they imagine. If the specific piece of furniture on which an actor sits is well selected, it will help the actor sense what to do and how to do it, just as hand properties do. Even more important is what a well-selected piece of furniture can do to encourage sensitive reciprocation between two actors. A suggestion given to one actor to use a chair in a certain way may immediately arouse ideas for adjustment in the other actor—adjustment that can set off a chain of physical illustrations around the set piece, which will communicate strong feelings to a watcher.

Creation of activity areas. Every area of your groundplan should be potent with "activity" possibilities, for they will encourage actors to use those areas for illustration. This is *organic blocking* in its best sense. Actors must have things to do, and you can help their motivation for crosses or uses of certain areas by providing reasons to use those areas. Downstage corners (foreground plane) that have uses other than merely sitting (telephones, desk work, bookcase) will suggest activities. It is important that the stage properties that define the downstage corners and create the "reality" of these locations be chosen in such a way that they strongly suggest activities and how these places are used in the life of the room—rather than being merely decorative. They must legitimately draw movements toward them, so that the actors' movements toward these places are organic and not arbitrary, for both the actor and the audience who observe. Upstage areas (background plane) can also be set up this way (cabinets, bookcases, drawer for concealing objects used in the play, worktables, sinks, refrigerators, storage areas, coatrack, dish shelf, private collection of objects, etc.). As with the downstage corners, upstage locations should legitimately and organically draw movements toward them, so that in the evolving series of movements in a scene, an actor's reasons for being in such a location or going to it are organically integrated into the logic of the scene. The midstage arrangement is the most important because most of the activity will take place on these planes. Achieve a variety in furniture placement by experimenting with all parts of conversational groupings. Increase your lines of tension in the placement to ensure full exploitation.

Variety in using pieces of furniture is a necessity if the illustrations are to be fresh and alive. Sitting on the backs of sofas or on tables is, of course, valid if the given circumstances permit characters such behavior; but chairs and sofas can be used in dozens of ways without employing exceptional uses that call attention to themselves and break our belief in the scene. As with hand properties, the director must be fully aware of the characteristics of the set properties he introduces for actor use if he is to exploit them. Fresh uses of beds, desks, stools, cabinets, and so on all lie within an actor's imagination, and the director can make them come to life with perceptive suggestions.

EXERCISES

1. You and two other members of the class "play" on and around chairs without moving them, each person doing something different with his or her chair at the instructor's signal.
2. Try the same exercise with a table and a chair. Each person should continue to work independently.
3. With you as the leader, have the class improvise a usable groundplan. Criticize and revise the plan to get as much ingenuity into it as possible. Now have two people use the groundplan, changing locations on signals from the instructor. Have the class judge the freshness of their uses of the set properties.
4. Repeat Exercise 3 several times, each time trying to find ingenious uses of furniture pieces. Have your classmates, acting as directors, suggest specific uses to the two individuals.
5. Ask two people to improvise a dramatic action around and on a chair. Warn them that they must not point up the functional use of the chair but must employ it only in finding contact with one another. *Let the chair tell them what to do.* Repeat the exercise with a table, with a sofa, and with other items.
6. Combine the use of hand properties and set properties in the same improvisation as outlined in Exercise 5.

12

Picturization

Helping a Group Intensify

This chapter will discuss picturization—the projection of group action. In Chapter 11, you learned that gesture pertains only to the individual; picturization, however, concerns a group of actors in which each actor uses the gestures appropriate to his own character.

Definition

Picturization is storytelling by a group of actors. It is brought about by the combined use of composition (the arrangement of the group), gesture (the individual moving within his own sphere), and improvisation with properties (objects added to composition and gesture) for the specific purpose of *animating the dramatic action.* Picturization, then, *is a still picture containing detailed illustrations, brought about by individualizing and personalizing composition through the use of gesture and properties to tell the story of the group.*

Concept

Picturizations are what we actually see in the performance of a play, the same pictures we see in real life when two or more people are involved in a close physical relationship. Again, you must remember that a *staged scene of a play is composed of a succession of still shots, with a new composition born every time the physical relationships of the basic elements are changed.* We use the term *picturization* in order to say that we have added the *storytelling details* of gesture and properties to composition. Remember, though, that composition is an abstraction—we never actually see it in its clear form except in exercises, nor do we see gesture stopped and held as in a tableau. In actual practice, when we set up compositions, "we wipe gestures from our eyes" in order to see whether we have established a good composition, then "we put them back in our eyes" to see if we are making a good picturization. Can you see the logic of this reverse order?

Picturization means that each actor in a group is presenting the dramatic action of his character with the decorum of that character. *The aim is to create the appropriate psychological relationship between characters,* because out of this relationship the strong feelings to which an audience reacts emerge. Remember, *only when a group of actors plays the action intensively will feelings emerge.* So the actors must find the proper character-mood-intensities for the picture in order for it to project the desired emotional truth. And remember also that picturizations are *visual* illustrations—only part of the full illustration that involves speech as well as movement.

Techniques

Good picturization involves expert use of a well-conceived groundplan, because the obstacles in such a plan will suggest all sorts of picturization ideas to actors. Thus, the groundplan is again a primitive means of communication. As understanding of the action grows, actors will become more and more intensively physical and in greater detail. If the basic composition is right, fresh ideas about gesture (the individual in the sphere) will emerge, and along with them, the improvisational use of properties. Thus, picturization will grow. Following are some specific suggestions:

1. Encourage picturization over and around obstacles (see Figure 42). Remember: *Obstacles prevent climactic compositions and thus intensify conflict.* They also help emphasize actors by taking on animate qualities in compositions.
2. Encourage space separations between characters, and the use of different planes, levels, and body positions (see Figures 43 and 44; *A*, *B*, and *C* are characters).
3. Look for intimate climactic picturizations (see Figure 45) and encourage actors to touch one another.
4. Look for the appropriate character-mood-intensities of the different characters. This procedure will declare the tension levels in the pictures by encouraging the actors to find illustrations at the levels of their nervosity in the scene. All pictures will contain character-mood-intensities of some sort, but the major problem is finding the *appropriate* intensities so that the illustrations will tell the truth. Here, gestures play an important part in picturization values.
5. Exploit gesture in every possible way by encouraging actors to vary their illustrations within their spheres by taking them, on occasion, to the full limits and withdrawing them to the opposite extreme.
6. Encourage the continuous use of triangles in setting up compositions, but vary them in as many interesting ways as possible. *There is nothing so dull in picture making as the repetitious use of triangles of the same size and shape.* Remember that a good composition must be at the base of every good picture, so make your composition first; then add details.

FIGURE 42

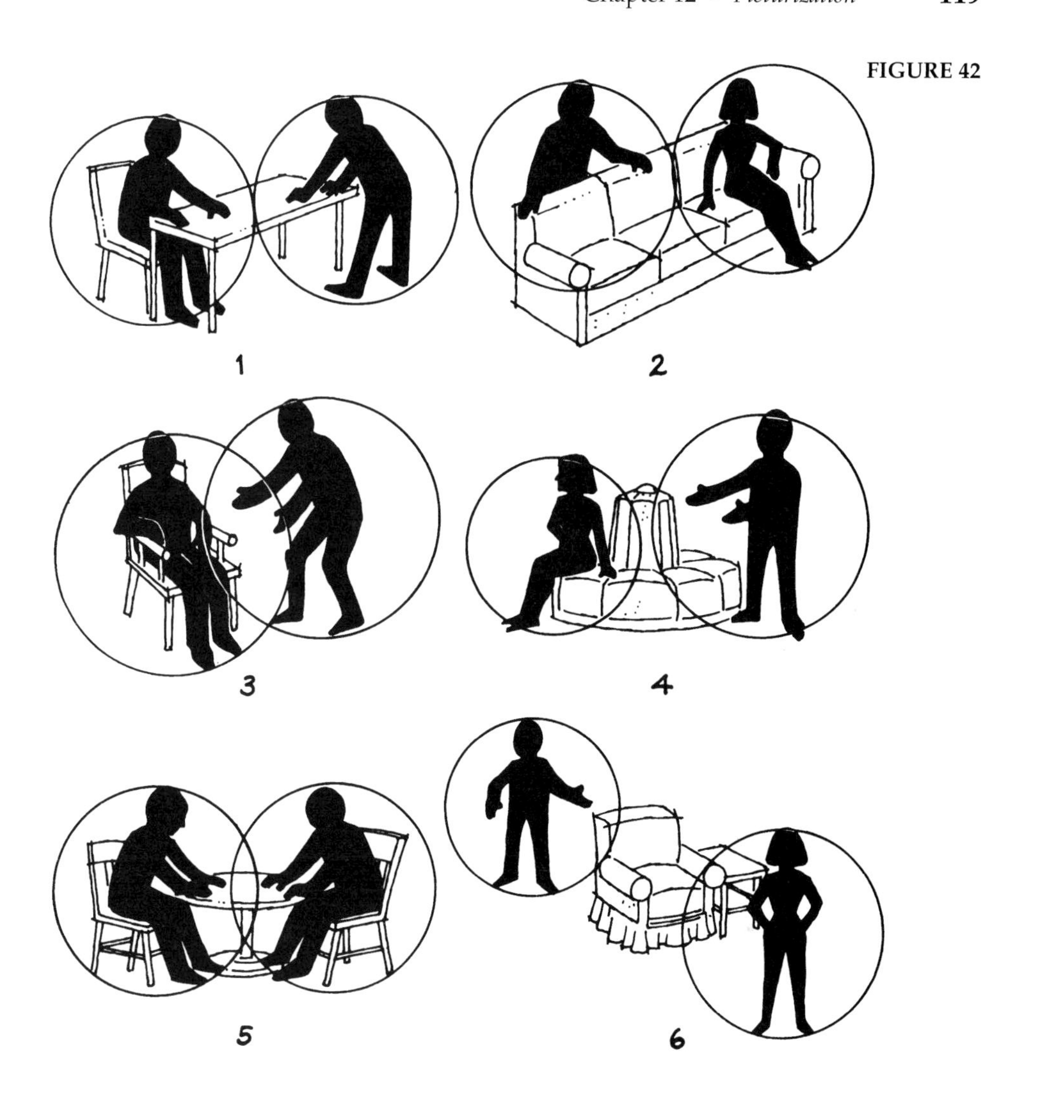

FIGURE 43

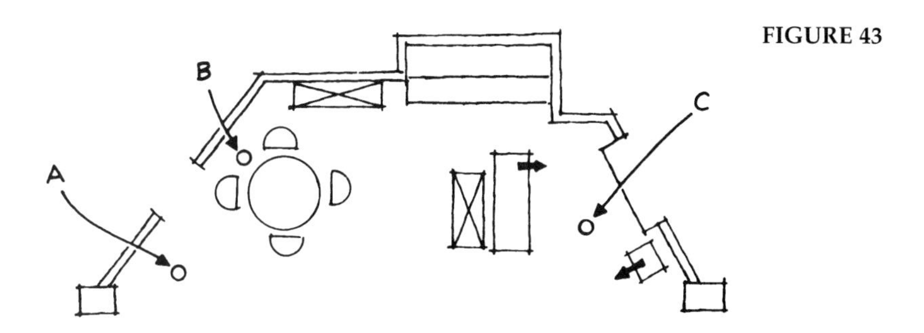

FIGURE 44

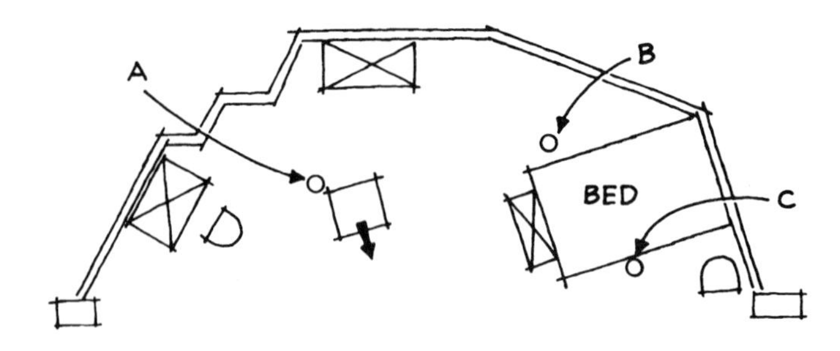

FIGURE 45

7. Encourage the use of hand properties, because they have high picture-making potential in forcing body positions, levels, and so on.
8. When you have exhausted all the director-actor communication possibilities for making good pictures by ensuring that the actors understand every detail of the action, you can turn to the secondary functions of picturization, which include:
   a. *Balancing the stage.* Remember that your picture on the proscenium stage is in a frame, and it is possible for you to make a visually beautiful picture if you follow some of the rules of good perspective painting. Picturizations thus have pictorial values that can give pleasure to an audience, whether it is conscious of them or not. Study the groupings in Renaissance paintings to see how the masters made exciting picturizations.
   b. *Exploiting the stage cube.* Remember that you are composing pictures in a cube and not on the floor of the stage. Thus, you can find many unusual storytelling pictures through the use of high levels such as stairways, balconies, and so forth. Learn to exploit the contrasts in levels to the fullest.
   c. *Exploiting the extremes of the stage floor.* This means using the full depth of your groundplan by encouraging actors to play the upstage and downstage extremes and by using the full horizontal width through all insistence on far-right and far-left positions. If you play the extremes, you will have the other places to go to; if you do not, your pictures will seem cramped and underillustrated.

EXERCISES

1. Arrive at a picturization by (1) starting with composition, (2) adding gesture, (3) adding hand properties, and then (4) adding picturization. Improvise the following:
   a. A group of three decides on a given circumstance and an action.
   b. The group sets up a composition, being extremely careful to keep the neutrality of composition.
   c. The group now moves the composition to a previously setup groundplan and uses one of the furniture pieces as an obstacle.
   d. Each person, in turn, adds gesture to his part of the composition by experimenting until he finds fresh gesture, and then holding it in tableau.
   e. At least one person (possibly two) works with a hand property.
   f. When the individuals have added gestures and hand properties, they adjust to one another (in terms of the dramatic action) and form the picturization.
   g. The class now identifies the picturization as accurately as possible. What story does it tell? What is its emotional level? The class also comments on the various stages of the exercise.
   h. Repeat this abstract exercise (abstract because it isolates the stages in forming a picturization in a mechanical way) several times because it will clarify all the stages that lead to good picturization.
2. Improvise picturizations that involve furniture pieces and hand properties with two or three individuals. Three teams will use the same furniture pieces and hand properties, and then change pictures at the instructor's signal. Note how each group will do something different. Have the individuals work for as fresh an expression as possible.
3. Improvise picturizations with three or four classmates in a present groundplan. *Shift pictures at the instructor's signal, with the class closing its eyes so that it will see only picturizations and not the movement from one location on the stage to another.* Repeat in other groundplans.
4. After you have looked at the photographs in this section, play the Game of Visual Perception on a "live" level by setting up the same picturizations you see in the photos. Describe the values in each.
5. Repeat Exercise 4 by using the photographs at the end of Chapter 10.

GAME OF VISUAL PERCEPTION: PICTURIZATION (see Chapter 8)

1. Analyze photos 15 through 26 in terms of the elements of picturization at work in each caught moment. Comment on specific ways gesture informs the bodies of the actors to make each composition come alive in terms of evocative, detailed storytelling.
2. How do photos 16 through 26 illustrate picturizations in productions? For each photograph, answer the following:
   a. Who has the center of attention?
   b. Do you see the added strength of eye-focus?
   c. What function do the characters in the background provide?
   d. What are the functions of the pieces of furniture?
   e. Can you see triangulation?
3. What is the psychological drama (story) being played out in each photograph?
   a. Can you see how picturization creates the dramatic moment?
   b. Has group intensification really taken place?
   c. Why is each photograph effective as a photograph?

PHOTO 15 *Dementia* (Fernandez)

PHOTO 16 *Curse of the Starving Class* (Shepard)

PHOTO 17 *La Victima* (El Teatro de la Esperanza)

PHOTO 18 *Romeo and Juliet* (Shakespeare)

PHOTO 19 *Romeo and Juliet* (Shakespeare)

PHOTO 20 *Orestes 2.0* (Mee)

PHOTO 21 *Orestes 2.0* (Mee)

PHOTO 22 *Orestes* (Euripides)

PHOTO 23 *Measure for Measure* (Shakespeare)

PHOTO 24 *Death of a Salesman* (Miller)

PHOTO 25 *Othello* (Shakespeare)

PHOTO 26 *Jack or The Submission* (Ionesco)

13

The Dynamic Tool of Movement

Up to this point in the discussion of the visual tools in director-actor communication, we have been concerned with how you, as the director, can help actors penetrate the subtext of a play through suggestions that have been, with the exception of gesture, primarily of a static nature. The intention in this chapter is to reveal the *dynamics of movement as the most powerful* of all the tools in *organic blocking*.

Definition

Movement is the actual transit of an actor from one point on the stage to another. Although it includes gesture in that the body sphere is always animated during the process of movement, it is a separate tool from gesture in that the actual *distance* traveled, the *route* of travel, and the *speed* of travel all declare specific values, in themselves distinct from gesture.

Concept

Think of movement as continuous lines on the floor of the stage between points (see Figure 46). When a point is reached, an actor stands still and we have a composition. Movement thus takes place *between* compositions. In order to see movement on the stage—that is, in order to see its meaning—*the distance traveled must be five feet or more,* for anything less will look like gesture (the body in the sphere). Movement, then, is climactic, because all the other tools—groundplan, composition, gesture, picturization—must be operating before movement can take place. And because movement is climactic, it is the most overtly powerful of all the tools of director-actor communication. Because it is large, because it is continuous, and because gesture animates it, movement can convey illustrations to an audience

FIGURE 46

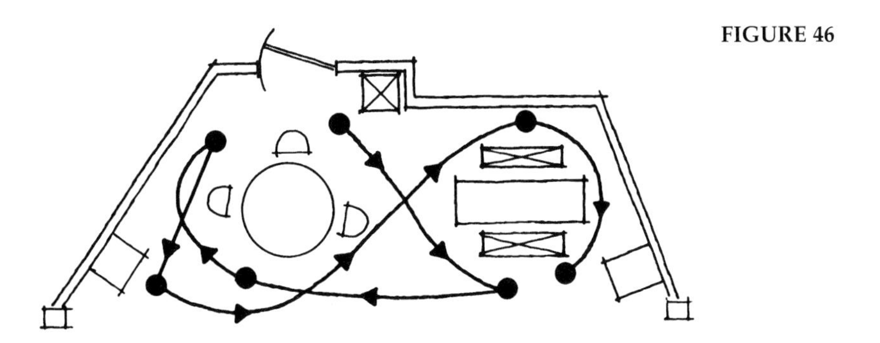

quickly and with force. An actor walking conveys a very different idea from an actor running or sauntering; and walking *toward* an actor means something very different from walking *away* from him. Movement therefore has tempo values; it takes place in time.

EXERCISE

Illustrate movement by setting up two points and having someone pretend he is rolling a ball with himself inside it from one point to the other. Repeat with two or three individuals, each taking a turn at doing this, and using three or four points as destinations. Repeat a third time with the individuals holding compositions long enough for each, in turn, to speak a line of numbers dialogue.

The Director as Choreographer

In a more restricted sense, a play performed on stage looks like a dance. Just as a dance starts and stops, a play alternates between movement and composition, with gesture working continuously. Thus, a director tries to find the appropriate movements to punctuate the still shots. If he and the actors find them, their production will have the appropriate animation—the rhythms—inherent in the playscript.

In the movies, we see many close-ups that punctuate the long or medium shots—shots that usually contain movement, either that of actors in transit, as movement is defined here, or that of the camera moving. *But on the stage, compositions act as close-ups and movement as the long and medium shots.* Yet, a playgoer always sees both at relatively the same distance from his eye, whereas movies can vary the size of images greatly. In this comparison, the stage is enormously limited. This limitation can be overcome, in part, only by intensely articulate and highly selected movement that is potent with meaning and ideas. Because of its dynamics, then, all movement must be inherently motivated directly out of the dramatic action; *it cannot be laid on but must be generated from within.* For this reason, some directors prefer to have the actors improvise their own movement because it can flow freely from their inherent comprehension of the action. This approach also has limitations, however, because actors often prefer gesture to movement for illustration. The director must therefore learn to motivate actors to articulate specific dramatic action through his suggestions for movement.

Kinds of Movement

Although all movement must be motivated by the dramatic action, it is important to note the different kinds of movement in order to see the full range of this valuable tool.

Playwright's Movement

Playwright's movement is formally prescribed by the playwright—what he considers the basic playscript requirements. It includes all entrances and exits, as well as those movements to locations on the stage prescribed by the author as necessary for the completion of certain business absolutely requiring that location by the dramatic action. Thus, if an actor must climb a scaffold to man a machine gun mounted thereon because the playwright has located his action there, an actor is performing *playright's movement.* If actors are required to dance, to play a game that requires movement, to participate in a military parade, to fight a duel, to crawl around on hands and knees looking for dropped jewels because a character has instructed them to do so, they are performing playwright's movement. As you may note, these movements are quite arbitrary in their demands. However, except for exits and entrances, most playwrights prescribe a minimum of this kind of movement. Be wary of directions for movement written into a printed play, for they are very likely to be the movements inserted by the director of the first production of that play on a specific groundplan and not by the playwright at all. (Do Exercise 1 at the end of this chapter.)

Technical Requirements

The choreographing of a play is not entirely free improvisation but is partly mechanical, because two hours of staging a play, often in one location (one setting), creates an immense traffic problem. How to get actors on and off the stage quickly and efficiently, particularly if there are many characters, and how to bring about the performance of business in appropriate areas of the stage are of utmost importance to the director. Thus, parts of playscripts must be blocked by directors, either in their minds or on paper, to be certain that they are exploiting their groundplans in the most imaginative ways.

In this regard, a director will occasionally require an actor to move arbitrarily from one location to another, and only then look for the motivation to support it—motivation that can always be found if the actor is imaginative enough. The actual placement of a piece of business may be extremely important to the revelation of character, so the director arbitrarily locates the scene for his actors and then decides, with the actors, how they get there. Actors may thus be required (1) to cross the stage at a certain time, (2) to uncover from behind other actors who may stand in front of them, (3) to close in or spread out as the business requires, and to do other such movements. This manipulation is always essential when several actors are involved. *The intention is to make arbitrary arrangement, when motivations are added, look like spontaneous improvisation.* In arranging group scenes, a director may want to distribute the actors in a particular way to show balance or imbalance. The movements by which they reach their assigned points, though otherwise motivated, are probably technical movements. *Probably* is used here because actors can frequently reach assigned positions through primary dramatic action. The skillful director will use technical movement only as a last resort when the use of primary dramatic action simply will not solve the traffic problems. (Do Exercises 2 and 3 at the end of this chapter.)

Movement Derived from Dramatic Action

Approximately 95 percent of all movement in staging a play *is derived from the dramatic action—what the subtext tells the actors and the director to do.* Actors who know their trade will move spontaneously and knowingly out of their strong feelings about the action in a play. The director's job in that case becomes one of suggesting more or less movement, more selective movement, more or less speed on certain movements, and often the specific destination of these movements in order to indicate to the actors the next important composition. *Beginning actors* on the other hand, *are movement bound;* that is, they will not move unless required by the director to do so, because they have not yet learned the illustrative values of movement. In handling such actors, directors often suggest much of the movement that will eventually be absorbed into the performance. If it is used skillfully, it can open up the subtext to the actors in a very real way—the outside-to-inside approach, organic blocking. However, if is not well conceived, it can impede actors' imaginations.

What is difficult about all of this—whether the actors develop movement on their own or the director suggests it to them—is finding the *appropriate* movement directly inherent in the playscript. As stated several times in this book, every line of dialogue is a word-statement of a dramatic action and a dramatic action is the forcing by a speaking character of another character. Thus, it is in the forcing or in the reception of the forcing (adjustment) that the movement inherently lies. For this reason, we use verbs to express dramatic action, for a verb is a statement implying activity. We note this point readily in such obviously active verbs as *run, jump, tear apart, rip, cry, grab, pull, caress, kiss,* and so on, because these verbs are verbs of *visual activity,* a class of verbs we avoid when writing down dramatic action (see page 33). The verbs we use to express dramatic action are not nearly so obvious. Note that there are no obvious visual hints in such verbs as *plead, command, seduce, adore, hate,* and all modifications of such verbs; yet, they contain movement (and gesture) in exactly the same way as the others, although we do not associate typical body behavior with them as we do with *run* and *jump.* If you always think of verbs as possessing inherent movement, you will see how actors and directors can readily devise this sort of illustration. (Do Exercise 4 at the end of this chapter.)

Thus, the director must study the dramatic action of a play intensely, for he must be certain that, whether an actor presents a movement or he suggests it to the actor himself, the truth is being told about an action. Movement can tell a boldfaced lie; it can even tell the opposite of what is intended. Therefore, both director and actors must be certain that actions that go "toward" and actions that "retreat" actually do so in the visual movement unless opposite movements are consciously intended for very specific reasons.

There are only two directions of movement on the stage: *the advance* and *the retreat.* That is, the advance or retreat of one character toward another as he pursues the dramatic action. Whichever one is used depends on the meaning of the subtext. Movement is played like a cat-and-mouse cartoon, with characters switching to play "Cat" or to play "Mouse," depending on the meanings of the actions. One character will always be the aggressor and one the pursued; and the change in roles will occur very frequently, perhaps as often as every minute or two. (Do Exercise 5 at the end of this chapter.)

Mood Values in Movement

Movements (1) occupy space when actors move from one location to another, (2) require time periods (duration), (3) are large and dynamic, and (4) can vary greatly in their rates. They have many mood values that need the most careful control if they are to be continuously expressive. Following are some of the values you must consider.

Length of a Movement

Long movements tend to be weaker than short ones, unless they are used with the greatest care; yet, they can have strong mood values when used in the appropriate places. Remember that all movements, if they are to be seen and recognized as movements, *must traverse five feet or more.* Continuous short movements, however, unless specifically intended, have a choppy effect, something like a series of simple sentences. Learn to vary the lengths of movements with the moods you want illustrated. On the whole, inexperienced actors tend toward short movements; therefore, when working with such actors, you will need to show them how relaxation and ease can be illustrated in generous movements.

Movement and Space

Although movement technically occupies space only when it is being made, it possesses the psychological value of tying areas of the stage together, thus making it seem as though movement occupies more space than it actually does. Learn to exploit this value by interrupting long patterns of movement with momentary compositions that will occur each time an actor stops. *Traveling the diagonals of the stage* will give the feeling of occupying the upstage areas and the far corners of the downstage areas. If the movement zigzags with interrupted stops, it will appear to occupy the stage. The mood values of small-space occupation are quite different from those of large-space occupation. You must learn to use each appropriately.

Size and Dynamics

Movements vary in size according to the number of gestures employed while making them. If an actor plays his character-decorum and his character-mood-intensity appropriately, he will vary the size and dynamics of his movements. Encourage the use of the sphere (gesture) while moving, increasing or decreasing the size of a movement and thus affecting the mood values it reflects.

Rate or Tempo

The rate of speed of movements is most important in expressing mood values because audiences are so easily affected by rate. The major problem with actors lies not just in helping them discover when and where to move but in how to vary the tempos of the movements in line with the character-mood-intensities of the scenes. The tendency with inexperienced actors is to take all movements at the same rate of speed, so that movement as illustration becomes quite ineffective. *You must therefore be certain that actors move at their appropriate character-mood-intensities,* a condition that will come about only if they understand their dramatic action thoroughly. Two characters never have the same rate, but each moves according to his nervosity. Only by understanding this concept can actors learn to make moods through the use of movement.

Movements in Series

You must learn how to plan movements so that they are joined in a series, with each move proceeding from the logic of the previous one. Thus, movements are more interconnected than they would seem to be, and moods can evolve out of their accumulation. If you learn to play this "chess game" sensitively, you will find that you can control the moods of a play more through movement than through any of the other visual tools.

Movement in Relation to Speeches

Movement is so dynamic, so eye-catching, that it exerts great power over line-reading illustration. Thus, the exact point at which a movement is made becomes extremely important, something that you and the actor must decide together. To accent a line, the actor moves *before* he says the line. To accent a movement (that is, to have the movement actually say more than the line), the actor moves *after* the line. It is for these reasons that actors tend to move on the lines, because by making such movements most of the time, they can then save the pointing of a line or movement for special moments. However, you can readily see that unless your actors are fully aware of the values of *pointing,* many of them will not use movement as illustration at all, and thus you will lose the most valuable tool in your directing kit. Therefore, you must learn to mix up the speech-movement relationship and to exploit it in every possible way. (Demonstrate with numbers and dialogue.)

Quantity of Movement

At first, you will not need to worry about putting too much movement into a scene, because you will have difficulties in finding enough of it. But after you understand the value of movement and learn the knack of arousing such illustration in your actors, you will learn to select all movements with extreme care. *Excessive movement (that is, movement on nearly every line) can kill the other tools of expression, but insufficient movement will mean underillustration.* You will also learn that experienced actors do not need as much movement as the less experienced because they know how to exploit *all* the tools of illustration and not just one or two. But to help the inexperienced, you must learn how to suggest movement to them, for these suggestions will build their confidence by giving them something specific to do and will lead to the use of the other tools, as well. *The quantity of movement, then, must be determined not only by the character of the play you are producing but also by the quality of the actors you are using.* You must learn to judge both with care and objectivity.

Because young directors tend to ignore movement as a tool of illustration, you are encouraged at this point to *work as much movement into a scene as you possibly can, and then remove, at a later stage of rehearsal, what you consider excess.* Movement can be your most potent tool in helping actors discover the dramatic action. When they move, they feel on the outside the way they should on the inside, and that feeling will give them a strong hint about what they should be doing in the dramatic action. This is an example of *organic blocking* put to work. (Do Exercise 6.)

EXERCISE

1. Examine a class study play by first making out *all* the directions in the script that prescribe movement, except for "playwright's movement," as described earlier. Now underline all entrances and exits by noting the beginning of units where characters either leave or enter the scene (French scenes). How many are there? What other movement does the playwright formally prescribe in the action? (Look for the use of objects that the playwright has specifically placed and then incorporated in the required visual illustration.)
2. Select a play for study that requires a group (such as *Riders to the Sea* at the point where Bartley is carried in and the villagers follow), and actually block the entrance of the group with live actors. Who will enter first? How many together? Where will they move to on the groundplan? How will the principal characters adjust to this entrance?

Now arrange an exit. What problems does this arrangement involve?

3. Improvise a living room/dining room scene with six to eight characters (*Ah, Wilderness!* is a suggestion). Play an action in the living room, and then move the actors to seated positions around the dining table. Note the extra movements required to bring this change about effectively and efficiently. Improvise the same action, but use the whole groundplan for the first action before moving the group to the table. What problems does this procedure involve?
4. Assign verbs to a classmate. Have him or her improvise movements to illustrate each verb.
5. Improvise an action involving two actors. Using number dialogue, have them play the action. Did they use much movement? If so, was it meaningful? If not, why not? Now play the same action with the aid of the instructor who urges movement, when necessary, from the sidelines, and who also, with a signal, demands that the actor playing "Cat" start playing "Mouse," and vice versa.
6. Each student, working alone, blocks the movements in a class study play. In class, one student directs live actors through two or three units, using his preconceived movements. Class discussion follows. Repeat several times.

14

Coordinating the Blocking Tools in Director-Actor Communication

It was emphasized in Chapter 7 that a separate treatment of each tool would be necessary in order to see the values and strengths of each in director-actor communication. Although isolating them has made them more abstract, the better you learn to see in great detail everything that happens in a physical way on the stage, the easier it will be for you to see the simultaneous use of these tools. So, while you are learning, you must run the film in slow motion if you are to isolate these tools at all. Yet, we know that the strengths of a scene's moods depend greatly on highly selective uses of these visual tools. A director who fully understands them will know how to exploit them.

Coordination

Coordination means using all the tools with as much variety and freshness as possible, a technique that can come about only if you constantly remind yourself of the many tools at your command. The most frequently neglected tool is movement; the dullest is usually the groundplan; the tritest is hand properties; the least utilized is composition. Not until you have all the tools working for you will you be of genuine help to actors in search of dramatic action and how best to illustrate it.

The director's job is to make a scene work by *"bringing out" the actors through appropriately illustrated reciprocation* of dramatic action. Once you fully comprehend that dramatic action cannot be conveyed movingly without convincing and believable visual illustrations employing all the tools, you can begin to consider yourself on the way to becoming a director. Play production is the articulation of idea, not the invention of the idea itself—something the playwright has already done.

Use of the Tools on Other Stages

You must give the proscenium stage all your attention at this point if you are to learn in a progressive way, for *all the tools are readily adapted to other stage forms*—arena, open-thrust, forestage-proscenium. (These adaptations will be given special attention in Chapter 19.) For now, you must concentrate on how to help the actor on the proscenium stage through the use of the tools of communication. Don't confuse the form of the stage with this central purpose. The strongest director is one who knows how to bring the actor to his highest achievement.

Paper Blocking

Again, some professional directors take a negative attitude toward blocking plays, saying that they leave most stage positions and movement up to the improvisation of their actors. However, they fail to mention that professional actors, through multiple experiences, know how to show themselves to best advantage on the stage—an awareness amateur actors seldom have. Don't let such statements mislead you; learning about how to direct is quite a different process than leading skilled performers in a professional production. Do your homework first.

Although a director in training should gradually move toward the goal of controlled improvisation with actors, he should practice *paper blocking* as a necessary step in learning the values of all the tools of communication. Paper blocking is the homework preceding rehearsal periods. The learning director can improvise in the quiet of his study without all the confusion and speed of a rehearsal situation, where he will likely be more self-conscious and less able to concentrate than the actors with whom he may be working. *Because his job is to help actors, he must be, in one sense, a big jump ahead of them in his knowledge of the playscript and what he wants done with it.* The learning director's blocking homework, then, is a playing of the scene in his own imagination: what he thinks it might look like visually. By giving himself time and privacy, he can experiment with several ways until he arrives at what he considers to be the best decision.

Paper blocking is in no sense an arbitrary director's decision that he will force on the actors, but a preexamination of possibilities for director-actor communication. Instead of leaving himself with only one way to illustrate a scene, a director has investigated the possibilities widely enough to enable him to move in several directions with actors, although he may personally think that one is superior to the others. *Paper blocking opens up a director's imagination instead of closing it,* for a dozen suggestions are far better than one. Moreover, the job of rehearsal is to keep the actors working. If they must wait around while the director makes up his mind about how he thinks a play should go, actors will be tense and will not concentrate well. Imagination in rehearsing is often released in the appropriate speed and rhythm of a scene; too much slow-moving playing may dry up the actors' imaginations.

The Promptbook

The *promptbook* is your original design for a live production of a play. After you have studied Part III, your knowledge will be much more inclusive, but at this point, the promptbook must be based on what you have learned in Parts I and II. Thus, it is a testing of how well you have grasped the concepts of play-analysis and the six blocking tools, as well as the techniques for making them work for you. Again, this procedure will open your imagination, not close it.

In order to provide sufficient space for all the necessary notations, make a working promptbook by taking the playscript apart, if it is a printed text, and mounting each page on an 8½" × 11" sheet of ruled paper. One procedure, if you are working with a printed script, is to cut windows in the paper so that both sides of the text are visible, thus requiring only one playscript. Now insert a blank page between the pages of the text so that each page of text has its own work page. You should make a practice of binding the promptbook in either a hardbound notebook cover or a strong folder-type cover with metal fasteners. A director, as with any craftsman, is known by the condition of his tools—in this case, his promptbook. Therefore, don't be sloppy about making this primary work tool that will undergo a great deal of use.

Groundplan Design and Testing

Because a groundplan for a Realistic staging is the floor plan of a walled setting, the plan should show the lines of the enclosing walls, doors, windows, levels (platforms), and all furniture pieces. *Always make an accurate drawing to scale.* Freehand improvisation will only get you into serious trouble—you will not be accurate with the space relationships and will be misled by what you think you have instead of by what you actually will have. Figure 47 is a sample drawing, but *you should follow the principles you have learned in your scene design class.*

FIGURE 47

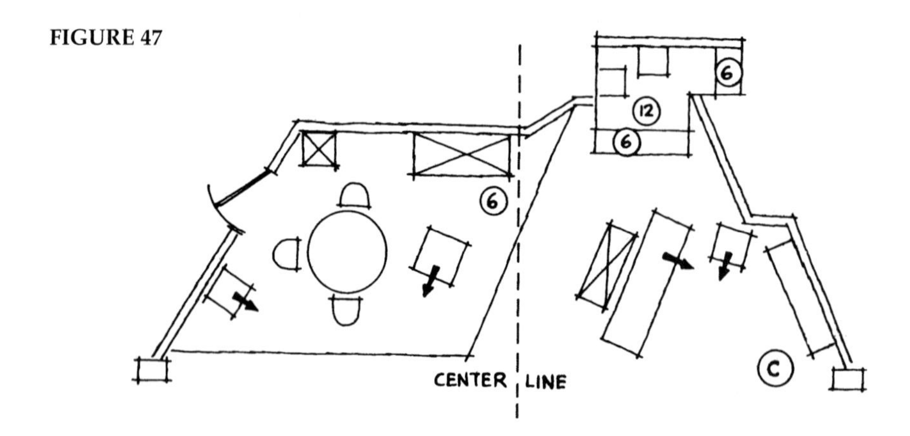

You must take the greatest care with the groundplan, following explicitly the procedures discussed in Chapter 9, for all the other director-actor communication tools will either depend directly on it or be strongly influenced by it. Remember: A dozen groundplans are better than one in trying to find the best choice, because your imagination and improvisational force will be released. Select the furniture pieces with unusual care in the interest of projecting how they can act as "activity centers" in stimulating actors to fresh illustration.

Test your groundplan by answering the following questions:

1. Does it have a minimum of five to seven acting areas?
2. Does it have strong upstage and downstage movement possibilities as well as stage right and stage left possibilities?
3. Are strong diagonals possible?
4. Have you created tension in the placement of your furniture pieces?
5. Is it an obstacle course?
6. What is the potential for strong compositions and picturizations?
7. Is it ingenious?
8. Will it provoke actors to fresh and imaginative illustrations?
9. *Have you avoided the no-room?*

Perspective Sketch

A *perspective sketch* of the groundplan is needed at this point to show more nearly what the groundplan looks like in the stage cube. Does your plan exploit levels as well as give ideas of proportion, balance, and so forth? It will tell you whether the room looks like a room and whether the areas have all been exploited. The mood of the *setting*—and it is now a setting with the walls added, except for color treatment and modifying details—will be declared largely on the basis of the distribution of furniture pieces, the sense of space created, and the size of the setting.

Composition and Movement Notation

Now that you have the groundplan designed and the promptbook ready for use, you are in a position to record your compositions and movement suggestions in a detailed way. You will already have many ideas in mind from your work on the groundplan, but your intention now is to assess the groundplan in a specific way by seeing how well it will work continuously throughout the scene. If you have done a good job in design, you will find that this detailed procedure will move rapidly and excitingly. *Do not labor over making everything work, for if you move too slowly with this sort of notation, you will lose the rhythm of the scene* and what you intend doing with it; blocking is like a chess game that you always project five moves ahead. Remember that the blocking you "see" will now meet its crucial test only when you suggest it to the actors who will play the scene, and that the intention of advance planning is to put yourself in as flexible a position as possible.

FIGURE 48

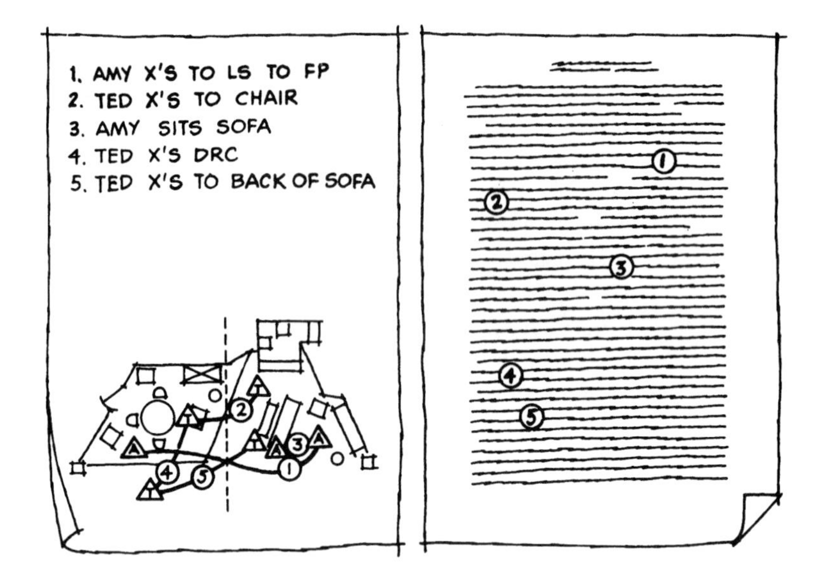

Now enter on the upper half of each blocking page all the movements for that page of text (see Figure 48). Number each movement on this page consecutively and then place the same numbers in the text. By setting down the movements, you will automatically imply the compositions and also, at least in your imagination, some projection of the picturizations. Ensure there is a copy of the groundplan on the bottom half of each of these facing pages. *Draw all the movements* for each page on this copy groundplan, and indicate each character by a triangle with its initial inside (△T). Show the direction of each movement by arrows on the lines and by the same number of the movement you have used in the written directions and in the text. A different color for each character will aid in keeping them separate.

Although gestures cannot be shown, as ideas come to you, they can be noted on the blocking page. Similar notes can also be made for improvisation with set and hand properties.

Master Movement Plan

When all the detailed blocking has been done for each page of text, you should *enter all movement on a single groundplan,* this time by using enlarged dots to show compositional positions (see Figure 49) and colors to show movements. When you finish doing this procedure, the drawing will look like a scribbled mess. Yet, it can reveal very quickly your exploitations of the groundplan—whether the movement, and thus the composition, has been concentrated in only one or two areas; whether the central planes have dominated, thus reducing the vertical use of the groundplan; whether the full groundplan has been utilized; and so on. This check is quick and reliable to see how well the groundplan has been thought through. Figure 49 is an example that shows the exploitation of all the areas.

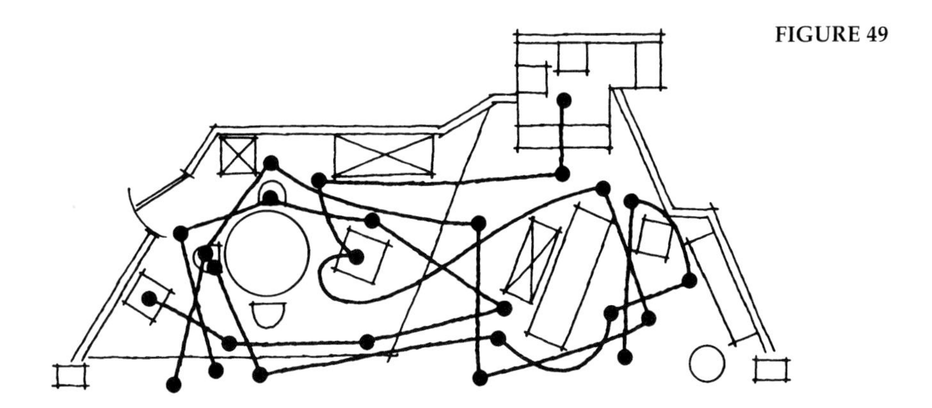

FIGURE 49

List of Properties

You have already made decisions on set properties when you designed your groundplan. At this point, you should review them carefully to be certain that you have selected the most activity-exciting furniture pieces you can think of that apply specifically to the given circumstances you are trying to suggest. *Strive for freshness and ingenuity; triteness and dullness are sure death as far as director-actor communication with the groundplan is concerned.*

Finally, select with the greatest care the hand properties you think might stimulate actors. Verisimilitude (the appearance of being true or real) to the given circumstances is again necessary, but remember that it is secondary and that the primary value of a hand property is to aid an actor in his use of gestures. If too few properties are used, a scene will very likely be underillustrated, but too many can distract an audience by throwing emphasis on the properties themselves. So you must give your *appropriate* list your primary attention, with the accepted intention of adding other properties later as they are needed or withdrawing those that prove to be inadequate.

EXERCISES

1. Using a common study play (a one-act play), prepare a promptbook incorporating the following:
   a. Playscript and blocking pages
   b. The full play-analysis you did at the end of Chapter 6
   c. Groundplan to scale
   d. Perspective sketch
   e. Blocking notations for the entire play
   f. Master movement plan

   (*Note:* If these exercises have been done with a study play en route, all that needs doing at this point is the master movement plan.)
2. Discuss *coordination* in all of its aspects.
3. Discuss *organic blocking* as a primary procedure in working with actors in training.

15

Helping Actors "Speak" a Play

Just as Chapter 8 alerted you to How well do you see? this chapter alerts you to the most important aspect of directing: How well do you hear? What have you learned in your classes in voice and speech? *Have you really learned how important speaking is on the stage?*

You are about to tackle the core craft of good theatre: speaking a play with dynamic intensity and reaching an audience—moving it, persuading it, keeping its attention. How much can you help on this job? After you have tried to work with this aspect of directing, you will look back at the visual as readily controllable; but now, you are treading on the real heart of acting and you may have a very difficult time helping actors.

This is where many would-be directors fail: They do not see their job of helping actors speak well, but instead rely only on the visual aspects of stage use. But a good director will perceive his job as that of a *listening* and watching critic who can help actors greatly in bringing out a play for an audience.

Listen to actor-playwright-director William Shakespeare on good and bad acting as well as the visual-aural balance in production. In *Hamlet,* he talks to the actors who are about to present a play he has selected. Can you see him at the rehearsal, just like your own, jawing at the actors about how they ruin plays? Listen carefully:

> *Ham.* Speak the speech, I pray you, as I pronounced it to you, trippingly on the tongue: but if you mouth it, as many of your players do, I had as lief the towncrier spoke my lines. Nor do not saw the air too much with your hand, thus, but use all gently; for in the very torrent, tempest, and, as I may say, the whirlwind of passion, you must acquire and beget a temperance that may give it smoothness. . . .

Do we see why Shakespeare thinks "mouthing"—that is, swallowed, obscured, unarticulated delivery—is ruinous? And how wild gesticulating merely exaggerates passion in a physical way and is empty. He goes on:

> Be not too tame neither, but let your own discretion be your tutor. Suit the action to the word, the word to the action; with this special observance, that you o'erstep not

> the modesty of nature; for anything so overdone is from the purpose of playing, whose end, both at the first and now, was and is, to hold, as 'twere, the mirror up to nature; to show virtue her own feature, scorn her own image, and the very age and body of the time his form and pressure. . . .

Can you hear his complaints about acting? Be dynamic, he says, and use moderate activity, but be truthful about human nature, because physical exaggeration will obscure what you are trying to say about human beings.

Shakespeare then talks about how actors insult both a play and the playwright:

> And let those that play your clowns speak no more than is set down for them; for there be of them that will themselves laugh, to set on some quantity of barren spectators to laugh too; though, in the mean time, some necessary question of the play be then to be considered: that's villainous, and shows a most pitiful ambition in the fool that uses it.

Don't make up speeches or insert gimmicks, he says, but stick to the playwright's words. And above all, don't "play" with an audience, because it will distract them from the main line of the play. Again: "That's villainous, and shows a most pitiful ambition in the fool that uses it."

Do you see Shakespeare's balance between what is visual and what is oral? He sounds like a tired director who has gone through this many times. How modern he is, how adept a director he is.

Note how Shakespeare contrasts what an audience sees with what it hears. He lets the two complement each other. It is not because he is writing plays in verse; we have the same problems with lowly prose today. Shakespeare is merely telling us how condensed and concentrated good dialogue actually is.

We have become so accustomed today to the power of the visual that we have literally forgotten that *great acting before our time was spoken acting*. There is no question that the twentieth century discovered through the camera a more highly developed sense of seeing than any other age has ever experienced. We look at everything, even such strange things as microorganisms, enlarged thousands of times or representations of such abstractions as sound waves and heartbeats.

The theatre, consequently, has an enormous task in competing with this sort of visual assault on our senses, because we can never see acting on the stage in close-ups. Stage makeup has always been used to enlarge and simplify features of the face, or masks have been made with typical or symbolic meanings. Even if a member of an audience sits close to the stage, say within the first five rows, he will certainly see the actors in much more personal detail, but he may not actually receive any more of the play than those sitting several rows to the rear or in galleries above. There is certainly a limit to the size of a playhouse, but that limitation is not made on the basis of the visual; rather, it is made on the basis of the oral—what can be readily heard.

Good directing, then, provides an aural (hearing) as well as a visual experience for an audience. *A play is not a motion picture on a stage; it is a sensual experience that reaches us through the ear as much as through the eye.* Without the sensitivity to and delight in the musical aspects of the human voice in the theatre, a director will have great difficulty in communicating to an audience.

The craft of theatre-making, then, does not lie in the visual alone, but in its balance with the oral-aural experience. Because the visual close-up is not possible in the theatre, the only thing that can take its place besides the body is the actor's voice, because it comes from deep inside him. That voice is what moves us. And how very rare that experience is.

So much attention is placed today in actor training on the interior approach in order to develop subtextual awareness that young actors lose sight of the fact that without a voice and the capability of using it, they can get nowhere on stage. Small, realistic voices are possible in motion pictures and television, but certainly not in the cavern of a theatre. The voice, therefore, is an actor's prized possession, for it is his principal tool of communication. A director who does not comprehend this fact is simply bypassing his most potent means of reaching audiences. *Acting is speaking in a very real sense.* Instruction in acting cannot take the voice for granted but must make voice development a dominant part of training.

To repeat, oral delivery is perhaps the major difference between the amateur and the professional actor. "Talent" is often designated on this basis, for the voice speaks from inside the nervous system of the human being; it "drags out the guts," so to speak, and forces hearing on the basis of its revealing intimacy. In this sense, the voice has a greater capability than the visual close-up, since it can move more deeply simply because it becomes a heart-to-heart contact between actor and members of an audience. *A character virtually lives in his human voice and not merely so much in what he looks like or illustrates visually.* Simply stated, the mature art of acting is speaking.

EXERCISES

1. How do you rate the speaking in the British comedies seen on public television? Except for the differences in English speech, would you rate the speaking capabilities better than that in U.S. sitcoms? Compare the speaking in *As Time Goes By* with that in *Suddenly Susan* or another sitcom. Why are Judi Dench and Geoffrey Palmer rated highly as comedians?
2. Is the speaking in motion-picture comedies better than that in television? Why?
3. Why are soap operas easy to understand as speaking plays?

Speaking: The Heart and Soul of Good Theatre

Playgoers frequently complain that they cannot hear young and inexperienced actors because they mumble and do not speak up. But more than likely, the fault is not low volume, for there are many things that prevent hearing besides the actor's actual volume-articulation capability. Chief among these are (1) the distraction of the visual, (2) the deemphasis of the actor as speaker, (3) the actor's faulty speaking of the subtext, and (4) an audience member's actual capability of hearing.

The oral-aural process is given the best chance to work in the absence of distraction, for hearing a play well is a matter of intense concentration by both the actor and the audience. In one sense, a member of an audience has a right to blame an actor if he cannot hear, although the director and, through him, the designers often may actually be the guilty parties. The director's job is to hold the audience's attention by reducing distractions to an absolute minimum. The motion-picture director is able to control this by means of close-ups, careful editing, close "miking," and high-volume projection that cuts out all other sound interference. The close-up specifically lets us watch both the mouth and eyes of the actor in great detail, and we hear better because we are better lip-readers than we think we are. But the stage actor is seen in his entirety from head to foot with no cuts, no changes. There is no instant replay as in televised football games or retakes as in movies. Once done, it's done.

The Actor's Speaking of the Subtext

An actor may possess a fine voice and excellent articulation and yet be quite incapable of being well heard and understood by an audience. *Much of the problem may lie in his failure to understand the subtext.* If an actor speaks the way *he* thinks and feels, he may not speak at all in the way that the character he wants to portray thinks and feels. Finding the character means finding the subtext, and this is where the director plays an enormous role in the oral-aural process. After all, it is his job to help the actor find the subtext.

Because of its careful selection and intensification, prose dialogue is not an exact reproduction of everyday speech, but it is close to everyday speech. And because of this closeness, it is often assumed that if an actor comprehends the dramatic action behind the actual words of a dialogue, he can make the words provided by the author his very own; that is, he can speak like the character. Although there are definite pitfalls the actor can fall into if he relies only on this one approach, there can be no question of its basic validity, because dramatic action is *character.*

This is precisely the core use of the director's intensive work on play-analysis, particularly his detailing of the dramatic action in verbal form, as described in Chapter 4. In his communication with actors, *he probably will not use the exact verbs he has set down in his play-analysis,* for they may be too pure, too formal, too literary for ready communication; however, the director will be able to imagize and stimulate in many different ways because he knows what must come out. The flexibility of his communication with specific actors is very great, and in working closely with them, in sensing and building on every contribution an actor may make, he can shape the action as he thinks necessary.

To repeat the point of the discussion in Chapter 4, *the director's most important job is to bring about reciprocation between actors.* Each actor must understand the feelings of his own character, but he must also be highly sensitive to what other characters are doing to him. Sensitive directing is ensuring that each actor is hearing the forcings of others, perceptions that will lead to subtle adjustments before action is returned. Only in this way will emotion emerge from a scene. To restate an important point: *Acting can be described as primarily the process of subtle adjustment.* Actors play off one another with strong recognitions and discoveries. Thus, the adjustments may often be more important than the forcings in keeping an audience's attention.

"Hearing" the subtext, then, is at the very core of reciprocation, and the director is the outside person who can be certain that this part of the acting process is fully exploited. Communication to an audience cannot be made by each actor working separately but only when there is high communication between two or more who adjust like the characters they are playing.

A practical example of how an audience reacts when it is deprived of the subtleties of subtext is in the experience with foreign movies where subtitles are printed at the bottom of the screen in English. We are afraid to look at the words for fear of losing the action illustrated in eyes and faces. In English-language movies, we have no such problem, if the director has done his job on the subtext, because we can absorb the text and subtext simultaneously.

Speaking the Text

As you can now see, "speaking the text" in Realistic plays means conveying the subtext (the "covered-up" text) in very subtle ways. You will see this whole process reversed when you begin dealing with plays of past ages in Part III. You will find that subtext is much reduced in those plays and the text speaks to the dramatic action quickly. However, the attack here is on modern drama, where the actor is required to give both. Too often, prose dialogue is taken for granted because of its similarity to real life. Yet, only when directors are aware of its subtle complications and its artifice can they bring about the necessary hearing in an audience. If an audience is to hear easily and well, actors must do a great deal of word and line pointing, *textual emphasis;* and the director must be constantly on the alert to be certain the actors are doing so. Here are a few suggestions:

1. Apply what you have learned in a course in interpretive reading concerning emphasis, contrasts, and echoes (repetitions of words or phrases).
2. Insist that all proper nouns (persons and places) be given special emphasis, with perhaps the slightest pause (a *caesura*) before the word, a technique you often hear good newscasters use. You will do the same thing with verbs because they create the action.
3. Insist on accuracy in the text, which also means the employment of an author's punctuation, because that discloses what he thinks is the sense, as it does in all good writing.
4. Discourage corruption of the text by such means as substitution of or addition of words. Good dialogue is highly economical, with every word selected and necessary. "This is a very difficult line for me to say," says an actor. "Can I

change the order or substitute these words. . . ?" More than likely, he does not yet understand the subtext or he is emphasizing the wrong words in the text. Because the author heard it, the actor can probably hear it *if you help him find what is underneath the words.* If you learn to spot the emphasis in a line—usually centered around the verb—you will be able to spot the subtext, and out of that subtext will emerge the meaning of the line, which can then be conveyed to an audience *if the right words are stressed.*

5. Alert the actor to the *pauses* in the dialogue, for they are tied closely to adjustments in the acting process. Their effect is very great, not because they give lifelikeness to speech, but because they *point and emphasize what is spoken.* Do you hear the silences in dialogue? They create the rhythm by punctuating the sound. If the audience is to "hear" the silences, you and the actors must hear them first. Help your actors find them and you will discover new meanings. If properly placed, pauses can sustain attention in an audience more readily than sound, because no one knows what will happen next.
6. As you learned in Chapter 3, dialogue is written with the emphasis toward the end of the line, which means that the *line is constructed climactically by placing the emphasis near the end.* Even though actors comprehend the subtext, they may fail to deliver the line with the strength of emphasis intended. *Pitch drop occurs when an actor loses vocal force before the ending of a word or sentence and drops the pitch,* thus destroying the hearing of this part of the line. Actors who are trained in subtextual acting become very self-conscious when a director points to such faults by correcting words or phrases. If it is only an occasional dropping of a word or line, it is better first to look into the subtext for such failures, because the actor may be missing the emphasis in the action. But if the failure is frequent, the actor is not fully aware of the climactic construction of dialogue and needs orienting on this point. A rehearsal technique used by some directors is to correct these failures through the use of written notes during the polishing period, when words, phrases, or line corrections can be absorbed readily by an actor because he understands the subtext; the written notes also communicate well because the actor can quietly be alerted to his problem.

The speaking of verse dialogue will be discussed in Part III, where the acting of plays of past ages is considered.

Character Decorum in Speech

In Chapters 4 and 11, *decorum* was defined as a character's outward show—what he literally looks like to others. This outward show also includes what he *sounds* like. Decorum is always a specific reflection of the given circumstances because environment defines social differences. We easily recognize it in speech, and perhaps with greater force, because characters, like people in real life, may refine their body movements but seldom change their strongly molded environmental speech patterns. A director must give primary attention to such physical verisimilitudes.

A not uncommon practice in playwriting, especially in plays before 1950, was for playwrights to record in writing as accurately as possible the actual sounds of speech they intended for certain characters. Good hearers such as Bernard Shaw and John Millington Synge were very successful in this sort of sound transcription, but many writers who could not hear as well went no further than a generalized substandard language. More recently, many writers have not attempted to transcribe at all but have left the sound in the hands of the directors and actors, assuming that their awareness of given circumstances will lead them to the appropriate sounds. Unless a director is fully attuned to the dimension sound can add to production, he will lose one of his most important tools of communication. If he pays attention to this problem, he will know that significant meanings can often be conveyed through sound itself, aside from the words and the subtext.

We are therefore concerned not only with dialects (departures from "General American" as a standard for speech), but with all speech we hear on the stage. Actors may have a full comprehension of the subtext in a Realistic play and yet not be able to convey convincingly the speech-decorum aspects of a character. We simply cannot believe an actor playing a highly refined, urbane, and mannered gentleman who speaks with a distinct country accent; nor can we believe an actor playing a rough peasant who speaks with the cultured sounds of city refinement. Realistic drama forces this demand on actors and directors, and to sidestep is to avoid the verisimilitude required by Realism. Nowadays, directors may cast actors on the basis of their speech characteristics alone, preferring to work back into the subtext with the "outward show" in the sound already certain of adequate acceptance, for few actors can handle both refined speech and substandard speech effectively. In the commercial theatre and in the motion-picture industry, rigid casting lines are often observed, employing actors who can simulate country or urban speech, or who can give the "sounds" of dialects or cultivated speech. How an actor "sounds" often seems to be more important than how he looks.

Of more concern to the director than the special problems of dialects is the level of *good* speech, for it is the only requirement in a wide range of modern drama. The only determining factor in good speech, in the absence of any established American stage standard, would seem to be *an absence of any readily recognizable local dialect.* The vowel structure in good speech would be close to what we recognize as the best urban speech of educated America—the speech we frequently hear from our best national network radio and television newscasters. To go further would rule out the wide range of acceptable American speech.

Speech decorum, in the sense it has been described here, may actually be more of a casting problem than one that can be remedied during a rehearsal period. However, a director must be thoroughly aware that an actor cannot communicate to and be heard by an audience without distraction unless he can reflect the speech decorum of the character he is trying to represent. All a director can do is to hold an actor to the sound he had in mind during the casting period, although he may be able to improve it extensively by working with the actor on vowel modifications and technical approaches for producing better sounds. A director's best communication to an actor, however, may be in his expert conveyance of given circumstances that may stimulate an actor into adjusting his character's speech decorum on his own. But this decorum can be brought about only if an actor has a highly developed hearing capability—a relatively sophisticated talent that can make him sensitive to his own speech and how it can be adjusted. Speech is not changed by telling an actor what he is doing wrong, simply because he cannot hear his own speech unless he has been trained to do so, as actors should be. Good speech, as well as good reproduction of dialects, can result only from an extraordinarily developed sense of hearing.

Projection

Projection is a very real problem for directors working with young actors because most new actors have not yet realized the level they must achieve in this technique before they can call themselves actors. The professional actor claims his rank as a professional on high-performance capability in this aspect of acting; and he may very well continue working for years with voice instructors in an attempt to improve his capabilities.

Unfortunately, far too much actor training in the United States does not insist on intensive work in projection, as it does in England, France, and Germany; and too many educational theatre directors take a lax position regarding this aspect of play production. There can be no assumption that, because an actor understands the dramatic action, he will be readily heard, for much prose dialogue can be as difficult for an audience to hear as dialogue in verse.

Projection training is, of course, part of actor training, and we are treating it here only as it concerns production. However, because directors must constantly meet this problem head-on, even though they cannot teach projection in more than a nominal way during a rehearsal period, they must recognize its great importance to the effectiveness of a performance. Projection is a technical problem in communication, and the director provides the listening ear to monitor the actors.

The real problem for the director is bringing a performance to a high level of projection without making the actors so self-conscious of this technical aspect that they lose the high concentration needed in playing the subtext. One approach is to begin the rehearsal period with production techniques by using material other than the text, although it means delay in the work on the actual play in hand. But once the actors are aware of the director's ideas about projection, especially while everyone's ears are free of the text, problems can be met later on because a talking position has been established without fear of upsetting concentration on the subtext. As this chapter has already pointed out, an actor who understands the subtext has already greatly improved his projection position. However, there is a great deal more to mastering the problem.

If you listen to first-rate actors in a stage performance or even in recordings of stage plays, you will be most respectful of their technical capabilities such as articulation, vowel choice, use of regionalisms, pronunciation, relaxation, quality, volume, pitch, a quiet head, energy, and confidence. And you may be most of all impressed with the way action, feeling, intent, and thought permeate and "color" the speaking of a well-trained and talented actor.

- *Articulation.* Speech is placed forward in the mouth cavity where the articulators—teeth, tongue, lips, and gum ridges—can be exploited fully. Good actors are remarkably energetic in the mechanical employment of their articulators by vigorously moving the jaw, lips, and tongue. Moreover, placing the speech forward overcomes the possibility of sound being buried in the back of the mouth, with a resulting loss of quality. English and German actors, as well as French classical actors, are among the very best in this respect. Directors must insist on energetic articulation of sound. Also, actors must avoid run-on or continuant sound, a significant failure because it obscures clear articulation.
- *Vowel choice.* Except in dialects and substandard speech, the term *vowel choice* pertains to the articulation of the vowels associated with what is considered to be the best American speech (speech without marked regionalism). These vowels are not nasalized, nor are they tense or flat. In the scale of the phonetic alphabet for American English, this means a "soft" [æ], or a sound nearer the halfway vowels of New England speech [a] and [ɒ] but not the Italian [ɑ], except in those words employing that vowel in General American speech. Directors must help young actors eliminate characteristic regionalisms, such as the substitution of [I] for [ɛ] in such words as *president,* [æ] for [ɔ] in *water,* and a high tense [æ] in *calf.*
- *Use of regionalisms.* Good actors do not employ regionalisms except in the use of dialects. Directors should be ever watchful for such characteristics as the southern dropped ending [n] instead of [ŋ], the intrusive *r* of New England speech, the added vowels of southern speech (Bill should not be [biIl] but [bIl]), and so forth.
- *Pronunciation.* Good directors, when in doubt, use dictionaries as a guide to correct pronunciation.
- *Relaxation.* A tense speaker is very hard to hear. Because body relaxation can improve projection tremendously, directors must encourage actors to relax; a relaxed actor can speak at very low volumes and still be well heard if he has excellent articulation.
- *Quality.* Relaxation and voice training will improve voice quality, although quality at its base is an inherent *talent* in an actor. In the Realistic theatre, however, the odd-toned voice can be exciting, especially in character roles; on the other hand, straight roles require a better-than-average quality that an audience can tolerate through a full evening. This is particularly important where low-pitched qualities have much to do with good audience hearing.
- *Volume.* Actors do not reach audiences on the basis of high volumes but on the basis of line sense (subtext) and articulation. Only occasionally is volume actually used as a dramatic technique, and then, above all, the actor must exercise the greatest care to articulate the words, for it is easy to blast the "hearability" of a word with excessive volume. In general, good actors speak with

fair volume, but it always appears easy and unforced; forced volume is a great distraction to an audience because the audience can hear the actor pushing, as distinct from playing his character. Actors learn to vary volumes because they can convey subtle dramatic meanings by doing so; but they are very careful not to jump in and out of volumes in an erratic manner because such sharp contrasts can destroy hearing.

- *Pitch.* An important factor in hearing an actor is his use of pitch. Good actors do most of their speaking within a surprisingly small range of pitch—perhaps even as narrow as up or down three notes on the musical scale from their median range of pitch. This might at first seem like a monotone to you when you think about it. But listen to a good actor and you will hear that his steadiness and ability to be heard in delivery lie in his narrow range of pitch, which leaves the rest of his range—perhaps as much as three octaves—available for special moments. Thus, he plays a scene primarily in his normal range, except for the climactic points when he will extend the range as much as the character-mood-intensity of the action requires. An actor who speaks lines with sharp variations in pitch in the interest of being dramatic is very hard to hear because a listener's ear cannot make pitch adjustments quickly enough to follow the speech. This fault is common in inexperienced actors and is one to which directors must constantly be on the alert.
- *A quiet head.* When he is speaking, a good actor always holds his head as still as possible without being stiff or rigid. This rule is an absolute necessity in being heard. Forget the short quick movements of the head by TV performers who "bob" to keep the scene interesting. Stage actors talk to 1,000 or more people without electronic support for their deliveries. An actor who bobs his head will also "bob" the sound; he may also use erratic change in pitch because he wants to be very dramatic. *Let the speaking do the work in acting* is the expert advice of the good actor. Use visual illustration when not speaking. Directors must have faith in the dramatic action and in how well-spoken dialogue can transfer it. Overacting always destroys hearing because it creates distraction.
- *Energy.* The mark of the professional actor is his ability to keep the energy that is behind his acting at a high level. *Acting is energy transferred to an audience.* This energy is really what the spectators have come to feel, what they want to experience during an evening, whether they know it or not. Poor speaking betrays poor energy in the actor. Directors must get the actors to speak with the energy of their entire bodies and not just with voices from their heads alone. A performance is a tiring experience for a good actor because he works with his entire muscular system as well as his nervous system. "Speaking from the guts" is no mere expression; it is the essence of projection. Also, keep in mind that rested actors will be much more capable of high energy levels than tired actors, for good voices depend on good health. When playing a series of performances with young actors, directors must insist that they have adequate rest.
- *Confidence.* How well an actor is heard depends much on his stage confidence. If he loves to play, if he knows what he is playing (subtext); if he exerts

his strong will as an actor, he will probably be heard. *Communication is the desire to reach others;* confidence is akin to command, and good actors command their audiences who hear them.

EXERCISES

The purpose of the exercises that follow is not in any way intended to do more than the chapter tries to do—that is, make you fully aware of the director's responsibilities in the oral presentation of a play. Separate classes in interpretive reading, voice production, phonetics, and regional speech are so widely offered in training programs that it is expected directors in training will pursue, perhaps extensively, the content of these areas so necessary to their work. Without a full comprehension of voice and speech, a director cannot hope to make an effective production with actors in training.

The following exercises, then, are suggested in the interest of pointing out the ever-recurring problems facing the director in any nonprofessional production. The instructor is urged to use his own range of examples and illustrations to augment an understanding of the often neglected content of this very important chapter. Remember, the most frequent complaint of the audience at amateur productions is: "I couldn't hear the actors." As a director, you must make sure the neglect is not your own fault.

A good collection of recordings is necessary for the following class exercises:

1. Listen to a recording of a Shakespearean play with Laurence Olivier or John Gielgud cast in a leading role. Analyze the articulation and range of pitch.
2. Listen to a recording of a modern play. Analyze the articulation and range of pitch.
3. Have two actors who have no previous knowledge of the play read the opening scene of Murray Schisgal's *Luv* to the class. They should characterize the roles only as much as one hour of rehearsal will allow. After hearing them, play the recording made by the first New York cast (Eli Wallach, Anne Jackson, and Alan Arkin). Was the sound a surprise? What does the sound mean to a production of this play? Are the actors illustrating the given circumstances of this play? What about the dramatic action? Other recordings suggested are:
   - *The Glass Menagerie* (Williams) with Jessica Tandy, Julie Harris, and Montgomery Clift
   - *The Young Man from Atlanta* (Foote) with Shirley Knight
   - *The Road to Mecca* (Fugard) with Julie Harris and Amy Irving
   - *The Master Builder* (Ibsen) with Maggie Smith and Michael Redgrave
4. Play the final scene of Le Gallienne's *Hedda* or the Michael Redgrave–Maggie Smith recording of *The Master Builder.* How do the actors play both the text and subtext?
5. Play a recording that employs either an American or an English dialect (Irish, Cockney, Bronx, or Brooklyn speech are good choices). Pick out all the characteristics of the dialect—for example, vowels, pitch lines, substandard English, rhythm structure, and national character as expressed in optimistic or pessimistic sound. Repeat with other dialects. What basic elements are present in all the dialects?
6. Play a word-tossing game. One actor says a word with a certain vowel and another replies with the same word and a different possible vowel (meaning that the word so pronounced must still be acceptable pronunciation for some group.) Can a third actor participate? A fourth? Now try varying the principal vowel in the following sentences: (1) *I have to laugh to see the calf go down the path to take a bath in an hour and a half.*

(2) *The rains in Spain fall mainly on the plains.* Each actor uses the same principal vowel sound in all the appropriate words. How many possible variations can be made on these lines? What would the use of each vowel mean in a set of given circumstances?

7. Play the dramatic action with a common phrase, with each actor delivering the same phrase with a different action. Try: *I like you* or *I'm going downtown.* Have the class identify the dramatic action behind each reading.
8. Devise a dozen word games for class participation. They are fun to play and they will train your ears to hear sensitively.

16

Directing Is Working with Actors—2

Now that you've begun to understand several aspects of director-actor communication, including the essential concept that staging is not only a mechanical process but also a way of communicating with actors (as well as with audiences), you are ready to consider a range of points having to do with directing the acting in a stage production. Although some of you may have an intuitive sense about directing actors, most directors would agree that effectiveness in directing actors requires a good deal of experience over a number of years to see firsthand the dynamics of interpersonal communication that is at the heart of this most central of directorial functions. Indeed, becoming a fine director of actors is a lifetime proposition and you will probably keep learning as long as you do it. Suffice it to say that effective directing of actors is something that you are not likely to master in a single scene or a single academic term, but a skill that you will develop over time.

Helping Your Actors: Some Thoughts to Keep in Mind

In order to provide a great deal of information in a relatively compact format, what follows is a survey of points having to do with directing the acting, things a director should be aware of in working on a scene or a production. By keeping these points in mind and trying to incorporate them into your work, they will become second nature to you and a regular part of how you think about directing actors.

Adjustments. These are the reactions that characters/actors (that is, it happens on both levels) play as they receive action from each other in an exchange. Much of what constitutes good acting and what convinces us occurs in these adjustments—it's part of what persuades us that something was felt or heard. Are the adjustments being played? Are they being directed?

Discoveries. It's easy for actors not to play the discoveries in a scene because as real people (actors) they already know the story and have absorbed the discovery into consciousness. However, the characters in the play don't know the story (at least not its twists and turns because it is unfolding as they live it) and the discoveries that happen are new to them. The discoveries move the story forward and are its point of articulation and change. Are the discoveries being played fully with the consciousness of the character in the situation (rather than the actor who may "know" too much)? Are the discoveries being directed fully? Staged as vividly as their importance warrants? (Which is not to say huge, necessarily; a discovery may register in quite a subtle way, but its vividness has to do with the freshness of the discovery and truthful playing rather than with size as such.)

Talking and listening. Actually to talk to someone on the stage and actually to listen to each other is not an easy thing to do because of the actor's self-consciousness of being onstage, in a performance. However, if the actors don't really talk and listen, the characters' intentions, along with what they are saying and what they're receiving, will not register—either for them or for the audience—and the story disappears along with any sense of truth or reality in the playing. Good directors help actors to talk and listen, that is, with the necessity of communicating as it happens in life, rather than in reciting something learned and consequently "safe." In life, we talk and listen because our needs compel us to do so. So it should be on the stage.

Hearing and seeing. This is the twin to talking and listening. Hearing and seeing are essential to discoveries and adjustments and consequently to a character's pursuing the dramatic action. Seeing is necessary for the motivation of most movements. Hearing and seeing on the stage are difficult for most untrained actors because their concentration is fractured by a very high level of awareness of being onstage in a performance rather than immersed in a "real" situation. Consequently, they can't really hear or see what is happening in the give and take of playing, and audiences sense this quickly as the onstage experience flattens out and deadens. Good directors help actors to find the kind of concentration that allows them, as characters, actually to hear and see what happens in the interplay onstage.

Staying in the "now." Helping an actor stay in the "now" of the character's thinking, action, and given circumstances of the instant is essential for the director. If the actors are not in the eternal, evolving "now" of the dramatic moment, the audience quickly discerns the performance is just that, a performance that is more rote repetition than magical re-creation of experience. Concentration, thinking, seeing, hearing, listening, pursuing objectives, all within the given circumstances of the scene—all of these are essential to staying in the "now." Helping the actors find this level of involvement in the re-creative process of acting is one of the most valuable things a director can do.

Reciprocation. Reciprocation is true playing together, interacting in the moment in an ongoing chain of give and take, adjusting, or reacting. Attaining a high degree of reciprocation in the acting is one of the key goals of the director. Be alert for actors who may tend to play "by themselves" and not be as open to reciprocation as they might be. Such actors sometimes achieve some remarkable things in their playing, but ultimately the total work, the compelling, spellbinding experience that can come from actors fully involved with each other in the playing, will not be as full as when a high degree of reciprocation is achieved. This can only be there consistently if it is a primary value for the director.

Basic idea about acting—covering up versus revealing. What is the actor's basic idea about acting? Usually this is an unconscious attitude, but it greatly affects the way actors go about acting. Is this basic idea, essentially, about "putting on" and "covering up" or is it about "stripping down" (the human heart and psyche) and "revealing"? This has a lot to do with casting and what you look for in an actor. Some of each instinct is likely necessary—for an actor to characterize someone quite different from himself, he will have to assume traits and decorum that may be quite removed from his own being. But even so, eventually, the actor must reveal a human heart, illuminate another soul, and nothing should obscure what lies at the end of the actor's quest, the compelling creation of a character. The ultimate goal is revelation. Helping an actor to reveal the human rather than to cover up out of some misplaced fear of being "seen" too intimately in a psychological way is one of the most essential things a director does.

Characterization. The actor must characterize. Although certain characters may be quite close to the actor in terms of age or behavior, ultimately the actor should not reduce the character to himself, but create the character with as much fullness and specificity as possible. The actor must make choices about who the character really is, and how the character thinks, behaves, sounds, walks, looks, and so on. Does the actor tend to play the character totally "straight" without characterization? Does the actor tend to reduce the character to himself? How can you the director help an actor to engage this essential work and refine it as much as humanly possible in the time available?

Decorum. Closely related to characterization, decorum is the outward manifestation of character—how the character dresses, walks, talks, behaves, and the like. Is the decorum rich in detail and interest? Is it evolving in the rehearsal process in a way appropriate to the world of the play and the given circumstances? Good directors help actors develop appropriate decorum for their characters. This is a subtle process; the director probably cannot or should not prescribe decorum if the acting is to be convincing and arise from strong internal and imaginative sources in the actor. But the director can do a great deal in terms of subtle suggestions and in creating a world where certain behaviors and decorums are appropriate for the characters who inhabit that world. Good directors create rich worlds that become organic to the acting (one mark of poor direction is that the play seems as though it is taking place "no place in particular" or could be almost anywhere).

Playing given circumstances. Are the actors playing in relation to the given circumstances of the play, the story, the previous action, the specific world of the play? Or are they playing essentially in relation to the world we all inhabit as individuals when we come into the rehearsal hall on a given day? If the actors (and director) are not playing in relation to the given circumstances set up by the play, the work will not be convincing and the actors cannot, ultimately, structure the thinking and doing of the characters. Given circumstances of time, place, previous action, and so on *shape the character's thinking and the range of options* the characters consider as they grapple with their problems. If the head of Ibsen's Nora in *A Doll's House* is not permeated with the given circumstances of her situation, the character and the play's action make no sense. Effective directors help the actors find and "live" within the given circumstances.

Structuring the thinking. Directors can help the actors develop thinking appropriate to the characters in given sets of circumstances. The director does this by gently identifying elements of thinking and behaving that betray the actor's circumstances and world rather than those of the character—and by helping the actor to enter imaginatively into the given circumstances of the play. This is a kind of "balance" not unlike that of the gymnast on the balance beam—the director helps the actor find a kind of footing in the alternative reality of the play; all the while both are aware of the actual reality of the everyday world outside the rehearsal hall. In this sense, a director helps the actor build up the ability to stay in the reality of the play for as long as it takes to perform the character. Much of what constitutes rehearsal is the slow evolution of this alternative reality. Imagination is the key, and the actor needs to gain the ability to enter through a portal in his imagination into the alternative world.

Units (or beats). Have you directed (and staged) the play in terms of the basic units of action? If you have not, you will be attempting to tell the story "in general" rather than in its specific, sequential steps, and you will not be helping the actors find the dramatic action. The probable result is playing the play in big swaths of story or chunks of action, that is, with a generalized "sense" of the action, rather than a fascinating, exquisite chain of moments that "happen." This will obscure both the story and the action and make it very difficult if not impossible for the actors to act. If you know the unit structure of a scene (sometimes called beats or similar names in various terminologies) and of an act, you can avoid falling into the swamp of "impressionism" in your directing—that is, directing your impressions of the story, rather than the specific moments that make up the story itself. One of the most useful things a director can do for actors is to help them find the units in the action. Once again, subtlety is everything—it is rarely effective to sit and mark out unit boundaries with actors. But helping them find the changes in the dramatic action, those "joints" that define unit changes, is everything and will be an enormous help to the actors in deciding how to play the scene.

Events. Have you helped the actors experience the big happenings of the scene as "events" that are landmarks in the unfolding of the story? Or, less desirable, is the substance of a scene homogenized into some kind of "normalcy"? In most good plays, characters experience extremes of one kind or another and the dramatic action doesn't have to be loud or overt for this to be so—Chekhov showed how hearts can break in even the simplest, quietest moments. In *Uncle Vanya* when Vanya fires the gun at the Professor, it is surely an event in the play's action, no doubt an overt one, a landmark in the unfolding story of the play. But in the quiet moment when Sonya learns that Dr. Astrov does not love her, it is also an *event* in the play's action, a most important one. Events such as these ultimately make up the story, the experience that the characters encounter and grapple with. Good directors make sure the events are really there, that they really *happen* for the characters and for the audience. If the director can help the actor to live the events, the actor will have a much easier time of living the reality of the character's situation. Don't let some misplaced sense of achieving a believable "normalcy" on the stage water down or blot out these events that mark the characters' lives.

Physicalization. This subsumes the whole range of concepts put forward earlier such as composition, picturization, movement, and the use of objects—the idea being that all of these are ways to physicalize the action and as such are invaluable means of director-actor communication. It's worth restating this basic premise at this point because absent a rich use of physicalization, what results onstage are "talking heads" in which the text is essentially narrated or recited for the audience and the experience to be had is dry, not alive, not "happening." The goal is for the clash of forces in the play to be illustrated for the audience (don't get hung up in any pejorative nuances of the word *illustrate* that may be in your thinking), and this can happen only if the actors inhabit a fully realized physical dimension. Remember that theatre is a sensual experience, involving sound, vision, and movement (and sometimes even smell). Good directors create experiences that can be had only in the theatre. If it can be gotten from reading, then why theatre at all? Don't seek refuge in your head from the sensual and physical dimensions of this most alive art form. Embrace and delight in what you and the actors can find in creating the physical dimension of a play.

Character arcs. Major characters have an *arc* through the action of the play. They start with a beginning polarity (a set of attitudes toward themselves, their world, their relationships, their prospects) and they arrive at an ending polarity. The director must help the actor start at the beginning point and arrive at a different polarity with the thinking and feeling of the character fully realized in terms of each pole. Directing and acting a given scene are closely tied with recognizing where the scene is positioned on this arc for each character. Do you have a clear understanding of each principal character's arc through the action?

Playing the end too soon or knowing too much. Closely related to the concepts of the arc and staying in the "now," a common problem is that the actor, unlike the character, knows the end of the story and has a consciousness permeated with this knowledge of how things end up—consciousness the character does not have until the very end. Characters in plays are like human beings in life—we don't know how our stories are going to turn out, nor should the character. Our thinking and our grappling can only be that of a given moment in time. It is all too easy for actors to play the end of the story from the very beginning (*Hedda Gabbler* being a classic example of this challenge). If this happens, then the actor's thinking is suffused with where the character ends up, rather than where the character is at a given point. Set the polarities clearly. The dramatic action is what produces the change, the grappling and "battering" the characters undergo in their struggle. It takes discipline and confidence for the actor to play the given moment and the given scene, secure in the knowledge that the rest will come, that the action will build up, the story will unwind. Young actors often try to play the whole thing at once: the whole character, the whole story, the whole effect. It can't really be done that way and for those who unconsciously try to do so, the outcome is to produce a generalized blur that is uninteresting and untrue to the moments.

Power balance. Is the power balance between characters in a scene appropriate to the play? Through the vagaries of casting or rate of development in a rehearsal process, sometimes this power balance can be skewed or even reversed. (We are speaking of power between the characters here, although the relative strengths of the *actors* play a part in this equation as well.) If an imbalance persists throughout the rehearsal process, it will impede the full development of the dramatic action.

Objectives and problems. This staple of acting theory and practice is essential for directors to master: the idea that characters are pursuing objectives with the actions they take and that they seek to overcome obstacles in their path and solve the "problems" that confront them in the action and basic situation. The more firmly the director has a grip on this, the more likely it is that the director can be truly helpful to the actors (and that is the ultimate goal in directing actors—to be helpful to them). It is useful to think about the action in a scene in terms of problems, inherent for each character in terms of the *opposing character.* Each character must "solve" these problems through a series of actions. Don't fall into the trap that can sometimes arise with actors, trying to evoke a kind of overall "normalcy" onstage, as mentioned earlier. It's true that part of what convinces us as audiences is believability and the illusion of reality, but remember that characters in plays are embroiled in conflict. The best way to achieve this believability is to help the actors find the conflict that ensnares the characters—don't direct them toward playing where the characters have no problems in the "now," no barriers or obstacles. The result would be acting in a void and the antithesis of drama where characters are often in a difficult situation, no matter how muted or sublimated it may be. If the objectives and problems are not clearly acted, the story doesn't come through and the action will appear "unacted" as a result.

Aggressor in the action. This is closely related to the concepts of playing objectives and power balance in a scene. In a given unit of the action, is the appropriate character "leading" the action, that is, being the aggressor as the action dictates? If not, the action cannot be played effectively by any of the actors in the scene nor perceived accurately by the audience.

Choices. One of the most valuable things you can do as a director is to help each actor arrive at the best choices she or he can possibly make. Ultimately the actor must make the choice, because it is the actor who must live it, inhabit it, and make it work in performance, but the director can be immensely helpful in helping each actor arrive at the best choices possible. Ultimately these choices make up an actor's performance and determine what will be achieved in the work. But what kind of choices are these? Well, everything from choices about decorum (outward show of a character), to characterization (how the actor sees the character and what the actor creates in bringing the character to life), to the interpretation of the action in a scene (what the character is really doing in terms of objectives, adjustments, etc.). The difficulty comes when the actor doesn't make choices or makes weak choices or, sometimes, when the actor doesn't fully commit to the choices that are made, even if he senses they are the right ones. A great performance arises from a series of great choices. The director should help each actor find the most workable and revealing choices and then help each actor test these out in the rehearsal process.

Upper and lower levels in action. Particularly important in plays that are based in Realistic style of one sort or another is the idea that an upper level or façade conceals a lower level where the "real" action, the dramatic action, resides. The director must ensure that both levels are happening simultaneously in relation to each other, because the former contains and conceals the latter, while the latter animates the former. The upper level or façade is the text of words (created by the author) and the activities (mostly created by the actors and the director, based on the author's text). In Realistic drama, characters are often engaged in a fabric of everyday activity, which gets ripped open at climactic moments by the force of the struggle transpiring on the lower level, beneath the surface of everyday life. If one or the other level is not fully realized, then the other level is not fully in focus either and the acting cannot do justice to the play.

Function of a role. This pertains more to the director than to the conscious process of the actor, but it has tremendous import for the outcome of the acting in a production, as well as implication for the direction of the acting. The function of each role in the scheme of the play's dramatic action overall must be clearly seen by the director and fulfilled in the acting of the play. If the basic function of a role in holding up the house of the play's dramaturgy isn't brought to fruition, the house will fall down (or sag, to extend the structural metaphor further). This may be particularly important for a director when working with an untrained or marginally talented actor or an actor having great difficulty in realizing a role. If the *function* of the role can be carved into the experience of playing for the audience (and the other actors), even if the actor in question does not realize a high degree of success in creating the character, then the story of the play can still sometimes be put across effectively. And even with a balanced cast of talented actors, the director will find that fully realizing the function of each role will be central to unlocking the full power of the play.

Actors as co-creators. Directors who have great success in directing actors see the actors as co-creators in the great adventure of making a play "work." Particularly if the principal actors do not rise to the level of being co-creators with the director, the ultimate result will not be as compelling as it otherwise might be. This involves the director's basic attitude toward acting and working with actors. The main idea is that actors (and the same thing applies to designers and other key collaborators) have specialized imaginations and gifts, which must be unleashed to rise to their fullest potential. It is the director's special gift to be able to lead this work and help others attain their best in a concerted, group effort. A pitfall, of course, is if the director accepts "anything" under a misguided sense of egalitarianism. The director's end of the bargain is to get the very best possible from each member of the team. Learning how to do this takes time, but it is one of the most rewarding things about directing. Remember that a talented, committed actor or a talented, committed designer can take the role or the design further than the director can. The goal is to unleash that talent, to *direct* its trajectory rather than trying to substitute for its functioning.

Creating a productive rehearsal atmosphere. How can you as the director create a rehearsal atmosphere that is the most productive and moves the work forward each and every day? This is an essential thing for you to understand and achieve in your rehearsal process.

Structuring a rehearsal process. How can you, the director, best structure a rehearsal process to come to terms with the demands of a particular play, a certain group of collaborators, or a given set of circumstances, such as the amount of rehearsal time or conditions? Wise use of time is supremely valuable to all undertakings, and especially so in rehearsing a play, in which time is finite and an opening performance is usually fixed on a calendar. Try to see the process as a whole and make wise decisions on how much time to spend on different aspects such as table work, improvisations, searching scene rehearsals, and run-throughs. Remember that the actors need enough time to "put it all together" and get the piece up to something approximating playable performance pitch *before* the play goes into technical or dress rehearsals when the addition of those new elements may "break the actors' stride" for a day or two before being absorbed.

Daring. How can you as the director create an atmosphere and a set of working relationships with the actors in which they are encouraged to dare and extend their limits? This is the only way you will ever get close to the human experience contained in a fine play. The extremes of experience contained in a *Hamlet* or a *Three Sisters* or an *Endgame* (or . . . you name it) is such that unless the actor gets out on the edge of experience and is willing to risk (not physical risk, but in terms of revealing the human condition), then the play's vision of human experience will not come through. It is a steady process of pushing further and going deeper throughout the rehearsal process. This will not happen if the actors and the director do not dare—with their own talents, with their choices, with the content of the play. Sometimes you gently have to remind them of why they were drawn to acting in the first place and remind them that only they can do what actors alone can do, that is, make the human experience come alive in front of an audience. Sometimes you have to help them have the courage and the strength to contain the pain of a Lear or a Blanche or a Mother Courage, to let the experience pass through them so that others can see it, feel it. Grotowski and others have shown us how actors are "holy" in this regard, how they are vessels for making the invisible become visible and palpable. They are the only ones who can do this. But it takes daring to attain this level of performance—and directors, good ones, are an essential part of the process.

Ensemble. One of the ultimate goals in working with actors is to achieve seamless ensemble playing of a high order. You must look at your actors as the process goes along. Are they tending to play separately or are they finding how to play together? Achieving ensemble is one of the great joys of this collaborative art form, and you must ask yourself how you can help your actors to achieve this ideal. Getting there involves everything from understanding the dramatic action, to the function of roles, to making an atmosphere in which everyone wants to do his or her best. It includes things such as fostering citizenship and professionalism as real values in the group. From you it requires true leadership, being able to enunciate a vision and help others to surpass themselves in attaining it—and ensuring that everyone has a real stake in the outcome. Ensemble is one of the lasting rewards of a life in the theatre.

Talking too much. You may be surprised at how little actual talking some very effective directors use in their work. Talking excessively is a pitfall and sensitive directors learn to avoid talking too much. It can soak up valuable rehearsal time, it can be a diversion from the real work that needs to be done, it can make actors feel powerless to come to terms with all the director has said, and it can create a cloud of "things said," making it difficult for actors and even the director to discern the most important among them. Young or inexperienced directors may tend to talk a lot in a misguided attempt to demonstrate that they understand all the nuances of the play or that they know what they're doing. Don't fall into this trap. Use as many words as you need, but build the discipline not to go into verbal overkill—remember that talking is not the only way to communicate. (A good groundplan is communication, a perfectly chosen object is communication, a telling composition is communication, and a photograph or a painting brought to rehearsal may be superb communication.) And above all, remember that the actors have to *discover* and *do* in rehearsal, and the worst thing a director can do is to put actors into a state of continual passivity and "receiving" rather than "doing"—which is easy to do if you talk them to death. You should also be skillful in when and where conversations occur. You will discover that conversations during chance encounters or before rehearsal or as rehearsal is ending or even over coffee on the intervening day may lead to productive results without taking valuable rehearsal time—all options that directors with a problem in this area tend to overlook.

Ownership. It is vitally important that each member of the creative collective feels a sense of ownership in what is being made in the act of creating theatre. While the director may lead the process of discovery, the sense that the work "belongs" to the director more than to the actors is not helpful in the long run. The goal is that each actor (and designer, too) has a high degree of ownership in the process and the outcome—for what they make as individuals and for what the whole ultimately turns out to be. Achieving this will draw on your interpersonal and leadership skills, for you must simultaneously lead and direct, but do so in a way that empowers each individual and the group as a whole. Achieving this depends on everything you do and decisively on whether you can arrive at a way of leading the work of others and getting them to move past their perceived limitations. It is an incremental process. Start with something as simple as the words you use. You may find it helpful to banish the word *I* from much of your phrasing in rehearsal. For example, instead of saying "I want you to do this . . ." or "I need you to do that . . . ," experiment with phrases such as "What would happen if you . . ." or "Do you think she [the character] might be thinking this or that as she does this or that. . ."? This way you not only avoid the impression that actors are doing something for *you* as the director (which tends to increase your ownership and diminish their own), but a subtle tone enters into the discourse, which is all about experimentation and individual discovery. Remember when the actors *find* something on their *own,* they are more apt to feel a sense of ownership and the surge of confidence that can take them onward to even more and greater discoveries. Your challenge is how to foment this process rather than impede it.

Appreciating the actors. Finally, directors who are good with actors enjoy working with actors and appreciate them individually and collectively for who they are. You will find that each talented actor has unique qualities, qualities that can be brought out to the actor's best advantage (not to mention the advantage of the role and, dare one say it, even to the advantage of the director!). Don't make the mistake of holding actors to some imaginary ideals they may never fulfill. It's true that you and the actor need to be working toward a goal with the characterization and toward what the author has written, but on the other hand, learn to see what you are working with and find the joy in drawing out of each actor the best that he has to offer. For joy it truly can be, and in finding it, you will find one of the true rewards of working in the theatre.

EXERCISES

1. Choose two or more scenes from a study play such as *The Crucible* and have a class discussion focusing on the *discoveries* that the characters make in each of the scenes

chosen. *The Crucible* contains many good choices for this exercise, but among them you might consider the scene with Proctor in Act I, the Act II scene where Proctor returns home from town, the Act II scene where Rev. Hale visits Proctor and Elizabeth, a sequence from the trial in Act III, or the Act IV scene where Danforth visits the jail. (It is important to see that discoveries occur throughout in the play, including early, midpoint, and late in the action.) List the discoveries that each character makes in the scene. Discuss how this affects the character's thinking and how the actor might play the action. Assess what would happen to both the thinking and the playing if the discovery were *not* made or fully developed in the acting.

2. Now the class should have a similar discussion, but move from a printed text to viewing a well-acted and directed film. Good candidates for this are legion, but among the many suitable choices, you might consider the film version of *The Crucible* with Daniel Day-Lewis, directed by Nicholas Hytner; *Long Day's Journey into Night* with Katharine Hepburn, directed by Sidney Lumet; or *A Streetcar Named Desire* with Vivien Leigh and Marlon Brando, directed by Elia Kazan. Focus on particular scenes and analyze how the discoveries are played. Is it evident how the discovery affects the thinking of the character? Can you see how the discovery feeds the dramatic action and the actors' playing of it?
3. Repeat Exercise 2, but this time focus on how actors play the *adjustments* in the scene you have chosen for study. What things in the playing reveal the adjusting going on between the actors? How does this deepen the sense of believability in the scene?
4. Again, repeat Exercise 2, this time focusing on the *decorum* aspects of characterization. The classic film version of *A Streetcar Named Desire* might be particularly useful for this exercise, with the discussion focusing on the characters of Blanche and Stella, and Stanley and Mitch in terms of how decorum is an important part of the characterizations. For each character, make a list of four to six key elements of decorum and comment on how each element brings something to the characterization.
5. Choose a play where there are two or more film versions available. Good choices for this include plays by Shakespeare such as *Hamlet, Romeo and Juliet,* and *Henry V,* as well as modern works such as *Cat on a Hot Tin Roof.* Choose particular scenes from the play and then compare the available versions in terms of the *choices* made by the actors and director in each version. Can you see how each can be true to the play in a different way? Do you see how what is particular and defining about each is rooted in the basic choices the actors and director made having to do with what they chose to emphasize about the characters in a given scene and the action in that scene? Discuss how making strong choices about character and action in a scene is one of the most critical things a director does in a production.
6. We've examined how much communication with actors involves physical, nonverbal means of communication such as a good groundplan and organic blocking. But those physical means are, of course, part of an array of communication that includes verbal communication. One of the crucial things a director does is to find ways of communicating with an actor verbally without relying on a constant repetition of phrases such as "I want you to . . ." or "I need you to . . ." which tend to give the idea that the relationship is essentially about the actor serving the director. Make a list of six different ways that you, as the director, can make a suggestion to the actor *without using the word "I"* in the sentence. (Hint: think about ways that words and phrases such as "how," "why," "what if," and "do you think . . ." might be used.)

Major Project 1A

Scene Practice

Here you are—your first major project! Note that it has two parts: Project 1A is directing your own scene; Project 1B is testing your capabilities in communicating with other creative people by requiring you to criticize the work of other directors in this project. Don't fear the second part because the other director may be your friend, but look at it as a personal challenge all directors must face.

You have worked through Chapters 7 through 16 and have done many of the exercises or similar ones you or your instructor have devised. Consequently, you should now understand a major approach in this book: the application of the concept of organic communication, the kind of communication that works through the actor with the main purpose of arousing his improvisational sense and thus his illustrations and activity that will flow from it. You should also be fully aware that the director uses two main areas of communication-stimulation—the visual and the oral—and that only when communication has been achieved through *both* means can it be said that the director has "gotten through." If you, as a director, concentrate on the visual alone or the oral alone, you will quite likely make a poorly balanced playing, for both sides of an actor must be approached if his improvisational sense is to be aroused to the highest degree. The material outlined in this project—information that combines all the things talked about thus far in this book—will give you the opportunity of putting your skills in communication to work.

Getting through to actors is the major problem facing a director. In working it out, you must learn to use *all* the visual and oral tools of communication, not just some of them, and to use them in as many ways as possible, for the frustrations in the directing process result directly from the barrier wall that separates director and actor. You will also discover that unsuccessful student-directed scenes usually fail not because the actors cast in such scenes are weak and ineffectual but because the directors have not broken through the director-actor barriers with communication that reached them. Nor did the directors employ such basic means as detailed and delineated subtext, reciprocation and adjustment in acting, climactic illustrations of discoveries and adjustments, decorum, articulate conveyance of the text, and exploitation of the groundplan. *Not until you, as a director, learn to take the blame yourself for your own failures in getting through,* and do something about them, can you justly criticize actors for their shortcomings. You must learn your own responsibilities first if you are to learn how to lead others.

Director-actor communication, then, will involve the organic use of groundplan, composition, gesture, improvisation with objects, picturization, and movement as the six visual tools for getting through; and speaking the text and projection are the oral tools. Improvisational techniques can be used at all stages, for once you have learned to work with this method of direct communication, you will see how intellectual approaches, such as director-actor discussion, are much less effective ways of breaking barriers. You will also learn that showing an actor how to do it, no matter how exaggerated your illustration may be, is a last resort and not a primary method. After all, *your job is to bring out the creativity in actors* and not to tie them up in the restrictions of mimicry.

Scene Practice

Although you are not yet fully ready to stage a production (the director's function in design will be discussed beginning on page 185), you are ready to direct minimally staged scenes with live actors. The approach here, then, is to bring about a synthesis of all the techniques developed in previous chapters by discussing the director's job with the playscript before rehearsals begin, with actors during a rehearsal period, and with "scene critics" after the first performance. Scene practice is the goal you have been preparing for all along, but there are also techniques involved in it that must be carefully followed if you are to accomplish your goal.

Scene Choice

Scene choice is used here instead of *play choice* because it is assumed that young directors can profit most at this point by doing two or three 10-minute scenes from long plays before doing a one-act play, the challenge in Project 2. The reasons are very simple. Although a one-act play provides a unity—that is, it is all about one thing—it will not give you the opportunity to work on play-analysis in depth because the structural elements, particularly dramatic action and characters, are considerably limited. In contrast, the structural elements of major plays, from given circumstances to moods, are fully developed, even though a play as a whole may be of inferior quality. By working with long plays, you will learn much about complicated structures, the study of which should greatly increase your respect for the playwright as a craftsman of controlled improvisation. Finally, you will be able to direct one-act plays far better after you have wrestled with parts of longer plays because you will know more about structure and will be able to handle the particular problems one-act plays raise. It is commonly assumed that one-act plays are easier to direct because they are short; however, this assumption is a fallacy you will become aware of when you try one after working in depth on a major play. A short play is a tour de force that requires the most experienced sort of handling to bring it to fruition.

Suggestions for Selecting the Scene

Choose a climactic scene. Every play has a major climactic scene, but each act also has at least one—probably two or three—secondary climactic moment; thus, in every play you have several choices for this project. What distinguishes a climactic scene from other scenes is *discovery:* An important character, usually the principal one, will discover something new in front of the audience; that is, an important fact will be disclosed to him *through dramatic action* that will decidedly alter his basic course of action. How important a climactic scene is to the play as a whole will depend on the importance of the discovery and the way in which the informant makes information known to the character who receives it. Thus, the playwright excites the audience by the gradual process of building to the moment of discovery; however, the actor caps it for us by the strength, duration, and quality of his adjustment on its reception, a high point in the acting process. *The scene is climactic because the dramatic action has reached a peak in the discovery-adjustment cycle,* leaving the recipient naked, so to speak, for several seconds in front of the audience while he decides what to do; the audience feels the climax because it is suspended with excitement until it knows what course of action the recipient will take. Thus, a climactic scene is made up of (1) a slow build, sometimes very intricate, with intensive suspense before the release of the discovery; (2) the discovery; (3) the adjustment; and (4) the new course of action taken by the recipient.

Thus, you must exercise great care in choosing a climactic scene for a project. Other scenes may be effective after a fashion, but they will seem obscure to an audience, whereas a climactic scene will be received with comprehension and high interest because of the strong contrast among its units.

Do not choose a scene with the beginning and ending arbitrarily and formally established by a playwright. In other words, do not select Act II, Scene 2, of a play where the curtain (or lights) is raised and lowered at both ends. To all intents and purposes, this scene is a one-act play, and this will not provide you with the learning experience of a 10-minute climactic scene selected from the beginning, middle, or end of a continuous act of a play. When you choose a piece of an act, you will find out about the nature of climactic scenes because you will be forced to dig out what leads to a climax, what a climax is, and what leads away from it. Your awareness of unit division will also be intensified because you will learn that a scene choice with only two units will not work. Rather, you will have a better chance with three units, and an even better one with four or five, for a unit can be seen well only when it is placed in contrast with other units.

Do not choose a scene in which two characters discuss a third character who does not appear onstage during the course of the scene. Scenes such as this are usually transitions in which a principal character uses a secondary character as a confidant. Although the action of the play as a whole is advanced, such scenes do not make interesting choices for beginning directors, because they will usually lack the dramatic quality of direct confrontation and thus will become very difficult scenes to present successfully.

As a starter, choose a scene with only two characters. You will have all you can handle. You will also find that 10 minutes with two people in a play will usually rise to a sharp, dramatic climax, because the author has intentionally confined his dramatic action, probably to principal characters. This confinement will give you and your actors a tight unity around which to work, for you will need to lead into it (the beginning), bring about the climax itself with its usual big discovery (the middle), and bring it to a state of suspension (the end).

The choice should be from a Realistic play because this is the style of play studied in Chapters 3 through 16. Other play styles will be treated in Part III, but you must first learn to work with Realism as the dominant style before you try to work with departures from that style. You could, of course, go back to Ibsen or Chekhov and still fall within the category of Realism, but their plays are very complex, set as they are in late nineteenth-century Europe. It is also suggested that beginning directors in the U.S. may do better in first projects with plays of American authorship because these depict given circumstances closer to the directors' own cultural backgrounds. You must be certain to avoid all the Expressionistic or Symbolistic plays as well as those of the Absurdists. Realism on the stage *is observed* reality—that is, reality can be easily seen and believed as the appearance of everyday life.

It might be best to choose an interior scene. Your early experiences in directing should likely be an interior scene—such as a living room, bedroom, or kitchen—or a backyard scene where a groundplan can be arranged much like an interior setting although outdoor furniture is used. Avoid scenes such as those located in a woods, a beach, or any open space, because you must first learn how to use occupied space (a groundplan obstacle course) before tackling the complexities of open-space groundplans.

The choice should be made from the standard repertoire of plays by well-known authors. Learn from Bernard Shaw's quip in the mouth of one of his critics in *Fanny's First Play:* "If it's by a good author, it's a good play." There is much to be said for the successful, regularly produced author, for such dramatists have a command over play structure that lesser known or unknown playwrights usually do not have. (In your search, be sure to consider the many outstanding works by writers of color and women.) One of your intentions in doing a scene project is to learn as much as you can about play structure; the best playwrights are the best teachers, so choose their plays. Whether the play you select is by Tennessee

Williams, August Wilson, Wendy Wasserstein, or some other writer, make sure that it is a good play by an author whose work has stood the test of time and repeated production on the stage.

Limit the length of the scene by the number of units. A 10-minute scene will usually contain four to six units, all you need if you have selected it properly. You may be in trouble if the scene runs less than 10 minutes because the actions may not have developed intensively enough to make a satisfactorily unified statement.

Keep your audience in mind when you choose your scene. Although the primary function of scene practice is to further your own training in play-analysis and actor communication, you must remember that a play is not a complete form until an audience has received it on its own terms. Do not let audience consideration deter you in any way from choosing plays of high quality, because you will discover that such plays can be acted more effectively because they are inventive and rich in dramatic action. Nor do you have to worry about losing your audience because it may think your scene is too obscure, too hidden in the play as a whole. If you have made a solid choice by observing the two basic rules for the number of units (four to six) and climactic action, and if you have expressed it imaginatively and with feeling, any audience will be able to follow the scene. Remember: Directing is not book work; rather, it is communicating with audiences through actors and staging.

Editing the Scene Choice

The only sort of editing you should consider is altering distasteful words, such as profanity or words with overt sexual connotations. You are the judge of what your audience will shy away from, and you must make a decision accordingly about what to leave in and what to find a substitute for. You should not try editing a scene that is strongly marked by the continuous use of such language, because the playwright intended his language to exert great force; therefore, do not choose that scene. An *occasional* word can usually be readily replaced by a word of less strength. Isolated words will not reduce dramatic action, nor will their alteration much reduce the strength of a text. The important thing is to remove the distraction these words might cause to your audience. You must not think of such editing as prudish but as good sense in many situations; the world does not live on profanity or other types of abusive language. Furthermore, local audiences may be more conservative than those an author may have had in mind, and if they are shocked, they may fail to hear or see what is truly important in the scene. In other words, they may fixate on a word and become insensitive to the dramatic action.

If you edit a scene by removing lines, or by removing a character because "he has only two lines, and I don't really need him," you have seriously changed the author's intentions. Young directors, thinking that they can make a better scene of the material, frequently want to edit. You must suppress all such urges! You may want to remove lines or characters because you do not understand them; that is, you simply do not comprehend why they are there. You can be sure that the author considered all such alternatives when he wrote his play. Have faith in him: He is far more experienced at his trade than you are at yours. Stick exactly to the script. Furthermore, *do not select edited cuttings of plays for directing projects*—that is, cuttings made by editors who have deleted lines or characters within scenes to shorten the length. In the interest of making plays more appealing to a wider audience, they may have removed crucial dramatic action. Use only fully printed playscripts.

Staging a Practice Scene

Scenes can be performed either in the classroom or on a proscenium stage. You must not violate the proscenium line by advancing in front of it; always play behind it. That is essential. If you are using a classroom, set the proscenium positions by placing two chairs 24 to 26 feet apart, or the maximum width your space allows (less than 20 feet will cause problems), and then observe faithfully all the laws of the proscenium stage as if you were playing on one. (A good substitute for chair-walls is to use a twofold screen unit on either side of your stage.)

Abstract Forms of Staging

As was suggested in Chapter 9 on the groundplan, you should learn to work with whatever rehearsal-room staging is available. It is far more important to learn how to occupy space with chairs or odd pieces, and to learn the concept of the obstacle course as well as the nature of architectural mass and line, than it is to try to reproduce things exactly as they appear in everyday life. Use chairs as chairs, and tables as tables, of course; but if you and your actors use them properly, you can make them appear to be different sizes, different shapes, different textures, even different styles. You could let stacked chairs represent cabinets, bars, fireplaces, even tables, if necessary; chairs, side by side, might represent sofas; and so forth. Learn to get along on a few items, but *never forget that you are delineating space,* not leaving it empty.

The suggested items in Figure 50 are explicitly designed for a director's rehearsal use because of their wide range of deployment in proscenium staging as well as in other types. Note that they have a neutral quality and do not have to be used as literal representation.

The four screen units are provided to give a variety of wall ideas because walls help directors and actors to know the specific limits of their groundplans. (See Figure 51 for sample illustrations of their simplest use.) Wall units (note the two sizes of the screen units in the drawing) will also help enclose all your other pieces, as well as make your obstacle course specific. The stools, benches, and rock provide a wide variety of sitting positions. A round table is included in addition to the two square tables because it has different compositional possibilities than square tables have. The practical pylons in three sizes open up all kinds of groundplan arrangements; also note that they can be used in front (closed) or back (open)

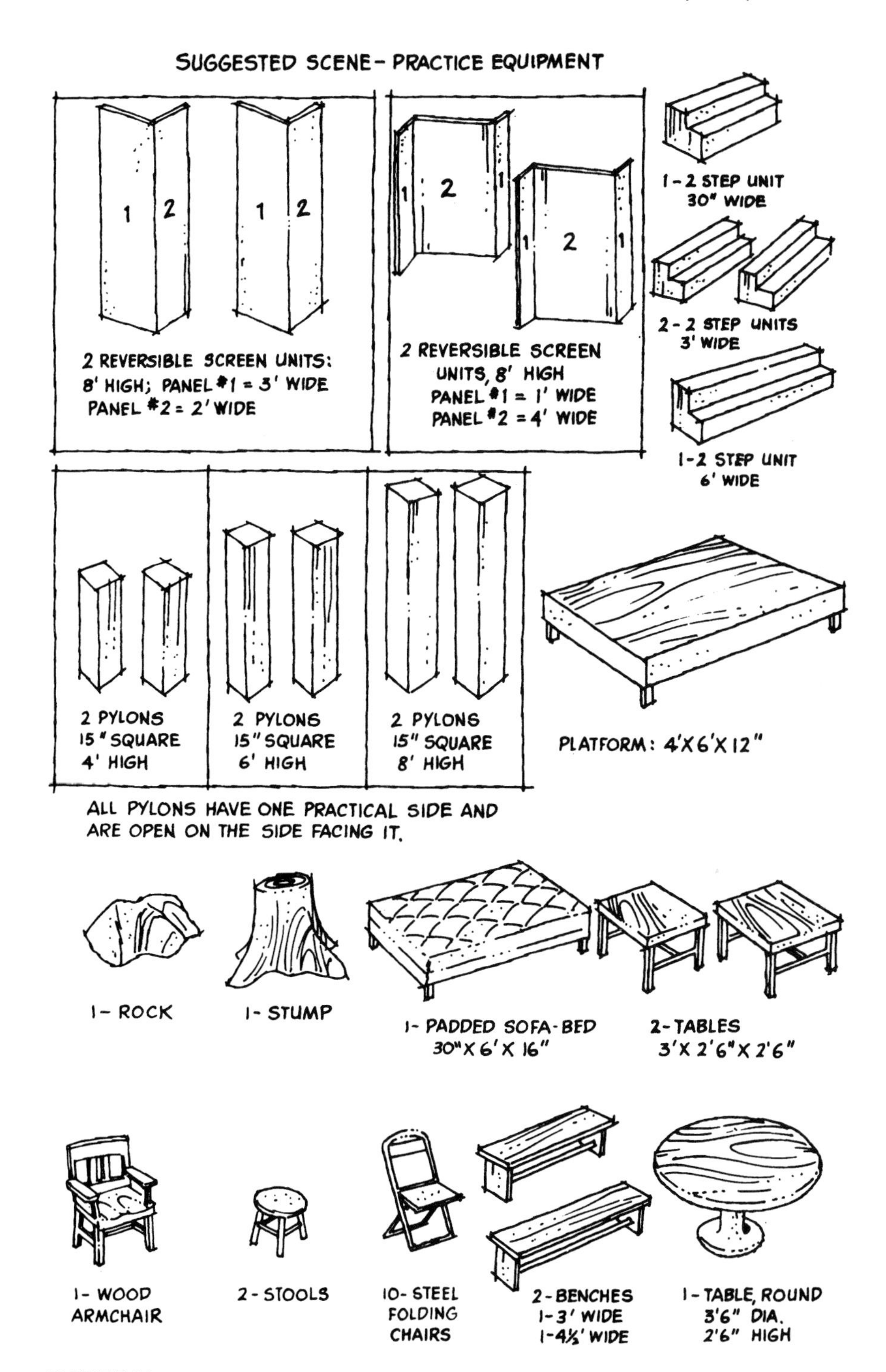
SUGGESTED SCENE – PRACTICE EQUIPMENT
2 REVERSIBLE SCREEN UNITS:
8' HIGH; PANEL #1 = 3' WIDE
PANEL #2 = 2' WIDE
2 REVERSIBLE SCREEN
UNITS, 8' HIGH
PANEL #1 = 1' WIDE
PANEL #2 = 4' WIDE
1-2 STEP UNIT
30" WIDE
2-2 STEP UNITS
3' WIDE
1-2 STEP UNIT
6' WIDE
2 PYLONS
15" SQUARE
4' HIGH
2 PYLONS
15" SQUARE
6' HIGH
2 PYLONS
15" SQUARE
8' HIGH
PLATFORM: 4'X6'X12"
ALL PYLONS HAVE ONE PRACTICAL SIDE AND
ARE OPEN ON THE SIDE FACING IT.
1- ROCK
1- STUMP
1- PADDED SOFA-BED
30"X6'X16"
2-TABLES
3'X2'6"X2'6"
1- WOOD
ARMCHAIR
2-STOOLS
10- STEEL
FOLDING
CHAIRS
2-BENCHES
1-3' WIDE
1-4½' WIDE
1-TABLE, ROUND
3'6" DIA.
2'6" HIGH

FIGURE 50

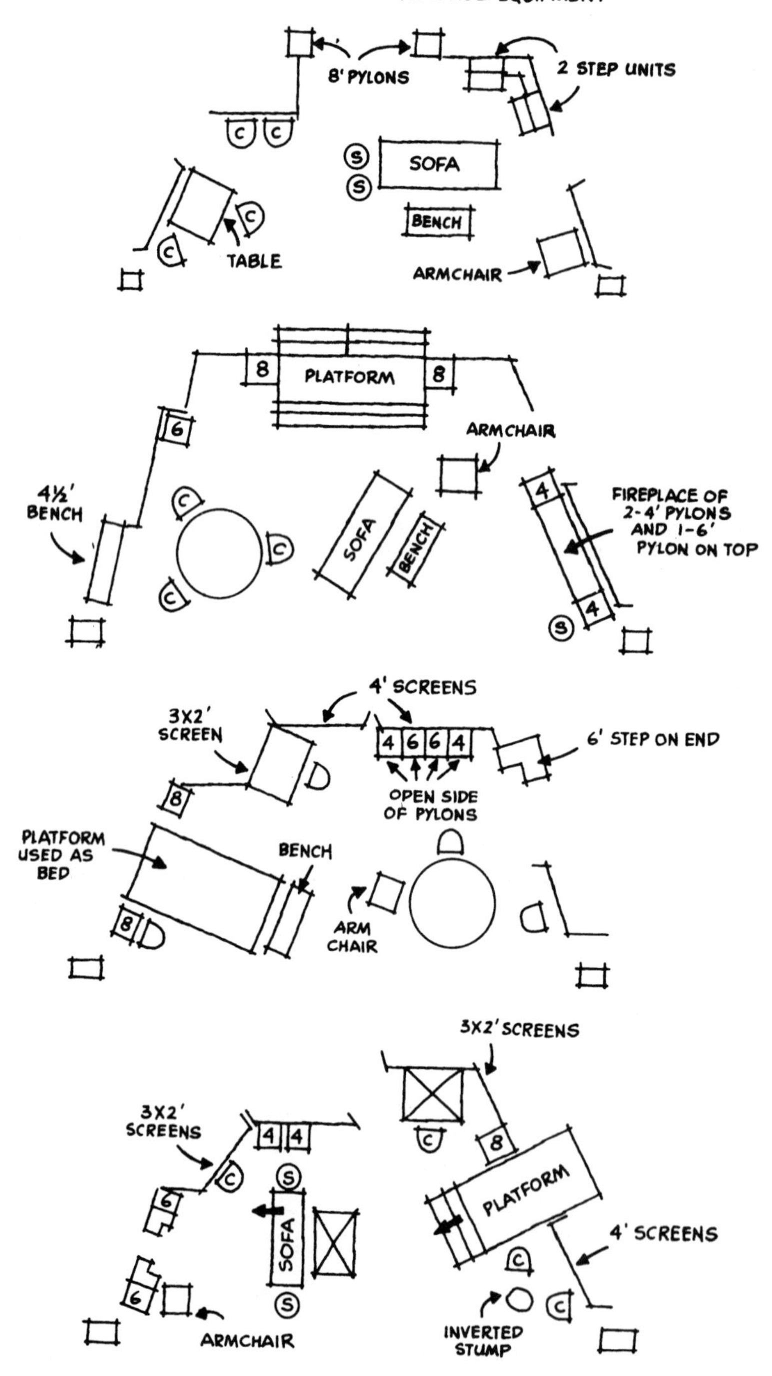
SAMPLE GROUND PLANS USING SCENE-PRACTICE EQUIPMENT
8' PYLONS
2 STEP UNITS
C
SOFA
S
BENCH
TABLE
ARMCHAIR
8
PLATFORM
6
ARMCHAIR
4½' BENCH
SOFA
BENCH
4
FIREPLACE OF 2-4' PYLONS AND 1-6' PYLON ON TOP
4' SCREENS
3X2' SCREEN
4 6 6 4
6' STEP ON END
OPEN SIDE OF PYLONS
PLATFORM USED AS BED
BENCH
ARM CHAIR
3X2' SCREENS
3X2' SCREENS
PLATFORM
4' SCREENS
ARMCHAIR
INVERTED STUMP

FIGURE 51

positions with different meanings respectively. The platform and step units will encourage the use of levels.

A word about the color of these materials: All the items in this rehearsal set *should be painted a neutral color,* perhaps a pearl gray, so that no single item has any particular emphasis through color value. You may at first think gray is too somber, but you will soon discover that it lends itself equally well to serious plays and to comedies. The intention of using little color is to reduce the materials to expressions of line and mass without the distractions of particularizing details.

Whether you use classroom furniture or the more elaborate rehearsal-room setup described here and illustrated in Figure 50, you must try to be as ingenious as you can, remembering that a groundplan is a tool of communication to actors and that actors will be only as free as your imagination encourages them to be.

Scene Preparation

Now that you have declared your choice of scene and know the circumstances under which you can produce it, you are ready to begin your scene preparation.

Do the play-analysis specifically as outlined in Chapter 6. *You will need to analyze the play as a whole for most of the preparation.* This point is precisely where many students fail; they think they can do a scene without knowing the entire play very well. Such a view is absolute folly, for a scene is only part of a whole, and without an understanding of the complete work, a director cannot illuminate the parts. Be sure to study in great detail the dramatic action of the scene you have chosen to stage, because all your other ideas will flow out of your understanding of this action.

Make your promptbook, as outlined in Chapter 14, at this time. It will contain all your suggestions for visual design, as you presently understand it, from groundplan through composition, picturization, movement, and improvisations with objects.

Casting

Acting instructors may possibly help you with the casting or arbitrarily provide you with a cast because they know more explicitly what they want their actors-in-training to gain from the experience you are providing. If you do not get such help, you will have to go through a minimum casting procedure with whatever actors are available. Casting will be discussed later in Chapter 26 as an intrinsic part of play interpretation, but at this point, you should be looking for any responsive and cooperative people, because your first job is to find out how to get dramatic action adequately rendered and not how to arrive at a delicately poised interpretation. This job will be enough for you to handle. If you are lucky enough to find actors who are able to project some of the decorum and qualities your characters require, you will be ahead in the game.

Above all, you should take care not to choose people who are much more advanced in acting than you are in directing, for you need to feel you are able to lead the process of work on the scene. You also need to feel free to experiment with all the devices and methods of communication. Actors who can too readily act the scene for you will deprive you of what you must learn about these approaches, and some may even take the scene away from you. You will also probably stand in the way of actors more advanced in their work than you are in yours by restricting rather than freeing them. Consider yourself lucky if you have a cast of two people—whether they have the right qualities or not—who are also eager to learn, eager to experiment, and strong-willed themselves. *Your job is to learn creative leadership*—how to draw out actors and free them to their own imaginations—not the practice of arbitrary authority. You will also discover that the right qualities are not as important as you may think they are. Actors *act* action and in this way make characters. If you can get the action acted, you will be amazed at how much the particular actor is buried and how much character actually comes across.

Rehearsing

Rehearsing a play is putting to work all the concepts and techniques discussed in this book up to this point. The rehearsal is your field of action, and you must give it every bit of imagination and energy you possess, for the success of the performance will depend on what happens here, not in the extensive paperwork preparation you have done. Rehearsing a play is a technique in itself that you must be aware of and learn to do with the greatest care. Your detailed organization here will release both you and the actors to your creative selves, making the rehearsals fun as well as profitable. Putting on a play is like playing a game in which you are the leader and can call the signals. It is also very much like a party at which you are playing host.

Suggestions for Rehearsals

Scheduling. A 10-minute scene from a major play requires a minimum of eight hours of rehearsal. Calendar time is very important because an actor needs a good deal of actual time to "try on" and "make comfortable" the strange garments of a character. It is therefore suggested that an hour a day over a two-week period is far better than two hours on one day, skipping the next, three on the third, and so on. The time between the one-hour periods will let both your imagination and that of the actors work on the play. In this way, rehearsals actually become experimentation hours based on assessments of the previous day's work and imaginings of what can lie ahead. There is also time to make brief suggestions to actors during the interim period, suggestions that can stimulate new directions or new experiments on the rehearsal itself.

Rehearsal plan. Each rehearsal should be designed to move your scene ahead as rapidly as possible, but you may want to begin with a prerehearsal warm-up to help your actors relax and concentrate. If you start each session of the rehearsal period with such warm-ups for the entire cast, you will find them more pliable and ready to act. Acting instructors often begin their classroom sessions with such warm-ups; ask them for specific instructions in order to keep rehearsal training in line with actor training.

Here is a suggested work plan for each successive day:

1. Read through the scene. Discuss briefly with your actors the whole play and the structure of the scene. Now tell them how you would like to stage the scene by setting up the groundplan and letting them "play" in it. Block the scene simply as traffic management so that the actors can "feel" their basic relationships.
2. Repeat the blocking of the first rehearsal. Now begin character development by helping the actors search out some of the dramatic action. Start improvisations now if your actors are capable in this technique. It is better to work on a unit or two than the whole scene.
3. Concentrate on the illustration of dramatic action (organic blocking) in the interest of unfolding the dramatic action and thus the character relationships. Continue improvisations.
4. With "lines off," improvisation with hand properties can be added to the other communicators, such as composition, picturization, and movement.
5. Run through the scene in order to assess the accomplishment of the dramatic action and thus the character development. Is actor reciprocation taking place? Is the groundplan working? If not, redo it, paying close attention to the number of acting areas, whether it is a good obstacle course, and whether it can excite the imagination of the actors. Are the *principal* discovery and adjustment in the scene being played with strength and careful pointing?
6. Reblock the scene as needed and work on dramatic action. Is the scene playing in units? Concentrate on actor reciprocation and on character development.
7. Make clear delineations in unit structure of the scene by working for mood and tempo goals. Concentrate on delivery of the text.
8. Do run-throughs, concentrating on rhythmic beats and pacing.

Note in this rehearsal plan, the director blocks the scene in the first rehearsal in the interest of direct communication. This use of blocking does not in any way rule out improvisational techniques for the purpose of scene discovery (see pages 177–178), though such techniques can be employed only if the actors and the director are already familiar with their use. If they are, improvisations become the method of direct communication. If not, use *organic blocking*. The purpose, however, is the same: the quick assimilation of the dramatic action by the actors while the scene content is still fresh. The sense of discovery is very important here, for the actors can see more clearly at this point the shape of the scene—the highs, the lows, the erratic points, the discoveries—than they will later when they have become too absorbed in the detail.

Speed. If you are ready with some suggestions of compositions and movements, the actors will respond quickly to the demands of the scene. Your intention in the first rehearsal is to tell the actors *the shape* of the scene through the communicators—groundplan, composition, picturization, movement, and tempos; music played out of rhythm is no music at all.

The lines should be learned by the fourth rehearsal so that the actors can put down the scripts and begin experimenting with illustration *at the same time that they begin listening carefully to each other.* Scene discovery, remember, comes in hearing an action and in making an adjustment. Line learning in this context can be seen as sense-of-the-scene learning, and there is little to be gained by slowing down this process. Find the subtext first, and only then will you be able to start work at pointing the text.

The run-through suggested in the fifth rehearsal is critical so that you can see and hear what has been accomplished thus far and where to go next. Do not interrupt the actors in this first run-through, but listen to it carefully, as if they were playing it before an audience. Use all your set pieces and properties at this run-through. The assessment that follows is your most important decision-making moment in the rehearsal plan. Is the groundplan working for the actors? Is the shape of the scene fully established in their acting? Is character development (given circumstances plus dramatic action) well underway? Does the scene build climactically through sharp delineation of the units?

The final work on the scene. Do not hesitate to find new compositions or movements, or to encourage the actors to find them, in the interest of stimulating new ideas; the actors will tell you instantly whether the new suggestions stimulate them. Shuffle up the groundplan on the same premise: The actors will now show you how to play the scene. Stretch out the scene limits by declaring the peaks and valleys much more dramatically and theatrically. And if the mechanics are stimulating ideas in the action, concentrate on character decorum, character-mood-intensity, unit division, and, above all, character reciprocation. *This last item, remember, is your reason for being:* to help *two* actors find the characters in each other.

The final periods begin with cleaning up the text and emphasizing the text in the interest of projection. It is your obligation, as the director, to be certain that a scene is well heard. Apply all the points discussed in Chapter 15. You can reach the actors easily by writing notes as they play the scene, underlining words or phrases in the dialogue that need pointing, and working continuously for the proper emphasis or flavoring of lines or entire speeches. Polish the scene in every way to eliminate distractions. Remember that the actors can now take directions easily and quickly, for they probably know more about the insides of the scene than you do. Insist on high energy and the proper starting points (character-mood-intensities).

Economy in director's suggestions. Do not talk too much. This rule is absolute. The purpose of rehearsal is to let the actors *experiment* with the acting. If you fill the rehearsal periods with your own chatter, the actors will want to talk too, and the whole thing will turn into a talkfest shambles. Actors must be kept busy acting, but not with talking about acting or analyzing the scene. Your directions, therefore, must be economical and explicit, quiet and assured, good-humored and alive. Remember, you are playing a game with the actors, and you, above all, must keep the rehearsal free and comfortable. "Why don't you try this or that . . ." is better than telling them what to do. But you must also insist on what must be done. Honesty is the best policy, because students working together will respect one another only on that basis.

Directions to individual persons. Devise your directions always in terms of the individual actors who are playing the roles, never in abstract terms. You must therefore watch your actors carefully, especially if you do not know them well, until you see what kind of suggestions seem to get through. The better you know your actors as creative people, the better you will know how to communicate with them. Some actors will need greatly exaggerated suggestions or images to move them; others will need only the barest suggestions. If an actor is already playing in an oversized fashion, make your images small and delicate. Likewise, revise your approach for the "small" actor. If you need to show an actor what you mean—a last resort—do so in very oversized terms so that he can get the *essence* of what you are suggesting, not the literal reality of that suggestion: Your intention is not to have him mimic you but to have him absorb your idea and turn it into his own feeling for illustration on his own terms.

Improvisation in rehearsal. Improvisations are used in rehearsal for the purposes of (1) freeing actors' imaginations, (2) effecting concentration, (3) uncovering dramatic action and character relationships, and (4) bringing about reciprocation between actors. The process is the usual game playing, this time with the material of the playscript before lines are learned or even well established in the minds of the actors. The intention is to draw actors into the given circumstances and subtext of a play by developing in them a high degree of concentration by letting them "feel" their way into close association with each other. Two actors thus make a magic circle of their reciprocal involvement; if such improvisations are done with seriousness and release, actors can literally feel the high-tension rubber band that always ties them together as characters. How much improvisation is actually used in rehearsal will depend on your knowledge and skill with this sort of communication device and on the needs of the actors: their abilities to concentrate and reciprocate, and how obscure the subtext of the play on which they are working may be to them. This is no place for a detailed discussion of improvisational techniques, but the following is a suggestion of the sort of thing that might be done.

An improvisation plan. One of the main problems with beginning actors is that of releasing themselves to one another on the intimate level, where dramatic actions take place in realistic plays. You must, then, design your improvisations with the purpose of breaking down barriers between actors in order to gain intimacy. Remove their self-consciousness by working with them in private. Reducing the light level in the rehearsal room will also help, for actors will feel less self-conscious and be able to throw off their personal façades in semidarkness. Now encourage your actors to sit close to one another on the floor and actually touch one another by holding both hands and looking into one another's eyes. After a communion concentration has been established (this may take several minutes), improvising on the material of the playscript can begin with number dialogue (see Exercise 3 at the end of Chapter 2) representing the dramatic action. Each participant should "feel" the sensations of *forcing* the other, of *adjusting* when it is his turn to be forced, and of taking his new action on the basis *only* of his adjustment. As the subtext develops in intensity, the two participants should pull or be pulled, never disengaging, and always responding to the pressure (dramatic action) of the other.

This type of improvisation can be varied by having the actors sit back to back, with arms interlinked. Or it can be played by holding hands over a chair, with each actor in his forcing action pulling the other to the edge of his balance (where he is about to fall). Both variations have the same purpose: "feeling" the force of reciprocal action. Such game playing will induce concentration because the participants will become involved in a physical way with each other and feel the intimacy of bodily force.

Once intimacy and the sense of reciprocal forcing have been established, the actors could try improvising the subtext without holding hands or arms. The obstacles in the groundplan can supply the same holding force if you encourage their use. You can also prompt such an improvisation from the sidelines if you want to push the actors into new areas of the subtext. The important thing is to have the actors hold the magic circle of their intimate relationship as long as possible; when it breaks, you will need to start them again.

Pacing. Are the rhythmic beats you noted in your play-analysis delineated and emphasized with variety?

You can learn a great deal about directing plays, and about pacing in particular, by watching a conductor of a symphony orchestra coordinate and control 60 or more musicians. Note the conductor's expertise in defining the sections of the music; how he builds the music architecturally by varying passages; how he handles the orchestra with discipline and authority, not as a dictator but as a knowledgeable leader. Watching other directors at work is not nearly as productive, because you cannot actually see what a director does with his actors in getting his effects. An orchestra conductor's work is constantly on display, however. Watch him in rehearsal—how he instructs his musicians and how he replays parts of the work to get the sound effect he wants. There is no guessing in the conductor's approach, because he has done his homework and knows his job as a leader.

Director's Self-Criticism during the Rehearsal Period

Here are some suggestions to help you assess your work:

- *Emphasize the "big moment."* Every climactic scene has a big moment that must be set out clearly and climactically. Have you pinpointed the exact moment in the script where it begins? It is your job to see that the actors achieve a high peak at the top of the scene.

- *Tell yourself the "long story."* Go over the entire story of a scene in great detail, *including all action and activity.*
- *Tell yourself the "short story."* Summarize the "long story" in two or three sentences.
- *"Play" the roles yourself to "feel" them.* When you are alone, use the technique of reading aloud each character *separately* while standing or moving about like an actor playing the role. Do you really "feel" the force of each action? When you have "felt" each part, read them together. Can you "feel" the see-saw battle going on?
- *Assessing the character-mood-intensity.* Are the characters playing their character-mood-intensities at the appropriate levels?
- *Assess the pacing of the scene.* Is the pacing in line with the development of the dramatic action? If you try stepping up the tempo a couple of notches, you will find it can probably move faster than you had previously thought.
- *Assess the violence level by the actors.* All climactic scenes contain a "violence," sometimes in words but frequently in physical activity. Is the violence freely demonstrated? Have you found the exact word or line when the character makes the climactic discovery and thus begins the violence?
- *Assess reciprocity.* Can you see the reciprocate? Can you hear it?
- *Beginning and ending.* Are they played fully and strongly?

Experiment

In a rehearsal period, nothing must be set in a final way until it works. You must be ingenious, a constant innovator, ready to shift and bend as the need arises. And you must instill this sense of creative adventure in your actors, for they will go beyond themselves if you do. Your job is to make them creative, not to show your own virtuosity. Art is made only in creative circumstances where the imagination can be released. The playscript already provides the springboard; you must provide the swimming pool, the sunshine, the crystal-clear water, and a good deal of the gaiety and laughter.

Performance

The audience will tell you very quickly and emphatically whether you have succeeded. You must always watch your scenes *with* the audience, listening as closely to the audience as you do the actors. Scene practice as outlined in this chapter should always be completed by playing for an audience, even if it is only the rest of the class. Introduce your scene quickly and effectively, telling the audience only what it must know to avoid basic confusions. Lengthy recounting of previous action is meaningless and will even put the audience off your scene. An audience wants to use its own imagination, its own capabilities, its own resources (not depend on someone else's). It will feel insulted if you imply (often by overplaying or overemphasizing points) that it is incompetent or insensitive. Reaching an audience is a difficult process, but the actor can do it very quickly and easily if he plays the action intensively and with sensitivity. An audience is not interested in actors per se, but only in the characters they create; they love those actors who arouse character images and strong feelings in them.

Good actors will always listen carefully to audiences before whom they play. This is why the theatre experience is an intimate one: The audience senses the actor, and the actor senses the audience.

Major Project 1B

Diagnostic Criticism

A *diagnostic criticism* is a written, and then oral, critical analysis of a scene directed by another director. Its main function is not to make you a book critic, but rather to intensify your skills in oral communication with actors and to improve your way of approaching self-criticism, by sharpening your critical faculties under controlled conditions. At first, you may feel uncomfortable about such give-and-take encounter sessions, but if you prepare your written critique well, the oral will go much easier. You will be learning how to listen to others, just as you expect actors and designers to listen to you.

Concept

Diagnostic criticism is your own analysis of another director's work, but it also gives you an opportunity to study other scenes and to develop your capabilities in finding *what went right* or *what went wrong*, simply because at this point you will tend to look more objectively at somebody else's work than your own. "I like it!" and "I don't like it!" are not valid criticisms, for they convey only feelings and not objective perceptions or insights. In one sense, diagnostic criticism is a scene produced in reverse, from final performance back to its origins, with all the significant intervening steps. *Your job is akin to that of a doctor who examines patients who are well and determines why they are well; but you are also the doctor who looks at patients who are ill and tries to find out what has made them ill.* Study of both patients is necessary because you need to recognize easily what works and what does not.

In this view, diagnostic criticism is the most positive criticism you can write for another director or receive yourself. Do not fear personal animosities if you are on the receiving end, for the diagnostic critic must prove his points, not merely voice them (as is often done by play reviewers in newspapers). Your capability at diagnostic criticism will greatly improve your capability as a practicing director because directing is expert seeing and hearing. *Being the eyes and ears for someone else also means looking back on yourself as a director.*

Production Plan for Diagnostic Criticism

Diagnostic criticism cannot be put to work effectively unless it is incorporated into an organized production plan that allows critics time and opportunity to do their work. In this regard, it is suggested that the class set up a rehearsal and performance schedule that will give assigned critics (perhaps two or three) copies of a scene several days prior to a scene performance. Thus, the critics will have time not only to read the entire play but also to consider in detail the particular scene to be performed. In this way, the critics come to the performance with some ideas about the scene and what can be done with it. Although critics should begin their written criticism as soon after a performance as possible, a deadline should be set no later than three days after the performance in order to keep the criticism as fresh as possible and also to give the experience a few hours of objectivity.

Outline for Diagnostic Criticism

Study the following outline carefully. Criticisms should follow this form explicitly. Please use the identical numbering system in writing your analysis.

I. *Action Summary.* Study carefully a copy of the scene *before* you see the scene performed. Number the units of action and give the action in each unit, *as you analyze it in the playscript,* by showing the reciprocal action in abbreviated sentence form: *A* (verb) to *B,* and *B* (verb) to *A.* Your awareness and perception of the action, as stated here, is the basis of your criticism, and it will partially inform the director about how you arrived at your conclusions.

II. *Technical Analysis.* Discuss the produced scene under the following headings:
   A. Groundplan
      1. Number of acting areas
      2. Usability
      3. Ingenuity
   B. Composition (discuss the use of areas, planes, levels, body positions, triangles, and so on, detailing several examples explicitly)
   C. Picturization (detail successful ones particularly noticed)
   D. Movement (select specific movements and comment)
   E. Improvisation with objects (detail objects used and the effective illustration they have made possible; discuss what objects might have been used to better advantage)

III. *Characterizations.* Discuss the acting of the scene by detailing what each actor has done and estimating the extent of the director-actor communication that has taken place.
   A. Character *A*
      1. Comparison of the ideal of the character as drawn in the playscript with the actor's characterization:
         (a) Delineate the character as *you* see it in the playscript.
         (b) Compare how well the actor accomplished this ideal (dramatization, discoveries, violence, etc.).
      2. Decorum
      3. Delivery of the text
      4. Believability
   B. Character *B*
      1. Comparison of the ideal of the character as drawn in the playscript with the actor's characterization:
         (a) Delineate the character as *you* see it in the playscript.
         (b) Compare how well the actor accomplished this ideal (dramatization, discoveries, violence, etc.).
      2. Decorum
      3. Delivery of the text
      4. Believability
   C. Repeat (A) and (B) for any additional characters.
   D. Synthesis (discuss here the reciprocation—how well the actors played together, their intercommunication)

IV. *Overall Evaluation*
   A. Moods created (list here the specific moods created)
   B. Tone (enter only *yes* or *no;* make no further comment)
   C. Qualifications (qualify (B) here)

Written Criticism Precedes Oral Criticism

The reason for written criticism is that it forces you to put into words exactly what you have noticed, both visually and aurally, about a scene, thus giving you specific practice in director communication. Merely "talking" your criticism—that is, doing it in a conversational way in the classroom—encourages looseness of expression as well as muddy thinking. (Writing it down will remove the totally vague and completely empty "I like it!" or "I don't like it!") If you write down your criticism in an organized way, you probably believe what you have written and can support it. Type the criticism and proofread it carefully, for your colleagues will listen to you only if they know you have prepared your criticism with great care.

When the written work has been completed, the criticism should be discussed *orally* in the group. Remember: The instructor will act as adjudicator between you, as the director-critic, and the director, and will insist on fairness and politeness (as will other members of your class). Oral discussion is the second most important thing you do in this technique (writing down your assessment is first). *A director must be verbally articulate,* and you can now speak your ideas because you are prepared to discuss them. You should also practice your verbal capability. *The purpose is to get through to another director without so irritating and antagonizing him that you fail to communicate.*

Note that the criticism begins with your own statement of the action. This sort of criticism is based on both your seeing and hearing the scene and on your study of a copy of the playscript itself. You should know the entire play, and you must be thoroughly familiar with the content of the scene performed. Put down the action carefully, as prescribed in the first section of the outline for diagnostic criticism, because all that you have to say can be evaluated explicitly against your concept of the action. If you see the scene before you record the action, you must be doubly careful not to let its presentation of the action sway your own opinion about what is going on. *The secret of good diagnostic criticism lies explicitly in your perception of a scene's action.*

Also pay particular attention to the section on characterization. Again, you must set down what *you think* the playwright prescribes the character to be before you comment on what a particular actor did in making his characterization. A clear analysis here on your part will tell you something about the director-actor communication in the scene—for example, Did the director get through to the actors? Other parts of the criticism will soon tell you whether the director understood the dramatic action. The synthesis in Section III, item D, of the outline is very important because the effectiveness of the scene will be declared specifically in the level of reciprocation with which the actors play.

Tone is used in Section IV, item B, to indicate total accomplishment of the aims of the scene. Did the scene work? Did it accomplish its basic intention in the play? Was the audience moved to laughter or to the serious moods intended by the playwright? This sort of statement is, of course, pure opinion; but you know the strength of your own feelings, and you were also aware of how the rest of the audience seemed to respond. Take a sharp stand on tone, recording "yes" or "no," and then support your opinion in Section IV, item C.

Directors Are Human Beings, Too

In writing this sort of criticism, always remember that you are writing to another human being—a director—who, like an actor, is very sensitive about his creative work. Practice your skill at writing an honest, careful statement without being cruel and arrogant. Do not generalize! Generalities hurt and confuse. Be specific and be direct, supporting all your points with carefully chosen evidence. The opinionated *are those who speak out of their emotions,* not out of their considered evaluation—a mixture of feeling and mind. Remember that you are making a diagnosis, not writing a diatribe against a production as if you were a professional reviewer with the intention of entertaining casual readers. You are a responsible person who respects the work of others, and your comment will be respected if it is offered with care and precision. Although you must always be honest and say what you think, there is no excuse for cruelty and dishonesty. Look for the best in others to find the best in yourself.

17 The Director's Design Function and Communicating through Staging

Directing Is Designing

This chapter and Chapters 18–21 are not about the director replacing designers and their creative work in making a production gleam and flow, but rather of opening up to you as director your options in staging and in how you can work with designers. Early in the twentieth century, English scene designer Gordon Craig, in a brief and very famous essay entitled "The Art of the Theatre," delineated two kinds of directors: the *artist-director,* who creates everything, including the playscript; and the *master-craftsman-director,* whom Craig defined as a designer-coordinator. Craig's artist-director came to life in moviemaking, where a tradition of writer-directors materialized to become a significant force in that medium, whereas the master-craftsman became the prototype for the practicing director in the live theatre. As Craig intended, the master-craftsman is an interpreter who keeps a very tight grip on all that happens on the stage, from the development of the playscript to the final performance, for in Craig's view only one person could be in charge. *This is the point of view in this book.*

Before you, as a learning director, can deal with very personal and individual ways of thinking about a play and expressing it in an exceptional way in production—the subject of Part III—you must fully comprehend the mechanics of the stage: how the stage can be used as a lively instrument of communication. *How you perceive the options open to you in production will make the difference between putting an audience to sleep and elevating it to excitement.*

The Director's Responsibility for Design

We live in an age of ash-pile theatre. Just as primitive societies throw out their totems after using them in rituals because they have lost their magic, we do the same today by throwing out production materials once they have been used or putting them in storage for future alterations. Ash-piling has thus made theatre much more costly than it once was. On the positive side, this means that every production is freshly conceived and creatively executed. Perhaps you have noticed the same thing happening in rock concerts, where those productions with freshly designed staging and lighting are more visually exciting and more enthralling overall.

Design as a Physicalization of Poetic Idea

Unless a director can control the visual and aural elements that constitute design, he is powerless in making an individual statement—a situation that would put us back in the dark ages of the nineteenth century where the "stage manager" merely gave an order to the stage carpenter to have the "dark fancy" set, or the "kitchen" set, or the "wood" set placed on stage at a given time. That sort of stock scenery, as you can readily imagine, had no individuality at all in terms of a specific play, but was intended to serve general purposes. Our present convention of making specific scenery for each play may seem terribly expensive and wasteful, but it is part of our theatre aesthetic that demands *individualization.* Therefore, as the principal designer, a director must take the responsibility for the individualized statement. *If he is an artist, he will speak freshly, for art is always a fresh, personal view.*

Directing, then, is not a mere manipulation of the actor and the physical stage; it is *considered* and *appropriate* manipulation, what Eric Bentley calls "the correct presentation of a poem." The concept is simply this: The playscript provides the dramatic action, and the director uses the many tools at his command to illustrate that action—his visual and oral tools with actors (which you have already studied) and his scenic production tools, usually with designers (which you will study here). Each group of tools has its techniques and its values. What the director must learn is how to use maximally all of these tools and not just a few, for the variety and complexity of his production effort will reflect what he knows about them and how well he can use them. Learn the *concept* underlying each technique, and you will then know how to put it to work for you.

The next few chapters in this book will greatly expand your functions as a director, for you are going to look at the director's relationship to the stage machine: the stage area, scenery, properties, lighting, costumes, makeup, and sound effects. The problems connected with using this machine are as complex as those in the director-actor relationship, because the stage machine requires a diversity of talents to bring out its highest potentials. When you do the whole job yourself, as you might in a small educational theatre setup or in a one-person community theatre operation, all you need do is argue out the designs with yourself and then carry out what your own imagination and your physical resources allow. But a director in this situation is bound by his own limitations, the same sort of limitations he would meet if he tried to act every role in a play. Consequently, unless you are totally familiar with all of your options in staging a play, you will not know how to work with designers in synthesizing a production when that time comes. Now is the time for you to examine your options, for you will use them all in Project 2 (beginning on page 262) when you design as well as direct your own production.

The Historical Relationship of Direction and Design

It was the problem of synthesis that brought the director into the theatre in the latter part of the nineteenth century. As has been pointed out frequently elsewhere, the contribution of the twentieth century to the history of the theatre was artistic play interpretation, an integration process of production in which the director figured prominently. As the twenty-first century unfolds, we look at theatre history not only as a thing in itself but also as a highly useful background for production; it has led us to revivals of both earlier plays and ideas about production on a scale no previous age ever has known.

Previous to the late nineteenth century, as was noted earlier in this chapter, stage design was more general than specific, more an appropriate background (and frequently an inappropriate one) for dramatic action than a *participant* in it. This approach directly reflected the concept of a play as a *presentation* in bold, broad lines. If the development of science and technology in the nineteenth century found its way directly into the theatre in forms that not only required that scenery appear to be like nature but that it create specific environments for specific plays. This scientific naturalism required much greater control of the stage machine as well as of acting, and it was at this point that the director was brought into the theatre as a much-needed craftsman. The *general* use of the stage soon became the *particular* use of the stage, and out of this was born twentieth-century stage production.

Nevertheless, even though the actor did not actually perform within the stage setting during the seventeenth and most of the eighteenth centuries, we know that some coordination took place—that someone placed the scenery and told the actors where to stand. We usually assume that this coordinator, where there was one, was either the stage manager or an actor-manager, but it could just as well have been the stage designer. It is not stretching historical projection out of focus to imagine that when Inigo Jones made his elaborate painted settings for his spectacular masques at the English Court in Shakespeare's day, he also directed the performers to certain positions in relation to scenery, which he probably designed with their positioning in mind.

Whatever total function designers may have served in past ages, in the late nineteenth century, they were brought under the control of directors who could then harmonize their creativity with that of the actors in the interest of making a total theatre experience. And so it remains today.

The Purpose of This Book Regarding Design

It has been generally assumed, largely because of the Stanislavskian wave in actor training, that director training should be primarily in the area of acting, with its subareas of voice, body, and movement. There can be no question that such specialization has its intrinsic values, for who will teach it if not the director? But this point of view also assumes, unfortunately, that designers will take care of the other aspects of production, that somehow visual design in the theatre is considerably less important than acting design. This assumption is very shortsighted because it overlooks the *concept of total theatre* in which the director as theatrical artist—the point of view of this book—coordinates both the acting and the visual presentation of a play's ideas.

The training of a director in all the areas of design is therefore essential, and it should be intensive training, not a haphazard process. Stage designing requires first an artist and second someone who can work within the limitations of the theatre. Stage designing is not the making of an arty background for actors, nor the operation of a technical machine. Instead, it is an organic expression of a high order. Stringent comment on the background and training of prominent stage designers, past and present, is reflected in the fact that when it comes to writing theatre histories, it is not directors who have made the major contributions but designers.

The following program of studies is suggested with the intention of alerting you, as a director in training, to the areas of study you should pursue, in whole or in part, if you are to be informed about the design aspect of your work. A well-conceived program would contain much of the following:

- A cultural history of specific civilizations (Chinese, Egyptian, Greek, etc.) in order to comprehend the meaning of culture in its social and intellectual aspects
- A survey of painting and sculpture; a course in life drawing; an elementary course in painting; an advanced course in art history
- Theatre history: theatre buildings, stages, scenery, and the like
- Costume history: a history of clothes as well as what was worn on the stage
- Elementary drawing for the stage: mechanical, perspective, and free rendition
- Scene design and staging materials
- Costume design
- Lighting design and engineering
- Sound design and engineering

Such training may seem extensive to a beginning director, but as you become more familiar with the complex, diverse problems of production in today's art-theatre concept, you will soon see the need for such a careful step-by-step building of your design capabilities.

The Purpose of the Exercises in Communication 3

Since it is assumed that you, as a director in training, are simultaneously pursuing some sort of training in design, and consequently are actively engaged in regularly assigned projects, no exercises in design of the usual sort are suggested in these next five chapters. Instead, two procedures are used: the first involves working through Chapters 17 through 21 with a *full-length, classroom play* for study as the principal device for emphasizing the director's options in design; and the second involves designing and directing your own live production of a one-act play as a summarizing project for Chapters 17 through 22. These two procedures, taken together, will take you to the second level of directing coordination and synthesis in play production. The third level—*style*—will be presented in Part III.

Finding a good study play at this point is essential because investigating a director's options in the area of design requires a play with multiple possibilities if you are to see the full range of the problem. Furthermore, a long play is suggested because you not only need to study this form as a contrast to the one-act play but you will also be able to see the concepts of coordination and synthesis in a large structure because of the scope it allows. Thus, you can make progress on two fronts. Although the class or its instructor can certainly make an independent choice, and may prefer to do so, for purposes of discussion here, all the exercises in Chapters 17 through 21 are focused on Arthur Miller's *The Crucible.* This play offers many advantages because of its undated content—despite the fact that it was written in the early 1950s—its multiact structure with different locations, its style of Realism that allows a fairly wide scope in staging, and the many problems in coordination and synthesis in design that it presents. Exercises with this play begin immediately at the end of this chapter. They do not attempt to be exhaustive in any way but merely guide you and your class to the sort of questions a director must ask himself.

The main intention of these chapters, then, is to ensure that you comprehend the relationship of the director to visual design by thoroughly understanding the concepts of symbolization, synthesis, and the communication process in design. You will not only need to discuss extensively all of the points in Chapters 17 through 21 in the classroom, but you are also encouraged to pursue these concepts in discussion with both directing and design students. Here is one place where directors can do a good deal of talking without getting into trouble.

In addition, *you should be certain that you understand one concept before going on to the next.* The material is laid out here in a logical progression, and you can advance only with step-by-step comprehension. Some of the points may seem obvious to you, but dealing with them is just where the difficulties begin; your theatregoing experiences up to this point have probably been quite unoriented toward design, and this lack of orientation may have led you to take a great deal for granted. You will need fresh eyes at this point in order to tear apart the obvious and to discover that it is not obvious at all, for someone has designed what you see and that means that decisions have been made about it. *Always remember that a design is a conceived plan, not an accident.* You will learn to see well only if you remove your own blindness; no one else can do that for you.

EXERCISES

1. You should begin your study of *The Crucible* (or other study play) by concentrating on its structure for design purposes. This sort of study is what directors frequently do in making a choice of a play for production; that is, it precedes a major play-analysis but it still enables a director to get a firm grasp of the play in order to make preliminary decisions about it. But you should by no means accept it as a substitute for a

full play-analysis, for you simply cannot direct actors without such study. Your first job is to read the play by recording the action in two ways:

a. Record the *story* of the play by writing down both previous action and dramatic action on sheets of paper. Record the previous action in red on one side and the dramatic action in black on the other, separating them with a vertical line. You can do this exercise easily if you make a note about what happens on each page of the playscript, and then carry this note over to your summarizing sheets.
b. When (a) has been completed, you are ready to go on to a director's scene-analysis. This is done by making a list of all the scenes in the play that are performed by the two or three most important characters. These are the major scenes in the dramatic action because the playwright has deliberately centered the forces of the play around these characters. These scenes are also climactic, thus containing the principal discoveries and consequent adjustments. Analyzing them will give you a quick grasp of the play's structure. (If you choose a study play with only two to five characters, be sure that you select the *principal* climactic scenes because the play will be made up of two- or three-character scenes). In *The Crucible,* you will find eight to ten of these scenes. Now write a comment about each scene with attention on two points: the scene's requirements in terms of acting and the scene's requirements in terms of staging.

2. When you have completed the two parts of Exercise 1, you are ready for a class discussion of the play. Proceed in the usual fashion for discussions of play-analysis, but instead of pursuing the seven major elements in detail, concentrate your discussions around specific points, such as:
   a. Why is *The Crucible* not a historical play? Why is it not a costume drama? How is it very contemporary?
   b. Who are the protagonist and the antagonist? Be sure you see Danforth's function in the play. Do you see Abigail's function as an instrument to effect the action? How do Proctor and Danforth clash head-on?
   c. Characterize Danforth. Can you see him as a politician rather than as a stern judge representing the church?
   d. What is the real witchcraft in the play? Should an audience believe in the witchcraft shown in Act I? What should an audience's reaction be to this act? Could certain lines possibly produce laughter? Should an audience hold the same view as John Proctor? Why?
   e. What role does Reverend Hale play in the action? What are his polar attitudes? Does he change? What are John Proctor's polar attitudes? What are Danforth's?
3. If you have done Exercises 1 and 2 carefully, you should be able to delineate the differences in structure between a long play and a short one. What does the long play allow in the way of character development? How many major characters are developed in *The Crucible*? How complex is the action? How many plots are there in *The Crucible*? (*Plot* means "separate lines of action": Abigail and the girls, Abigail and Proctor, etc.)
4. Read Gordon Craig's essay, "The Art of the Theatre." Discuss its contents in class.

18

The Director and the Stage Machine

Symbolization and Synthesis

This chapter is mostly about theatre aesthetics, the concepts behind all the practical work done in the theatre. We have become so accustomed in this day of science and technology to seeing things around us in only external ways—that is, in terms of what is useful or functional—that we find it very difficult to recapture the other kind of seeing we knew as small children but somehow lost when subjected to the controls and conformities of adult life. Yet, this must be done if we are to discover what art is all about. Wordsworth's "The child is father of the man" has very special meaning from an artistic point of view, because it epitomizes the very nature of the artist who must relearn or recapture the freedom and simplicity of childhood vision. The employment in actor training of improvisation and games has as its goal the freeing of the individual from rigid behavioral patterns and the releasing of the imagination as an active, living force. The same thing must be done for the learning designer or director. *In the art world, to see things eccentrically is to see them normally and freshly.* Without this free imagination, one is forever tied to accepted and prosaic realities.

Motion pictures prior to the 1960s and most television from its beginnings to the 1970s had enormous influence on this restriction in seeing, because they largely assumed that what we see literally and see quickly is all that there is. However, our vision has again been opened to the mainstream of the history of art forms by many works in both mediums that have penetrated surface realities to take hard looks underneath. Films, in particular, have won favor with adult audiences, not because of their sexual content but because of their mature themes and complex perceptions. These films have had an effect on the theatre by helping to force the theatre back into the mainstream of dramatic literature where revelation and poetic insights are a way of life.

Symbolization Is Theatre

Symbolization allows us to see life more clearly, more perceptively, by sensing it through the recognizable essences of things. This definition does not in any way rule out the use on the stage of what we regard as real objects. What it does force director-designers to do is use objects in *appropriate* and *contextual* ways so that their full values can be exploited artistically and the audience's vision be amplified. When used in these ways, the stage machine becomes organic: Not only are scenery, properties, lights, and costumes shown for what they are in themselves, but their life and vitality, their image-making powers, are greatly extended through actors who reveal their essences.

As a director, then, *you must learn the fine art of symbolization if you are to use the stage machine with any degree of sophistication.* You will find that you can reach audiences excitingly and with direct contact through symbolization where you have failed with the mere use of surface realities. *Design is not decoration but organic symbolization.*

Stage Convention

A *stage convention* is a contrivance with symbolic values. Continuous use of a contrivance so firmly establishes it in the feelings of audiences that they accept it as part of familiar stage form without any effort whatsoever. Audiences perceive its symbolic meanings and take it for granted. Conventions thus become deeply rooted, so much so, in fact, that artistic revolts are often needed to overthrow them. The raised platform is just such a form, as are the proscenium arch, painted scenery, the architectural stone wall of the Greek theatre, and the Shakespearean stage that projects into the house. The late nineteenth century went through a revolt in its attack on Romantic staging, replacing it with illusionistic conventions (like observed realities); and the twentieth century has gone through a similar revolt against the illusory theatre in its attempt to break away from the conventions of Realism.

A director must grasp the concept of stage convention and the force it exerts on popular audience feelings and comprehension. This perception is also a basis for understanding design.

Why Study Theatre History

This book cannot possibly provide an in-depth examination of everything a director must know about theatre architecture, the playing space, scenery, costuming and makeup, lighting, and sound. Each is a specialized study in itself and should be pursued with specialized intentions. What needs to be pointed out here is the nature of change in the design function throughout the history of theatre, and the necessity for a director's understanding of it. *The form of theatre does not change but only the conventions and symbolizations within that form.*

Changes are clearly marked by shifts in conventions, but the constant factor behind all the changes is *symbolism: Each age finds a characteristic symbolism for pro-*

tecting its ideas through its stage machine. Imaginative theatre historians, such as George Kernodle and Richard Southern, have pursued these changes in great detail, and you should study their books for specific illumination of the subject.

Consequently, what follows is a brief résumé of the interrelationships of the staging tools. They are discussed at this point in the interest of showing what the director must study of theatre history if he is to comprehend the theatre machine and thus have a sophisticated view of all his options.

Theatre architecture and the audience. The study of theatre architecture deals with the relationship between the playing space and *the audience.* Such study leads to the following:

1. An understanding of the basic arrangements of performance space in relation to audience space: whether each is contained in a separate "envelope" of space separated by a wall with an opening (proscenium arrangement), or whether the audience space and playing space are combined within one envelope of space with no barrier wall (various forms of arena and so-called "black box" stages, as well as "end" stages), or whether the playing space is thrust from one envelope of space into the space occupied by the audience (so-called "thrust" stages). Each of these arrangements establishes a different spatial relationship between the production and the audience—and the director must, over time, master the dynamics and optimal uses of each.
2. A comprehension of the "size" of plays and what this has to do with the arrangement of audiences.
3. An awareness of the effects of physical distance on the relationship of actors and audience.
4. A comprehension of the problems of acoustics and of an actor's projection arc (the maximum arc, from side to side, that a speaking actor can use and still be heard).

Playing space. This area of study is concerned with what is commonly referred to as "the stage." But because that term is so often confused with a raised platform, the broader, more conceptual term is used here. Any historical study of playing space would certainly reveal that actors have played on the following types of spaces:

1. On the ground level with the audience on the same level
2. On the ground level with the audience raised in graduated steps
3. On both ground level and raised platforms simultaneously
4. On raised platforms of varying levels, with the audience below or on various levels above
5. In circular, square, rectangular, or triangular arrangements

Scenery. In the broadest sense, scenery delineates the backing of the playing space or the occupation of the space itself. It includes permanent architectural façades, movable backing pieces, permanent or movable objects, platforms, and other devices within the playing space. Study of theatre history shows a wide variety of uses, from the architectural façades with movable pieces in the playing space to the latest devices of projected scenery, either stationary or moving, behind the actor.

Costuming and makeup. The actor has always worn something to declare his difference from members of the audience, although, as in the case of modern Realism, this difference is sometimes so subtle as to be almost imperceptible. But indeed there is a difference, because costume, like all the other tools in the stage machine, must symbolize. Costumes, as we notice through a study of theatre history, can make an actor look larger than a human being by raising him on stilts or increasing the height of his head with extended headdress; or they can make him look wider, and thus more imposing, by extensions of shoulders and arm garments. The actor's face and head can be changed into all sorts of shapes and meanings through the use of masks, wigs, and false hair or through its pale descendant, painted makeup. Some periods of theatre history used what was regarded as the best court dress; some have used archaeological and historical reproduction; and some have worn practically no costume at all in an effort to find a neutral body.

Lighting. The history of lighting in the theatre is not as extensive a study as is, for instance, scenery and costuming, but the director must be fully aware of what was done in order to more fully comprehend dramatic literature and historical stage production. The fact that audiences of the Greek theatre, the Roman theatre of Plautus and Terence, the medieval street theatre, and the Elizabethan public playhouse all saw plays in daylight tells us much about the workings of the plays and their productions. Likewise, to see the Renaissance drama in candlelight—as did Shakespeare's audiences at Blackfriars Theatre (one of the first indoor playhouses in England) or at the Teatro Olimpico, or at Drury Lane in Garrick's day—is to help us understand intimacy, confinement, and how "soft" lighting can create a rare beauty of its own. To be aware of the gas lighting of the nineteenth century is also to comprehend the enormous revolution in lighting when theatres shifted to electrical power and control. To view lighting only as it is used today is to miss its historical significance as a theatrical device and a manipulator of audience perceptions. Why burn torches in midday as was done in street theatre in the fifteenth and sixteenth centuries? In order to get to the "guts" of a play of any era, a director must study how lighting and other effects were used at that time.

Sound. The reed and stringed instruments of the Greeks; Shakespeare's live musicians above the stage and on the stage as actors; the Drottningholm's cannonball track above the stage to make thunder; the nineteenth century's orchestral background to the melo- (music) drama—all these are design ideas, some so thoroughly embedded that they become conventions plays could not do without. We are so accustomed to hearing music as part of a movie sound track that we take it for granted as a convention and we are startled to hear a film deliberately designed without such a score. Can you hear the sound of an actor's voice in a huge Greek amphitheatre? From a Roman platform in the context of a fair? From a scaffold erected on a street for the commedia del l'arte? From the intimate forestage of a 600-seat Georgian theatre? From the stage of an enormous 3,000-seat nineteenth-century stage? The motion picture is largely a visual experience: We watch the face and eyes of a character through close-ups, and in this way we come to know the character intimately. *In contrast, the stage is largely an aural experience, for we are moved intensely by the live human voice and less so by what we see.*

The study of theatre history, then, as distinct from the study of dramatic literature, is the study of variations in the use of staging concepts—variations that have been extensive. Thus, a director who is not also a student of theatre history can have only a superficial understanding of the major tools through which he makes his creative statements. You can readily see that this knowledge is necessary for the staging of historical drama, but you must also be aware that it is of enormous value in the staging of modern drama simply because of your knowledge of *what is possible* in making theatre can be greatly extended.

Synthesis

General Design versus Specific Design

Stage design means making something for the stage *by intention* rather than leaving the effect to accident. This definition implies that stage design is an art form, and consequently must have unity, coherence, proportion, arrangement, selection, economy, grace, and rhythm. A director's visual sense, like a costumer's or a scenic artist's, must be highly refined in order to be capable of perceiving the essential elements of form that contribute to the making of symbolic representations.

Design, therefore, is always a *specific thing,* though a particular design may be stated so simply that it appears to have a general quality. But if what is placed on a stage is too loose or too free, if it lacks an interesting arrangement of line and mass, we cannot, as audience, perceive it at all. Thus, if a director-designer simply places materials on the stage without conceiving their effect, he will not make a statement we can call design, for the materials will have no relationship to other aspects of the context.

As previously mentioned, the director's role in the theatre today is *to bring about a synthesis in design: to place actors in relationship not just to each other but to all the materials on the stage* in a coordinated design that could make the meanings of a play not only much clearer but also much more exciting. In the latter part of the nineteenth century, Appia and Craig developed the concept of synthesis—that is, that one person should do all the physical designs of scenery, costuming, and lighting. But what also became clear was that if that person were to control the physical production completely, he would also have to control the actors. Thus, the concept of the director as a master-designer was born. Since then, although the one-man autocrat has been rare in practice, the concept of synthesis has been well established, for it is the only way specific design can be controlled.

Looking back, then, is the best way to look forward and to bypass the prejudice that today's theatre is the only valid theatre. You must learn to see current changes as evolutionary, not new in themselves. Evolution is the name of the game: Think about how painted scenery has given way to no scenery at all; how stage lighting, as we know it today, has basically affected all staging; how costuming has moved from historical representation to symbolic enhancement; how acting elicited techniques of interior expression; how theatre architecture followed changes of staging; and how motion-picture techniques have modified stage production in all areas.

Balance and Imbalance in Synthesis

Balance is at the heart of the concept of synthesis. *Without balance in the media brought together, without the most careful joining of playscript, actors, and designs, there can be no synthesis.* This statement in no way implies that a production must have these in equal parts, resembling an undefined reddish mixture of vegetables in a juice blender. Instead, a production should be more like a well-conducted symphony in which the conductor brings out at appropriate times, and with appropriate strengths, the various components of his orchestra—the violins, then the horns, then the cellos, then the woodwinds—blending the whole into a sensitive, harmonic, and absorbing complex.

It is easier to see the nature of balance by looking at imbalance in production. Among the factors that contribute to imbalance, the following occur so frequently that they are worth pointing out as production traps: (1) self-conscious directing, (2) underdesign, and (3) overdesign.

Self-Conscious Directing

When we watch a production, if we are too aware of the mechanics, *too aware of a striving for effect*, we are watching self-conscious directing. Instead of being drawn into the inner story line and receiving the production with unbroken empathy on the level of our imaginations, we are disconcerted and distracted by a director who lays a production onto a playscript rather than *pulls it out of* the playscript. Thus, his blocking may be mechanically contrived rather than organically embedded in dramatic action, or the designs may be too self-conscious, drawing audience attention away from the actors. Directing is the art of *reducing distraction* in the imaginations of viewers in order to leave those imaginations free to do their own work. By pushing too hard for effect in the wrong way, the effect is lost. The focus of an audience must always be placed on the human values deriving from the playscript and not on the mechanics of projecting those values.

Underdesign. When a director is not thoroughly aware of what part visual design plays in play production, *he might settle for a much less effective statement than a play needs for its best fulfillment.* When this happens, such a production will lack vitality or enough symbolization to project the play into the imaginations of an audience.

Theatre as distinct from drama means the actual live presentation of a play before an audience through *theatrical* means; it is not merely a play read for an audience. The values are very different. Some critics of modern Shakespearean productions maintain that far too many are overproduced, that they cannot "hear" the play because there is too much scenic enhancement. What they are probably saying is that they do not like theatre very much as a production art but are enamored of the text as a piece of literature that must be preserved at all cost. If we, as an audience, get hung up over Shakespearean wordage, it may not be at all because of the elaborateness of the production but more likely because of the difficulty with an archaic language. Underdesign may perhaps make a Shakespearean production more easily heard, but it may lose the very essence of what is most Shakespearean about it, which only the "vulgarity" of theatre can reproduce. Underdesign and simplicity of design are not the same thing. *Simple design can be highly organic and can intensely arouse imagination.* The director's goal is to release imagination in an audience, and he must find the necessary symbols for doing that with each play he produces.

Overdesign. The greatest danger that occurs when a director works with skilled designers is *doing too much.* Each designer, as a matter of course, wants to make his own design as effective as possible; and when a costumer, a scene designer, and a lighting designer are also involved, the whole problem of balance is intensified. *The principal danger is that of overwhelming the actors,* who have difficulty enough in holding their own against the dynamics of visual effects. It is in controlling this situation, like controlling the balance in acting, that the director exerts a primary force on production. The great problem is that, as with actors, the director must work through the imaginations of others (the designers); and it is in guiding these imaginations, not in dictating their direction, where his primary work as a director-designer is done. *Overdesign can be ruinous because it stultifies audience imagination by depriving it of focus on the intrinsic values of a play.* An audience can all too easily be swept away by spectacle, with the consequent loss of the play as a total theatrical experience.

Counterpoint in Synthesis of Design

At first glance, it would seem possible for a director to achieve synthesis in the areas of visual design—set, costume, and light—by bringing the designers to the same point of view regarding the emphasis to be made in a production, and that all the director would need to do would be to declare the emphatic points. Such a procedure, however, does not exploit the design possibilities; in fact, it may actually stultify audience imagination and cause distraction by too obvious overloading at the points of emphasis.

Although a director and his designers must have a mutual understanding of a basic common direction, *full exploitation of visual effects lies not in the likeness of the designs but their difference.* You will understand this idea better after the discussion of the design process in Major Project 3. At this point, you should appreciate the fact that *arousal of imagination frequently depends on clash and conflict in the visual effects, not on repetitive or seemingly harmonious statements. As characters clash in a play, so must the various elements of visual design.*

A simple example of how *counterpoint* can work is in a production of a historical play that uses an abstract setting, realistic costumes based on clothing of the period, and lighting with strongly contrasted highlights and shadows—all to the accompaniment of modern jazz as musical background. As you can imagine, an audience will be disconcerted by the lack of expected harmony, with the consequent awakening of fresh imagery of all sorts. If the acting is strong and very much alive, this theatrical experience can be a truly exciting one. *The theatre is an attack on the senses as well as on the mind, and without sense-awakening approaches to design, the basic nature of theatre is lost.*

Counterpoint as a design approach does not in any way imply that all production must be highly melodramatic and theatrical; it merely suggests that different areas of design can do different things, and that *it is the total effect the director must work for—an effect that is disconcerting rather than restful.* The director who does his own designing must give intensive consideration to counterpoint because he is a ready victim to the obvious in design. Although he might think he is moving his audience with intensive design emphasis, he may merely be hitting an idea on the head with a sledgehammer and thus driving it away from imaginative audience reception. *Do not wallow in design emphasis; "counterpoint" it.*

EXERCISES

1. If you have not already done so, read Richard Southern's *The Seven Ages of Theatre.* This will give you an excellent idea of the concepts of symbolization and convention in various historical periods and in cultures very different from our own.
2. Apply *symbolization* and *stage convention* to *The Crucible* in a class discussion:
   a. Why is *The Crucible* not an everyday reality, but a symbol in play form?
   b. List as many symbols from the play as you can find.
   c. How is the title of *The Crucible* symbolic?
   d. What are the conventions in staging that can be used for this play?
   e. How would *The Crucible* have been staged in Shakespeare's day? Is that sort of production still valid?
3. How can *The Crucible* be overdesigned? If you read the reviews of the first production in New York, you would know why Arthur Miller restaged it in a much simpler way. What do you think he accomplished by doing so? Is underdesign of this play possible?
4. What counterpoints would you propose in staging *The Crucible*?
5. Discuss *symbolization* as a concept.

19

Director's Options

Choice of the Stage

The goal of Chapters 17 through 21 from a director's point of view is the mastering of the coordination-synthesis process in designing a production. Before you can approach the designer—either the designer in yourself or persons other than yourself—you must be keenly aware of the full range of possibilities and options open to you as a director. Many students study the areas of design through specialty courses without actually seeing how these areas overlap and how they may be similar in approach and arrive at similar concepts. But because the concept advocated here is counterpoint in design, the director must penetrate as deeply as he can into the various options available to him. The range is great, and when to use which ones is an important part of a director's decision making.

This chapter is a detailed examination of options in the choice of the stage. As you will note, this option, as well as those in the following chapters, is developed here in close relationship to the historical backgrounds outlined in the last chapter. The intention now is not only to show you how you can apply theatre history to the designing process but also to give you an active idea of how your imagination must work if you are to preside as the leader in the process of coordination.

One rule is necessary in approaching this and the following two chapters. *Do not take anything for granted, but argue it with yourself and with others* until you have declared solid positions of your own on each of the many options open to you as a director.

Today's Stage Machine

At no time has theatre had such a highly developed stage machine as today. Many recently built theatre plants, both for professional purposes as well as for educational training, not only have flexible stages where the architectural form of the stage can actually be changed but they also have two or three theatres of different shapes and sizes where different sets of aesthetic values prevail. However, today's problem does not lie in the flexibility of the machine but in the same old indecipherable question: How can audience imagination be excited?

The stage as a tool of production in today's theatre has probably undergone the greatest shift in concept of all the areas of design. Whereas past ages had fixed stages on which to mount productions, our age is characterized by its concept of flexibility; that is, it is now assumed that no one stage form can do the work for all the historical and modern drama being produced. Consequently, a major set of options open to a director lies in his choice of a specific stage form for a particular play. This fact does not imply that the theatre in which he works does not have a permanent stage form built into the structure, for it probably does (usually proscenium in style). But if a director is to follow recent methods of production, he will find himself altering the stage form to meet the requirements of the other options, or finding a place to play outside his established theatre.

Four distinctive architectural stages merit discussion here: (1) proscenium, (2) arena, (3) open-thrust, and (4) forestage-proscenium and end stages. The order of discussion does not indicate any preference but has been determined by logical progression. The term *found space* might have been added to this list because it is still in use these days, born as it was in the 1960s, to describe whatever audience-actor relationship a director decides to use, whether it is a theatre, a church, a hall, a garage, or whatever. It is not discussed here, however, because the use of such space, no matter what label may be attached to it, probably falls into one of the four major categories.

Proscenium Stage

Although the dominant hold of the *proscenium stage* as the principal convention for presenting plays in our time has weakened somewhat since the mid-1950s, especially in college theatre productions, it is still very much with us and probably will be for some time to come. New theatres are still being built with this stage as the architectural form as the values it offers continue to be appreciated. Because you are already familiar with many of its workings from your previous study in this book, it is being discussed here first.

If you comprehend the theory behind this stage, you will be better able to see the workings of the other stages discussed later in the chapter. Do not take the proscenium stage for granted because it is familiar to you, but read the following material carefully, checking it against your present knowledge of this stage.

The proscenium stage as a convention was and is basically *illusory;* that is, it has the inherent capacity of creating the illusion of the real world we see every day. It is not just a platform but a three-dimensional framed platform. We sit in front of it and are expected to believe that what we see taking place through that rectangular hole cut in the stage wall is so close to an imitation of life that we can forget we are in a theatre. This illusion is heightened because, if we use it strictly defined, we cannot see any changes of scenery made since "the wall" intentionally hides all the machinery, and either a curtain is closed or the lights are extinguished so that we will not be distracted. Furthermore, to reinforce the sense of illusion, the lights in the auditorium are turned off while a performance is in progress, so that we cannot see other members of the audience except for the backs of their heads as we sit behind them. In this sense, *the experience is something like reading a novel, something we do alone;* but by hearing responses from other members of the audience, we still feel part of a group.

This experience of the darkened, picture-frame theatre has been appropriated by motion pictures, which in many ways do a much better job because they can use unlimited scenic backgrounds, can employ the close-up (thus bringing the actor far closer visually to an audience), and can amplify sound so that hearing, even in delicate nuance, is never a problem. Movies can also maintain audience attention at a very high level through the techniques of moving the camera, montage, and making instantaneous changes of scene. *As an illusory device, the proscenium stage is now a poor cousin to the motion picture.*

Because of this competition with the movies, the proscenium stage in recent times has been pressured by other forms. The first wave of evolution came in the development of new scenic approaches that since the early twentieth century have almost replaced the nineteenth-century box-setting convention and replaced it with fragmentary walls, set pieces, and even projected scenery, or design approaches that emphasize the sculptural properties of the stage, as in the work of Meyerhold, Brook, and other innovative directors. Thus, this trend has altered an aesthetic that requires actual reproduction of places and has moved us toward a new one based on *suggestion* of those places, all in the interest of exciting audience imagination by forcing it to complete what has been left out. Architectural units—platforms, steps, and the like—have come into wide use in an attempt to create verticality on the stage and, in this way, to overcome its flatness—flatness because everyone in the audience sees the same dimensions from its frontal position. Although the ways directors and designers use the proscenium stage has undergone a continual evolution from the seventeenth century onward, the basic power of this arrangement of playing space and audience has proved its staying power. It is difficult to believe that other stage forms, valuable alternatives though they undoubtedly are, are likely to replace anytime soon the proscenium form, which took over 300 years to perfect and has proven adaptable to different design approaches.

Perhaps one manifestation of the movement away from the proscenium is the building of small playhouses—university theatres, for example—that seat only 200 to 500 spectators. Even though such houses may be built in the proscenium style, there is a question as to how conscious most of the audience actually is of the proscenium. The opening, though it may be of standard dimensions (32′ × 18′), is sometimes so large in this small theatre in relation to the audience area that the arch effect literally does not exist for most of the audience. Broadway play reviewers, a group that has not pushed the new concepts, have probably seldom truly experienced the closed, framed effect of the proscenium stage because, by sitting so close to the stage, they have literally been "within" the frame. It might be said that only the back-of-the-house or the balcony viewer has had much of a proscenium-arch experience today—the "removed" illusory experience. That theatregoers attending "thrust" theatres still prefer to sit facing the front of such stages, rather than on the sides, indicates the hold of the old proscenium convention.

Blocking suggestions. Both composition and movement on the proscenium stage have been discussed extensively in Chapters 7 through 14, where it was assumed that if the learning director understood the concept of the proscenium, he could easily move to other forms. In brief, the concept of composition and movement on the proscenium stage is illusory; that is, it must *appear* to be lifelike, although some very definite conventions must be observed.

Thus, as noted earlier, compositions on this stage are largely open to the audience, with the apex usually placed upstage. Actors can, of course, turn their backs to an audience, but such positions must be momentary, simply because an audience wants to watch the frontal actor in order to follow his reactions and because it cannot hear very well the lines that may be thrown upstage. Just as furniture pieces are placed in open positions, so must the actor place himself in positions of that sort as often as possible. But this opening front also necessitates deemphasis, which can be brought about by back positions, using the weak upstage corners, standing behind furniture, and so on.

One rule, however, seems to dominate the use of this stage: *No actor must appear to violate the proscenium plane by walking through it toward the audience or appear to be outside the prescribed lifelike lines of the setting.* This rule does not mean that actors cannot look directly toward an audience or face that way, but it does suggest that compositions should be arranged (with downstage placement of secondary actors, for instance) so that they will not appear to be in violation of proscenium logic. It does suggest that an actor who takes a position at either corner of the stage gazing out into space makes a poor composition because it implies that the actor is facing a wall (the imaginary proscenium wall) and is thus doing an eccentric rather than a lifelike thing.

The convention of the proscenium stage, then, is *an appearance of reality,* not reality itself. No matter how lifelike a play may seem on this stage, *it is never life itself.*

Arena Stage

In theatre-in-the-round, or *arena stage,* the audience tightly surrounds the acting area and exerts pressure on the playing by its close presence. Although this form has not established itself as a dominant stage form like the proscenium, arena stages have nevertheless become a recognized kind of stage in educational theatres and in several notable professional circumstances as well. Like the proscenium stage, it was used as an illusionistic stage in parts of its early history, but recent users have greatly extended its possibilities.

Another convention, however, operates in arena staging that tends to break down its illusory elements: Members of an audience can fully see and watch many other members of the audience. This creates the paradox of an audience watching lifelikeness of a very subtle sort take place in front of them at the same time it is participating in an obvious *communal* and obviously theatrical experience. When an audience surrounds a play, it is performing one of the oldest rituals of humanity: the tribe standing or sitting in a circle around its ritual dancers, its medicine man, its heroes who move around the fire in the center.

Thus, *the intimacy of arena staging is its prime convention,* for the audience can sense the actor in a very personal way: his breathing, his perspiration, his body sounds, even the shower of his spittle when he speaks vigorously. It is a kind of motion picture in live stage form. But the experience actually goes beyond that of the movie because it has no such barrier as the lifeless projection screen and can exhibit the flesh-and-blood actor in close-up to the voyeurism of an audience. The participatory-theatre experimentation of the 1960s greatly depended on this "touching" possibility of actors and members of the audience.

But how real is it all? Again, *arena staging gives only the appearance of reality.* The room created in the acting area may look like a real room, the food consumed by the actors may be real food, the costumes worn may be genuine clothes, the speeches the audience hears spoken in low tones and even whispered may seem realistic in the extreme. Yet, all this is not life itself, for a play is always an artificial thing that involves selection and exaggeration (less than life as well as more). One of the techniques in arena style is for the actors to begin playing at a low level—as close to reality as possible—in order to draw the audience into the illusion, and then to raise the level gradually in size and proportion until the acting resembles what is seen on the proscenium stage. *Theatre-in-the-round is not for the inexperienced amateur but for the capable and trained actor.*

Another convention that the director must be aware of in using this form is the specific location of the acting area. Should the actors stand on the same level as the first row of the audience? Should they be at least six inches or more below? Should they be a foot or more above the floor level of the first row? Such a decision is crucial because the separation of the stage from the audience, which lowering or raising can accomplish, will subtly modify the convention. The raised stage may so set an actor apart from the audience that the result is a *platform stage,* which may no longer be considered intimate or illusory. In this instance, the actor will loom over the members of the audience, some of whom will now look up at him. From this view, he may no longer appear to be just another member of the audience going through a dramatic experience but may now be viewed as a kind of *superbeing—an actor.* By raising the stage, the theatre-in-the-round may be converted from an illusory aesthetic to a nonillusory one in which the audience's experience can be very different. The surrounding location of the audience is the first convention of the arena stage, to be sure, but the second is surely *the level of the stage.* The director must be aware of the changing aesthetics when manipulating the playing area.

Moreover, the fact that an audience sits on four sides is no reason to limit set design to furniture alone. You should think of this stage as having all the potentials of a circus arena, with vertical exploitation one of its important extension possibilities. Thus, this stage, just as with the proscenium, becomes a cube that can be occupied dramatically and theatrically not only by actors but also by *look-through scenery.* Anything goes, as long as it stays within the logic of its aesthetic. Placing covered scenery on this stage would certainly obscure audience vision, but when skeletal frames are introduced you have both good vision and the suggestion of baroque scenery. Looking through such frames is no problem at all for audiences, for people actually see much in real life through interrupted views. You must learn to exploit this stage in every possible way, for the communal theatre has great potential for our times.

Blocking suggestions. It should now be apparent to you why organic blocking (using the tools of illustration for purposes of communication from director to actor) has been emphasized over the pictorial in the discussions on composition, movement, and so on earlier in this book. *If you understand the organic concept, you will have little difficulty in arranging on the arena stage everything from the groundplan to composition and movement.* The basic principle is still the same: *By arousing the imagination of the actor through ensuring his understanding of and sensitivity to given circumstances and dramatic action, the imagination of the audience can be stimulated to strong empathic action.*

The pictorial requirements in arena staging are fairly obvious. The four-sided audience demands a four-sided look by the director. Or better still: *Forget* the one-sided view of the proscenium stage and direct the actors into intense character-action relationships, and the compositions will largely take care of themselves. Two principles of all good composition should be kept in mind: (1) Play the limits of the stage on an obstacle course, avoiding climactic compositions as much as possible; and (2) play a cat-and-mouse game in composition; now one character pursues and the other retreats, and vice versa. Actors will frequently turn outward toward one section or another of an audience as the most natural thing to do in getting away.

If the center point of the stage is thought of as the center of a clock, variety in composition is infinite (see Figure 52). A groundplan can readily be designed that will fan out from the center (see Figure 53). The use of a center object approachable from all sides will avoid the deadlines of a cleared space and will provide the obstacle course so necessary in a dynamic groundplan.

FIGURE 52

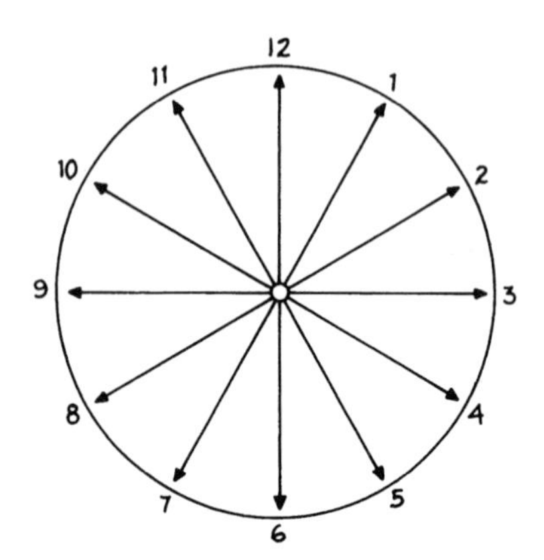

FIGURE 53

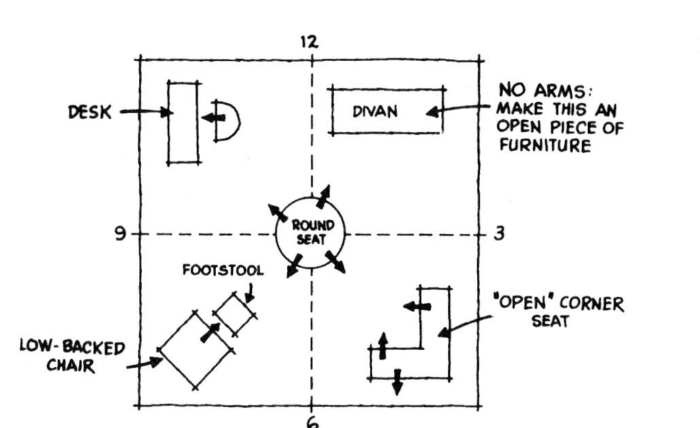

Note that Figure 53 has four major stage areas. By using the areas in combinations with only occasional use of one area, a dynamic interlocking of the stage will result, and all four audiences will see the play equally well. An actor's back facing one part of the audience is an accepted convention of this stage; but this rather extreme body position can be kept at a minimum by frequent shiftings to other body positions. When back positions must be used as the best illustration of a dramatic action, the *neutral corners* (entrances to the stage where no audience is seated) can be employed effectively. The problem of quick entrances and exits on the arena stage is always difficult because of the distance through the audience that must be traversed, but this problem can often be solved by occasional use of entrance-walkways as acting areas—an actor starting to speak on the way in, or stopping halfway out to give an exit line—or through the use of *vomitories*—entranceways underneath audience seating—where actors can enter the acting area directly without being seen. (The modern word *vomitory* comes from the Latin *vomitorium,* an architectural feature of the ancient Roman arenas that allowed for efficient and rapid movement of thousands of spectators filing into and out of the tiered bleacher arrangements surrounding the games space.)

Several additional points to keep in mind when blocking on an arena stage follow.

Compositions seen from across the space. The basic principle of "seeing" in this form is something like an "over the shoulder" shot from film or television; that is, the audience seated on one side looks past (or over the shoulder of, so to speak) the figure of the actor who may be closest and whose back may be turned to them *to the actor or actors facing* toward that observing quarter of the audience from *across* the stage. In this sense, in this form of stage, where the space is sculptural, the audience is always looking through a composition to see the fronts of the actors facing toward them. This means that it is relatively rare for an actor to face directly into the section of audience closest to him, because doing so would mean closing off, or showing his back to, the majority of viewers in the space.

Learning to compose with this in mind is essential for making effective compositions and picturizations in the arena.

Movement in arcs. Movements that curve or arc through the space (in conformity with the needs of verisimilitude or lifelikeness in the style of the play) tend to work well in comparison to straight lines because the curve opens up the face of the actor to more of the audience. In this form of stage, the connection of each audience member with the face of the actor carrying the dramatic action is something that continually needs to be "refreshed" and the director is always on the lookout for ways to do this, even in the momentary, fleeting passages of time subsumed in movement (perhaps particularly because movements come between the still, caught moments of compositions). Groundplans that are effective obstacle courses and that break up the space in interesting and believeable ways will greatly facilitate movement patterns that are other than straight lines.

Subtle turning. Similarly, experienced actors in this stage form learn to find ways to incorporate subtle turns into their performance, so as to keep themselves in a continual "opening up" to the different sides of the audience. If subtle turning changes of position are integrated with and arise from changes in the character's thinking or responding to what he hears on the stage, then the effect is invariably much more organic and thus not overtly noticeable to the audience as artifice. Finding ways to help actors do this in a natural, believable way is part of learning to work in this form and is invaluable in finding effective staging, particularly for extended moments in the play that may be physically static or still.

Size of compositions. In this stage form, compositions that become too small and "knotted" or closed off on themselves will be difficult for audiences to see into, essentially because the actors wind up blocking off each other from the lines of vision from various sectors of the audience. While still being sensitive to the verisimilitude required, it is important to keep the compositions large enough and open enough (often by having actors offset each other slightly rather than by facing each other nose-to-nose) to allow for audience members to see into the composition without actors' faces being blocked.

Again, it must be emphasized that the purpose of organic blocking is to *free the dramatic action. If the actors understand their intense relationships to one another, good blocking cannot help but materialize.* This blocking can then be modified to meet the demands of pictorial necessity and variety.

Open-Thrust Stage

Open-thrust is used here to describe a theatre setup in which audiences are seated on three sides of a raised stage, with *the stage backed by a wall on the fourth.* (Early examples of this form feaured a fixed architectural façade from which the stage thrust outward into the auditorium; later and more frequent examples feature a cavity from which the stage thrusts outward, with the cavity being used for variable rather than "permanent" fixed scenery.) It is "open" because no portion of the stage is concealed from the audience (like the arena); that is, everything must take place *before the audience;* it is "thrust" because it juts out from a concealing wall *into* the audience area.

This is the classical stage, the oldest form known. A version of it was used by the Greeks in the fifth century B.C., and it was also the stage of Shakespeare and of classical Chinese opera. Its revival in the twentieth century came about in part because of the increased emphasis on the production of historical drama that had been written for this convention. But there is good reason to believe that it has won acceptance in recent years more as a reaction against the relative two-dimensionality and illusory quality of the proscenium stage.

The dynamics of the open-thrust convention lie in its plastic, sculpturelike capabilities, for the actor is three-dimensional in every way. The theatre experience is thus greatly heightened in contrast to the proscenium style, for *it puts the live actor back on the stage in full force where his energy and radiance are dynamic realities and are not withdrawn or are not merely behavioristic experiences.* The open-thrust stage could have the same illusory aesthetic as is possible in arena staging when the actors and audience are arranged on the same floor level; but its *basic concept is that of a raised stage.* Thus, *the intention is not representational but presentational.*

Presentational is a term commonly used to describe the nonillusory theatre experience. This aesthetic—the oldest in the history of the theatre—makes no attempt to fool audiences into believing that they are looking at the real thing. "This is the theatre," it says, "and here is a stage, here are actors, and here is an audience, and what you see and hear takes place *only* in this theatre; it resembles life, yes, but it is definitely *not* life." Consequently, this stage is in sharp contrast to the concept of the proscenium stage where life and what happens in the theatre have been confused. *Theatre as a pure art form distinct from life and stated in obvious theatre conventions is at the basis of the concept.* The audience may become involved in a play, but it can never forget it is in a theatre—a place where one watches playmaking—and not a peep show for a slice of life.

The treatment of the area backing the stage is an important aspect of the open-thrust stage because it provides the background against which the play is seen. This may be designed as permanent architecture when the theatre is built, as in Greek and Elizabethan theatres; it may be partly architectural and partly painted, as in Chinese classical opera or in Japanese Noh staging; it may be even a curtained wall, as in the extant drawings of early Renaissance playings of Seneca and Plautus; or, it may be a cavity into which scenery is placed for a specific production. *Whatever form it may take, it provides a more or less permanent façade against which the play is performed.* Even in examples of this stage form where scenery specific to the particular play is built and placed in the cavity behind the playing space, there tends to be less changing of scenery than in the proscenium where the fly loft above the stage and extensive wing space are built to accommodate changing scenery. In the thrust form, greater emphasis is placed on altering set props on the acting platform that thrusts out from the backing, whether that be a fixed architectural façade or scenery unique to a particular production.

The open-thrust convention places great responsibility on the playscript and on the actors, and can free both from the confines of the visual statement of exact place. Thus, the "stageplace" can be anything the actors with their costumes and properties declare it to be. The suggestion made by some early twentieth-century scholars that signs were needed on Shakespeare's stage to tell audiences where scenes were taking place can easily be seen as nonsense today. We now know through the use of this stage that audiences can move quickly from one imagined place to another with only the slightest suggestion—that being either an opening line, a property such as a military banner, or an explicit costume such as armor. Modern plays present no more difficulties about place than do historical dramas, and, as a result, we have begun to question *the validity of exact place: Does it confine, more than release, an audience's imagination?*

Lighting has become an important convention in the use of this stage, particularly with modern plays, as we have not yet given up the convention of the rising and falling stage curtain in the proscenium theatre to mark interruptions in the stage action. Consequently, plays are still being written with this dramatic cutoff in mind. On the open-thrust stage, as well as on the arena stage, light control is presently used to function as the curtain, with actors entering and taking places in the dark and departing in the same way. When plays are written for it—and the experiments of the 1960s turned up a few—characters will probably be given reasons for entering the scene and leaving at its end, as in historical drama, and with this technique the lighting conventions could change radically.

Another modern convention that has been used occasionally with this stage is the vomitory, as described in the discussion earlier on the arena stage. Before the introduction of this convention, actors either entered at the rear of the stage or approached the stage through the audience, as in arena staging. The vomitory solved the problem of quick entrances because a large number of actors could access the stage area very quickly and then disappear at the end of a scene within a few seconds. The entrance and exit tempos of the proscenium stage were thus preserved almost intact.

The old convention of "scenes above," as in Shakespeare's theatre, has been retained with only minor modifications through the use of back-wall structures that permit actors to appear above the stage on scaffolding or through windows in the stage wall. *Vertical playing space thus becomes an inherent convention in this stage form.* Even modern plays with their simultaneous use of upstairs and downstairs can be satisfactorily accommodated through skeletal look-through structures placed in the acting area.

(At this point some mention should be made of a hybrid form of stage that is frequently encountered and can confuse this discussion unless the differences are clearly perceived. This is a three-quarter arrangement of audience seating surrounding a playing space on a flat floor more or less at audience level rather than on a raised platform. This form is best seen as a hybrid, combining aspects of the thrust and the arena stage forms, rather than a true thrust stage with its characteristic raised platform for playing (and with a consequent lessening of those aesthetic and perceptual qualities that flow from the presence of the platform). Because the raised platform is absent, this form tends to be closer, in audience perceptions, to the experience to be had in an arena arrangement with one side of audience seating removed and reclaimed for scenic purposes. This form is probably born out of twentieth-century experiments with arena form that were closely followed by the new open-thrust stages that also appeared in the middle decades of the twentieth century. What to call these hybrid stages is problematical, but they are not exactly the same thing as "pure" thrust stages with their raised playing spaces and they tend to be of a smaller, more intimate, less "heroic" scale than the classic examples of thrust stages. It is an important distinction to keep in mind when thinking about space and how different arrangements of performance-audience space have great impact on plays and the perceptions of audiences and performers too, for that matter.)

Blocking suggestions. Composition and movement on this stage follow the same usage as in arena staging, with one major exception: *The neutral rear side permits positions similar to those used on the proscenium stage—a pitfall for the inexperienced director because he too readily assumes he is working on a proscenium stage and encourages his actors to take much too frequent frontal positions.* This is catastrophic because it nullifies the function of this type of stage as a fully participative audience ritual and instead assumes the objective-observation function of the proscenium stage. Few experiences are more frustrating than seeing a production blocked on a thrust stage as if on a proscenium stage with little exploitation of the powerful possibilities inherent in the thrust arrangement. "Spin the wheel" and "face out from the center" are the major suggestions here. You must learn to see the acting from all three sides and to encourage actors to open up their illustrations to all three audiences and not to just one. If you follow the principles of organic blocking, as outlined in Chapters 7 through 14, you will have little difficulty in showing a play to a multiple audience.

Here are several additional points to keep in mind when blocking on a thrust-type stage.

Use of perimeter levels. The placing of steps around the perimeter of this stage will aid greatly in achieving variety in stage levels, particularly if two or three steps are employed. Lower steps can be used to deemphasize secondary characters and higher steps can focus strong emphasis on the principals. This is particularly useful in period drama such as Shakespeare and even modern plays such as Shaw's *Saint Joan* or the epic dramas of Brecht such as *Galileo* where the sweep of an entire society is depicted, often hierarchically, and the director can make great use of options (particularly downstage options in the thrust form) that allow for variation in head heights of figures in a composition. Closely related to the use of steps around the perimeter of the main playing platform, is the possibility of using the "moat" that may surround the stage thrust. This area should not be overlooked as a playing space, particularly for "passings through," blocking solutions to show characters in transit from one place to another. With all such peripheral locations, however, be aware that such use may present added challenges for the lighting designer (in terms of lighting the location adequately and minimizing spill into the audience), and you and your lighting colleague together will need to arrive at compromises and workable solutions.

Exploit upstage to downstage movement. Because it is so important in this form not to replicate lateral movement patterns from the proscenium stage, the director must take care to exploit the great potential for upstage to downstage movement in this arrangement. Remember that, for audiences seated "on the side," these movements will, in fact, have a lateral quality (at least more so than for audience members seated directly front and center). This will require that a logic of movement in the space be established that causes movement to flow from upstage to down and back again.

Quick downstage entrance and exit. As already mentioned, this stage form works best when there is a concealed entryway near the far downstage extremity of the playing platform. This vomitory allows for actors to make quick, sudden appearances or fast exits from the playing platform without having to make the sometimes long cross upstage and off that would otherwise be required. This also allows for variety in the structuring of the flow and pattern of entrances and exits. Be aware that the longer entrance and exit patterns through the upstage area can be used in such a way as to have a ritual, formal pattern if so desired (very useful for plays with kings, popes, funeral processions, and the like), while the vomitory option downstage can be ideal for quick or sudden appearances or exits. This quality, almost like a fast cut in film montage, can be particularly useful in a play by Shakespeare or any text where one scene must overlap another in rapid succession.

Remember, the center of the stage becomes the strongest position in this arrangement, because it is equidistant from all parts of an audience. You must learn to play the full limits of the stage space in order to enhance the climactic compositions when characters are finally brought together.

Forestage-Proscenium and End Stages

Although other terms might be used to describe these stages, *forestage-proscenium* and *end stage* are used here because they tell the way in which these forms have come about in recent years through joining proscenium conventions with those of the open-thrust stage. Nominally, the forestage-proscenium is a raised proscenium stage with a forestage erected in front of it—the same stage that was used in seventeenth-, eighteenth-, and nineteenth-century theatres when the pure proscenium stage was in its making. For this reason, forestage-proscenium might be regarded as a return to the past, because it again moves the primary playing area forward of the proscenium line after nearly 300 years of watching the play gradually retreat behind that line. However, it is closer to the fact to see it as a natural evolution from the pure proscenium stage.

As a modified proscenium stage, then, audiences will sit in the frontal position. The forestage-proscenium is an adapted form, for it is neither fish nor fowl but has elements of both. It has undoubtedly come back into use in an attempt to retain the scenic aspect of the proscenium, yet bring the actor closer to the audience.

The conventions on this stage are therefore obvious: The proscenium wall conceals the use of stage rigging for the spectacle of painted scenery, while at the same time actors, who in this convention play largely on the forestage, appear to be more sculpturelike and more three-dimensional to audiences. The proscenium arch itself is much reduced in value and may, by the judicious use of masking scenic pieces, appear to be blocked off entirely. A stage that seems to be very deep can thus be achieved, similar in kind, although not in dimension, to those of the late eighteenth and early nineteenth centuries, such as New York's Bowery Theatre with a phenomenal depth of 128 feet. The baroque scenic tradition can thus continue in full force on this stage, and the acting can be done both behind the arch and in front of it, allowing a director to greatly expand or contract his stage as he may see fit.

If the forestage is deep enough, this stage can also be brought close to the open-thrust aesthetic, for architectural back walls and curtained walls can shut off the upstage area. The only problem is the largely frontal audience. The use of additional projections from the forestage, which places the actor farther out in the audience, can help to remedy this situation, although such a stage can never achieve the same feeling provided by the pure open-thrust form.

Related to the forestage-proscenium form, but different still, is an arrangement frequently called an "end stage," probably because it features the playing space at one end or side of a contiguous space. This is similar to the forestage-proscenium arrangement, but there is no proscenium wall or arch. This arrangement features a playing space either raised on a platform or more or less flat on the floor equal to the first row of the audience. In this form, the audience and performers inhabit the same envelope of space because there is no proscenium wall to provide a division. This arrangement has proved a popular and utilitarian arrangement, particularly for "found spaces," that is, for theatres set up in spaces not originally built as theatres, such as warehouses, ballrooms, gymnasiums, and the like. Perhaps as a result of the connection to found space and the types of collectives who work in found spaces, this arrangement is often to be seen as the performing venue of avant-garde theatre and dance companies. One quality of such spaces that appeals to many is, in fact, its inherent *ad hoc* or improvised aspect, a quality of an artistic kind of roughness that can work very well for some kinds of theatre. In terms of family resemblance, however, it's important to recognize that it resembles the proscenium form in that the audience is all on one side or end, viewing the stage essentially from one angle of vision (rather than three or four sides). It also has some aspects of the thrust stage in that the absence of the division caused by the (here nonexistent) proscenium wall creates an openness and sense of overt theatricality that can be very appropriate for some forms of theatre.

Blocking suggestions. Proscenium and open-thrust blocking procedures must both be employed on these stages because of their combination of frontal and circular presentation, depending on which areas of the stage are in use. Proscenium blocking tends to work better in upstage positions because of the "hearability" factor, which must enter into any consideration of such a large stage space. Low volumes can be employed in extreme downstage positions but may not work at all when a scene is played upstage. Rather than create distorted hearing by raising volumes in the upstage positions and lowering them in downstage positions, the director can adjust the upstage or downstage blocking to meet the needs for volume, thus allowing the actor to concentrate on the dramatic action without worrying about oral projection.

As has been suggested, the spectacle and dramatic value of a full use of the stage space can be very great. The director must therefore learn to use the extremes of the stage from far upstage to far downstage, from far right to far left. The actual physical distance between actors can take on significant meaning when used judiciously. In contrast, the director will also learn to exploit the intimacy of far-downstage positions, which can be collected and tightened by selected lighting for effective presentation of intense dramatic ideas.

EXERCISES

1. *The Crucible* has been played in various productions on several different types of stages, including each of the forms discussed in this chapter. Discuss the following:
   a. Why does this play seem to be open to flexible staging? Do you think Miller conceived of it as a proscenium-style play, or did he deliberately open the structure to other staging possibilities?
   b. What are the advantages and disadvantages of playing *The Crucible* on (1) an arena stage, (2) an open-thrust stage, (3) a forestage-proscenium or end stage?
   c. How would you approach the blocking of *The Crucible* on any of the stages mentioned in (b)?
   d. Which of the stages would you choose? Why?
2. How can you vary the arrangement of the open-thrust stage? What would happen if you thrust the stage too far into the audience by making it much deeper than it is wide?
3. Discuss the differences in the effect the following arena stages would have:
   a. One that is 6 inches below the first audience row
   b. One that is 2 feet below the first audience row
   c. One that is on the level of the first audience row
4. Identify the stages represented in Figure 54. Note that each one is part of a circle with the degree markings representing the size of the audience areas.

FIGURE 54

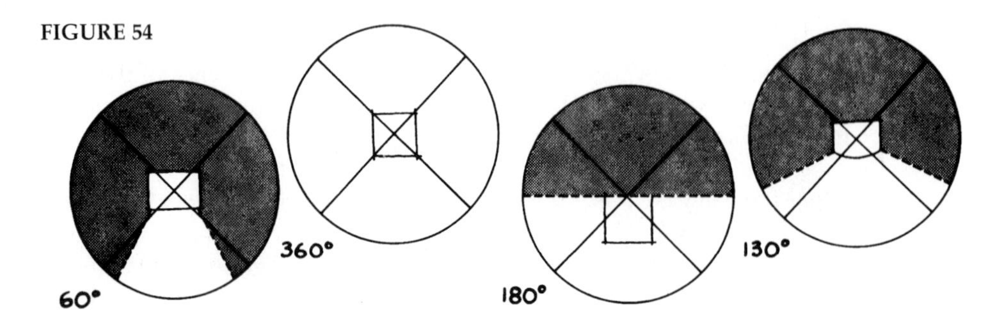

GAME OF VISUAL PERCEPTION: CHOICE OF STAGE (see Chapter 8)

1. What is the type of stage and the position of the audience in each photograph (photos 27 through 34)?
2. How does the three-dimensionality required on the proscenium stage differ from that on the thrust?
3. How is "intimacy" gained in each staging represented in photos 27 through 34?
4. Photo 31 shows a production in the arena form. Analyze what the photo reveals in terms of design and staging.
5. Photo 28 shows a thrust stage in use for a production of Marlowe's *Doctor Faustus.* Analyze the physical relationship of the audience to the stage, particularly how members of the audience would perceive actors standing on this stage. Photo 33 shows the model of a thrust stage design for a modern play, Sam Shepard's *Curse of the Starving Class.* What would be the effect of seeing a modern play like this one on a thrust stage?
6. What is the function of the steps in photo 30?
7. Why are floor treatments a part of a design plan? Ceiling treatments?

PHOTO 27 *Orestes 2.0* (Mee)

PHOTO 28 *Dr. Faustus* (Marlowe)

PHOTO 29 *Antigone* (adaptation, Keystone)

PHOTO 30 *Saint Joan* (Shaw)

PHOTO 31 *The Book of Days* (Wilson)

PHOTO 32 *The Illusion* (Kushner)

PHOTO 33 *Curse of the Starving Class* (Shepard)

PHOTO 34 *The Misanthrope* (Molière)

20

Director's Options

Scenery, Properties, and Lighting

Now that you can see how the director's design function requires some very important decisions about what sort of stage to use in presenting certain plays, you are ready to look at the options open to you in deciding what kind of scenic materials to put on the stage you choose and how to light those materials. It should now be obvious that you can exert important leadership in shaping the direction of a play's physical production.

Again, you must keep in mind that the content of these chapters is not intended to substitute for extensive training in design, but only to point out to you the many paths open in staging a play. The more you know about what can be done, the more inventive and adventurous you will be in producing plays, because reaching audiences with fresh imagery depends on knowing thoroughly the tools with which you work.

Options in Stage Scenery

If you think of scenery only as painted flats and drops, the term can be applied only to the pure proscenium stage and its forestage-proscenium and end stage variants. However, today this meaning is too narrow because the open-thrust and the arena can both use staging pieces that modify acting areas; and although these modifications may be simple, they are nevertheless scenic in concept. The word *scenery* is actually derived from the Greek *skene* and Roman *scaena,* both of which stages had permanent architectural façades before which the actors performed. *Scenery, then, is any device that makes a change in a stage, starting with the stage floor.*

From this point of view, it is obvious that the director and the designer will approach each stage form in terms of its own concept and conventions. *Thus, scenic design is both architecture and painting* and may be both at the same time. Five distinct types of scenery are delineated in the following pages: (1) painted, (2) architectural, (3) painted-architectural, (4) projected, and (5) fractionated.

Painted Scenery

You are probably most familiar with painted scenery, which dates in its continuous use from the sixteenth century. It consists of painted cloth mounted on frames, the type we still see in wing-and-drop settings, box settings, and set pieces (flats, ground rows, etc.) placed at any point on the stage. In its most common use, it is *illusory* in concept, with the intention of making such scenery appear to represent what we see in real life. Thus, it can be either *painted* architecture (interiors and exteriors), *painted* nature (wood scenes, etc.), or combinations of such content. In this sense, painted scenery is two-dimensional, like easel painting; but it is cut into many pieces and placed on the stage in such a way that it gives an audience an illusion of three dimensions, with depth as well as height and width. To heighten this three-dimensional effect, in its early usage the stage floor was raked upward from front to rear, thus forcing the perspective. As you can obviously see, such scenery required stage machinery (lines, pulleys, etc.) both for hanging it and moving it. Consequently, changeable scenery is associated with the proscenium stage, where *the proscenium wall is used to conceal all the machinery* necessary to make quick and effective shifts from one represented reality to another.

The fact that this convention would have such a long life in the theatre—a life unbroken until now—is not difficult to understand. The development of drama has been a gradual approach toward photographic reproduction—an approach that reached its peak in the latter part of the nineteenth century—and in this development the statement of more and more exact places became part of the stage aesthetic. The new staging (that is, the staging as it evolved in the last half of the twentieth century) has been a revolt against photographic reproduction of exact places, a revolt that has led to new stages and new scenic concepts.

The nineteenth- and twentieth-century box setting is painted scenery carried to the extreme of representation: the photographic reproduction of an interior. The painted walls and ceiling are made to look like the real thing in both color and texture; and the actual placement of the flats and jogs, slanted walls, slanted ceilings, exterior views placed outside windows and doors, and so on, are all intended to increase the architectural illusion to a point where it is difficult to believe that one is not looking into a real room. Yet, of course, it is all make-believe, with the intention of fooling an audience. The adding of architectural pieces to these painted flats—such as real window frames, door frames and doors, wood molding, and wood-beam ceilings—increases the illusion of reality.

If the director is thoroughly aware of the history of this tradition and of its full exploitative possibilities, he can understand more readily the departures from this convention, and he will also have a clearer idea of how and when to use such scenery in designing productions.

Architectural Scenery

Architectural scenery, as defined here, includes not only permanently built structures, such as the rear wall of an open-thrust stage, but also all structures that move upward from the flat stage floor and create a three-dimensional mass. As pointed out in Chapter 19 in the discussion on open-thrust stages, the rear wall of such stages *may be* part of the permanent architecture, like the altars in many churches, and arranged in such a way that it can serve a large body of plays as did the Elizabethan rear wall. It does not need to be a flat surface, but can be projected onto the stage, because the sides are open to the side audiences, as in Tanya Moiseiwitch's design for the stage at the Stratford (Ontario) Festival Theatre. Thus, the wall may contain not only doors for entrances but also raised portions and approaching steps. The wall is, nevertheless, a permanent façade. Although a few theatres have been built in this manner, it is unlikely that this will become the most popular of stage devices. However, the learning director must become fully aware of its concept and exploitative possibilities if he is to understand the nature of flexible stages.

Equally important as a concept is creating architecture through the use of platforms and steps. The baroque scenic tradition developed the concept of movable wings and drops and, later, walls and ceilings; the "new" staging of the twentieth century added the development of the stage floor, not as a painted or raked plane, which had been a convention for 300 years, but *as an architectural mass.* Platforms and steps are always fabricated with hollow interiors; but the fact remains that they occupy real space, which makes them architectural in every sense of the word. The new concept, then, is of a three-dimensional stage with the capability of making the actor *visible to the audience at any level* within the rectangular prism or cube that composes the stage area. To know the values of such dramatic capabilities is to extend tremendously the director's use of the stage.

Painted-Architectural Scenery

Much of today's staging is a combination of both painted and architectural scenery. This combination has probably come about because today's theatre is transitional with no single established form. Thus, we use what is effective in both types of scenery, rarely using pure forms. However, only through understanding the pure form can the director decide how best to exploit a particular play. A spectator's imagination usually is easily aroused by fresh, dynamic impulses, but it can also be stultified by a too self-conscious use of scenic materials. The process is, as it always is in art, one of selection.

Projected Scenery

Projected scenery has evolved out of the twentieth century's development of electric light and its projection. Designers are still finding new ways of making statements, a fact that indicates that its full range of uses is yet unknown. Among other things, designers have learned the following:

1. Projected scenery can take the place of both architectural and movable scenery as a backing for a scene.
2. Projected scenery can be used simultaneously in direct coordination with movable or architectural scenery when projected on a screen either built into other scenery or mounted in front of it.
3. Motion picture projection as scenery with actors moving in front of it can provide unusual theatrical effects. Some uses have coordinated the actor and such moving scenery, producing the effect of the actor walking into and out of the projected, moving scene.
4. Projected scenery can be changed instantly, and multiple quick changes of location, as in motion pictures, are possible as they never have been previously.
5. Projected scenery lends itself readily to abstractions, increasing the symbolic uses of backgrounds. When multiple, simultaneous projections are used, a montage effect is possible; thus, it can be idea-building.
6. Projected scenery is comparatively very inexpensive to use.

From the preceding list, it would seem that projected scenery has an active future ahead. However, one of the drawbacks of projected scenery is that it imitates too readily the motion picture, and this imitation takes the theatre closer to a form it is trying to escape. Yet, in trying too hard to escape, the theatre may be only bypassing its own destiny, for the future may depend on an even closer liaison between these two forms. Whatever the future of projected scenery may be, a director must be fully aware of the freshness of this scenic option and must learn how and where it can be appropriately employed.

Fractionated Scenery

Fractionated scenery is used here for lack of a better term to describe a popular form of staging that deploys several types of scenic pieces, some connected and some unconnected, with the intention of suggesting a room or other place with a minimum of scenic materials. Thus, such staging may use flats, cut flats (a piece of a wall), screens, platforms, step units, curtains, hanging drapes, suspended flat pieces of practical window frames, ground rows, selected rear backings, skeletal framings, or any other scenic devices.

A procedure used fairly frequently is to place a scenic piece against a skycloth in order to convey a sense of greater space or to give the impression of seeing inside and outside simultaneously. *Fractionated scenery is a direct move away from the representational effect of the box setting and a move toward simplified and abstract staging.* It dominated staging in the 1980s and 1990s.

There is no question about the advantages of this sort of scenic statement, because fractionated scenery possesses the power of releasing audience imagination by forcing it to complete necessary but omitted lines or to interpret and put to use any inherent symbolism that may reside in such fractionations. Therefore, the justification for such staging goes far beyond the practical limits of low-cost production or easy movability of such settings in a multiscene play. Simplified realism of this sort can release the poetry in a play by giving the audience a free-flight experience instead of confining it to prosaic realities.

Fractionated staging can thus employ all the previous scenic options: painted, architectural, painted-architectural, and projected. Its free form may well account for its frequent use in contemporary scenic design.

Minimalism

Minimalism, like fractionated scenery, is used here to describe a form of staging that eliminates painted or projected scenery entirely in favor of a limited use of properties, such as chairs, tables, and so on, placed against a neutral background. The stage space is declared by the use of enhanced lighting. Such staging not only declares specific stage space but it also throws the attention on acting and the enhanced moods of a scene. Such staging has appeared off and on since the 1920s, both as a means of saving money and as an expression of symbolic ideas. Representationalism has thus given way to presentationalism. In the 1990s, minimalist staging was used as a means of focusing explicitly on the acting without distractions of any kind. Dramatic actions and characters are thus given central focus, and place and time are left to the audience's imagination.

Combining Scenery and Stage Choice

This section would not be complete without brief mention of the random options in scenery available to a director on the various stages. Thus, arena and open-thrust stages can use look-through scenery as well as architectural steps and platforms. Painted cloths (drops) can also be stretched *above* these stages to achieve effects similar to the "heavens" in the Elizabethan public theatres, actually the painted underside of the penthouse structure. Not only can drapes or structural materials be suspended from above but they may also be pulled up from the stage floor, thus employing baroque scenery but placing it in a different context than on the proscenium stage. Trap doors can be employed advantageously on these stages as well as on the proscenium stage and its variants to lend a further dimension by implying other "places" beneath the stage. Moving scenery on turntables or tracks parallel to the curtain line can also be employed on the proscenium and forestage-proscenium setups to give the illusion of the actor moving great distances or changing places in transit.

The intention here is by no means to make an exhaustive list of possibilities in the use of scenic ideas on these stages; rather, it is to suggest the scope of designing activity in which a director must become involved. Part III will again consider these options in the discussion on individualization in stage production, but you should keep in mind that the stage as a machine can do anything you want it to do as long as you thoroughly know its limitations. Scenic design as a fresh statement can grow only out of your imaginative use of the broad range of materials available to you. You must study set design in depth if you are to become an effective director.

EXERCISES

1. *The Crucible* has been played on the proscenium stage with (a) highly developed, illusionistic box settings and (b) fractionated scenery made of curtains and screen units. Discuss the effect of each production. Which would you prefer? Why?
2. What colors and textures would you use on painted scenery for *The Crucible*?
3. If you were to stage *The Crucible* with projected scenery, what would you choose for the projections? What would be the effect of such a production?
4. If you were to stage *The Crucible* in an illusionistic manner, what sort of research would be needed to locate the appropriate set properties?
5. Would you use look-through scenery for staging *The Crucible* in arena style? Why or why not?
6. Could you stage *The Crucible* on either the open-thrust or arena stages with set properties made of plain, boxlike cubes two feet high, wide, and deep? What would be the effect? What other geometric forms could be used and what would be their dimensions?

GAME OF VISUAL PERCEPTION: SCENERY (see Chapter 8)

1. What is the function of the scenery in each photograph (photos 35 through 40)?
2. Why is "pictorial" scenery used less frequently in contemporary plays?
3. Can you see the following scenery in the photographs: architectural, painted, and fractionated? Discuss your answers.
4. Can you "see" the three-dimensionality of the scenic devices? Discuss your answers.

PHOTO 35 *Elektra Fragments* (adaptation, Hackett and Krajewska-Wieczorek)

PHOTO 36 *The Divorce Court* (Cervantes)

PHOTO 37 *Dementia* (Fernandez)

PHOTO 38 *Doctor Faustus* (Marlowe)

PHOTO 39 *The Price* (Miller)

PHOTO 40 *Blood Wedding* (Lorca)

Options in Stage Properties

Definition

As Chapter 11 has already pointed out in some detail, there are two kinds of properties used on the stage: (1) set properties, associated closely with the definition of acting space and scenic ideas; and (2) hand properties, actually held in the hand by actors or capable of being held in the hand. Both are extremely important tools for the director because they can determine in a primary way how actors will find their illustrations of dramatic action. To repeat the premise: *Imaginative use of properties, both set and hand, permits the actors to project sense imagery directly to an audience, who then puts that imagery to work in its own imagination.* Because properties are used in such personal and individual ways, the director even more than the designer must give the most careful attention to their selection.

Set Properties

In Chapter 9, on the groundplan, it was emphasized that set properties occupy space and therefore determine a very great deal of what happens in the visible acting areas. The actual selection of a specific set property may be the designer's decision but not before the director and designer have decided *together* how much space such a property will occupy and what its nature, and thus its usability, will be. Carefully selected set properties will delineate the specifics of an obstacle course, which will, in turn, declare emphases in compositions and the nature and kinds of movements. Set properties are often handled by actors because they sit on them, lean over them or against them, walk around them, or sometimes actually move them. They also become animate in certain compositions, and their mass and shape are always factors in this animation. Reread the groundplan section of Chapter 9 and you will appreciate even more, at this point, why the director must make set properties a primary part of his designing vision.

In brief, the obvious functions of set properties are to delineate given circumstances and to provide common uses. In Realistic plays they are invaluable in showing subtle gradations in environments, and in most other plays they provide similar information although not on such a refined scale. Set properties are functional in their common uses as chairs, tables, beds, desks, benches, stools, cabinets, and so forth, but above all, they serve as obstacles in a groundplan to keep characters apart and to make it more difficult for them to reach one another, thus creating activity and illustration. Well-selected properties can greatly stimulate an actor's ideas about illustration.

The options open to a director, then, would consist of quantity (the number of set properties that can actually be used effectively), size, shape, and mobility. (Can they be moved on the stage by an actor, or do they contain inherent movement?) A director also has a choice of real (archaeologically accurate) objects or abstract objects such as geometric forms. Whatever a director decides to do, he will probably select set properties in coordination with the scenery chosen for a particular play, because the design of one will tend to enhance the other.

Hand Properties

Hand properties as an element in design were treated extensively in Chapter 11. To reiterate: *Hand properties are the extension of the actor's arms and hands;* thus, they are subtle tools of illustration, for they possess capabilities of sensory illustration that the hands alone cannot provide. Any director who does not give primary attention to the selection of hand properties is merely ignoring one of the actor's principal tools of illustration.

For this reason, *the final selection is not a designer's decision but a director's, oftentimes in consultation with his actors.* Hand properties can be modified and even changed as actors use them during a rehearsal period; therefore, they should not be set permanently before rehearsals begin. Furthermore, they should be selected in terms of the particular actor who is to use them. Remember: There are no *general* properties, only *specific* ones. A designer cannot possibly be as aware of this fact as can a director, who should regard the choice of such properties as his own particular province and look to their actual selection with the greatest care. Be meticulous! No one else can be except the actor.

In summary, hand properties are occasionally functional in their common uses, provide specific reflections of the given circumstances of the play, enhance the individual actor as an instrument by giving opportunities for fresh illustration other than through the use of the hands, are capable of making light (candles, flashlights) and sound (snapping a book shut), and have inherent mobility (visible liquids, eyeglasses, telephones, automatic weapons, books, flags, fans, etc.). The options open to a director concern type (size, weight, and shape), mobility, archaeological accuracy, and abstraction (use of a stick for a gun, a cane for a sword, etc.).

EXERCISE

Make a list of hand properties for use in Act II of *The Crucible.* What items did you add to the list beyond those specifically called for, such as the doll, chains to tie Proctor, whip, and so on? What can be done with hand properties associated with the fireplace?

GAME OF VISUAL PERCEPTION: PROPERTIES (see Chapter 8)

1. What properties are actually required for each play in photos 41 through 44?
2. How can the hand properties in each staging be used to illustrate dramatic actions?
3. How do the environmental properties create moods?
4. Do the properties "help" the actors communicate dramatic actions? Explain your answer.
5. Which properties are symbolic of place and which ones are symbolic of characters? Do any seem to be intrusions or "laid on"?

PHOTO 41 *Ghosts* (Ibsen)

PHOTO 42 *K2* (Meyers)

PHOTO 43 *Tobacco Road* (adaptation, Kirkland)

PHOTO 44 *School for Wives* (Molière)

Options in Stage Lighting

Director-Designer Relationship

Lighting has become the most important aspect of staging today. As with the design of properties, a director has a primary and personal concern for what happens with stage lighting because *it is not mere illumination but specific illustration of a very subtle sort, the sort that can reach an audience's imagination more quickly and more subliminally than an actor often can.*

In everyday life, we know that light can stimulate delicate psychological feelings that affect us strongly; consequently, light in the theatre can affect us even more intensely because it has been intentionally selected. The director-designer relationship must be a very close one, indeed, because *lighting design is the actual extension of the director's most sensitive and most personal vision.*

The director's training in stage lighting should be extensive because he should not only be able to visualize the scope of lighting but also have a firm technical knowledge of how to achieve what he wants. Lighting designers can, of course, add greatly to the possibilities in any one situation, but unless a director knows this tool firsthand, he will not be able to communicate to a designer what he feels and sees in a play.

Variables in the Problem of Design

However a director goes about acquiring his training in stage lighting, he will most certainly learn a great deal about the following options.

Illumination. The basic function of stage lighting is, of course, to make the actor visible to an audience. At first, this remark may seem to you a simple-minded statement. However, such is not the case, for good illumination on the stage today means not only a large quantity of lighting equipment but also expert use of that equipment to heighten the effects of the actors *in movement.*

The problem is historical. When the English theatre moved indoors at the beginning of the seventeenth century, both actors and audiences illuminated with the same light provided by overhead and sidewall candelabra. Subsequent development in the use of the stage, along with the increased emphasis on illusion in the stage picture, brought about not only a gradual separation of the stage from the house, with separate lighting provided for each, but also eventually the convention of the darkened house. The control of light became increasingly important as candlelight was superceded by oil lamps, which, in turn, were pushed aside in the nineteenth century in favor of gas, which finally gave way to the incandescent lamp. The unusually minute possibilities for control afforded by electricity revolutionized stage lighting practice and provided us with the theories under which we are presently working. However, the basic intention has always been the same—to make the actor readily visible to the audience.

Greater control of light on the stage, however, has not necessarily meant a better theatre experience. "*Hearability*" (an audience's capability of hearing actors), for instance, has a great deal to do with visibility. We have learned that when low lighting is used to achieve certain effects of mood, *the capability of hearing is reduced.* It is not that an audience lip-reads what actors are saying, but more probably that feelings created by such light tend to cloud the hearing (a psychological problem). From another point of view, we know that too much light, now entirely possible because of improved lighting instruments and quantitative control, can reduce visibility; contour in the faces of actors is lost; thus hearing as well as facial projection are reduced. Color has been long used in stage lighting as a technical convention, but we have discovered that it can be very tiring on the eyes, thus reducing both hearing and seeing. From all this, it should be clear that good illumination is not just a matter of turning on lights; it is the result of careful design for the appropriate circumstances of a play. *Selective visibility* is a good phrase for it.

Source considered. One of the remarkable coincidences in the development of the theatre is the invention of the incandescent lamp at approximately the same time as the shift in playwriting to the new style of Naturalism. *Naturalism* means strict verisimilitude to nature, and in the theatre, it meant photographic reproduction. Only electric light made this goal possible. Lifelike sunsets and dawns became possible on the stage, and interior rooms could be lighted with accurate window effects, shadowed corners and ceilings, lamp effects, and lighted entranceways.

When wall switches were turned on, rooms were immediately flooded with light. Chandeliers, wall brackets, lamps, fires flickering in fireplaces, and sunlight and moonlight were the motivating sources of the light, and audiences looked at an appearance of reality and accepted all the logic of the sources within its own sight. Any violations of the logic could be quickly detected and could therefore become distractions. If the lighting design was logical, the audience accepted the *source considered* and took it for granted. In the representational theatre, then, lighting must have all the appearances of accepted motivation because we are familiar with what we see and we believe in its reality.

Source not considered. The wave of Naturalism temporarily sidetracked *the oldest theory of lighting from a nonconsidered source.* Again, at first you might think this theory means merely turning on the lights without specific motivation from lamps, sunlight, and so on, but it can mean much more than that. In contrast to representational light from a source considered, *nonconsidered source* is *presentational light,* or *light as it exists only in the theatre.* A spotlight that obviously comes from a projection booth at the rear of the house and is thrown on an actor is the most obvious example, but in general use, it means that a motivating source for light is unimportant and thus is not considered.

Such light can come from above the actor, with the instrument concealed from the audience and with the intention of providing an illusory effect; but because the light is not motivated from any logical source, it becomes purely conventional. *The actors are merely gathered in the light.* As an audience, we do not worry about where the light comes from—it just comes and we find other values to concern us.

Source not considered is the lighting used on open-thrust and arena stages and frequently on forestage-proscenium and end stages, because parts of the stage picture can be selected from the total possible picture for certain scenes, with the light areas changing from one location to another as various parts of a stage are used. Thus, large stage areas can be cut into small stage areas, and grand scenes and intimate scenes can be played in sequence. The audience accepts the convention and focuses its attention on the dramatic action and not on the appearances of reality.

Composition in lighting. Because stage lighting in modern theory and practice is provided by specific instruments and is not a general illumination from massive sources, the director-designer must be fully aware of the three-dimensional capability of lighting control. Actors and objects can be made highly plastic, with their depth emphasized. You will remember from the experiments in your lighting class that light thrown from the front tends to flatten faces, and that side light and back light will reveal their three-dimensional qualities. By manipulating intensity, direction, and color, the masses on the stage can be made more dynamic and more alive, simply by emphasizing their lines. Good lighting therefore has enormous architectural values.

Color or noncolor. Although there is always a certain amount of color in the electric light emitted from an incandescent lamp or other light sources, the consideration here is whether light should be projected through color media (gelatin or other filtering material) or left in its original state. The American theatre, in contrast to the European theatre, has tended to use color media much more extensively. However, the growing development in repertory programming in the United States (as opposed to the fixed staging of one particular production) has introduced, perhaps out of necessity as it certainly has in European repertory theatres, the nonmedia approach. Because the intention in this chapter is only to show the range of possible exploitation, which direction you go is immaterial as long as you understand the values of both methods of lighting the stage, so that either can be used in designing productions.

The color-media approach. As you have already learned in your lighting classes, white light is composed of red, green, and blue light. It is thus possible to give an appearance of natural light by throwing a combination of these colors, usually highly modified, on the actor. The usual procedure is to create a "living" quality by producing highlights and shadows—warm gelatins from one side, cool ones from the other. As you may know, blended light made of the same color components is often used, usually from the front by means of striplights or soft-light instruments, to soften the mechanical lines of the angular light but not in any way to destroy its effect.

Because the range of possible warm and cool colors can vary greatly, now the director enters directly into the decision making because the light can strongly affect the pigmentary colors in costumes and painted settings. A good lighting designer will, of course, consider what will happen when he sets up such a design. Unless the director is thoroughly aware of his coordinating function in this respect, he may lose the values of the other designs he has carefully nurtured. The worst that can happen is the graying out of pigmentation. Color media create many problems that necessitate an extensive knowledge of light on the part of the director if they are to be met head-on.

Color in light is also a matter of taste, as color choice is in scene design and costuming, because it possesses highly sensuous values. We can see this obviously in motion pictures and television when we contrast the effect produced on us by color film with that of the black-and-white convention. Color can greatly excite the audience, for it works on us much as any sensuous excitation—we vibrate in psychological response.

Perhaps light has played a larger part in declaring the style of Broadway theatre than any other element of design, for much of it has been erotic and sensual in its usage of gold, brown, orange, and amber light, sharply contrasted with heavy blues and purples. Whatever may have brought this usage about, it is apparent that heavy mood effects can be created entirely by the use of light alone and that the mood is in the color. A director must be thoroughly aware of the potential of color media if he is to control the values in lighting and the values in pigmentation of scenery and costumes.

The noncolor approach. The noncolor approach seems to provide more ready control over design as a whole than does the use of color. Although it allows close-to-true colors of costumes and painted scenery to emerge, there is a certain brightness, a certain coolness about unfiltered light that can reduce somewhat the psychological grip of actor-audience contact. Much can be said for the days of candlelight on stage, or even gaslight, because those media were soft light sources that tended to soften actors' faces and bodies. Unfiltered electric light, even with the use of properly adjusted makeup, has a flat, unrelieved quality.

A possible compromise lies in the careful use of softening filters—frosts or filters with a light tinge of pink or amber—or noncolor light softened with border striplights and back lighting. If instruments are property placed to produce excellent compositions, the light can be increased or decreased through these softening filters and the whole design can be brought into harmony.

Movement. You have learned that *changeable scenery* means the creation of new places through the shifting of flats, drapes, borders, wings, wagons, and other elements, sometimes directly before the eyes of an audience. *Changeable lighting* is similar, for lighting is the most flexible of all the elements of design in production with the same capability for instantaneous change that we find in movies. Lighting, then, can be said to have movement—akin to music in its inherent rhythm and sequence.

The obvious examples are in those lighting designs that incorporate sunsets or dawns: We actually see the light move in changing patterns and we realize that what we are watching is not simply a verisimilitude to nature but an artistic representation of natural phenomena. What is less obvious is our acceptance of changeable light to "open up" or "close down" scenes. *Controlled light has spatial properties that permit the declaration of infinite spatial relationships.* Thus, within the same scene, one can create different emphases through the use of lights, moving from one point on the stage to another, from one intensity to another, and from one dominant color to another.

The fade-out and fade-in of lighting provide the same function as the act curtain, although the speed of such changes can be adjusted dramatically with much more diversity than can be arranged with a curtain. One can also cross-fade, moving from one light pattern to another, a convention similar to the wipe of a motion picture. One can follow the actor with a follow spot, thus seeming to move his scenery with him, and one can isolate him completely from others around him and then have him seem to join the group again.

This inherent characteristic of movement in light can provide many theatrical moments, but when improperly used, it can be both self-conscious and distracting. Good stage lighting must seem to happen and must be exactly right for any given moment.

Moods. It is obvious from the previous discussion that light has a very great capability of arousing moods (strong feelings). Moods in lighting are *consequences of light,* the goals of the director-designer. Light can create the bright, happy moods of comedy or the cool, shadowed, dislocated moods of the serious and troubled. It can draw us into the illusory world of representation, it can arouse images of the world of fantasy, or it can make us accept explicitly that we are only in a theatre and that what we see can only take place there. We can be plunged into strange feelings of darkness or inebriated with great quantities of light. We can feel the enormous shock of symbolic color—red is blood, yellow is sunshine, blue is night, brown-orange is heat, and so on. Through the use of projections, we are allowed to sense much more strongly the idea of place without seeing its actual, three-dimensional reality. Light is not just seeing; it is feeling. *As the light goes, so go our feelings. A director is a maker of moods, and light is one of the strongest allies in that making.*

EXERCISES

1. What would be the effects if *The Crucible* were staged with each of the two approaches to lighting—that is: (a) color and (b) noncolor?
2. Is *source* considered a necessary concept in staging *The Crucible*? What sort of instrumentation would you use for an open-thrust staging of this play? What would happen to the flow of the play if you used area lighting, raising it in various areas as they became dominant acting areas and lowering it in others?

GAME OF VISUAL PERCEPTION: LIGHT (see Chapter 8)

1. What is the dramatic force of the well-lighted character in each photograph (photos 45 through 50) when contrasted with the low-lighted character? What happens beyond emphasis?
2. How is mood created through light in each photograph? Picturization?
3. Can you find a photograph elsewhere in the book that illustrates the difference in lighting for a comedy and that for a serious play?
4. Do you see how light actually controls space in each photograph? Does the designer light the place or the space?

PHOTO 45 *The Collection* (Pinter)

PHOTO 46 *Orestes 2.0* (Mee)

PHOTO 47 *The Council of Love* (Panizza)

PHOTO 48 *House of Bernarda Alba* (Lorca)

PHOTO 49 *The Play's the Thing* (Molnar)

PHOTO 50 *Kitty Hawk* (Jenkin)

21

Director's Options

Costume, Makeup, and Sound

Because costume is associated with the moving actor, it has a dynamic and "living" aspect among the visual designs. With this in mind, the director can be much more certain about how he can bring counterpoint into the total design if he first makes choices among the options outlined in Chapters 19 and 20. He will then know how close the costumes will be to the audience, what kind of scenery will be used, what color plan is intended for the settings, and what the lighting potential may be. The director can then make the major decision about how far to stretch or contract any or all of the designs, and costume in particular. The *makeup design* will, of course, have to wait for costume decisions, for it is inherently part of costume and should be designed in close coordination with it. The following discussion of the director's options in these two areas will follow that order.

The final decision that must be made in design coordination is what to do about *sound,* including the use of music. Because of its very important mood-inducing characteristics, sound must wait until the director knows what can be achieved through visual effects. Consequently, the last section of this chapter will be devoted to the director's options in the use of sound.

Options in Costume

Definition

We are so accustomed to thinking of costume as period dress—actors dressing up in clothing much removed from our own time—that we are apt to misinterpret the basic concept of costume. Although it may be defined in several ways, one of the best is to see *costume as live scenery worn by an actor in a particular role in a particular play.* Acting is impersonation, not reality; so is costume, for it is the exterior reflection of the actor's impersonation of the person he is portraying. Just as the playscript is an artificial device because it involves specific selection and arrangement, so also is costume: The designer (or the actor in other eras) has to choose the particular and appropriate dress for a particular circumstance. Costume, therefore, is an integral part of production design, and the director must pay the most careful attention to it.

How strange you probably feel when you try on someone else's clothing—and you likely feel even more self-conscious the more personal the items of clothing because they may actually bear the scent of the owner. What you are feeling is the strength and individuality of the person to whom the clothing belongs. In this sense, costumes *belong* to other people, and the actor's job in his process of impersonation is to make "the dress" belong to the character he creates.

As with the other tools of production, the intention here is to discuss costume, not as training in depth, but only as one of the director's possibilities in production—how a director looks at costume and what his options are in applying it to stage plays. It must be assumed that your overall training will involve an intensive study of clothing as well as costume design and its construction, for only in such a study can you really comprehend the range of this complex craft. Without this knowledge, you will be forced to rely entirely on the work of others, an approach that can be disastrous as far as production idea and unity are concerned.

Capabilities of Costume

A director should be fully aware not only of the nature of costume but also of its capabilities as a tool of production. What follows is a summary of the main ways in which costume can directly affect production.

Given circumstances. Because costume is "scenery on the move," it has the inherent capability of locating the time and place of a play with some accuracy. Thus, it is quite possible to reflect economic circumstances as well as social, political, religious, and climatic aspects of a given environment. In particular, it can bring onto the stage all the rituals in a given circumstance: the synagogue or the church, the evening dress of the military or the diplomatic corps, the pomp and circumstance of court ritual, or the decorations of a country wedding. Dress can tell us immediately where we are and can provide much of the detail affecting a particular environment.

Character and dramatic action. Costume particularizes and individualizes because dress moves with the characterization being made by an actor. Because the personal choice of clothing is a suitable reflection of the individual who wears it, the director-designer must always look for the specific idea, rather than the general. Costume design involves more than ordering dress from a rental agency where the materials are assembled as general items with very little regard paid to individuality because they are to be used over and over again in different ways. Rather, it is the result of the particularization of character, usually with a specific actor who is to play the role in mind. Using the general design of a costume house may be a quick way out of a tight circumstance, but the loss of individuality—of character as it is perceived by the director and designer—is the usual result. The same failure in design is also possible when dress is pulled from a stock wardrobe, unless the director and costumer undertake the crucial and time-consuming problem of design—the search for fresh and individual statements.

What does clothing say? Does it say it in the specific terms of the dramatic action embedded in the playscript? What do the appearances of a character have to do with the actions he takes at the strongest moments of forcing? Does he look different on the outside from what he really is on the inside? These are the questions about the dramatic action that must concern the director. In real life, we find much concealment, much covering up; so, it is logical that we find the same types of concealment in plays. A brutal king might be an elegant dresser, but he also might be a careless one. The convention of dark clothing on a nineteenth-century villain might become light and colorful dress on a contemporary character. *Because dramatic action frequently deals with the opposites of appearances, the intention of costume design may often be simply to surprise an audience into unexpected revelation.* In Edward Albee's *Everything in the Garden,* for example, the suburbanites, who dress casually in disarming sportswear that reflects excellent taste, are also capable of murder when the secrecy of their lives is endangered. *Costume is character* and thus shocks audiences.

Form, color, and texture. Form in costume means silhouette or shape. It is the sum total of the lines of a costume; thus, it is the most basic aspect of a design. The lines may follow the contours of the body; or they may create artificial lines related to the body but nevertheless distinct from body lines; and they may do both at the same time. Thus, we have the changing aspects of the fashion—the relationship of the physical contour of the body to materials in order to alter the exterior line. Because form is basic, it is more general than either color or texture; but without the basic architecture there would be nothing on which to build specifics. Costume begins with form.

As already pointed out in the discussion on scenery and lighting, color has strong sensuous, even sensual, values: We find it exciting, often erotic, and in some way theatrical. As we move in color in real life, so also we move on the stage where there has been no possibility of passing through a black-and-white convention as in movies and television. The director who misses the option of using color knowledgeably in costuming is simply missing an important emphasis in design.

The same can be said of the texture of materials, for without texture and color, we cannot see contrasts or find emphasis. Texture gives boldness and clear statement by providing the necessary exaggeration that makes possible the projection of ideas from the stage. Cloth can vibrate: It can seem to stretch or hold rigid positions; it can lie in soft folds or be pressed in such a way as to seem firm and unyielding; it can have great bulk or be nothing at all. We see and feel texture, just as we see and feel color.

Movement. As already pointed out, costumes are not static; rather, by their nature as coverings for human beings, they are dynamic and movable. Only the few items that seem to be arbitrarily fixed—for example, tights, corsets, metal armor—violate this characteristic. And because costumes move, they convey to viewers the many images inherent in flexibility, images that range from stiffness to complete freedom and flow. In this sense, *a costume lives if the actor inside it is fully aware of how the costume ought to move.*

For this reason, matching footwear to the style of a costume is very important. A body moves as its feet move, because the whole body structure depends on what happens from the ground up. An actor cannot make a costume move in its inherent logic unless he can "walk" the costume properly. A director must have a full awareness of the capabilities of costumes (including wigs and hats) if he is to create the appearance of logical and living clothing on his actors. *Part of his job is to show actors how to wear their dress in the appropriate way.*

Composition. Because costumes are seldom seen alone on the stage, the art of costume design is to foresee all the possible compositions (actor groupings) that might turn up in the staging of a play. The problem is much more complex than arranging scenery because costume is always dynamic—it can move with the actor to any position on the stage—and yet, it must always do its most effective work no matter where it is. To the costume designer, *the effect of the ensemble is as important as the individual costume.* It should also be of prime consideration to the director because his *compositions that reveal the basic action of a play can literally be destroyed, or at least greatly weakened, if the costume ensemble is not properly designed.* This is why the director and costumer must work very closely together.

Composition, in its simplest form, means placing the strong costumes—those striking in color, mass, line, texture—on the dominant characters and designing the dress of the secondary characters to recede away from the primaries, with those of third and fourth importance definitely placed on the fringe of the design. Because color is so powerful as a centering force in composition, it is usually made the springboard in design, with the other design elements following closely on its heels. The color palette—the arrangement of the entire ensemble in gradations of color—thus becomes a significant principle in the technique of costume design.

It is for these reasons that the director must be absolutely certain that his costume designer sees the play as close to his own vision as possible, because the costume designer, like the lighting designer, is an alter ego of the director. Without this parallel viewing, the director has no control over the subtle physicalization of the moves a character makes, because an audience will actually see most gestures and all movement *through* a costume; thus, it should not be a barrier but must be a helpful illuminator. The relationship of the director to the costume designer must be a free and fully creative one.

Mood. Because costume is worn by the moving actor, it is a more intensive and continuous conveyor of mood than either setting or lighting. Our feelings as members of an audience are definitely aroused by costume, even though we are not conscious of how the effect is made (nor should we be). Again, we can see that costume *is* character, for we are led away from the actor and toward character through the particularizing aspects of good costume design; in the end, it is character that moves us. If a costume is stronger than an actor, however, it can readily seem self-conscious and be distracting, a condition that definitely reduces mood possibilities. Costume must be an aid to feeling and not an inhibitor. *Every aspect of costume design can evoke mood: form, color, line, mass, texture, and movement.*

Some Suggested Options in Costume Selection

Overdressing versus underdressing. It should now be clear that the line between overdressing and underdressing is a subtle and delicate one. If a costume is "right," it can do an enormous job in helping an actor; but if it varies too far on either side of the scale, an actor must work *against* his clothes. Finding the right balance depends on successful communication between director and designer.

Neutral dress. *Neutral dress* means literally no costume effect at all—a very difficult possibility in design, because any clothing an actor wears takes on some meaning. Perhaps the dress that would be closest to neutral is the leotard—a thin cover for the actor's body. It can be called neutral because it has no movement of mass in itself—what moves is the actor alone. If all actors in an ensemble wear the same color of leotards, color will not be an individualizing factor in the composition. The actor is thus left free to express his "body idea" without assistance from the amplifying and illusionary effects of costume.

Archaeological clothing. *Archaeological clothing* refers to stage dress that comes very close to the reproduction of the real clothing of any period. At its poorest and least communicative, such dress is actual reproduction; *at its best, it is modified and artistically conceived, although it is still closely related to the basic historical design.*

Clothing worn in modern Realistic plays is usually archaeological, because reproduction or the use of real clothing is one way of gaining verisimilitude. Yet, a director and a designer quickly learn that photographic reproduction will not stimulate imagination in an audience unless such clothing is most carefully selected in terms of its overtones or symbolic values. Modern dress, because it is more subtle than that of other periods, is therefore among the most difficult costume designs to achieve. When the clothing is well selected and arranged, thus becoming costume, it can perform the same function for a modern character as historical costume can for a character in a play of another era. In this sense, Realism is an enemy of costume design because the tendency is for directors to accept reproduction rather than design.

Ritual and rite. Many plays contain actions that revolve around formal ceremonies or deal with characters closely associated with such ceremonies—gods, priests, hangmen, lawyers, warriors, and so on. Because such characters are symbols in everyday life, they must be treated as such on the stage. Just as a director would be extremely careful in reproducing a religious ritual, so he must also exercise expert judgment and care in the design of the dress that illustrates such rituals. In the imaginations of a general audience, the dress becomes the ritual itself.

Fantasy clothing. This refers to that class of plays in which dress must be invented. What do the devils look like in *Doctor Faustus*? What will people wear in the year 2100? What do the fairies wear in *Midsummer Night's Dream*? What does the Alien from Outer Space look like? Children's plays are full of this sort of costume requirement, and many adult plays include abstractions. Without a lively imagination about such costuming, a director cannot make the points he sees in a play. Can he help a designer without doing a design? This question is a real problem.

Summary of costume options. From the preceding discussion, it should now be clear that the director can move in multiple directions in making decisions about design. But instead of searching for historical accuracy, he will probably follow the usual route of adapting historical clothing by finding and reproducing its essence; or he may dress his play in *contemporary modern*—another way of saying modern dress; or he may use the fashions of a period quite different from the one associated with the play. If none of these options seem to fit the bill, he may turn to neutral dress or abstract form. The intention will always be the same, however: to reveal the interior meanings of a play through the outward show.

Rehearsal Techniques

Approaching costume. The rehearsal period is the time of experimentation when an actor searches for and, it is hoped, discovers the character he is trying to play. One of the best aids to his imagination is the "feeling" of a character's dress, because it can show him how the character moves, how he gesticulates, and often, in a detailed way, how he feels. An actor can discover these things because the restrictions of a character's dress may differ sharply from what the actor normally wears in everyday life. *Clothing is the shell of a character, and the actor must discover the qualities and the nature of that shell.*

Rehearsing in the final costume that an actor is to wear can be very helpful, for it is director-actor communication in a very real sense. If you, as director, do not know explicitly how a costume should move, enlist the aid of the costume designer to help you instruct the actors.

Shoes. Because a character's body movement is declared by his feet (how he stands and moves), appropriate footgear worn in rehearsal is of specific help to an actor in devising his characterization. An actor in a Wycherley or Molière comedy should wear the high-heeled shoes he will wear in performance; or, if he is to wear boots or heavy shoes, he should work in them as early as possible. Women should wear high heels if the costume will eventually require them, or sandals if those are the requirement. The actor who feels the effect of the footwear, who lets it work on his imagination, is telling himself much about the person he is trying to play. At first, the footwear will seem awkward and unfamiliar, but this is precisely why it is the very best moment for an actor to discover the new things the footwear does to him and to his characterization. If he makes imaginative discoveries, an actor will forget the difference from his everyday wear because he will have incorporated ideas about how his feet move into his moving character. For this reason, athletic shoes should be banned from rehearsals, unless the character would wear them. *As the shoes go, so goes the body.*

Other dress. Period plays should be rehearsed as soon as possible in the basic costume, which may amount to no more than long skirts, coats, flowing shirts, or head wear. Underpinnings are very important because costumes move on the basis of what is worn beneath them. Restrictions of any kind—an amplified stomach, armor, corsets, tight vests, stiffened garments, and so forth—will tell the actor much about how his character will move. Directors who do not insist on this kind of help early in rehearsals will face actors at dress rehearsals and performance who have not absorbed ideas about the clothing: The actors move, but the clothing does not, or vice versa. Communication is a subtle process, and the director must use every device to help his actors find their characters. Costume is one such device.

EXERCISES

1. If you were to stage *The Crucible* in archaeological clothing, what would be the symbolic meaning of the play? What would it be if you used highly simplified dress—that is, if you followed the lines of historical dress but reduced all decoration to a minimum? What sort of dress would you choose for arena staging? For open-thrust? Would nearness to an audience make a difference?
2. Why would a low-key color palette be a design idea for *The Crucible*? Would you decide to go in that direction? Would there be any difference in this choice when considering proscenium-style or arena-style productions?
3. How would you dress Danforth? How would his dress differ from the other clergy? Would he be more urbane, more sophisticated, more vain? What could you tell us specifically about him through the dress that he wears?
4. How would you dress Proctor in Act IV? What would Elizabeth wear in the same act? What about Tituba? What could you show beyond the specific images of physical torture and deprivation?
5. If you dressed *The Crucible* in dress approaching the archaeological, would your men need wigs? If you decided on a much simpler dress, would Danforth still wear a wig? What would be the minimum treatment of hairstyles?

GAME OF VISUAL PERCEPTION: COSTUME (see Chapter 8)

1. Can you see the line (silhouette) of each costume shown in the photographs (photos 51 through 54)? The texture of the materials employed? The possibilities for animation of the costume?
2. Can you see character-illustration in each costume?
3. Pick out one costume and describe its inherent capabilities for enhancing dramatic moment.
4. Can you see the difference between serious and comic dress?

PHOTO 51 *True Love* (Mee)

PHOTO 52 *True Love* (Mee)

PHOTO 53 *The Wonderful Wizard of Oz* (Skotnicki)

PHOTO 54 *Lady from the Sea* (Ibsen)

Options in Makeup

In today's stage practice, makeup has two significant functions: (1) to assist the statement of an actor's characterization and (2) to counterbalance the effects of stage lighting. Both of these functions fall into the director's hands because the first is closely tied to how he thinks an actor can best illustrate a character, and the second is closely related to the lighting problem. The costume designer is also much interested in makeup because of the good and bad effects that hairstyles (including facial hair) as well as facial coloration have on a costume as a whole; and the lighting designer is interested because the colors and textures of makeup can either complement or seriously hamper his design. Thus, it is up to the director to coordinate all three specific interests as well as those of the actors who not only will be wearing the makeup but also will be executing the actual agreed-upon design.

Stage makeup is the appropriate application of color—pigmentary color, the same as is used in scene painting and costuming—on an actor's skin with the *intention of exaggerating the facial features in order to make them appear specific and emphatic.* The actual design of a makeup depends on how the directional light is used in a particular setup—where it comes from, its color, its intensity. Good makeup is never noticeable to an audience except in those plays where it is used as an obviously stylized device, for it is part of the actor's face and is therefore part of his reality. Consequently, makeup cannot be a laid-on stage tool but must be organic in that it expresses the actor's characterization in the context of the stage lighting. Because it is the director's job to coordinate makeup on a technical level with costume and lighting, the usual procedure is for the director, in consultation with the costume and lighting designers, to design for each character a facial mask—what he looks like—so that this problem is considered systematically. Actors can then execute their own makeup and can be confident of their adjustment in a specific design.

Good makeup exploits given circumstances as a matter of course (time, place, social level, etc.) because they are the outward visual show of a character. The actor asks himself: What do I look like? And this is also the director's question, because *makeup can tell an audience—especially through the use of hair—about the degree of character conformity or nonconformity, about his vanity and his awareness of others, about his sense of personal style.* Makeup provides an audience with its primitive visual idea of a character, the frame of reference from which the dramatic action can emerge. In this sense, *makeup bridges the gap between a character's costume and the physical character in the body of an actor.*

A director's options in makeup design, then, rest primarily on what happens in the lighting and costume designs. The more he understands about lighting, particularly about the specific effects of light colors on pigmentation colors, the easier it will be for him to effect the appropriate coordination. Exercises in a laboratory lighting situation where makeup can be introduced should be of great benefit. Likewise, the more he knows about hairstyles and styling, the better he will be able to coordinate costume effect with character expression: You will therefore need to study hair in its relationship to costume, including basic knowledge of how wigs are constructed and worn effectively.

Good stage makeup is the result of a director's specific seeing, for many possible effects are lost by young directors who look at makeup as a general tool instead of a specific one. Learn to plan designs with the greatest care and with an eye toward theatrical possibilities. We have lost the art of makeup in the modern theatre, not only out of disuse but also out of negligence. With no one usually assigned to design this area of expression, it has been left in the hands of actors who simply cannot see themselves, or with a director who does not assume it is one of his primary coordinating responsibilities.

In brief, makeup expresses character, complements lighting, and exaggerates, emphasizes, or distorts facial structure (through the use of putty or other structural additives). The director can call for historical accuracy in terms of hair fashions, for abstractions such as the use of symbolic colors or designs, for no makeup at all, or for the use of masks. The latter are as much employed in our theatre today as they have been in any theatre of the past with the exception of the Classical Greek (where they were used exclusively), for we have found them extremely useful in expressing symbolic ideas.

EXERCISES

1. What would you suggest for makeup on a proscenium stage for Act IV of *The Crucible* to assist the costumes you devised in Exercise 4 on page 245? On an arena stage?
2. How could a change in makeup for Proctor and Elizabeth between Acts III and IV help the actors and reveal the story?
3. How would the hair of the village girls be designed in Act I?

GAME OF VISUAL PERCEPTION: MAKEUP (see Chapter 8)

1. What is the function of the masks in photos 56 and 57?
2. In what ways would you regard makeup as masklike?
3. Why are masks so dramatic? Can they "create" mood? How do they signal style in a production?
4. Look at other photographs for "straight" makeups you think are effective. What do you think would be the makeup requirements in photo 56?

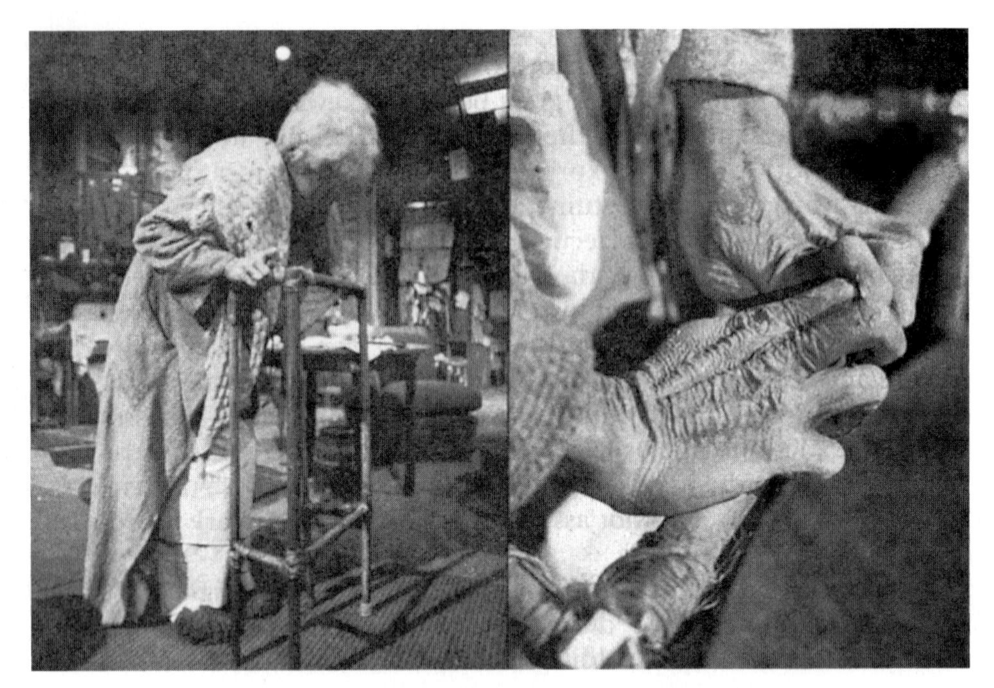

PHOTO 55 *The Effect of Gamma Rays on Man-in-the Moon Marigolds* (Zindel)

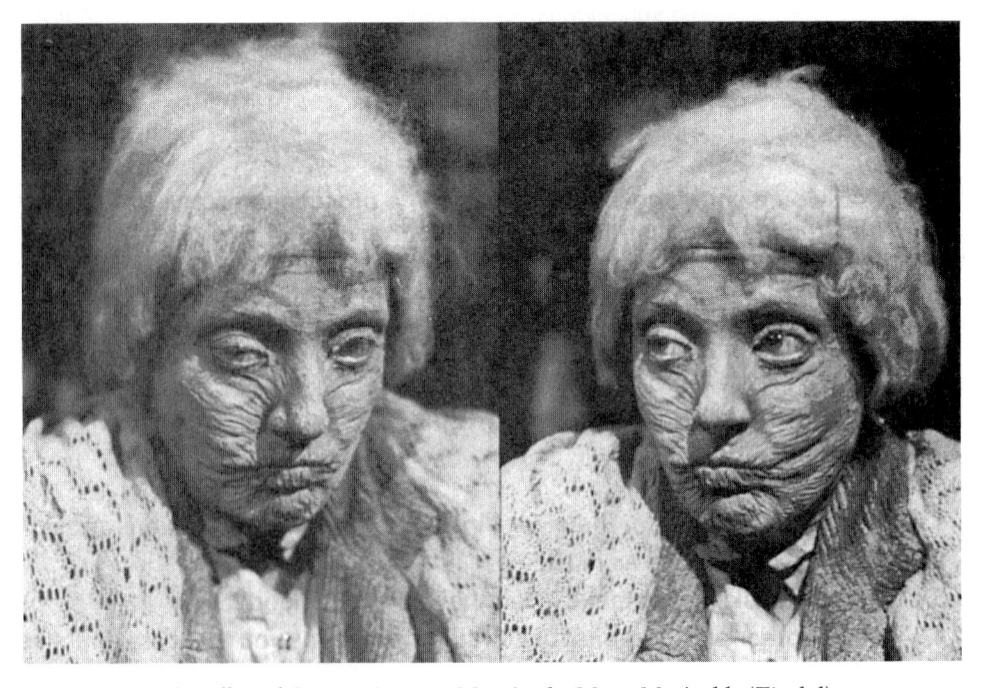

PHOTO 55 *The Effect of Gamma Rays on Man-in-the Moon Marigolds* (Zindel)

PHOTO 57 *Jack or The Submission* (Ionesco)

PHOTO 58 *Beehive* (a composite musical)

Options in Sound

The point has been made several times in this book that the theatre is more of an experience in sound than in sight, for it is the actor's voice that finally moves us, wrenched as it is from the heart and the body. We are, of course, easily excited by the visual, particularly because of its sensual, erotic capabilities; but we are not apt to be so deeply moved by what we see, except in an actor's spontaneous use of gesture and movement in support of vocal sound.

It is not at all surprising, therefore, to find that supplementary sound has been used throughout the history of the theatre. Music has always played a part, sometimes accompanying the actor's voice either directly when he sings or indirectly as background to his speaking—a convention employed on the stage for 2,500 years before it was adopted by motion pictures as one of its primary conventions. Another use of sound—sound effects—has been developed extensively in the Realistic theatre, although certain effects such as thunder or cannon shots have been in use since Elizabethan times or before. And more recently, we encounter the use of comprehensive, complex "soundscapes" made possible by the development of new digital technologies in recording, control, and synthesization. Even more than with background music or sound effects as they have traditionally been used, such soundscapes can provide heard environments for the production in ways only imagined before the development of these new technologies. Nevertheless, the goal remains the same: the use of this aspect of design to enhance the expressive potential of the play and performances in production. *The director who is thoroughly aware of how to exploit sound is well on the way to making total theatre.*

Music

The director is usually his own sound designer because most theatre setups do not include a musician as part of the permanent staff of designers. Even if such a person were included, the coordination would have to be as close as that of the director and lighting designer because *music is as personal and as delicately sensitive in its capacities for arousal of the imagination as is stage light.* Music can often be a distraction rather than the intensification it ought to be. A most meticulous approach is therefore necessary if it is to be used as a helping tool.

The director must be as knowledgeable as possible about music of all kinds and always alert to the potential of different kinds of music for possible use in the theatre. A knowledge of different kinds of music (classical, world, jazz, popular) is one of the most valuable assets a director can have. Broadening and deepening this knowledge not only provides the director with useful knowledge; the actual process of thoughtful listening over a period of many years (the rest of the director's life, in actuality) brings additional benefits. Making this kind of listening a regular part of your life can help develop aural sensitivities to nuances of all kinds in sound, including rhythm, as well as helping the director experience flights of fantasy in ways that enrich the imagination. Thinking about music should be a way of life for a director in the theatre.

Music in the play. Many plays are written with a specific musical requirement—a song, a dance, an instrument—that necessitates its performance on the stage in front of the audience. The problem is a double one: to find the music itself, if none is specifically provided, and to work out a way in which it can be done, either by the performers onstage or by the subterfuge of a substitute offstage. Finding appropriate music is often very difficult, a problem that frequently can be solved only by having the music composed especially for the production in hand. *The latter approach has the merits of free flight on the part of the director because he can work closely in a stimulative way with the composer,* accepting or rejecting what seems right or inappropriate as he would do with a lighting designer. But this approach also has its own inherent problems if it is not to be a distraction.

Music within a play must somehow catch the beat of the particular moment of its use, because the playwright, if he is a good one and not just a maker of entertainments, has included it not as a decorative device but as organic material intended to heighten, intensify, or fill a gap where spoken words cannot do the work. Often, the words of a song will be the key to the musical line the playwright hears. Or he may have suggested titles of specific songs, in which case the director must search them out in order to hear their ideas and rhythms; although he may decide for a number of reasons, including the capability of his actors who are to perform them, to have *similar* music written. Whether he uses something from the music library or has it composed, *the director must be constantly alert to the fact that such insertions in a play are dramatic actions in themselves and must produce the same effect as actions in the dialogue of the play. Music has subtext as well as text.*

The performer, if he is actually to perform the music "live" onstage, is often the key to what can be done, for his talents will determine how far the music can go and still be effective. Actors frequently have musical talents; but whereas an individual's acting capability may be particularly suited to a particular casting, his musical talents may lie far afield from the necessary requirements. To work around this situation, it has been frequent practice to place a live piano or other instrument offstage with the actor dubbing onstage; or to have an actor speak the words of a song, or half speak or half sing them. But these substitutions are poor seconds, for a live musician onstage can provide fine moments if he is truly an actor; however, if he is not, he can be a genuine distraction. Insertions of music into a play are difficult to perform successfully unless the director has solved all the attendant problems.

Background music. *Background music* is the mood music used as background to acting with which you are so familiar in motion pictures and television. In those media, it is firmly established as a convention. But it has not been so used in the theatre since the passing of nineteenth-century melodrama (drama with music) early in the century. Perhaps it lost force when the motion picture took over as the popular entertainment. But more likely, it had served a purpose in the theatre of another age and was abandoned when other conventions for obtaining mood effects were developed—lighting, for instance. Nowadays, it is occasionally used and then usually with a logical offstage source of motivation. In this instance, music may emanate from an offstage band or orchestra that is related to the action in some way or from a single instrument played by one of the characters in the play. *Good dialogue, because it is also good sound, does not need musical support to enhance its mood qualities,* whereas in film-script writing, where dialogue is often secondary to visual effect, the work is done partly by spoken words, partly by the music, and mostly by visual storytelling. *The theatre is a place for sound, but the legitimate play is not musical theatre; its own inherent sound values must be carefully discovered and preserved.*

Music between scenes. This convention has continued in the theatre since Shakespeare's day because it can provide the mood-bridge from one major action to another. *Such bridges can tie diverse sections of plays together, especially when changes of location are involved.* A few seconds' wait while the scene is changed is a very long time in the theatre, and music can help to pass this time by bridging, in the imagination of an audience, the closing mood of one scene and the opening mood of another. One technique used is the overlap: beginning the bridge music a few seconds before the end of one scene and continuing it for a few seconds after the start of the next. Used in this way, the music not only helps the work of transition, but it also acts as relief from the spoken play—a resting moment for the audience. In addition, it gives a sense of quick passage of time. The theatres of the seventeenth and eighteenth centuries, and even much of the nineteenth century, used these bridges to cover the changing of the scenery before the eyes of the audience. But with the use of the act curtain and the darkened theatre as devices for separation between scenes, the convention was continued in the interest of occupying the audience. The use of this convention is, however, a matter of the director's interest and taste, for some directors prefer a "clear" play—one that stands alone on its own organic sound. The strongest argument in favor of bridge music is that the theatre is a sound experience, and the assault on the human ear can be more complex, more arresting, than it can be with only the actor's voice.

The problem of finding appropriate bridge music is as difficult as finding appropriate musical settings for songs in a play, for *the bridges must reflect the beat of the play.* This requirement does not mean that the bridge must be the same beat, for *effective bridges are often counterpoints to a completed scene or even to the play as a whole.* It is the search for counterpoints that encourages the use of modern jazz or other modern music as bridge music in productions of classical drama. The counterpoint is what the director is after, for he wants to shift the audience's mood quickly from one emphasis to another; he may even want his audience to think and feel modern though the material of the play may belong to another age and time. If a director uses classical jazz in Christopher Marlowe's *Doctor Faustus* or a Bach chorale in jazz style in Shaw's *Saint Joan,* an audience can partially sense the modern quality and meaning of each play and be divorced from any preconceptions about it, for the music has been used to jolt the audience out of its expected responses and to give the play a sense of present context.

The possibility of distraction with bridge music can be great. The director must therefore exert every care to be certain he has found the appropriate bridges in terms of the meaning of the production as a whole. Sound is as subtle as light and can easily throw an audience in a wrong direction.

Sound Effects

The use of offstage sound effects, with the exception of thunder and firearms, is largely a convention of the modern Realistic stage. Such effects are an extension of onstage illusion because they give weight and quality to offstage places, even though such places can exist only in the imaginations of an audience. The development of radio broadcasting in the 1920s and 1930s as a total assault on the ear undoubtedly had a good deal to do with the development of sound effects on the stage, for the theory was the same: Excite the imagination through the use of familiar sounds. Thus, productions of Realistic plays often require the arrival or the departure of wagons, horses, cars; rain and thunder effects; crickets and night sounds; sirens, airplane engines, bombs, guns, blasting, cock crowing, clocks, bells, and so on. Closely tied to this use of offstage sound is the use of onstage radios and television sets with their voices and sounds from elsewhere, and the use of onstage telephones, which allow audiences to imagine what the caller has said while the visible actor speaks his part of the communication.

These conventions are still effectively in use, as in such plays as Ionesco's *Rhinoceros,* with its terror-arousing sound of offstage rhinoceroses. The imagination of an audience knows no limits in the hands of a director alert to sound possibilities in the theatre.

Although not nearly as sensitive as music in the effect it will have on an audience, sound effects must be carefully selected in order to evoke clear and precise imagery. Bells of different pitch and volume have different symbolic meanings; the age and style of automobiles can be pictured by the proper selection of sounds; the mood effects of a storm in contrast to a rain can be very different. The problem is one of appropriate selection. The careful director will enhance a production, but the careless one will merely add distraction. Again, a play production is an experience in sound as well as in sight.

"Soundscape" Environments

With the development of digital technologies in sound, it is possible to process sound, music, and sound effects in ways hardly imaginable before these technologies expanded the range of expression possible to achieve in the theatre. This may include the processing of sounds in mutations or transformations. (For example, the reverberations of the murder weapon firing as well as of the doors of a cell block closing may be morphed in such a way that one grows into the other as the production progresses.) Other examples: a blend of music and electronic sound effects melded into a sound environment that is akin to light in its seamless presence and expressive potential. Even the actor's speaking voice can be involved in expressive strategies making use of digital processing. For example, the real-time continuous alteration of an actor's speaking voice, including its timbre and timing, can now be manipulated. (In a production of Ionesco's *Macbett,* for example, the witches may speak, through wireless microphones and digital sound processing, in ways not possible to achieve with the unaided human voice; sounds for these creatures can be achieved that are truly of another dimension of reality.) The director should be aware of developments in this continually evolving area of technology and consider ways they might be used in the theatre. And, as with all aspects of design, they should be used not as ends in themselves, but for the way they can extend the expressive potential of the production.

Sound Equipment

The director must be thoroughly familiar with the use of all sorts of sound equipment. Depending on how much design or technical support is available to the director in a given situation, he may actually create his own tape or compact disc for use in rehearsal or production. The director should be familiar with ways to transfer music and effects from sources to either tape or compact disc, including ways to access the various cues instantaneously in rehearsal or performance. Whether this involves cutting and splicing tape or "burning" compact discs for a particular production, the director should be equipped with the knowledge and experience to provide sound for a production if the circumstances are such that there is not a collaborator in this very important area of production. He should also be familiar with the capabilities of speakers and their offstage or onstage placement to achieve the best effects. Finally, he must always supervise the setting of the volumes himself in order to bring the electronic sound into balance with actors' voices. The fidelity of sound reproduction is an essential in the theatre of our time when excellent equipment is readily available.

EXERCISES

1. Each member of the class brings in his or her choices in music to use in the production of the play. Discuss each person's choices.
2. Would the use of bridge music increase the effect of the play? If so, what would you choose as music?
3. What sound effects are needed for *The Crucible*? Would you use live or recorded sound?

22 Helping Audiences Receive a Play

Responsibility to Audiences

It is the audience that really matters, not just what you have created on the stage. They are not just a bunch of lunks sitting out there waiting to be entertained but an active, alive group of imaginations ready to receive. It should now be clear to you that *a director's primary field of action is multiple communication,* first to his actors and designers, and then, through the imagery they create and he helps to select, to his audience. The actors and designers are his media, and only through them will his *vision* of a play take shape and be able to reach others. A play is not complete until an audience acts on what the playmaker has made.

Do you understand what an audience is and how it works on a play? Most people who choose to go to plays do so not because of the talents involved in the production but because they love the energy and vitality of live actors, and they enjoy being in a group experience with those actors with nothing inhibiting the reciprocity between them. As one great actor, Liv Ullman, says, from the actor's point of view, "It is the sense of freedom that comes in the silence and laughter from the audience." The craftsmen have all done their work with commitment, and out of this has come something fresh, whether drama or comedy—a living, breathing, changing experience the audience may remember all their lives. Don't cheat them. It is up to you.

Motion pictures have always done most of the work for audiences by holding their attention through continuous changes of environments, long shots, close-ups, and multiple scene changes. To study a motion picture in detail involves not only seeing it in general but also seeing it specifically by counting its multiple scene and camera changes. D. W. Griffith, an early giant in moviemaking, revolutionalized the whole process with his Civil War epic, *Birth of a Nation,* in 1915, by joining together (editing) nearly 1,500 such changes, instead of stopping, placing the camera, and starting it again in a new location after a change in scene, as had been the usual method in story films.

An orchestra or pianist *in each theatre* provided musical backgrounds for these silent films, as they had for stage productions since the eighteenth century. But when sound came along, a film could combine seeing and hearing simultaneously with a continuous sound track, not just behind actors' dialogue but as a complicated score of both musical and sound effects. Consequently, motion picture audiences could be mesmerized by this continuous attack and did little on their own during the course of a film.

Far more is required of a theatre audience because each individual in the group must fill in imaginatively all the spaces suggested by the actors and the staging. This is the game: freeing the imagination.

A director should get in the habit of thinking not about *an* audience or *the* audience but *with* an audience, for out there is a collection of individuals who receive a play and "work" with it, each from his or her own perspective, mind, and spirit. It is the quality of an audience that makes the reception of a play possible at several levels. Listen again to Hamlet's "Speech to the Players" and note what Shakespeare thinks about actors who ruin his plays. It is the playwright in him who talks. The speech is addressed to actors, but it contains many warning signs for the director.

> O, it offends me to the soul to hear a robustious periwig-pated fellow tear a passion to tatters, to very rags, to split the ears of the groundlings, who for the most part are capable of nothing but inexplicable dumbshows and noise. I would have such a fellow whipped. . . . Now this overdone, or come tardy off, though it make the unskilful laugh, cannot but make the judicious grieve; the censure of the which one must in your allowance o'erweigh a whole theatre of others.

To see an audience as a dynamic part of play production, a director must be alert to the full process: *A playwright imagines an improvisation and gives it form through his use of given circumstances, dialogue, dramatic action, characters, idea, moods, tempos; a director then reimagines and recaptures the improvisation; he then helps the actors and designers to discover the improvisation he sees and feels in the way he sees and feels it, and to re-create it through themselves, thus giving it intensive personal life. If the images they create are strong enough and appropriate enough, the improvisation will be projected in such a way that viewers can receive it and act on it by reimprovising what they have seen and heard in their own terms (vicarious experience).*

Thus, a play is not an object transferred in a direct way but a series of improvisations capable of producing images, and consequently strong feelings. In this sense, it can be said that a *play hovers in space between the stage* (playwright, director, actors, designers) *and the audience,* with the latter receiving it only if it has been released in terms the audience can understand (see Figure 55).

Audience Spaces and Capabilities

As you learned in earlier chapters, a director has a number of options in the choice of stage for his productions, with each type of stage having specific characteristics. But you must also be aware that the sort of communication described previously can be seriously hampered by audience locations in reference to such stages. The gulf of a wide apron, an orchestra pit, or a very large house, for instance, reduces all of this reciprocal communication proportionally—the greater the actual distance,

FIGURE 55

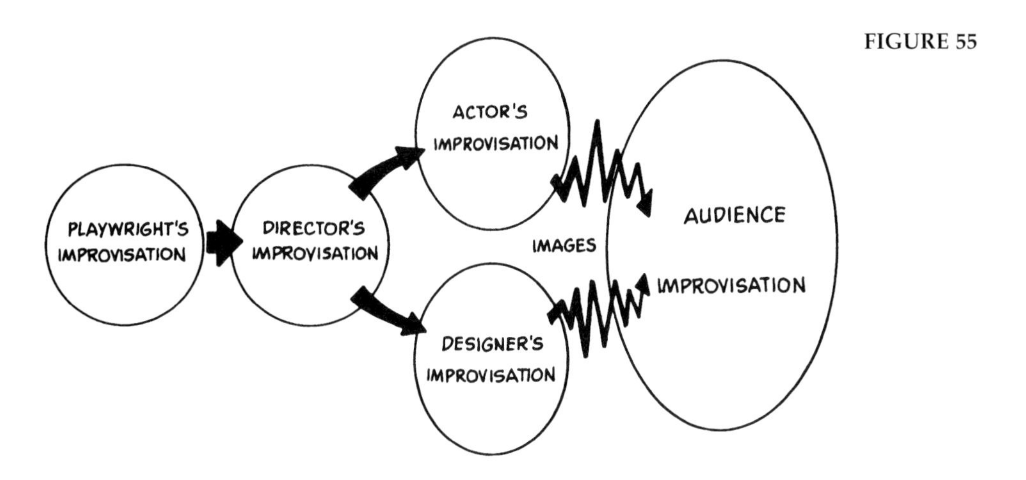

the more difficult the reciprocation. An audience seated in the balcony simply does not experience the play at the same level of intensity as do those sitting close to the stage. This fact is reflected in the various ticket prices for different parts of a playhouse: One gets the kind of play one pays for. A theatre in a democracy, then, really ought to be a small playhouse, not a large one built for the purpose of getting everyone inside who wants to come.

In another sense, a member of an audience can unfairly blame a production and those who have made it because he is totally unaware that he is incapable of receiving it, despite the fact that it may have been perfectly delivered. Mature plays are stories "told" to an audience, and to assume that they are going to reach everyone at all ages and with all backgrounds is assuming far too much. If someone in the audience cannot hear a play well, it may not be because of poor delivery by the actors or because the dialogue is difficult as language, but because that person is not mature enough or experienced enough to comprehend its content. The individual may understand the superficial elements but not the complexities.

Often, plays that may look utterly simple in their reading—*Oedipus Rex* or *The Bacchae,* for instance—can be most complex at their cores. Hearing, then, involves audience capabilities as well as director-actor capabilities. But with comprehension pushed aside, it is quite possible that audiences have lost the "knack of hearing" in the live theatre of our time because of the visual onslaughts of television and motion pictures. The use of electronic amplification in Broadway musicals tells us much about the loss of the human voice in the live theatre.

The Director as Audience

Although the director's primary job of communication is to get through to the actors, you have now reached the point where you should be able to understand the director's second job: to be the eyes and ears for an audience. This second important function of the director is being mentioned only now not because it is less significant than the other but for fear you would see this sort of work as the director's primary job and would therefore fail to understand that if you do not recognize the actors as media, you cannot get through to the audience at all. Arousing the appropriate dramatic action in a group of actors is a very difficult process, and you must know thoroughly how that process works before you can judge the quality of what is released to the audience's improvisational sense. Only now are you ready to consider this second major function of the director: *judging the effectiveness of the transfer.*

It is precisely at the point of transfer where the director performs a primary critical function for the audience, because now he is concerned not just with getting across the footlights but with *the appropriateness and effectiveness of the thing being transferred.* Is it the right statement? Is it intensive enough? Is it completely believable? Is the reciprocation between the characters of the desired sort? Is it moving? Or, if the play is a comedy, does it provoke laughter? What is the audience forced to do? Has it been put off balance? Will its curiosity and attention be maintained at a high level? Can it receive the ideas and images as presented? These are only a few of the dozens of critical questions that a director must ask himself of which the sum total will be: *Does it work?* In other words, the director is so much the eyes and ears of an audience that his responses should forecast those of an actual audience. As he responds, so will the audience.

What a terrifying responsibility it is to be the monitor of success for a group of creative people, each one hoping to show himself to his best possible advantage. After being immersed in the enormous detail of rehearsing a play day after day for several weeks, a director must set himself apart—that is, he must become objective about the subjective creation in order to examine what he and the others have made.

So begins the critical function of *selection.* Some professional directors would say that this is their primary work, that because professional actors know how to act and how to do their homework (bringing in something to look at), the director's job is mostly that of selecting the best that can be provided or of suggesting ways of playing scenes that will improve the selection. However, such a procedure will not work with learning actors, for so much more must be done to make the acting effective. It is also doubtful that even competent professional actors can find the *appropriate* action in a play without a good deal of director-actor communication regarding the contents of a playscript and the emphasis a director wants to give it. No matter what level of actors a director may be working with, the final question is always the same for a failing scene: Why does it not work?

Here begins the diagnostic process that must be highly developed in every director: discerning why a scene fails and then, like a doctor, prescribing a remedy. The process goes on continuously throughout a rehearsal period and particularly in the closing days: the process of judging the product and selecting what works from what does not, and all this based on whether the director, as the eyes and ears of the audience, responds favorably or not. Somehow, a director must be moved to laughter or to strong feelings in the spirit of whatever a play requires as he watches a run-through; if he does not react so, he will probably find that his potential audience will also respond negatively. This is why diagnostic criticism is so important to the learning director.

How to be objective, then, about your own work (the total product you see and hear on the stage) is a state of mind and feeling. The critic in you may take a long time to develop, for many young directors cannot make the jump readily from the inner to the outer look. Yet, jump you must if you are to evaluate what you are doing as a director. At best, you are the patient at the same time you are the doctor.

Major Project 2

Designing and Directing Your Own Production

You are now ready to undertake the difficult process of making a synthesis—*something new.* It will be "new" because it goes beyond simple coordination of the parts and involves *your personal selection* of the pieces in *appropriate amounts.*

In working out this project, *you will do all the designs completely by yourself, because every learning director must discover firsthand the complex problems facing designers in the various areas.* Later, at the end of Part III, you will learn how to work with designers. But at this point, you must learn all you can about the processes of design. In addition, as you do this project, you will be debating with yourself the procedures you would use if you had designers. You must learn how to free the design part of yourself, which is subjective by nature, so that you can take an objective view of what you are putting together in your synthesis. *You must free yourself before you can free others!*

Practicing Fully Designed Play Production

If you have had sufficient formal training in all the design areas, as you should have had by now if that training has accompanied your instruction in directing, and if you have done many of the exercises in Part II on *The Crucible* or another study play, you should be in a good position to undertake a directing-design project *on your own.* As was suggested earlier, although you may sooner or later work with designers, *a director-in-training must go through the full process of design a few times by himself; that is, he must do all the designs in order to understand the concept of synthesis.* The content of this brief section, then, is devoted to a step-by-step process of designing your own production.

PROJECT A: SELF-EVALUATION IN THE DESIGN PROCESS

1. Before you begin work on a live production, you should practice coordination and synthesis in visual design and sound design by doing a project specifically with that focus. The class should choose a one-act play (perhaps the one studied in Part I) and observe the following rules:
   a. Each student should do all the work alone and without advice or consultation of any kind. Remember that this project is a test of your imagination and skills.
   b. Follow the procedures outlined in the previous sections concerning coordination in Chapters 14, 17, and 18.
   c. Prepare your designs with a specific proscenium stage (or classroom modification thereof) in mind, for that is the type of stage you should understand best through your work in Part II.
   d. Do only Realistic design—that is, designs extracted directly from what you see about you in everyday life, although you may use fractionated scenery rather than a box setting if you prefer to do so.
   e. Make design plots in all six areas: (1) setting, including groundplan and an elevation sketch *in color;* (2) properties, both set and hand; (3) lighting; (4) makeup; (5) costume; and (6) sound. Make all set drawings to scale and do renderings of costumes, makeup, and so on, in color. Make complete lists of all materials required.
   f. Be accurate, be neat, and be comprehensive.
2. When Exercise 1 has been completed, you are ready to make a class evaluation of what has been accomplished. Compare the individual projects and note specific differences. Each area of design should at first be treated separately but always with an eye to how it relates to other areas. The focus of the discussion should be placed on two primary points: freshness of the ideas presented in the designs and the problems of coordination. Having everyone design the same play has the definite advantage of showing you where you stand in the development of your capabilities in designing. Therefore, each member of the class should evaluate the following:
   a. What is my present capability as a designer in each design area?
   b. How can I develop my skills in each of the weak areas?
   c. What is my comprehension of the principles of coordination and synthesis?
3. The class should now *review the entire process of production in as detailed a way as possible, including all of the concepts and approaches outlined in this book up to now.* You should give particular emphasis to the functions of play-analysis and to the relationship between the director and actors. Intensive discussions of acting are most valuable at this point, particularly if the emphasis is placed on methods of communication. The problem of design can also be given emphasis by encouraging students in the class who are specializing in design to discuss the ways in which they work and the kinds of communication that get through to them.

PROJECT B: YOUR OWN PRODUCTION

1. You are now ready to do the major project: designing and staging (with the help of your cast) a Realistic one-act play of your own choice. A one-act play is suggested because it will still provide you enormous opportunities without getting mired in the difficulties of a long play. And Realism should still be the style of your choice because you have not yet studied the problems of departures from Realism as discussed in

Part III. Perhaps you may wish to undertake a "new" play written by one of your fellow students. Much can be learned from such collaborations that will prepare you for the big project at the end of Part III. But be certain the play is Realistic in style.

2. The production should also be confined to the Realistic style, although you may now wish to experiment on an open-thrust or arena stage. *Minimum staging* provides the full opportunity of handling actors in the unity of a complete play without introducing the complications of full settings and costumes. If possible for this project, minimum lighting and sound equipment might be employed, thus giving you the opportunity of putting to work your lighting, sound, and makeup designs. If hand-property substitutes can be found, this design can also be fully used. Costumes should be whatever the actors can provide after close consultation with you. Minimum staging permits a good basic production experience without the complications of set and costume building.
3. A detailed preparation, including the *play-analysis and all the designs, together with the list of materials needed,* should be submitted for approval to your instructor in advance of the rehearsals. You should then cast your own play, if possible, and proceed with production.

EVALUATION

After the completion of Project B, a thorough evaluation of your work should be made, considering the following points:

1. The Playscript
   a. Comprehension of the dramatic action
   b. Understanding of unit divisions as illustrated in the playing
   c. Sensitivity to moods and tempos
2. Design Areas
   a. Validity of design ideas, with each design examined separately
   b. Ingenuity in the designs
   c. Skill in execution (shop experience in technical skills)
   d. Leadership ability in handling a work crew
3. Acting Area
   a. Achievement of an exciting choreographic pattern (composition, picturization, movement)
   b. Skill in communication (achievement of reciprocation)
   c. Development of characterization
   d. Achievement of "violence level" and climaxes
   e. Performance of the text (the "oral" play)
4. Tone Achievement
   a. Accomplishment of mood goal

Part III

Interpretation

A Matter of Style

I told you my belief in the Renaissance of the Art of the Theatre was based in my belief in the Renaissance of the stage-director, and that when he had understood the right use of actors, scene, costume, lighting, and dance, and by means of these had mastered the crafts of interpretation, he would then gradually acquire the mastery of the action, line, colour, rhythm, and words, this last strength developing out of all the rest. . . .

Then I said the Art of the Theatre would have won back its right, and its work would stand self-reliant as a creative art, and no longer as an interpretative craft.

—Gordon Craig, "The Art of the Theatre"

23

Style Is Individual Expression

You are now ready to puruse the second part of this text (see paragraph 2 of Chapter 1), the very heart of play directing: the nature of style in a playscript and how you can individualize a play on stage. Chapters 1 through 22 have given you the basic tools of directing, and now you are ready to make a play come alive by seeing more deeply into its many workings and how you can shape them in your own individual way.

When New York's Theatre Guild was first being put together back in the early 1920s, the people who set it up—Lawrence Langner (businessman), Philip Moeller (director), Augustin Duncan (director), Lee Simonson (designer), Helen Westly (actor), Rollo Peters (actor), and very shortly thereafter, Theresa Helburn (manager, playreader, director)—saw their primary mission as that of turning "plays that mattered" into first-rate entertainments. In other words, they saw the paradox of theatre: It is intended to entertain, but it is also intended to move people's minds and feelings. To them, this was what was new and refreshing about their plan, because they saw an audience "out there" that was starved for good theatre. As the years went by, they proved their premise many times over, not only changing the face of the theatre on Broadway but also setting a pattern for resident professional theatre and educational theatre in colleges and universities across the United States.

"Theatre that matters" is the premise of this book. Moving audiences is partly leading them, with significant plays, into paths and levels they have either not previously experienced or not recently explored. Theatre may be a big laugh, but it can also be a chuckle, a smile, or, on the other hand, a deep concern, an ache, a tear, a gasp—all so deeply satisfying one never forgets the experience but keeps it on the edge of memory like a dream that will never fade. This part of the book is all about how to do this, all about producing plays that matter and *how to make them "your own."*

Form and Content

Up to this point, the discussions of play-analysis and staging have concentrated on the two basic elements of all the arts: form and content. For the purposes of this book, *form* is defined as the shape and structure of something, whereas *content* is the material being shaped. These terms were not used in earlier discussions because it was best to define *structure* and *material* in a more intertwined way without drawing hard lines of distinction or attaching labels. Moreover, it was assumed that you would only be baffled by this labeling and could best discover their meanings in the process of doing. You now have enough background to differentiate the meanings of these words and to see how they apply to directing. Understanding them is very important in defining the concept of style.

The study of play structure in Chapters 3 through 6 examined the *form* of a playscript, breaking the play-analysis into six pieces: given circumstances, dialogue, dramatic action, characters, ideas, and rhythmic beats (tempos and moods). In this way, you are examining the entire *dramatic content* of the play. The content was thus revealed through an analysis of form. Likewise, when you studied the process of stage production, you examined the form of staging through the six visual tools: groundplan, composition, gesture, improvisation with objects, picturization, and movement; the oral tools: speaking the subtext, speaking the text, decorum in speech, and projection; and the stage tools of the stage, scenery, properties, lighting, costume, makeup, and sound. When all of these elements of form in staging are employed appropriately, one has a *theatrical content.* Thus, form and content exist in staging as well as in the written play. The major point about form is that although content cannot be revealed without it, form is still *general,* rather than a specific statement of content.

Style

Style is what makes form individual and specific. The purpose of Part III is to help you specifically pin down style in your awareness so that you can see the possibilities in both playscripts and their production on an entirely new and different level. You probably remember high school performances that were dull and boring although you may have responded favorably, as did the parents present, out of loyalty and a sense of belonging. Occasionally, something clicked and held your attention. That something was probably brought about through style. The college productions you see are apt to hold your attention more continuously because many directors and designers working at that level know how to present a play with style, and they have the actors and staging resources to make it possible. Successful professional productions are marked by their individuality—their style—and it is the style that is discussed by everyone, including the critics, when they talk about such productions, whether they know what style is or not.

Audiences always respond to individualization because subtleties move them, whereas general statements do not. The main problem, therefore, is how to elevate the generality of form into the individuality of style. Part III tries to answer this problem by showing you how to *recognize style in a playscript* and then how to *make a style-analysis.* The discussion then turns to production, with the intention of showing you how the director is a stylist and how he makes style in play production. Exercises are included in some of the chapters, some of them based on new plays and some on dramas of other ages, all leading to Major Project 3: directing a full-length play with designers.

As you will note, many of the examples of Part III are drawn from significant historical and modern plays on the assumption that at this point you have a fairly good background of dramatic literature. You should view Part III, then, as advanced study in directing, although you will not not be able to comprehend the content unless you have worked through Parts I and II with attention and care and you have accumulated some experience from the live directing projects suggested in Part II.

It is here the hard work begins. Many young directors do not progress much beyond the directing level of Part II because they are too eager to get into play production and do not realize that there is still much preparatory work to be done. You will note that Part III ranges much more widely than the previous parts of this book, and you will thus need to do a great deal of thinking and talking about it. *If you want to be a good director instead of a merely adequate one,* you will have to give close attention to the many special studies outlined in the following chapters, because *successful directors are stylists who make things of their own.*

What Is Style?

It is easy to recognize form, but style is much more difficult to delineate because we perceive it on an emotional level without being conscious of what we are really seeing until we *make it conscious.* In addition, our recognition of a style often depends on comparison—namely, experience with many different objects in the same category. We all know what an automobile is when we see one because that is form; we can easily tell the obvious differences among motor vehicles, trains, airplanes, and boats because we know the differences in their forms and functions. Even a young child with several of these objects as playthings can categorize them as modes of transportation, even to the extent of pointing out their obvious differences in form. Moreover, when the field is narrowed to motor vehicles, for instance, there is still little problem for most people in noting differences among passenger cars, pickup trucks, trailer trucks, and motorcycles. When we further reduce the field, most people begin to encounter difficulties in recognition. Because you, in particular, may be interested in cars and have looked closely, when you discount the differences in engineering performance, can you delineate the differences, for example, in sedan models among (1) BMWs, Mercedes-Benzes, and Jaguars; (2) Hondas and Toyotas; or (3) Fords and Chevrolets? Can you separate the differences in the models in each group? If you can, you are involved in differences in style, or *styling,* as the automobile manufacturers say.

Yet, this example will not do for objects of art. Commercial design, whether of a toothpaste carton or a box of cereal, involves a certain amount of style because manufacturers want you to recognize an individual item on a crowded shelf, with the style intended for reproduction in thousands, sometimes millions, of the same item. Yet, despite the quantity of reproduction, such items have an individual look and can be delineated readily from other items in the same form.

In art, we are concerned with extremely narrow categories, usually only a handful of items with the same individualized look. Thus, we can talk about Cézanne's style as differing from Van Gogh's, about Brahms's symphonies differing from Tchaikovsky's, about Ibsen's plays differing from Strindberg's, about Arthur Miller's plays differing from Tennessee Williams's, about Sam Shepard's plays differing from Edward Albee's. We also have differences in stage productions by directors Mike Nichols and Daniel Sullivan, and in movie productions by Ingmar Bergman and Robert Altman.

Four points can be made about the preceding pairs of artists. First, each pair represents the same art form. This fact is important to our understanding of style because we can understand this concept much better if we stay within specific categories.

Second, notice that the two people in each category are contemporaries—they did their work or are doing it in approximately the same period. The important thing about dating art is that each age (an age can vary from 20 to 50 years) establishes its own variations and refinements of form by setting up something that can be recognized as the *style of the period,* the individualization of that age. Thus, we can speak of Elizabethan style, French Classical style, Romantic style, Realistic style, and so forth. When we consider drama, we note that each period has made general modifications that all dramatists of that period use; by noting these characteristics, we can delineate the style of a period. We can also do the same for production by labeling the styles Elizabethan platform staging, seventeenth-century Italianate, nineteenth-century Romantic, or twentieth-century Realistic. By these designations we may take a different look at each one, no matter whose individual work we may be examining.

Third, notice in the pairs listed that names of people have been used because this is the only way we can delineate the most subtle aspects of style. "Style is the man," goes the adage. This saying means that every creative artist will make individual alterations within the general style of his age, individualizations that people who look closely at art will recognize as unique in the artist—truly *his signature to the work.* Style may have broad meanings when designating historical periods, but it can also have a very specific meaning in referring to the unique work of individuals. In its most refined sense, style is the significant aspect in the definition of art itself—that is, something unique and highly individualized.

Finally, notice that the artists are paired according to how they make contact with spectators or audiences. Cézanne and Van Gogh make direct contact through direct showings of their work in museum galleries. However, Brahms and Tchaikovsky as well as Ibsen and Strindberg and Miller and Williams must depend on interpreters to present their works, because the forms in which their works appear are incomplete *without performers and audiences.* Bergman and Altman are part creative writers and part interpreters, because they usually create both the form and content of their movie scripts and go on to interpret them through the form of cinematic staging. Although their work is in movies, both Bergman and Altman are examples of Gordon Craig's artist-director; while stage directors Nichols and Sullivan are what Craig labeled master-craftsman-directors—that is, directors who act as interpreters of the work of others. However, no matter what the relationship may be between the creative and the interpretive, all the people mentioned here have developed a recognizable style all their own. To clarify this point, we have given examples of various art forms along with categorical differences in style for each pair of artists, with the implication that each artist will make his own personal and individual statement. *Style, then, is both the individualization of art form and the way of moving spectators* (those who only look) *and audiences* (those who both hear and look).

Interpretation Is Criticism

Interpretation is the director's goal because, as a master-craftsman-director, he *interprets* the work of the playwright rather than creates the playscript himself. To carry out this function, he becomes the primary critic in the theatre. To understand his work better, it is most useful to compare him with the other "interpreters" who work in and around the theatre—namely, the newspaper reviewer and the dramatic critic. All three are essential to a vigorous and active theatre, but each has a distinctively prescribed job to do.

The Newspaper Reviewer

Most of the comment about the theatre we read in newspapers and periodicals is not criticism at all in the strict sense of the word. Rather, it may be better labeled *reviewing,* because its primary function is to look at a produced play in its final form and in its natural habitat—the theatre—and then judge its merits and failures. Consequently, the 500- to 800-word review we read in a newspaper shortly after a first performance of a play is the opinion of a trained and experienced viewer who is reporting his or her reactions to the play, the acting, and the directing to a waiting public, who, in turn, enjoys the reviewer as an entertaining writer and often listens closely to his or her advice on whether to spend money and time on a particular play.

Such brief and personal news reporting serves the theatre by spreading word about a produced play. But such reporting also harms the theatre when the reviewer sets himself or herself up as the primary interpreter by substituting personal opinions about what he or she thinks a production should have been. Instead of focusing the eye of the reader on what is there, the reviewer may point to what he or she thinks should have been there. The reviewer who does this moves into the director's realm of interpretation and thus becomes an armchair director.

The Dramatic Critic

Another level of criticism is closer to the function of the director. Although dramatic criticism has appeared more or less regularly throughout the history of the theatre, it has never been so much in vogue as it is today. Dramatic criticism, as opposed to the reviewing that you find in newspapers or magazines, is in-depth examination of a play or a body of dramatic literature or issues of performance. Frequently using theoretical approaches, in addition to the evidence in the dramatic texts themselves, the dramatic critic searches for new insights into the workings of plays or phenomena of performance, with the findings often worked out at length in a substantial essay or book. Although newspaper reviewers are usually sophisticated viewers with a wide range of theatre-going experiences to draw from, their educational backgrounds may be quite different from those of dramatic critics who are often academics, versed not only in vast expanses of dramatic literature, theater history, and performance traditions but also in a range of critical theories, including such approaches as feminist theory, postcolonial and transnational studies, intercultural studies, and the like.

Plays are created structures that have meanings. Dramatists deploy different strategies to work out the meanings, interests, and visions that gave rise to writing their plays. Sometimes the meanings and workings of a play may be quite clear, while at other times these meanings and workings may seem, at first, elusive, although their power can still be felt. In this sense, plays are a kind of poetry, even when they are written in prose, and playwrights are poets who communicate to others through metaphor, symbol, and other strategies beyond the surface meaning of the dialogue. And this definition of dramatic poetry is all encompassing. Whether the play is actually written in verse or the prose lyricism of Tennessee Williams, whether it employs the complex, allusive imagery of Heiner Mueller or the clear political point of view of Edward Bond, the play is still a dramatic poem. And as with poetry, it usually takes sustained engagement on the part of its interpreters to come to terms with its content and its dramatic means. In this search to understand meanings and forms, dramatic criticism can be very helpful to the director, although it can never supplant the director's responsibility to interpret the work.

A learning director should cultivate the habit of reading dramatic criticism as a way of developing his own sense of what to look for and how to find it. However, when he does so, he will also find that the director's reading of dramatic criticism has limitations. Because its primary intention is to illuminate the mysteries of drama, in may turn out to be just another interpretation. The critic has looked intensively at the play to support his or her own ideas about the structure and meanings, and has shown textual proof to validate those views. However, the critic can easily be led astray by placing too much emphasis on what he or she has taken for proof. Unveiling the mysteries of poetic experience requires exceptional vision indeed; such vision is rare, and so are good dramatic critics.

The Director as Primary Critic

Despite the presence of the reviewer and dramatic critic, *the director is the primary critic in the theatre.* The function of criticism is to interpret and illuminate a work—a perfect description of the director's job. In comparison, the dramatic critic works only with the playscript, which in itself cannot be complete because by its nature it requires actors and production to give it full life; the reviewer works with the finished production and *provides a criticism of the director's interpretation* while at the same time he tries to fulfill the nominal responsibilities of a dramatic critic by examining the playscript. *Only the director works in a firsthand way with both the playscript and the production.*

This function is nowhere better delineated than in T. S. Eliot's essay "The Function of Criticism." In that work, the celebrated poet-playwright-critic is talking about literary criticism, but it can be just as readily applied to directing. In it, he draws a sharp line between two major approaches to criticism. The first, the intuitive approach, he labels *whiggery*—that is, what proceeds without principles from the "inner voice":

> "If I like a thing, that is all I want," so the argument goes; "and if enough of us, shouting all together, like it, that should be all that you (who don't like it) ought to want. The law of art . . . is all case law. And we cannot only like whatever we like to like but we can like it for any reason we choose."

Such practitioners, Eliot maintains, are not concerned with literary perfection but only with momentary and personal values. The second approach (to Eliot, the only valid one) *is more analytical, more conscious criticism,* the sort a superior writer must apply to his own work, for the critical activity finds its highest, true fulfillment in a kind of "union with creation in the labour of the artist."

At one time, Eliot took the position that the only critics worth reading were the critics who "practiced, and practiced well, the art of which they wrote." Later, he modified this view in the interest of finding a more inclusive frame, and he then concluded that the most important qualification for a critic was a "highly developed sense of fact." This allowed him to permit inclusion of critics who write about the works of others; but he points out the rarity of good practitioners: "For every success in this type of writing there are thousands of impostures. Instead of insight you get a fiction." *The best critic is one who sees a work of art steadily and sees it as a whole.*

In applying this distinction to the director, whiggery would seem to be as unacceptable an approach to directing as it is to criticism. How a director feels about a play will certainly affect his treatment of it because he is dealing with art and not science, with intuition and not scientific fact that must be explicitly and fully explained, with the behavior of human beings as set out by the playwright and not with puppets. Nevertheless, *a predominantly subjective approach to directing is incompatible with the director's function* of finding unity and order in the playscript, in acting, and in design because he must constantly exercise his objective, analytical, critical view in order to control his media, which are subject to constant variations. As a stimulator of ideas, the director is involved in getting from the playwright the strongest play—if it is a new one and he can control its development—and in arousing the actor to his best performance and the designer to his highest level of creativity. The director's success is also tempered by his mastery of the physical materials of the stage. Among artists, he might be compared in some respects to the architect, who is also concerned with the limitation of materials and the ability of the craftsman on whom he must depend for the execution of his ideas.

In summary, because the master-craftsman-director is the subject of this discussion, you must assume that *the director's function is largely one of interpretation,* that his primary concern is *about* something that someone else has already created (the playscript), or, as in the case of the actor and designer, something that someone else is about to create.

Something to Say

Because the primary job of the director is *interpreting* what has already been set out for him in a playscript, how can he make an individual statement that can be classified as style without violating the integrity of the playscript, especially when *the temptation of not telling the truth is always there*?

The answer is relatively simple although the achievement of style is not. The assumption is that a director will be in command of a production, of both the actors and the designers, and that he fully comprehends the *form* of the playscript and its *style. A director's style will be stated in the individual qualities and emphases he gives to the form, content, and individual style of a playscript through the production elements at his command.* The director's statement of style evolves as he makes decisions about which direction he will take with a play. Here are a few of the basic questions that will have to be faced, and out of the answers will come his style:

What is the dominant idea in the play?

Whose (which character's) play is it? *(This is a very important decision about character emphasis.)*

What *actions* should be given the most telling emphasis?

Is the production to emphasize text or subtext, and in what balance?

How can the given circumstances be individualized?

What dominant moods can emerge?

Who shall be cast? (texture and balance)

How shall the design be stated? (as Realism or as a departure from Realism)

When it comes down to the fine points in a play, there is no absolute interpretation. Its ideas will fall within a narrow range, but it is just that narrow range that is left open to the director and out of which will come his individual statement—his style. *Style is beyond form and content; it is something personal to say.*

Style Is Today's Statement

To reproduce a historical play exactly as it was first presented is impossible. Even if all the information were available, we would not want to do such stagings because audiences simply would have great difficulties in understanding them. If you have seen motion picture revivals of 70 and 80 years ago (Sarah Bernhardt as Queen Elizabeth, for instance), you will remember how the audience probably laughed at what looked like odd, elaborate behavior of the actors and at the overly exotic qualities of the settings and costuming. *You were watching acting and design styles of another age,* and the audience was not able to reconcile it with its own prejudiced, highly indoctrinated, well-conditioned conception of style.

Style Is the Primary Means of Immediate Communication

Photography has made it possible for us to see more clearly than ever before how quickly styles change. From the new millennium, we look back at photographs of the styles of the 1960s and 1970s and find them outdated, just as people from the 1960s regarded the 1940s and 1950s, and so on. Style says something to us quickly and easily. This characteristic is readily illustrated in dress, whereby new styles quickly become old styles in a continuously changing, arbitrarily forced world of industrial design. A designer makes a new-look dress; other designers more or less copy the creation to set the fashion, and when others follow in numbers, a fad is declared. A style remains in fashion only as long as it is not replaced by a newer style with more ready communication.

Avant-gardists are the makers of new styles because they are always in search of a fresh means of communication, a new way of saying something. The speed of present-day electronic communications has reduced the length of time a style can stay in fashion. Not long ago, style seemed to last for several years, perhaps as much as one or two decades; now the "new" is given such quick circulation that a style's lifetime seems to be markedly reduced. Last year's avant-garde in the popular music field (the latest new sounds, rhythms, and words) will be superseded this year by another style that will soon become the craze or the rage, words that to you may sound quite out of style.

An awareness of the immediacy of style—that is, its quality of being contemporary—is most important to the director. His job is to *get through to an audience no matter when the play he is producing was written.* The problem is always one of communication through style. The director not only has something to say because he sees it vividly in the context of his own time, but if he is to communicate to an audience, *he must also say it in the immediate terms most understandable to his audience.*

It is the living, breathing immediacy of style that makes it one of the director's primary tools of communication. Although the *adaptation* of historical styles will be treated in a later chapter, it is necessary to note here that, no matter how an adaptation is made, *if the style is too unfamiliar to an audience, it may not be very effective because the theatre demands group recognition.* There is no harder demand on any artist than this because the tendency is to play it safe—to be conventional and not to strive for the new. But the new can also be a real obstacle to an audience when a director decorates it on the assumption that a different staging will get the idea across. Consequently, the director may lose faith in the play itself, and instead of showing its inner heart and being, he might present his own reworking as a substitute. Remember: "All that glitters is not gold!"

Thus, the range of style for the director is a rather narrow one, because he must constantly fight the paradox of *reaching an audience on the level at which it can understand him* while at the same time trying to find new and exciting ways of communicating. As a popular art form, theatre in the past usually lagged as much as a generation behind the other forms while it was waiting for the general audience to catch up. Today, this is no longer the case because, with urban culture and electronic communications before us, the new quickly becomes old.

24

Style in Playwriting and Playwrights

The purpose of this chapter is to pull together many of the ideas and bits of information you may have garnered from your courses in dramatic literature. To some of you, this may look familiar, and thus redundant. But if you will read the chapter carefully, you will see that it is about the special way a director looks at plays and playwriting in order to put them to work for him. This will challenge the critic in you.

The *form* of drama in Western civilization, as distinct from theatre production, has always contained the same basic elements since its beginnings in the fifth century B.C.: given circumstances, dialogue, dramatic action, characters, idea, tempos, and moods. What has made drama seem different over its 2,500-year history is the rearrangement in value and emphasis of these basic structural elements. One age, from Ibsen to 1960, for instance, gives great prominence to given circumstances, with detailed emphasis on previous action; whereas another, such as the Elizabethan Age, ignores this aspect almost completely. Dramatic action is relatively simple in some periods (Greek) but complex and extensive in others (Jacobean). Characters are largely primal types in some periods (Greek) but intricate and highly detailed in others (Ibsenite-Chekhovian-Strindbergian Realism). Dialogue is in verse form in some, with emphasis on variety in meters (Spanish Classical), and in prose, sometimes quite elaborate, in others (English Restoration Comedy).

These variations in the basic elements of dramatic form are what distinguish the drama of one period from the drama of another. You should remember, however, that categorizing is only a general sorting of the thousands of plays we wish to know better. The only way to be sure of what a person has in hand is to take a particular look at a specific play through play-analysis. Playwrights, we like to think, are free improvisors like other artists, and only at certain times have they been expected to conform to established rules prescribed through one sort of pressure or another (as in Neo-Classical). We are so accustomed in modern times to think of playwrights as free spirits that we seldom realize how many restrictions on form and "community style" actually bind them. As with entrenched governments, revolutions by playwrights or theatre people, sometimes physical ones, are necessary to overthrow overused forms. Victor Hugo's revolt against classical French drama with *Hernani,* J. M. Synge's and the Abbey Theatre's similar revolt with *Playboy of the Western World,* Ibsen's and Strindberg's overthrow of nineteenth-century Romantic drama in their shocking Realistic plays of sex and marriage, and Pirandello's overthrow of Realism are all obvious examples.

The Playwright and His Choice of Content

One of the oldest ways of specifying differences in the content of drama is type designation. Ever since Greek Classical times, drama has been divided into categories as a way of grouping plays of like intent and similar structures. Although tragedy and comedy (the two major types) had different origins in the ancient Greek world, with separate heritages of rituals and mythology, by the fifth century B.C. they were brought together within the same *general* form, with both employing dramatic action, characters, idea, dialogue, choral groups, music, and spectacle; both types were performed in the same religious-theatrical temple, as well—the Dionysian theatre.

The difference between these two major designations lay in how the basic elements of dramatic form were used and the kinds of emphasis given to each element. This method of play description has been so useful that present-day dramatic critics wrestle with the same basic problems that faced Aristotle: (1) What makes each type work? and (2) What kind of emphasis must be given to each element in each of the two structures to achieve the total composite effect required by each structure? Consequently, an extensive literature has developed around the theory of drama in the attempt by each age to define these composite types. Critics know that the types work in the theatre, and the theoretical discussion is directed toward penetrating their poetic mysteries.

A learning director cannot advance very far into the realm of style unless he comprehends a good deal about these composite types. *What makes an audience laugh?* and *What can move it deeply?* are the most important questions a director must answer for himself. An extensive knowledge of the composite types may not only unlock historical drama for you in a very direct way but it may also give you the key to modern drama. With a strong awareness of types, you can then proceed to unfold for yourself the ways in which each individual playwright attacks his problem—what the playwright's style is all about.

The intention here is not to provide a theoretical study of the composite types but merely to describe these types in a general way in order to alert you to basic differences. Your course work in dramatic literature will help you develop your understanding in depth, and you will add greatly to this understanding through regular practice in play-analysis.

Again, you must remember that each age has made its own description, sometimes *pre*scription, of these composite types. It is therefore impossible to treat them briefly without including points that some ages would take strong exception to. Nevertheless, here are some general statements.

Serious Drama

Tragedy has had the most intensive treatment of all the composite types. In general, however, all ages and cultures have seemed to agree that it is serious throughout; that it deals with man's relationship to forces usually outside his mundane, domestic world although they may be secret forces inside himself; that it is about a better-than-average man, frequently highly placed in society, who makes a discovery that brings about a great change in his life, usually resulting in his death. Furthermore, the man *usually,* but not always, comes to a knowledge about himself in relation to the outside forces; that what happens as a result of the discovery affects all that he holds most dear in his life, but he has the great courage and strength to face his destiny. Very important to this description is that members of an audience may be greatly moved to pity him for his suffering and, at the same time, may fear that the same thing could happen to them. Finally, the language in which these plays are written is heightened beyond that of everyday speech and frequently is set down in verse.

Tragedy is about violence and suffering. These aspects are what make it so compelling in the theatre, for they can take us to the periphery, to the very brink of life's experience. During a lifetime we all go through a certain amount of suffering and may even have an experience approaching violence, but few of us ever experience life even near the level of the tragic hero. Yet, we recognize that it could happen, that it is possible; it is just this possibility that makes tragedy so utterly believable.

Isolating the violence is a key to understanding such plays, for it allows working backward from the climactic peaks in order to discover more readily what led to them. *As a director, you will want to give violence great prominence, because through the very force of its presentation, an audience can experience the intense emotions of the aftermath. Great drama is always about the great passions in life where the desire to maintain integrity supersedes all other desires.* Consequently, producing tragic feeling on the stage is a very difficult matter even when you understand what violence is and what precedes and follows it.

Today, we have many problems in labeling our drama as tragedy because emphases differ from those of the classical forms. *Serious drama* or *a play* seems to be a more apt description because it exhibits no pretentions about the contents, which may include some humor. Today's drama shows the principal character in conflict only with other men or with groups in the society, and not with forces beyond earthbound human contacts, as did the Greeks. And although it may not end in the hero's coming to know his own weaknesses, it contains the same basic elements as classical tragedy: fierce integrity on the part of the hero, which leads him to a do-or-die position, and the violence he must undergo when he makes his principal discovery. *Only when you make an exhaustive play-analysis of a serious play can you see why it is truly serious and what the consequences will be to an audience that views it.* Your directing skill will be marked by your perception of serious drama and the intensity with which you show it on the stage, for serious drama presents intellectual and emotional challenges to any director who undertakes it.

EXERCISES

1. Is Ibsen's *Ghosts* a tragedy? Explain your answer.
2. What is a tragic hero?
3. Because discussions of serious drama can be profitable, devote as much time as possible to thrashing out its complexities with your classmates. If possible, each of you should do an analysis of a serious play of your own choosing, with the focus on what makes it serious.
4. The principal characters in Arthur Miller's *All My Sons, Death of a Salesman,* and *The Crucible* all die. Are these plays tragedies? Why or why not?

Melodrama

The word *melodrama* has been used for nearly two centuries to describe those plays in which theatrical "activities" dominate the dramatic action. These activities tend to make the action superficial, which, in turn, reduces the development of character. Such plays live in large part on their external excitements, resulting in the capabilities of holding audiences in firm grip because their danger levels are both high and obvious. *Melodrama,* since its earliest usage, has meant "drama supported and enhanced by exciting music," a perfect description of today's detective and police thrillers on television. Classical tragedy also had music, but it was used in support of choral songs and not merely to excite the emotions *behind* stage activities.

To see melodrama only in the light of those travesties of nineteenth-century "mellers," where the villain operates the buzz saw while the heroine advances toward it on the log rollers is seriously to malign it as a composite form of drama. The term *character melodrama* is frequently used not only to denote the stature of the better plays but also to describe an entire range of dramas that cannot fall into the category of serious play or tragedy even though the moods of such dramas are indeed serious. They do not qualify as tragedies because their actions are always man-versus-man in his dealings in everyday life: The protagonist must overcome his antagonist as in tragedy but for superficial gains—money, property, upholding the law, and so forth. Although such plays deal with psychological aspects of character, they do not penetrate deeply enough to be intensive perceptions of life. Instead, they play on our sense of personal security, our prejudices (we tend to destroy those things we do not understand), our morbid curiosity, our moral codes, and our personal search for excitement to relieve ourselves from the boredom of everyday life. Most of what we see in television drama is really melodrama.

A director must learn the sensitive skills of staging melodrama if he is to learn how to direct the intensive activity, often melodramatic, in the serious drama. A director should therefore get into the habit of looking at all plays as melodramas if only to see how the excitements in them are created and what levels they reach. Without this skill of expressing external dangers, a director will never know how to project the quiet, interior dangers more deeply and subtly embedded in serious drama. The rhythms and tonal pitches of melodrama are the best possible avenues to learning what the term *theatrical* means in the theatre—a high sense of personal (audience) danger. You should direct melodramas, then, before you try to direct highly serious plays.

EXERCISES

1. *Hedda Gabler* is sometimes labeled a melodrama. Why? Be very careful not to belittle characterizations in that play.
2. Why can *Macbeth* be labeled, as it sometimes is, a tragedy with melodramatic overtones?
3. What is melodramatic about Sam Shepard's *Curse of the Starving Class*? What is melodramatic about Tennessee Williams's *Sweet Bird of Youth* or *Orpheus Descending*?
4. Do a written analysis of a melodrama of your own choice, proving that it is a melodrama or how it compromises the form. Here are some suggestions of categories: *Ladies in Retirement, The Cat and the Canary, Rhinoceros,* and *The Zoo Story.*

Comedy

The most difficult of all the composite forms for a young director to understand is comedy. Serious plays are more a matter of feeling than of mind, and both the young director and the young actor can comprehend that form on the basis of their past emotional experiences in everyday life, though perception in depth requires experiences in depth. *In contrast, comedy is more a matter of the mind than of the feelings.* To find a joke funny, one must perceive the incongruities that are presented in the joke: It amuses precisely because *A* is not congruent with *B;* but we must know both *A* and *B* intimately in order to note their incongruities.

The director is constantly confronted with the fact that *if he and his actors are to make an audience laugh, they must first understand the jokes themselves.* In this sense, comedy may seem to require greater maturity not only on the part of the director and the actors but also on the part of the audience, although the actors may have great capacities to communicate comic ideas and thus simplify comprehension on the part of the audience. What may be obscure on the printed page can appear both obvious and funny in the hands of comic actors—the instruments through which the incongruities are conveyed.

Although there are many levels of comedy, ranging from humor (the audience *likes* the trapped character and laughs with him) to satire (the audience looks objectively and closely at the trapped character, usually disliking him and laughing at him), comedy as a composite type has specific, identifiable emphases within the basic elements of dramatic form. A good comedy throws a strong emphasis on a character who is simplified in such a way that we can readily see the distortions that have made him a fool in other men's eyes; we can see them, that is, if we understand what is considered normal behavior in the society reflected in the comedy.

Norms, then, are very important in comprehending comedy. Thus, the action in comedy consists of a string of incidents that reveal the fool in situation after situation where he always shows the same distortions, the same variations from what is considered normal behavior. Consequently, the fun of a comedy usually consists of the reactions of the other characters to the continuing stupidities of the principal character until he finally sees how distorted he is, or, more usually, the others decide that it would be heartless to make him face his realities. In this sense, comedy is a social leveler because it shows average or less-than-average people caught in their own foolishness. It is based on the principle that no man knows what he is, that he cannot see his real mirror image but only what he wants to see.

Comedy thus produces laughter on the basis of distortion in character—a blind spot in the character's own view of his actions. Comedy can be gentle if the audience is led to sympathize with the behavior of the character, but it can be very cruel when a character gets no such sympathy and is laughed at.

The ideas behind this category of plays all concern man's adjustment to the social patterns in which he lives. Given circumstances play an important part in setting up a comedy, for what may be funny in the context of restrictions of one social group may not be funny in another context at all. From Shakespeare's *Much Ado About Nothing* through Molière, Sheridan, Bernard Shaw, Noel Coward, and Edward Albee's *Who's Afraid of Virginia Woolf?* satirical conflict between the sexes in and out of marriage was the major holding force in comedy. After 1960, the genuine comedy of dialogue and ideas had become scarce in the United States, though it still appeared in the plays of Neil Simon, Woody Allen, A. R. Gurney, John Guare, and a few others. The old approach also still seemed to work in such films as *Nine to Five* and *War of the Roses.* In the theatre, however, perhaps because ideas of marriage had moved in new directions, together with the fact that playwrights were no longer writing in this mode, comedies were rare indeed. But there is still validity in the comedic idea that women are creatures of common sense, and men are the distorted ones in a world largely of their own making: What seems to them so perfectly logical and so right can be taken for granted.

Dialogue is given significant emphasis in comedy. In high comedy, we have conversation at its cleverest and wittiest. Thus, language is not just a conveyor of action, but a delight, an entertainment, in itself. We love word play because we all use language, but we all do not have the capability of putting it together in amusing ways. However, though the young director must be highly aware of the text in a comedy, he must also pay the most careful attention to the subtext because what is truly funny will be there. As with the other forms, comedy is still a matter of dramatic action.

A knowledge of comedy from a theoretical point of view is invaluable to a director, for he will sooner or later tangle with this composite type. Among the valuable principles he will learn is the one that always causes trouble if he does not know it: *Characters in comedy are all deadly serious about their points of view, and the principal fool is the most serious of them all.* We laugh at characters in a comedy because they take themselves so seriously. The young director will learn that comedians do not pretend to be funny, but that they are so caught up in the distortions they are playing that they are absolutely convincing in every aspect of those distortions. *Good comedians are thus not laughing at the characters they are playing but are being those characters, a fact that makes us laugh all the more.* An actor who plays a comic role in such a way as to show that he finds the character funny is seldom funny to an audience.

Directing comedy, then, involves knowing what is funny and then playing the action very intensively. Life is comic when we perceive the incongruities, and so it is on the stage.

EXERCISES

1. Why are the following plays comedies?
   a. *Man and Superman* (Shaw)
   b. *The Show-Off* (Kelly)
   c. *The Circle* (Maugham)
   d. *Everything in the Garden* (Albee)
   e. *Lost in Yonkers* (Simon)
2. Analyze a recent joke you have heard. Exactly what makes it funny?
3. Analyze a television sitcom in the same way.
4. Do a detailed analysis of a comedy of your own choosing by citing all the points that prove it to be a comedy.

Farce

Just as melodrama is a diluted form of the serious play, so farce is a diluted form of comedy. Again, as in melodrama, the basic elements of the master type have been simplified and the emphasis has been placed on the external aspects. In addition, just as tragedies may contain some scenes where melodrama takes over in the interest of intensive physical illustration (Shakespeare's *Macbeth* is a good example), so comedies may contain scenes where farce is used to intensify the illustration.

Farces are usually packed with laugh-getting situations and business, for the emphasis is thrown on simplified characters, ingenious involvements, and physical illustrations. In television, such plays are often labeled *situation comedies (sitcoms).* Although the characters are close to the realm of comedy by being distortions of life, they are meaner, more superficial, more puppetlike. It is precisely because they take life so seriously and can see no other avenues but their own that we find them funny. Excellent examples of farce are the motion picture reels of Laurel and Hardy, where both characters are of below-average intelligence, both are clumsy and awkward, both are sober and serious, and both work industriously with failure courting their every move. We see ourselves in their farcical antics because we all have a certain amount of the same problems in everyday life; but at the same time, we can laugh at them with sympathy not only because they are below-average ("meaner") men, which brings out our own feeling of superiority, but also because we are distanced in a very specific way and made to see only certain things.

Farce takes on the look of *exaggeration* because of its simplified structural elements, but we can also see and easily recognize the incongruities in characters and actions because the actors hold them out to us in very clear ways. Although tragedy and comedy can be read from the printed page with a certain amount of reward, farces require acting to give them specific life because the funniest moments may be involvements with stage properties or machines or physical contact among the characters. Only occasionally do we have farces that depend on language as one of the major emphases, and in these cases, the fun is still in the acting, for it is the actor's sense of timing in line delivery that will provoke the laugh.

Good farce on the stage is rare in our day because movies and television are more capable of presenting the contrivances of farce. But wherever a director picks up his knowledge of the dramatic values in farce, if he understands this composite type well, *he will be able to augment his sense of illustration in directing the higher form*—comedy. Fools are fools, and in working with comedy, a significant moment of farce that is still in taste and in line with character can often bring audiences to a clear understanding of the blocks in characters. Farce may be a lesser form of comedy, but it has the greater capacity of arousing audiences to explicit laughter by bringing them into the peculiar realm of fantasy that surrounds a farcical moment. An audience is simply lifted out of its sense of reality and led to believe in, if only for a few moments, the rarified world in which the farcical characters live.

EXERCISES

1. Explain what is farcical in the following:
   a. *The Importance of Being Earnest* (Wilde); is this play a comedy or a farce?
   b. *Misalliance* (Shaw); *Noises Off* (Frayn)
   c. *The Bald Soprano* (Ionesco)
   d. The most recent sitcom you have seen
2. Why is the play of "Pyramus and Thisbe" in *A Midsummer Night's Dream* a farce?
3. Is Beckett's *Happy Days* a farce? Why or why not?
4. Do a written analysis of a farce of your own choice, proving from the structure that it is a farce.

Other Composite Types

Although there are a number of labels in use to describe other composite types (*tragicomedy, absurdist comedy,* and *black comedy,* for instance), what they tend to do is cross the lines of the major ones previously described, thus delineating new composites by rearranging the emphases. At best, such labels are merely descriptive. Once the director understands the nature of composite types and how the principal ones are composed, he will realize that the game of close identification can be infinite, simply because there are so many possible arrangements of the pure composites. Serious plays, for instance, may contain comic moments, just as comedies may contain serious moments (see Polonius's speech in *Hamlet,* Act II, Scene 2). *All labeling will therefore contain a certain amount of readjustment to this mingling of emphases, for few plays precisely conform to the strict definitions of the pure forms.* If you keep in mind that the director always deals with specific plays, and that the major categories are abstractions, you will not get caught in the dangerous game of labeling plays, thinking that you have a better understanding of them because you have assigned them to categories. You must also keep in mind that changes in drama come about when playwrights break the narrow prescriptions of composite types.

EXERCISES

1. How would you describe the following composite types? Try to use specific labels although they may be made by combining some of the four composite types already delineated.
   a. *Much Ado About Nothing* (Shakespeare)
   b. *The Misanthrope* (Molière)
   c. *A Month in the Country* (Turgenev)
   d. *The Cherry Orchard* (Chekhov)
   e. *Idiot's Delight* (Sherwood)
   f. *Juno and the Paycock* (O'Casey)
   g. *A Man for All Seasons* (Bolt)
   h. *The Boys in the Band* (Crowley)
   i. *Rhinoceros* (Ionesco)
2. Make a list of as many plays from the modern repertoire as you can think of that seem to cross the lines of the pure types. Why do we have so many today?

Understanding Playwrights and Their Contexts

It is dangerous to rely on historical sources in an attempt to understand those many plays that deal with history, simply because playwrights do not write history but use it only as background. Nevertheless, a knowledge of history—and this knowledge includes backgrounds in our own time—is an essential tool for the director.

A well-known American dramatic critic once remarked that he could not see how directors could direct or critics could write about plays since 1920 without having a lively understanding of Marxist philosophy and all of the forces working out of it. Although he was no Marxist himself, he felt that political ideas involving either favorable attitudes toward Marxist philosophy or condemnations of it were everywhere in modern drama, and a director or critic could easily miss them unless he was politically oriented. What this critic implied by his statement was that a director cannot modify or adapt historical drama to his time and tastes without knowing a good deal about the historical background out of which the plays of that period were written; knowing an author's bias or lack of bias toward what he took as historical fact can tell us much about the individual direction he may have taken in a play.

A director, then, must also be scholar, though he may think that label too pretentious. But whatever he calls himself, he certainly must do a great deal of probing into backgrounds if he is to understand the drama with which he works. If a playwright is still alive and willing to offer assistance, conversation with him can easily solve the problems about background; but if this is not possible, a director will need to do a lot of spade work. To know an author and his sense of history as well as to know the historical background of his plays is to understand the circumstances in which the author's style took shape. *Biography and history are therefore essential working tools in directing.*

Biography as Source Material

Because playwrights tend to write about the things they feel strongest about, biographical research can often turn up parallels in an author's own life to the content in his plays. Understanding the playwright in Jean Genet also requires comprehension of Genet as a thief, as a convicted and sentenced criminal, as a hunted and haunted man, and as a homosexual. The same necessity for inside awareness applies to Sartre, Shaw, O'Casey, Brecht, O'Neill, Hellman, Albee, Shepard, Fugard, Churchill, Wilson, and others, and any other playwright whose works a director wants to produce.

Certainly, we can be misled fairly easily by biography because at its base it is only an interpretation of someone's life, or what the biographer thought it to be. Autobiographies are usually even more risky as dependable sources. But by reading such background materials carefully and by exercising your own sense of logic against the myth-making or image-making that may go on in any particular study, you can sift out significant points. More recent biographers have turned away from mere reporting of incidents and toward a sort of literary psychoanalysis. But the traps in this approach may be more frequent because the projections are more speculative, though the insight is keener and more revealing, and thus more illuminating to a director.

What is perhaps most directly useful about biography is the context out of which a particular playwright works. If a biographer has done his job, not only do the social, economic, political, and religious worlds in which an author lives and works stand revealed, but also the way he may have participated directly in dealings outside of his life in the theatre. Playwrights are public personages, and, as such, they become involved in human relationships and commitments that reveal them as individuals. Consequently, what they write about for the theatre may be very closely tied to their everyday behavior and social participation. This interrelationship was particularly true among twentieth-century dramatists; but as we learn more and more about historical figures—Molière or Lope de Vega, for instance—we can see how they, too, were motivated in their writings out of the personal and public contexts in which they lived.

To be a director is to be highly curious about human beings. It follows that a director is not merely interested in the imaginary characters in the plays he mounts on the stage but is intensively sensitive to the revealing moments in the lives of the people with whom he works most closely, his blood brothers—the playwrights.

History as Source Material

Again, it is necessary to point out that a director's pursuit of the historical background out of which a play is written can be very misleading, but with the exercise of great care, it can tell the director a good deal about a play. Two aspects of historical review must be considered and clearly separated by a director. One is what the director accepts as historical fact *today,* and the other is what the playwright accepted as historical fact *in his day.* These two points of view may be in complete disagreement, and the director must keep them distinctly apart. We have been so influenced by nineteenth- and twentieth-century interpretations of history, many of them based on new scholarly discoveries, that we are all too ready to apply them to the thinking in other ages.

The safest approach to the study of historical backgrounds is to read contemporary (contemporary with the playwright) or earlier accounts of events used in plays that might have been available to the authors who wrote them. In this way, a director more easily can see what led to a playwright's interpretations of the events, and the resulting prejudices can stand revealed. Understanding Goldsmith's *She Stoops to Conquer,* for instance, can be much more lively if a director understands Goldsmith's immediate sense of history, his feelings about the new changes taking place in the late eighteenth-century society he wrote about—a class society confronted by humanist influences stemming from the revolutionary ideas associated with a slowly emerging philosophy of democracy. There are many lines in this play that must be interpreted in the light of eighteenth-century thought and feeling if they are to get through to today's audiences with force, clarity, and good humor. Likewise, you will know a great deal more about Lope de Vega's *Fuente Ovejuna* if you try to discover why the play seems to be filled with what we take to be democratic sentiments. Or about Marlowe's *Doctor Faustus* if you ask yourself: Why was he so angry? Why was he so angry at the Roman Church? Or about Shaw's *Man and Superman* if you ask: What is the difference between Jack Tanner's political philosophy and Straker's? Or about Brecht's *Mother Courage* if you ask: Did he warp historical fact to make his play apply to the war-torn Europe of the 1940s? Or about John Osborne's *Look Back in Anger* if you ask: What was Osborne so mad about when he wrote the play in the mid-1950s? Or about Shakespeare's *Henry VI* if you ask: What did he know about Joan of Arc beyond hearsay? Or about Gardner's *Conversations with My Father* if you ask: What did he know about American Jews?

Wherever the search may lead a director, he must always keep in mind that his intention is not to infuse a play with his own interpretation of history but to better understand an author's sense of what he was using as background. *The intention is not to uncover an author's errors in historical fact,* although that may be quite revealing, *but to see fully what the author found dramatic and exciting in his vision of humanity placed in the historical context in which he told his story.* Plays are largely about a *peripheral* situation surrounding historical events, but to see the periphery more clearly you must comprehend the core. *A director is not a historian or an archaeologist in a technical sense, but he must have a lively feeling for history and how it works in plays.*

Other Works by a Playwright as Source Material

In the study of one particular play for production, if a director studies three or four additional plays by the same playwright—plays written in approximately the same time period—*he will usually turn up most of the essential characteristics of that playwright's style.* This is not to say that playwrights repeat themselves in content, although this can occasionally happen even with the better ones, but it does suggest that because style is a very personal thing, it can become inherent in a whole body of work.

Thus, we talk about "an Ibsen play," "a Chekhov play," "a Shaw play," "a Williams play," "an Albee play," "a Shepard play," "a Churchill play," and by these designations we mean a characteristic style associated with each writer, such as the following:

> Each playwright probably chooses his themes from a certain range.
>
> The dramatic actions he devises are probably either serious or comic, or perhaps both.
>
> The given circumstances he arranges probably deal with people from a certain class who hold attitudes inherent to that class, and with much previous action or little previous action, depending on the emphasis he, as a playwright, gives to environmental control.
>
> The characters he draws in detail are scaled to the action.
>
> The dialogue he sets down has certain specific and individual markings because dialogue is the expression of his subconscious self, despite his conscious use of techniques in its composition.
>
> The moods and tempos he pulls out of all this particular usage will be individually marked in as positive and identifiable a way as the works of a musical composer.

By looking closely in this manner at a playwright's individual characteristics, the examination of several of his plays *written in approximately the same time period* can establish the general style associated with his work; and from this general description, the director can move to specific elements in the particular play he wants to produce. *Comparative analysis is one of the surest ways of pinpointing style,* for what goes for one play probably goes for another *if their time of writing is fairly close together.*

The period of composition, then, is a very important consideration because the works of some writers span several decades during which time their style changes. If we are to understand changing style in a playwright, *we must compare works from different periods of his writing.* Ibsen's playwriting, for instance, spanned half a century. To understand the body of his work and be able to place any one play, we must know that his earliest plays can be loosely characterized as romantic-historical dramas; that he followed this style with the allegorical dramatic poems of

Brand and *Peer Gynt;* and that he followed these in turn with the Realistic plays dealing with the contemporary society he knew. Later, the style of this middle period gave way in the late 1880s to a new one in which symbolism played a dramatic role, and finally in the last plays to a style some critics have termed Expressionistic. Thus, it would be quite wrong to define Ibsen's style only in terms of *A Doll's House* or *An Enemy of the People.* We can, perhaps, group all of Chekhov's plays together because they were written within a much narrower time span, although perceptive students of his dramas usually see differences between the early and the late plays.

Do playwrights consciously look for new ways and thus new styles to express themselves? Like the rest of us, they are strongly influenced by the real world, and it would be strange, indeed, if they did not move with the times. *In one sense, this is what art means: the fresh revelation of man in the context of his time.* When we say that the plays of a certain author mirror his society, we mean that he found an individual way—his style—of telling his audiences about themselves, so that they could see clearly what they were compelled, involuntarily, to watch and listen to. With study, we, too, can see that society clearly.

The more a director knows about a playwright's other works—his poetry or fiction—the more easily the playwright's style can be detected and pinpointed. Of particular value are his theories of drama and the practice of playwriting. Like most working artists, playwrights resist telling us how they make plays because they recognize that creative art is subjective, and that revealing the creative process in oneself is an extremely difficult, if not impossible, business. Yet, when they do write critical comment, as have Jonson, Lope de Vega, Molière, Hugo, Shaw, Chekhov, Maugham, Anderson, Miller, Williams, and many others, they must be listened to with great attention, for what they have to say may be of great import to their plays when you contemplate production.

Style in Translations and Adaptations

Strictly defined, a *translation* is a literal and literary carryover of a playscript from one language to another, with the translator paying strict attention to accurate word or phrase duplication. An *adaptation* is a loose carryover of a playscript in an attempt to recapture its spirit and feeling in language inherently possessing the capability of reaching audiences for which it is intended. In an adaptation, scene and line alteration is entirely possible because the intention is to transfer a play, not as a piece of literature, but *as a piece of theater.* It is readily apparent that these two processes are different in their intentions and thus in their final products. *The director's problem is to be able to perceive the quality of the transfer, no matter what method is used.*

Whether you are dealing with a translation or an adaptation is a most important consideration in perceiving style, for you will be entirely at the mercy of those who carry over plays written in languages with which you do not have a firsthand acquaintance. Since style is the inherent individuality in a work, how can you, as a director, possibly know what the individuality is unless you have either a firsthand command of the language in which a play is written or great faith in the capabilities of a translator or adaptor? Much attention has been given to this aspect of play production in recent years.

As the world has grown closer together and as we have found great value and interest in one another's plays, *theatre people have recognized that foreign-language plays do not transfer on the stage through words alone, but that far more intensive revelations of the works are necessary if the characteristic styles of the playwrights are to be captured.* The trend in American theatre has been away from translation and toward free adaptation, not only of contemporary works but also of Greek drama and of French classical drama. However, there may be poor adaptors, just as there are poor translators. In fact, some adaptors treat works in such a loose manner that the original work may be quite mutilated.

The process of adaptation is a most difficult one. After Lillian Hellman had adapted Jean Anouilh's *L'Alouette* for the American stage under the title of *The Lark,* she said she would never tackle an adaptation again because it was the most difficult dramatic composition she had ever done, with none of the compensations of free creativity. To understand the kind of work she did, you will have to compare her version with Christopher Fry's "translation" of the same work for London production. You should also note that the New York production was a success, whereas the London production failed. Can you see why?

The search for style, then, in foreign-language plays depends a great deal on what a particular translator or adaptor has discerned about the style of the original. If either is both a perceptive playwright and a critic with the capability of looking closely and "telling the truth," a director may find the style close to the original; if either does not know how to make the transfer, the director who uses such translations or adaptations will, in T. S. Eliot's disparaging phrase, "make a fiction" of the original work.

In approaching foreign-language plays, then, a director should examine closely all of the translations and adaptations available to him as well as a text in the original language. This means careful comparison, sometimes of several works. Translations are frequently helpful because, although they may not be readily "playable" on the stage, they provide clues to what adaptors have left out or changed. If possible, the director should work with a language consultant who can make fresh translations of contested passages or explain why translators or adaptors have chosen the language they use. In some cases, a new adaptation will result because the director sees in a playscript dramatic possibilities that other translators or adaptors have completely missed. At the very least, out of this comparative examination a director will learn the strength of the playscript with which he is dealing, and he will be able to penetrate the stylistic characteristics much more readily. *With foreign-language dramas, the director plays the role of detective even more than he does with plays in his own language.*

A word should also be said here about what some people see as the curious phenomenon of plays written for the London stage, in English of course, that do not succeed with U.S. audiences, and vice versa. The difficulties encountered in this exchange of plays in the same language points all too clearly to the very real problems in transferring drama from other languages. Failures in transfer can be explained only from the viewpoint that plays are deeply embedded cultural mirrors that require sensitive understanding of the culture out of which they are written if they are to be fully comprehended.

In particular, because contemporary drama looks so closely at cultural environments in its attempts to unravel psychological problems, unless an audience can feel the environment of the play through its own parallel and sympathetic environments, it remains insensitive to the dramatic action in a play except on a superficial level. This failure to feel environments has also happened to the European politically oriented drama of commitment since 1920, such as that of Brecht, which escapes many U.S. theatregoers because they cannot sense the dark intensity of the environment out of which these plays appeared. Similarly, the changes in English society, including the breakdown in the class structure, are unfamiliar and not well understood by audiences in the United States. English audiences are similarly subject to miscomprehension when it comes to looking at American plays. If you read the reviews of the London production of Arthur Miller's *Death of a Salesman,* reviews that obviously show a poor perception of intense U.S. concerns, you will know more about the problems of cultural transfer.

EXERCISES

1. Compare translations and/or adaptations of the following:
   a. Ibsen: *A Doll's House, The Lady from the Sea, The Master Builder, An Enemy of the People*
   b. Chekhov: *The Sea Gull, The Cherry Orchard*
   c. Strindberg: *The Father, The Ghost Sonata*
   d. Pirandello: *Six Characters in Search of an Author*
   e. Williams: *The Glass Menagerie* (variant versions in this instance)
   f. Anouilh: *The Lark*
   g. Albee: *Everything in the Garden* (Should this be viewed as an adaptation of the English play by Giles Cooper on which it is based?)
2. Can you add a few others to the above list?

25

The Director's Analysis of Style in a Playscript

This chapter deals with the crux of our discussion of style: how to do a style-analysis. Once you have learned how to do this, you will no longer approach plays in a general way but will always look for the specifics of individualization. You will learn to characterize the plays of a certain author as you would characterize one of the persons he may draw in a play. Further, you will learn to separate one play from another in the body of his work because you will be looking very closely at the plays' specific characteristics. His plays will become personalities to you as readily identifiable from each other as are your close friends. Once again, *a director always directs a specific play, never a general play.*

What to Look for in Analyzing Style

Style-analysis is based on play-analysis; this implies that you should not undertake it until you have completed an intensive analysis of the content of a play—a play-analysis—in the usual manner. You will be tempted to try to do both analyses, the play-analysis and the style-analysis, simultaneously, but if you do, you will miss significant information about the play. If you think of the first analysis (the one outlined in Part I) as *play description* and the new one outlined here as *style-analysis,* you will better understand why the first analysis must be done before undertaking the second.

A list of suggestions about what to look for in making a style-analysis is presented here. Many of them have been discussed in detail in the previous chapters, so this can serve as a summary review. However, there are many new suggestions that may, at first glance, have the look of play-analysis but that go far deeper into the individualities of a play. Be sensitive to their differences if you are to understand the level on which you are now working.

Near the end of this chapter you will find a a worksheet for style-analysis that you should add to the form for play-analysis at the end of Chapter 6 (pages 55–56). Used together, these two outlines cover all the major points of a play's form, content, and style.

Looking Outside the Play: Sources and Backgrounds

1. Date the play both in its general historical period in relation to other plays and in the body of work by the specific author under consideration.
2. Study the author's background through biographical sources. Try to relate him to his time and try to see him as an individual working in a general cultural and aesthetic pattern. Probe his personal life for reasons why he should write the sort of play he does.
3. Study at least three or four other plays closely associated in time to the principal play under study. If the playwright's career has been a long one, examine other plays written at least a decade or more before or after the principal play. Study other works by the playwright, such as his poems, novels, short stories, essays, and, if available, any dramatic criticisms he may have written either about the work of other playwrights or about his own. Criticisms of this sort are invaluable, because they may illuminate the playwright's specific intentions in writing his plays and whether he carried them out, or they may defend his work in a most revealing way. Introductions to plays often contain such inside views.
4. Carefully examine all available editions, or, if a play derives from a foreign language, study the available translations and/or adaptations. Read any commentaries that accompany them in the attempt to understand what a particular editor, translator, or adaptor had in mind when he undertook the editing or the transfer of a work. These introductory essays frequently contain valuable insights into various aspects of play structure that, after your own study, you may accept or disregard for good reason.

   The translations and/or adaptations *should be studied for their actability in terms of the playwriting craftsmanship exercised in the transfer.* Compare lines and speeches for economy in word usage, imagery and poetic value, and simple craftsmanship in technical details, such as building to the ends of lines and speeches. Examine comparatively the available translations or adaptations for mood values, theatricality, and all the dramatic values you think are commensurate with the play.

   If a historical play in English is under consideration, you should look at all published editions or, if available, at unpublished manuscripts. Not only do playwrights change their own work before publication, but editors often make extensive changes depending on where they obtained the work for publication. Many plays have been published—historical as well as modern—as acting editions; that is, they are versions used by acting companies in actual stage productions, and they consequently reveal any additions or cuttings that may have been made in mounting a specific play. Such acting versions appear throughout English drama, from Marlowe's *Doctor Faustus* to Farquhar's *Beaux' Stratagem* to Williams's *The Glass Menagerie.* Only by careful examination of all available editions can you really know what sort of playscript you have under study. This may leave you in some confusion as to what to do, but at least you will be making your own decisions affecting style and will not be so apt to be misled by others.

5. Study the historical context of the specific play's setting. Where did the author get his material? Are the sources available, as are Arthur Miller's for *The Crucible*? If so, read the sources and, while doing so, try to decide why he selected the material he did and why he treated it as he did. Bernard Shaw's *Saint Joan* and Jean Anouilh's *The Lark* are both about Joan of Arc and both draw largely from the same sources, yet each is different. Shaw's play, by his own confession, is a direct interpretation of history. Anouilh is not very interested in history but is greatly concerned with recapturing the poetic nature of the mythology surrounding Joan and her spirit as a French symbol in the context of a confused France following World War II. Lillian Hellman, in adapting Anouilh's play, made a third version—a melodrama that tells us more about her feelings concerning the Spanish Civil War of the 1930s than it does about the context of Anouilh's play or about the historical fifteenth-century context of Joan. What would you decide after reading the historical backgrounds?

    Remember that you are not going to write your own notions of history into a play. The sole purpose of such study is to understand as thoroughly as possible what an author thinks and feels about any background material he may have used. Your own study must be pointed toward revealing a playwright's awareness of history and how he approached his use of it.

    Historical-sociological research may also be of immense value in working with all kinds of plays, including fairly recent ones. How did people live? What were the mores in real life that the author mirrors, and how did they guide people's actions and behavior? What is the play's context in which the author places his action? *Note that the dramatic actions of many plays depend on revolt against a society's existing requirements for behavior.* If a director has a more lively understanding of moral, religious, and social patterns, he will be better able to see the rigidities that must be overthrown. And with comedy, how will a director know what is funny unless he is knowledgeable about the patterns that make a character so ridiculous in the eyes of his contemporaries?

6. Finally, when you have completed your other studies, you should study the dramatic criticisms written about a play—what others have said about it. This study should wait until you have made your own play-analysis so that those criticisms do not interfere with your own critical views. But sooner or later, you must make comparisons, if only to pit your own conclusions against other interpretations. Instead of weakening your own ideas, countercriticisms should actually strengthen them because you will then have a critical "audience" with whom to fight. Directing is setting out one's own interpretation with strength and decision. It cannot help but advance on firm ground if

weak and vague comprehensions are thrown out in the "critical battle" and the strong ones are given purpose and direction. A strong director—the nature of his job says that he must be strong—is also a strong critic because he has faith in and has made a decision about his own interpretations or critical statements.

Looking Inside the Play: Inherent Style-Analysis

Again, you must keep in mind that what follows is only a list of suggestions for helping to discover the *emphasis* a playwright may give to the basic elements in play-analysis. *His style will be defined by his particular use of the elements he considers most expressive of his ideas.* All plays will have all the elements, but individuality will reside in the particular use of those elements. A playwright may emphasize one element over the others and thus declare the play "environmental," "a character piece," "a mood piece," "an actionist melodrama," or any combination he desires. A director can either emphasize the playwright's values or go his own way in choosing the dominance. But an audience will react either positively or negatively to whatever is declared, because the option of endorsement is in each audience member's mind and heart.

Given Circumstances

1. *Environmental Facts.* What level of society does the author write about—lower, middle, or upper? Does he show strong interests in political or religious backgrounds? What are the mores issuing from these environmental factors, and how strongly does the writer impose them on his characters? Is environment assumed (the royal court in *Hamlet*), or does the writer specifically and intentionally set out a mass of detail (small-town life in *Ghosts*)?
2. *Previous Action.* Does the author use a minimum of previous action to tell his story *(Macbeth, Delicate Balance, The Homecoming)*, or is a great deal necessary *(Hedda Gabler)*? Where does the playwright begin his story: near the beginning so that he can show all the incidents *(Hamlet)*, or toward the end, just before the final major discovery *(Oedipus, Who's Afraid of Virginia Woolf? Cat on a Hot Tin Roof)*? More recent plays (since 1960) seem to have reduced previous action to a minimum in comparison to the way Ibsen and those who followed his techniques handled it. Departures from Realism tend to treat previous action only fragmentarily because the intention is not psychological development in depth but the unfolding of the action of the moment *(The Adding Machine, Our Town)*.
3. *Polar Attitudes.* This is a most important stylistic declaration because *the points of view a playwright's characters will take toward the environment will, in turn, tell us what that particular writer considers important in the society he mirrors, and from that will come the actions of the play.* All plays are about revolt of some sort, about a character's overthrow of or submission to the restrictions that have fenced him in. Thus, as was shown in Chapter 3, the attitudes toward

the environment at the opening of a play set up the initial pole in the major character (or characters if two are under consideration), which will be changed during the course of the action, resulting in a new attitude and thus a new pole at the end of the play. Plays take place between these two poles. *The style may be declared,* then, *by what sort of poles an author sets up* and, particularly, by how he has individualized them so that they are fresh and therefore have the potential to move audiences. We are seldom moved by the trite; much of a writer's capability will lie in his devising of the polar structure. Because the initial pole will initiate the action, what sort of pole an author chooses will declare a point of style.

Dialogue

The way a writer handles dialogue can certainly declare the outward appearances of style; because dialogue also contains the action, the most careful scrutiny of this basic element is absolutely necessary. Along with the usual study outlined in Part I, the director should pay particular attention to those *idiosyncracies in line development that bear the personal touch:*

1. Look for specific choice of words, with close attention to repeated words that may contain strong moods or even symbolic values.
2. Look for choice in phrases, especially if the play is in the Realistic style and the speech is intended to reproduce folk idiom. Does the playwright use key phrases to set off the speech of certain characters in idiomatic fashion?
3. Look for poetic overtones in word and phrase choice declared by the use of imagery. How elaborate are the images? How frequently do they occur?
4. Is the dialogue *economic* as a container of the action? How much room does it allow for acting? Does it tend toward the literary?
5. Does the playwright intend textual dominance or does the play exist more on intensive illustration of the subtext (Shaw versus Pinter?)
6. If the lines are in verse form, what is intended in the way of rhythm delivery? Eliot, Fry, and Anderson, as well as recent versions of Greek plays and plays by Molière, among others, all require special handling because of the verse forms. Are you sensitive to the styles?
7. Reread and restudy Dialogue: The Façade of the Playscript in Chapter 3 to ensure that you are aware of the nature of dialogue.

Dramatic Action

Again, you should be certain that you understand the basic characteristics of dramatic action discussed in Chapter 4 before you proceed. Now look carefully for the following:

1. How complex is the action? Is it (in Aristotle's definition) simple or complex? (*Hamlet* versus *Mother Courage*?) Has the playwright written his play around

a very simple unity of action, or does he have a multiplicity of incidents affecting two groups of people (double plot) only casually related but who must be brought together in a final synthesis *(Henry IV, Part One)*?

2. How are time and place handled?
3. Whose play is it? Only by an intensive analysis can you sometimes determine this question in plays in which two or three people seem to play very strong roles. *One character, however, must dominate.* Therefore, it is essential that you decide which one, for the author's style will be exhibited in the subtlety with which he handles such characters and the care with which he delineates them.
4. What is the *type* of the action? Here is a basic declaration of style. What sort of serious play or comedy does the author write? If you can describe it, you are describing a point of style. If the category is comedy, does he specialize in dialogue? In situations? In irony? In youthful caprice or in mature foolery? Is he a satirist? If you categorize him by the type of drama he writes, you will be able to pinpoint his style more clearly because you can compare his treatment of that type with that of other playwrights.
5. A major aspect of style lies in the sort of actions a playwright chooses to show on the stage. We say that drama is the showing of the strange, the unusual, the extraordinary, but what we mean by these words can differ greatly. We tend to regard as extraordinary those actions in real life in which we do not all participate: murder or violence, torture, sadistic cruelty, family destruction, and so forth. It is possible to bring any or all of these onto the stage, although in some historical periods they were banned. But are they the extraordinary?

   Much modern drama converts peripheral action into the extraordinary—not the obvious we can all observe but the subtle, marginal action we seldom pay attention to in moments of great stress. Thus, when we see an automobile accident in the street, a normal person's attention is apt to be caught up in the details at the center: the injured, the ambulance personnel, the police, the wrecked cars. *Peripheral action in this instance would be the actions outside but near the core of the accident:* someone in the crowd who reacts out of mental recall or guilt, someone not associated at all with the accident who reacts in a certain significant way, and so on. These are what good playwrights are apt to find most interesting. Thus, we do not usually need to see hard violence on stage, because the truly exciting moments are on the edge of the violent activity; and it is this marginal activity that holds our attention in the theatre. Here is the point: Authors declare themselves stylistically through the sort of actions they choose to record in the theatre.
6. How does the playwright make discoveries in the action? What characterizes the climaxes? Is the playwright truly theatrical?
7. Try to find the rhythm of the action. Here is a subtle delineation of style that is inherent in an author's work, something that can be very revealing of an author's individuality. If you can find his rhythm, you have pinned him down.

Characters

A playwright's style is frequently known by the sort of characters he draws. One of the common truisms about Bernard Shaw is that his characters all sound alike—they all seem to be talking as Shaw talked. This is a generalization to describe a point of Shavian style, for with few exceptions, the characters in Shaw's plays, no matter what level of society they come from, all talk in a dynamic, articulate way; there are no dunderheads, no inarticulate people, no low-energy types. Here is a point of style that a director must not only be aware of but learn to utilize to full advantage. In contrast, although Tennessee Williams's women might be grouped together as psychoneurotics—a point of style—the problem in style-analysis comes in trying to separate them to discover their special and distinctive psychoneurotic qualities. Like Ibsen, Williams has specialized largely in drawing female characters, but the life of each play will rest on the delicate shadings he gives to each character. Note Ibsen's specific attack. To describe his women as suffragettes or "new" women is to fail at delineating their differences. It is true that many of them are in revolt against the hard, Victorian, conformist world made by men, but you will find that they differ extensively once you examine them in depth. Ibsen's approach to playwriting often led him into drawing antipathies: Once he had developed a woman from one point of view in one play, he would follow it from just the opposite in another. Although they both drive men to their ruin, Hedda Gabler and Hilda Wangel *(The Master Builder)* are very different.

Style in characters, then, lies in the sort of people a playwright is interested in and wants to say something about. He does not select his people at random and by accident but chooses them from among those he knows best, those he has studied in real life and can see clearly. In this respect, there is no gap between William Congreve and Somerset Maugham, both of whom wrote comedies of manners about English society, because each wrote about the sort of people he saw about him. To hold our attention, plays must reveal humanity; thus, it is the particular eyesight a playwright possesses that will or will not open up life to us. We are not talking about photographic reproduction here but about perception. *Style results in perceiving clearly,* first by the playwright and later by the director, *for the clearly perceived statement can be singled out from what is generalized and poorly observed.*

What often holds our attention in the theatre is not the people we know but those we do not. The new have something of an exposé quality about them, and for this reason, new playwrights are always finding their way into the theatre; they are able to show us new people, new in the sense that they are freshly perceived. The interest in folk plays in the United States during the 1920s and 1930s may have come about as a reaction against middle-class drama. Was the middle-class audience that primarily supported the theatre bored with looking at its own kind? Did it find in the simpler life of the lower class something that was not only absorbing but also revealing? But look what happened when playwrights began to tell the truth about the lower class—that it was poverty-ridden, that poverty could be totally destructive, and that the middle class was an actual enemy because it shut itself off from the lower class and forced its continuance. Here was the shock drama of the 1930s, found again in the 1960s, that took seriously the characters caught in these given circumstances. The movement of audiences away from such truth telling is a matter of theatre history.

Here are some things to look for that concern style in character drawing:

1. Does the style lie in the *desires* of the characters—*what they want*?
2. Does the playwright deal with eccentric or rarely seen characters who hold audiences with great fascination (Jean Genet in *The Balcony, The Blacks, The Maids;* Mart Crowley with homosexuals in *The Boys in the Band;* Jerome Ragni and James Rado with the hippies in *Hair*)?
3. Is it possible, in controversion of Aristotle's *Poetics* and Maxwell Anderson's "The Essence of Tragedy," to write successful tragedies about evil people? Who declares what evil is? And once we see "evil people" in explained circumstances—what makes them think and behave in the ways they do—can we then see them in any other light but as human beings who may not agree with the way the majority thinks and feels? Are gangsters such as Bonnie and Clyde the evil ones, or is it the society that made them the villains? The classical definition of evil seems to have altered, for in recent times there seems to be no fence between good and evil. Humanity can be anything, and absolute goods become only what the majority at any one time says they are.

Thus, *the problem of human values can become a matter of style.* Playwrights in revolt will give their characters those values necessary to achieve their ends. Consequently, the theatre in our time often holds our attention because age-old values that people have long believed to be true are debated and even discarded. *Our most energetic modern theatre concerns characters who are caught in this revolution in value judgments.*

Idea

One of the crucial points about style in drama is that ideas in plays *become lost in time.* When we lose the context of a period, we also have great difficulty in reestablishing the ideas that made the plays of that period live in their day. Until fairly recently, the production of historical drama was approached only as storytelling drama with no other purpose than to show human motives and actions. In this sense, they were dead plays, because they were far removed from the heat and conflict of our own day—the quality in present-day drama that holds our attention. Nowadays, many directors approach the old drama quite differently because they have come to believe that such drama can also exist on the idea level if the ideas can somehow be pulled out of them. Such directors believe that these plays are no different from modern plays but only seem so because the ideas cannot be "felt" easily. At the basis of this approach is the concept that plays always have underlying ideas and are written out of an assumed context that their audiences take for granted. Thus, in this view, it is not that the historical dramas lacked ideas, but that *the contexts in which they were written have been lost;* and if directors can only discover the contexts, they can find out what made them vivid and living experiences to the audiences who saw them and, consequently, bring them alive for audiences today.

Therefore, the point of style—whether one is considering modern *or* historical plays—is what the playwright chooses to write about. *What are the ideas in an author's plays that make him distinct from other playwrights?*

The implication here is that no matter when a play was written, *a director must search for the idea at its core if he is to fully comprehend that play.* In today's approach to production, it is not the updating of plays that interests directors but why they were written in the first place. To discover the idea behind a play is to discover the need for producing it. Productions that lack this purpose will be diffuse and vague.

It is also true that many plays are unified primarily by idea, especially contemporary drama. *Hair,* the rock musical of the 1960s, for example, is not held together by its story but by its theme or concept. Often, such plays do not have characters in the usual sense; that is, the actors do not pretend to be someone else. Instead, they are agents of the play, and thus of the idea.

EXERCISES

1. To understand Ibsen, read a play from each of his four periods and compare the ideas in each.
2. Perform a similar experiment with Chekhov, although you will find that his plays are written over a shorter time span. Why are the ideas in each of his plays harder to separate?
3. Now look at the ideas Edward Albee uses. How do they differ from the ideas of Harold Pinter? Samuel Beckett? Bertolt Brecht? Eugene Ionesco? Sam Shepard? (Note that each playwright in this group is characterized stylistically by the ideas each develops in his plays.)
4. What is the idea in Euripides' *The Bacchae*? Read some recent criticism of this play to compare with your own ideas about it. Do you have any comprehension of what Shakespeare wanted to do with *Henry IV, Part One*? *Othello*? *As You Like It*? What was Molière's idea in *Les Précieuses Ridicules*?
5. Study the ideas in Brecht's *Mother Courage* and *The Good Person of Szechuan.* How do they specifically mark his style?

Moods and Tempos

Although moods and tempos derive from the more basic elements of action and characters, they can explicitly mark style. The making of moods is the goal of the playwrights, as it is also that of the directors. Some playwrights—Chekhov and Williams, for instance—have such lyrical capabilities that the moods they create tend to dominate their plays, and we characterize them explicitly as mood dramatists. This designation means that their most prominent mark of style lies in *the quality of the moods* they make. But all plays reach and hold audiences through the power of the moods they are able to evoke, with one fact quite clear: Moods must be inherent in the playscript, for they cannot be overlaid during production.

The first good reading of a play should tell you about its moods. Now is the time to note whether the moods are unusual and vigorous enough to declare a point of style. Later, after you have studied the play, you may find it more difficult to decide.

Tempos can be treated in the same way—by early discovery. Writers are characterized by their sense of rhythm in the same way we distinguish composers of music. Can you recognize anything distinctive in a play you presently have under consideration? Do you sense the strong variations in tempos? Is your playwright musically minded? What can be played very rapidly? What must move very slowly? Are there strongly marked differences in contrast throughout? Does the author have a marked sense of pause?

If you can detect the moods and tempos in several plays by the same author, you have probably found his basic rhythms. Some directors specialize in staging the plays of certain authors simply because they feel themselves in close harmony with an author's rhythms. But finding such rhythm is no easy matter. Because moods and tempos are more subjective than the other elements, it is often difficult to know, as a director, whether you have caught the style-rhythm of the author or are merely showing your own style-rhythm. A director has as many problems with letting his own personality show at the expense of a playwright as an actor has in trying to create a characterization.

Synthesis of Style

It is obvious that by summarizing all the points of style you have collected in this advanced level of play-analysis, you will be making not only a style-analysis of a playwright's work in general but also a style-analysis of a particular play. One point is very important: Work on this summary statement *must be done in stylistic terms* and *not* in terms of basic play-analysis. In other words, style-analysis *assumes* a knowledge of form and content; if you have made a form-content description first (basic play-analysis), doing a style-analysis will be relatively easy. Therefore, always study the play first in terms of form-content analysis before trying to set out the style-analysis. *If you do not work in this order, you will miss important aspects of style because you will not understand the content well enough to collect all the elements.*

The study of style in a particular play, then, is the study of its individuality. Before you write a job recommendation for a person, you first have to know a good deal about that person; *a style-analysis is a personal recommendation of a play in the most specific and heartfelt terms.*

Following is a suggested procedure for making a style-analysis. As you will note, it is a summary of the content of this chapter. Therefore, the purpose of this worksheet is to help you discover a play's style by pinning down its individuality.

Much of what you will find difficult to do here you will later do very easily and quickly when you have acquired experience in style-analysis in depth. But now is the time to teach yourself efficient procedures for the careful scrutinizing that discovery of style requires.

Worksheet for Style-Analysis

I. *Introduction*
   A. A style-analysis should not be made until a play-analysis, as outlined in Chapter 6, has been completed, because the content of this second analysis must be based on the accumulated content of the first. If you do a careful in-depth play-analysis, you will have the facts necessary for answering the questions introduced here.
   B. Never force your play-analysis when you are looking for answers to the questions on style. *If your proof is not readily available, it may not be in the text of this play.* Be honest with both yourself and the play. Remember that the style of a playscript is based explicitly on what is there, not on what you imagine is there, although you may have to use your imagination extensively to pin down the explicit.
   C. The order of development of a style-analysis is the same as for play-analysis. Stay with that order and you will better understand the relationships of the basic structural elements in a play.
   D. Your intention in a style-analysis is *to look for the individualities* in a playscript. But remember that your author will have some of the same aspects of style as his contemporaries. These aspects are part of the statement of style and should be recorded as such. This approach is particularly essential in defining Realism, where you will too easily take many stylistic devices for granted because they seem to fall within common usage. Therefore, be certain to look closely for variations in that usage.
   E. The form of the style-analysis worksheet is arranged to cover the seven basic elements of play structure. The questions in each section are intended as suggestions and reminders of what to look for. The actual completion of such a worksheet should take the form of essay answers, but they must be brief, clear, and exactly stated. Do not use the questions as ends in themselves, but rather as springboards to guide you to your own perception.

II. *Given Circumstances*
   A. *Environmental Facts.* Is specific emphasis placed on any one of the categories? (Your answer here may well tell you the particular sociopolitical bent of your playwright and the play you are dealing with.)
   B. *Previous Action.* How much is used? Is there a specific emphasis on a certain kind of previous action? How is it inserted into the play: all in the first part or sprinkled throughout? How expert is the author in presenting previous action through present dramatic action? Where does the dramatic action begin in relation to the previous action: near the beginning with minimal previous action or near the end with much previous action? What sort of thing is recalled: situations, character delineations, psychological flavorings?
   C. *Polar Attitudes.* What sort of poles has the playwright set up? Are they fresh? Are they obvious? Is the principal character readily declared through your analysis of the poles? How many characters are given polar positions (potential for change)?

III. *Dialogue*

What is distinctive? Has the playwright a "listening" ear? Does he use words in an individual way? Beyond the basic dramatic actions, what marks the speeches? Does he use characterizing phrases and repeat them? Does he use monologues (Chekhov, O'Neill, Osborne, Shepard)? What marks the length of the speeches? Is he witty? Of what does his wit consist? If it is other than prose, what characterizes the verse form? Does the playwright have a genuine ability for using verse forms, or are they laid on? If a line were to be quoted, what would declare its individuality? Does the playwright have a poetic quality, a sense of mystery, in his dialogue? How obvious is the dialogue?

IV. *Dramatic Action*

A. *Unities.* Does the author observe or violate the unity of time? Of place? Of action? How tight is the unity of action and what makes it so? Does observance of the unities give the play an artificial or a natural flavor? How far-ranging is the action? Are there many minor plots or only a few? How tightly are the minor plots connected with the main plot or with each other?

B. *Type.* What is the type of action? How can you support this emphasis from the detailed action? If it is tragic, what specifically makes it so? If it is comic, what specifically makes it so? If the emphasis is divided, how is this division done? Why? Does the action declare the play a melodrama or is the action only melodramatic? Why? Is the action farcical or comedic with farcical moments? Why? If the action is tragic, how does it stand up against Aristotle's definition in the *Poetics*? If it is comic, how does it stand up against Henri Bergson's definition? Against George Meredith's? If you label the play serious, why?

C. *The Ending.* How is the ending of the action handled? Do the characters make discoveries about themselves? Is a *deus ex machina* used?

D. *Technical Development.* How are the climaxes handled? Are the methods of discovery logical and exciting? How quickly does the first action begin? How would you describe the surges in the play?

V. *Characters*

A. *Choice.* What sort of people does the author write about? Why is the author interested in these people? How conventional are the characters? Are they conformist or relatively free? Are there any fantastic or allegorical characters? Why are they used?

B. *Development.* How finely drawn are the characters? Are they types or individuals? Why?

C. *Values.* What motivates the author in drawing his characters? Does he let them go free? Are they positive or negative people? Why or why not? If the play contains a hero (tragedy), what makes him one? If it contains a fool (comedy), what makes him one?

VI. *Idea*

A. *Choice.* In comparing this play with others by the same author, what sort of ideas does he like to treat? Is the idea in this play fresh or worn? Why?

B. *Validity.* Is the author an original thinker in any way? Does the idea have validity today? Why or why not? Is the author moralistic in the presentation of his idea or purely objective?

C. *Motivation.* Does the author seem to care strongly about the idea in his play?

D. *Quality.* Is the idea poetic? Is it purely practical? What is the potential of the idea for surviving?

VII. *Moods*
Is the play a "mood" play; that is, is it distinctly marked by mood dominance? Do moods tend to dominate logic? How do the mood-arousing techniques used by this author differ from those of another? How much does word choice have to do with mood arousal? Does the author use theatricality or business for mood arousal or does he generate the moods directly from clashes in the dramatic action? Are the moods odd or relatively usual?

VIII. *Tempos*
Does the author have a musical sense? How can you prove the answer from the playscript? How sharp are the variations in tempo? Does the author tend to use erratic tempos, fast tempos, or are they slow and stately? What kind of music does the playscript suggest to you? How individual, how original is the author's musical sense? Is the rhythm of this play typical among the author's works? Can you describe his rhythm?

IX. *Summary of Style*
You should now make a summary statement of the style by noting the points in your analysis that you think have the greatest emphasis. If you can integrate them in a conclusive statement of this sort, you will pin down your play as an individuality, for the summary is the epitome of your style-analysis.

You will have to practice style-analysis extensively until you see clearly what you must do and why you are doing it. The tendency at first will be to revert to play-analysis, because it is easier to deal with form readily perceived than to deal with content in an overview. But with practice you will learn to separate the two levels of analysis and become much more articulate at the higher level.

The exercises that follow are intended to enrich your experience in style-analysis by leading you into divergent areas of play structure, beginning with the plays more familiar to you and progressing to the more difficult and removed ones. As you will note, the exercises are presented more as challenges than as specific problems to be completed. Remember: Although the exercises begin at the style-analysis level, it is expected that you will first complete a play-analysis before beginning the second level.

EXERCISES

1. Do a style-analysis of *Riders to the Sea.* Can you see it as a play about three women instead of Maurya alone? Is the play a tragedy? If so, how does Synge get his tragic effect?
2. Do a style-analysis of *Ghosts.* Is this a romantic story about the sins of a father, or is it an attack on a blind, middle-class morality upheld by a confused and weak clergy? Is Pastor Manders a villain or a comic fool?
3. Do a style-analysis of Chekhov's *Uncle Vanya.* Is it a comedy or a tragedy? How can some critics say that there is very little dramatic action when every page seems crammed with it? How does Chekhov handle dialogue? How does he handle mood values?

4. Do a style-analysis of Shaw's *Man and Superman.* How does Shaw handle dramatic action? Why is there so little of it? Is there great activity in the dialogue? What sort of characters does Shaw deal with here? Why? Is the play all "Shaw-talk," or are distinctive characters developed? Why is the play a comedy?
5. Do a style-analysis of Pirandello's *Six Characters in Search of an Author.* How does Pirandello tear apart the premises behind Realistic psychological drama? Is the play structurally classical in its use of the unities and denouement?
6. Do a style-analysis of Rice's *Adding Machine.* Why is it categorized as an Expressionist play? What is the play's intention? How are dialogue and character handled? Is the play a comedy?
7. Do a style-analysis of Brecht's *Mother Courage.* Why does the dramatic action seem to have no climax but seem to be joined end to end? What is the function of the songs? How does Brecht use given circumstances to make his play meaningful today?
8. Do a style-analysis of Ionesco's *The Bald Soprano.* Can you see it as a conventional, classical comedy with a well-developed, logical action, conventional character types, climax, and denouement? How can you be easily misled by the dialogue?

26

Style in Production

Making Decisions

Now that you are much more aware of style in playscripts and can identify a playwright's individualization, you are ready to attack your own problems of making style in productions. *The goal is to make something you can call your own while maintaining the integrity of the play and the playwright.*

When applied to play production, *form* means the *general* shape of the staging, as opposed to *specific* shape. Form implies that a playscript has been physicalized on an available stage, that it has been given some sort of scenic investiture, that it has been costumed and lighted (perhaps only with daylight), and that it has been acted at least in a minimal way. All staged plays, including historical ones, have form because they observe the basic premise that makes the theatre a live ritual and different from the other arts—namely, that a play is a story devised for presentation on a stage by actors before an audience. As pointed out earlier, basic form in production has remained unchanged since the fifth century B.C.; it is production *style* that has changed.

Style in production, as in playscripts, means *specific individuality,* a major step beyond form. As discussed earlier, style is defined as *both the general characteristics of staging in any particular age and specific characteristics of an individual production.* General characteristics are those conventions in staging that each age has developed and kept in use for a period of time (Elizabethan style, Restoration style, Realistic style, etc.). Specific characteristics are what a director implements in staging a particular play.

Today's director, then, serves as more than just a coordinator in play production. Instead, he is a stylist and an individualist. However, at the same time, because the theatre has always been and always will be a group art, he must learn how to lead his fellow craftsmen to creativity beyond themselves if he is to make the unique production he envisions. Are you both a dreamer and an adventurous leader?

Production Style and the Choice of Dramatic Emphasis

The crucial point in style-making comes at the very beginning, when the director makes a firm, basic decision concerning the kind of statement he wants to make about a play. Every other move in this complex "chess game" will hinge on this decision. The director must therefore do his homework thoroughly so that he does not discover later in the rehearsal period, when it may be too late to redesign the production, that he has gotten off on the wrong track. As pointed out in Chapter 25, a thorough play-analysis topped by a style-analysis can lead to sensitive decision making, because what your dramatic imagination may see in a play can be quite different from what someone else sees. *Your individual perception will be the basis of your style.*

Two basic decisions must be made: (1) Whose play is it—that is, which character is dominant?—and (2) What is the spine of the action?

Before we are aware of style, we are apt to assume that plays have limited basic meanings and that the principal characters are always declared. Thus, *Antigone* is about Antigone, *Macbeth* is about Macbeth, *Tartuffe* is about Tartuffe, and *Ghosts* is about Mrs. Alving. This assumption may be true up to a point, but beyond that, individual opinion comes into play because a director makes the play he sees and feels. All he must do is place a very strong actor in what appears to be the second role and a new play can emerge. Why can't Cassius, instead of Brutus, dominate Shakespeare's *Julius Caesar*? Or Mark Anthony? Can't Creon become the principal role in *Antigone,* Lady Macbeth in *Macbeth,* Orgon in *Tartuffe,* Oswald Alving or Pastor Manders in *Ghosts*? Is Anouilh's *Becket or the Honor of God* about Becket or about the king? (Note that Laurence Olivier switched from Becket to King Henry after playing the first role for many performances.)

Plays, you may argue, are about both the protagonist and the antagonist and both must be given equal positions. However, doing precisely that may weaken a play's structure. It will be better to settle on the character and give him prominence in every way. This will prevent begging the issue and will present a clear point of view. You may be prejudiced, but audiences can either argue with your view or see something new in it. When Tyrone Guthrie cast an African American actor as Horatio in his Minneapolis production of *Hamlet* in 1963, he greatly changed the significance of this supporting role and, along with it, the usual concept of Hamlet as a character. What would you make of the play on those terms?

Characters are, of course, *the result* of the action in a play, for we see what they are primarily on the basis of what they do. Therefore, character and action are intertwined in such a way that one declares the other. Once a character has been established, he cannot be artificially manipulated; that is, he cannot be made to do things in violation of his character without stretching our sense of logic to the breaking point. Yet, it is possible to let actions lead our imagination in certain directions by building up evidence in those directions.

When Olivier made his film of *Hamlet,* he shocked critics and audiences alike with his strong emphasis on the Freudian aspects of the characters. Is Hamlet in love with his mother? Through a succession of scenes in which the camera probed Hamlet's subjective self, Olivier placed major emphasis on this point. When the same actor played Othello as a native African, with characteristic physical features in face and body, he created a fresh view of a character in action—a fully declared style for the play. At a time when many people feared but at the same time were intensely curious about interracial marriage, he played on the full value of that fear-curiosity and thus startled his audiences into view vision. *Romeo and Juliet* played by teenagers, as it was in Zeffirelli's Old Vic production in 1960 and his movie version in 1969, gave audiences quite a new experience with the play.

What can be done with *Hedda Gabler*? Is there only one way to treat it or are there several possibilities? Consider these:

> Hedda is played as a Medea-like woman who revels in her dominance of others whom she craftily destroys.
>
> Hedda is played as a nymphomaniac who brings about destruction of others because of the sexual denial of her marriage and the restrictions society has placed on her.
>
> Hedda is played as a woman, perhaps homosexual, who hates and despises men because she considers them inferior and who goes under only when she finally meets an equal in Judge Brack.
>
> Hedda is played as a masochist, as a suicidal paranoiac, who destroys everything about her, including a possible child before birth.
>
> Hedda is played as a selfish, self-centered virgin who cannot stand violation of herself in any possible way.
>
> Hedda is played as a "good" woman.

All these are options open to a director in his decision-making role. What his individual decision turns out to be will determine the style of his production.

Up to this point, serious plays have been under discussion, but you must be aware that decisions about comedies and farces may be even more difficult to make because the director must decide what is really funny in a play and how he can convey that joke to an audience. Comedy exists in the theatre only when a director and actor understand the incongruities; only then will they know how to reach audiences with the fun of a play.

Deciding whose play it is and, accordingly, making gradations in the comedy are absolutely essential if a production is to have stylistic unity. Feydeau's *A Flea in Her Ear* cannot exist on its second-act chase scene alone but must be carefully constructed as both a comedy of manners and a comedy of character in the first and third acts. *She Stoops to Conquer* is not just about Tony Lumpkin's high jinks but must also be about Mrs. Hardcastle's pretensions, Mr. Hardcastle's puritanism, and Marlow's impotence with well-bred women. If young Marlow is played straight—that is, as only a bashful young man—the principal comedy may not come through nearly as well as when he is played as an experienced London rake who moves unerringly among servant girls, or the demimonde, but turns to rubber when confronted with middle-class "goodness."

If a director does not discover how to make *The Importance of Being Earnest* "talk well," he might better delay production until he does, because it depends extensively on verbal wit. Is Sheridan's *School for Scandal* about Joseph Surface? If he is made the central fool in a slippery, falsely pious way, not only can he be drolly amusing like Tartuffe but he can also cause the other fools to stand out clearly. Without solid building of character based on decision making about character, comedy can never work, for people are amused primarily by the incongruities in human behavior and not by the situations in which characters are caught.

Whose play is it, then? This is a decision of major importance, and you can make this decision only by making the most personal and intensive examination of the action in a playscript and the characters that grow out of it. Once you know who will dominate and why, you can determine the specific line of action you want to emphasize and in this way declare the *spine* of your production. Each character will relate to this spine of action exactly as you intend him to relate to the principal character. You will now have a specific and personal way to tell the story of the play on the stage as you see it.

Although the Stanislavskian technique of declaring the spine by using the infinitive form of the verb is rather involved (see the essay by Elia Kazan, "Notebook for *A Streetcar Named Desire*," in *Directors on Directing*, edited by Toby Cole and Helen Krich Chinoy, Allyn & Bacon, 1963), you may find it useful to reduce your decision on the action to this highly abbreviated form of summarizing. Whatever method you use, *the purpose will be to crystallize your own personal vision of the action* so you can easily hold on to this central drive that will declare at the base your style of production.

Production Style and Casting

The style of a production will depend significantly on how a play is cast. Strong actors who are appropriately cast can declare the emphasis you have in mind. However, if they are inappropriately cast, they can warp it. Casting is the basis of interpretation and it plays an intrinsic part in making style. Whoever plays a role will endow it with his specific personality, no matter how carefully the chosen actor works within the confines of the actions. By nature, actors possess radiance and that radiance will suffuse the action. Who the director selects will declare the overall style more than any other factor.

Casting in a professional theatre production is very different from what you will be doing with amateur actors; decisions in the former ride on celebrated names and the desires of the producers. With movies, a casting office is usually involved to sort out available actors. You will have to make all of these decisions on your own, recognizing that casting is a delicate process of matching weights and qualities, partly subjective and partly objective. *Casting projects the future of a production,* a gambling process in which a director tries to foresee what will happen by balancing certain actors with clearly defined qualities against other actors with different qualities equally well defined. It is all weights and measures.

However, if the director has done his homework on the play and if he has a fair choice of actors from whom to select, the style he envisions has a good chance of emerging. Success in this aspect of production can come about only if a director has a firm idea in mind of what he wants; haphazard casting can lead only to confusion.

The following are suggestions for the casting process, all of which affect style in one way or another.

Orchestrate Voices

A cast with a variety of pitch differences will not only increase the "hearability" level but will also readily declare character qualities. We take for granted that characters in operas are written for certain voices—tenors, sopranos, bassos, and the like—but we are apt to forget that characters in plays have similar pitch requirements, although the range when compared to opera castings can be much greater and is not as stereotyped. Hear the play "in concert" during a final casting session *not by looking at the actors but only by listening to them* if you want to know what it is apt to sound like four weeks hence.

Size-and-Shape Type Casting versus Antitype Casting

Style in production often depends on the unexpected. Visual stereotypes may be necessary in some roles, particularly those that exert no particular force on the action and act as instruments to the main action. However, individualization in casting major roles may turn a worn play or a worn idea into a fresh and vitalizing experience. *Antitype* casting is casting against what seems to be prescribed type. From modern psychological drama we have learned one important principle that pertains to all drama: What people look like on the outside does not at all prescribe what they are like within. Consequently, in casting historical drama as well as modern plays, directors have turned away from nineteenth-century type casting and more toward antitype casting.

Where does the truth lie? In describing the sorts of actors he would like to play his roles, Bertolt Brecht specifies "potato faces" for his women. He is suggesting that it is impossible to portray the peasantry who populate his plays with conventional types, and that truth lies in the rugged edges actors bring to a play rather than in their physical attractiveness. Julian Beck in his Living Theatre productions took the same position: Truth, and therefore beauty, lies in the spiritual values one holds and not in the visible physical realities; therefore, what we take for physical ugliness may possess inherent beauty. Further, it is possible that only by being "turned off" by unsympathetic exteriors can we begin to see the beauty behind those exteriors. Whether you agree with Brecht or Beck, you will discover that a high potential for production style lies in antitype casting, just as you will find that certain plays (Feydeau's or Oscar Wilde's, for instance) cannot do at all without conventional beauty in their women as well as their men.

Special Qualities Reveal Action

The previous discussion declares the necessity for a director to cast a play in such a way that it can augment what he believes to be the emphatic action. Only then can he ensure that his point of style will be preserved. A large variety of actors can play a specific dramatic action fairly convincingly, but only a few will possess those essential qualities that will endow the action with moving overtones. Leading actors in the professional theatre know this fact, and they avoid roles they feel they cannot fulfill in this special way. In the amateur theatre where the director has a great deal of control, he can usually cast the actor who can best illuminate the emphasis he has in mind.

The search for special qualities, then, is the major attack in the casting process. Actual selection may revolve on whether a role should be played by a "cool" or by a "warm" actor, because these qualities cannot be acted but will be inherent projections. Some actors can project more intellectuality than others; some project pure animality and nothing else. Some actors have natural decorum in voice and gesture for projecting upper-class roles, whereas others simply cannot reflect such conformist qualities of behavior. What can be achieved in style will depend on what a director can project of his action-emphasis through the actors he selects in casting.

Overcoming Blocks

What stands between a director and adventurous, more exceptional casting and thus clear declaration of style are the blocks of (1) playing safe; (2) forming preconceptions about certain actors; (3) seeing and hearing too many actors in casting sessions, which results in a sort of blindness and deafness; and (4) failing to make objective assessments before final decisions are made.

To help you overcome your blocks, you need to develop specific techniques that will lead you away from subjective viewing and toward objective assessment. Five- to ten-minute auditions with material other than the play being cast can help objectify the process. Get yourself into the habit of making a new tryout card for each actor on which you can record his voice quality and speech pattern, his sense of the dramatic and the theatrical, his capability at improvisation, his dominant qualities as you can see them on the surface, and his capability as an actor in general. After the preliminary auditions, read each actor in several roles, particularly the one you think him least qualified for, and then make specific comments on his card. Use closed tryouts (one actor at a time) in the interest of keeping an actor from copying others reading for the same roles and of relaxing him sufficiently so that he can show you who he is. After this initial assessment has been made, you can hold group readings or improvisational sessions. You also must arrange your early tryout plan in such a way that you are always seeing actors as individuals; later, when you see and hear them in groups, you will be able to see how each actor affects the balance in the group—what he can contribute that will be individual and therefore partly declarative of style.

A highly useful technique for sorting your actors is casting sheets on which you can list in numbered columns (1) the characters in the playscript (men and women collected separately), (2) a brief physical description of each character along with any special qualities essential to the role, (3) names of all actors who can possibly play each role, (4) first tentative decision, (5) second tentative decision, (6) third tentative decision, and (7) final decision. You should gather all this information on two or three sheets of paper so that you can look at the entire situation easily and comparatively. Items 4 through 6 will indicate each reassessment you make as you progress through the casting period. Before you make a tentative decision, take a long, hard look at your choices: Are they fresh in qualities and ideas? Can you hear their voices in your mind's ear, and are they the right ones? Are you being adventurous in leading young actors away from their tired stereotypes and toward sensitive and individual statements? Are the protagonist and antagonist in strong contrast? Are there possibilities for development of each actor as an actor during the rehearsal period?

The intention of all of these questions is to make you aware of what lies ahead, what an audience will eventually see and hear. Above all, if you want to declare individuality in your productions (that is, make style) you must be as adventurous in casting them as circumstances will permit, because fresh statements are always the ones that communicate most easily to audiences.

Production Style and Pointing the Dramatic Moments

Now that you have cast the play and moved into the rehearsal period, you are faced with many new decisions in effecting the dynamics of the play as you see it, and consequently the style that will emerge.

Violence, Energy, and Size

A distinct mark of style in play production is the *violence level.* Most young directors are afraid to open all the stops for fear such a procedure will result in overplaying and thus make the illustrations appear stagey. You should take just the opposite point of view, while recognizing at the same time that opening the stops does not necessarily mean playing at high volumes but often just the opposite. *Good actors move audiences precisely through the intense level of illustrations they give to the violent moments—the climactic peaks of a play.* At these peaks they expend enormous energy by using their bodies as great and powerful instruments of communication. If we watch them closely, we also note that gesture has either increased or decreased markedly, for illustrations of violence require size in acting.

How you show violence on the stage will reveal your sense of style. You must never fear overplaying; it can happen only if the actors do not believe their dramatic action or fail to act reciprocally. Conversely, you should not underplay because it will never move an audience beyond itself or carry it into the astounding mysteries of the passions of life. Nor must you think that violence, energy, and size apply only to great drama. These elements must be used in all drama, serious or comic. *Audiences come to the theatre to feel energy vicariously;* this identification is what actually thrills them because it makes them perceive that such energy is also possible in their own lives. If you miss this inherent point about the need for acting, you will never touch audiences.

To make the "theatrical moment," make it in big, bold strokes (high volumes or low volumes, big movements or practically no movement at all). In your study of the playscript you should mark (in red pencil) the big moments in three stages: (1) how they are approached, (2) the exact points of climax, and (3) how the characters move away from them. Then, in rehearsal you can help your actors see their great importance and can find the violence levels they require. Some professional directors use this power as the core of their work with the actors because it "phrases" a plan and "paces" it through *contrast.*

The Light Touch

Style is also revealed by getting a play acted with a *light touch.* Can you project violence fully and still do it with a light hand? This is the paradox. A light touch depends partly on directing techniques but much more on a director's natural sense of *taste.* It does not at all mean a withdrawal from intensive dramatic moments or a backing away in any sense from the fact that the theatre is a robust, knockabout business. What it does mean is that audiences are neither deeply moved nor made to laugh in the theatre if the acting is too heavy, stolid, or predictable. Theatre is an art form that dances and sings and is full of surprises; it is not a sluggish battle between fighters, but a sparring match between boxers. *A light touch means a seeming lack of effort that permits the audience to relax into the play.* Poorly performed plays never allow the viewers to relax, because the plays always seem in danger of going awry.

Building imagination depends on a director's sense of taste, a quality that can be cultivated if he has an inclination to find out what it means. *Good theatre always has taste, because acting at its best is not reality but ideality.* Because selection and emphasis are possible in theatre art, what can be *suggested* is usually more powerful than what we encounter in much of everyday life. A director who plays music and lets his actors dance, both seriously and joyously, can make his points of style with clarity and feeling.

Tempos

Finding the appropriate tempos (see "Pacing" in Major Project 1A) for a production is to discover an inherent way to project style. Tempos are always a matter of feeling and are deeply embedded in the personal nature of style. How a production moves will declare its style because rhythm is the basis of comprehension; we vibrate emphatically if we catch the rhythm, and only then do we believe a dramatic action to be right and true. It is like singing a song at the proper speed.

Actors are frequently excellent musicians, but the primary job of determining tempos lies with the director because only he can control multiple-actor situations. As noted in Chapter 5 in the basic discussion of tempos, a play has a surging effect in its structure of action, like surf rolling in on a seashore where the waves grow larger and larger until they finally culminate in a climactic wave, which is then followed by a relative calm before the next surging begins. The director's job is to find these surges and to pinpoint their beginnings and endings.

The emergence of style depends on whether a director can build the surges accumulatively with variations in tempos, pauses, and climaxes in such a way that a performance becomes a rhythmic whole. Each performance must achieve this effect or the style will be lost. This is why plays that have long runs must be frequently redirected, with redirection actually the process of rediscovering the rhythm that has been lost. Top-flight baseball players, for example, lose their batting rhythm from time to time, sometimes for weeks or months, and go into a slump. Their recovery depends on again finding the split timing (the inherent rhythm) that first established them at the top of their trade. So it is with actors in an ensemble: Once the rhythm is lost, it must be rediscovered or the audience's concentration will be lost.

The Amount of Actor Illustration

If you were to see a production of *Racine* or *Corneille* at the Comédie-Française in Paris, you would be struck by the quietude with which the actors perform their roles. This quietude is a point of style because it assumes that French classical drama gains its greatest effects from line delivery and not visual spectacle. Some plays such as *Le Cid* may be spoken in a hushed sound, only a few steps up from whispering, with the actors making very few movements or gestures. Such a style results in a dynamic and exciting theatrical experience because the verbal delivery is so unusual in the context of minimum visual illustration. Only at the Comédie will you hear a performance like this, and you will be struck by its unique quality of style.

How much a director gives an actor to do or encourages him to develop will be a major point of style. Directors in the United States tend toward relatively heavy visual illustration, keeping the stage constantly busy. English directors do somewhat less, with a leaning toward economy and sparseness. French directors do least of all, in comedies as well as in serious plays, preferring their classical emphasis on the spoken play, whether modern or historical. How much visual illustration you use will depend on your inherent sense of rhythm and what you think your particular audience needs to keep its attention and concentration at a high level. Overillustration may make a play seem choppy and insecure, whereas underillustration may make it seem vague and undeclared. The only way out of this dilemma is to use *appropriate* illustration. Therefore, each play will have its own rhythm of illustration built into it, and the director must find this quality and develop it in his own terms and in those of his expected audience. For the most part, learning directors tend to underillustrate or to emphasize small, detailed movements at the expense of larger, more dynamic surges. You will, of course, discover how to handle illustration only through experience, but you must recognize at this point that style will emerge only when you use appropriate illustration.

Style will depend on the kind, quality, and quantity of illustration your production contains. You must learn to compose a play's illustrations so that there is always room for the "bigger and better" ahead. Quiet beginnings can lead to dynamic endings, whereas the reverse may result in boredom. Learn to build climactically; much of the secret of audience control will lie in this capability.

Production Style and the Choice of the Designs

The Metaphor

Many directors and designers build productions around metaphors because these images are, at the base, style oriented. If the metaphor is a good one, it can have continuous application with many overtones throughout the areas of design or will at least work well in one area. The production style can therefore flow from such an image.

If the playscript of *The Beaux Stratagem,* for example, is thought of as a clever chess game, with scene after scene of subtle maneuvering, it can be carried into production with a painted floorcloth made to look like a chessboard. Scenic pieces can then be whisked on and off like moves in the game, with each new setup forcing a new play by the characters involved, and so on. A metaphoric approach of this sort certainly has limitations, but it is possible for an exciting stylistic production to emerge. However, a director should never force a designer to work in this way unless he has been so trained. It is better for the director to create such an image for himself and then use it as he can.

Dominance in Scheme Making

Production style depends greatly on physical production—what it looks like and how it works. Because a play is always seen as a fluid progression, a tight interrelationship in the choice of stage, scenery, properties, light, costumes, makeup, and sound is absolutely necessary if a style is to emerge. What the director must bring about is a production scheme that works because it enhances the actor as the principal instrument in the storytelling. It is the director's job to decide what should be dominant in a production scheme and then to tie in the other designs to that dominance.

The Mermaid Theatre's production of Henry Fielding's *Lock Up Your Daughters* used a marvelous stage machine: a high platform raised on a pedestal with two swinging arms, each having platforms and steps, with the entire structure mounted on a turntable. This machine not only allowed multiple locations both on the stage level, steps, and above on the movable platform, but it also provided extensive possibilities for movement in a lively and vigorously busy play. *She Stoops to Conquer* was played on a modified Elizabethan stage with a sharply raked forestage, side entrances, inner-below entrances, above positions, and a neutral area surrounding the whole as a place for the garden scene. By avoiding the usual eighteenth-century arrangement of wings and backdrops, the play was seen in a fresh way on what amounted to an Elizabethan stage.

Mart Crowley's *The Boys in the Band* was also staged on a modified Elizabethan stage with the scene "above" (the bedroom) approached by means of a curving staircase. Even more stylistic was the use of a Serlian adaptation: Real furniture was placed against wall units covered with photographic murals of real rooms with furniture. The effect was super-Realism. Equally radical was the production of *Hadrian VII,* which was staged in curtains with the exception of one interior scene (the attic). *Hair* revolutionized the American musical by not using conventional scenery at all except for a small scaffolding at the rear of a huge stage space and a few carry-on pieces. An unusually complex lighting design "in space" declared the style.

Many more examples of style can be given to illustrate how various directors and designers have seen plays in action and what they have chosen to dominate the physicalization. In the constant search for style, a new convention has appeared: *The more limited the scenic investiture, the more important the lighting becomes as emphatic design.* This convention, in turn, has forced changes in what to do with the lighting. Should it be full of color or should it be primarily white light? Should backlighting be employed as a basic principle? Should the quantity of light be an important factor in the style? All these questions directors will have to answer for themselves as each production is undertaken. In costume design, we are beginning to relearn earlier ways as we tackle the problems presented by the open stage with its strong sculptural demands.

The significant point in this discussion is to show once again the necessity of seeing interrelationships in design and how a director can make something fresh out of old theatrical devices. People no longer seem to be content in the theatre with the aesthetic of "peeking in" on humanity, which was the controlling convention of box-set Realism in production. As the revelatory power of Realism has been absorbed over time, much of the artistic search in the theatre has had to do with realizing the theatre theatrical; that is, finding ways of making theatre that recognizes theatre as theatre and its image-making potential as starting points for the production. Much of what has been innovative in theatrical direction and design throughout the twentieth century and into the current one, has had to do with the theatre's image-making potential. Audiences, who have absorbed the lessons of Realism's specialized kind of seeing, have generally responded favorably to this kind of heightened image-making in the theater, for it allows them to participate more directly in the theater event as their imaginations are stimulated by design approaches that are something other than literal Realism.

Counterpoint in Scheme Making

It is important at this point to reread carefully the section on the *counterpoint principle* discussed in Chapter 18 to see how counterpoint is essential in the development of a production style. Design that proceeds from a single impetus will lack contrast and even necessary conflict. A director must see that each design fulfills its particular values in a production and that it exerts the force of its own individuality, its contributing point of style.

Results of Good Scheme Making

A production must move. This is a basic fact about the theatre, a fact that no director can ignore. *Pacing a play also means pacing the scheme of production* because style will be the rhythm of the whole. In multiple stagings, where several sets are used, the quick change, perhaps in front of the audience, is an absolute necessity. In this sense, we are back to the seventeenth-century masque tradition and its influence on movable scenery: We want the change as part of the theatrical experience. To lower the curtain and take an intermission for changing scenery (the practice of the theatre of illusion) is no longer feasible in a theatre that places a great deal of emphasis on things happening in a spirited tempo. *Style will depend on a workable production scheme.*

Tempo. Can all the designs be moved with the necessary speed to provide the appropriate tempo necessary to convey the style? The director must decide what the overall tempo should be and then see that designing is done in accordance with it. A clearly defined tempo in a production scheme will give an audience both a sense of security and rhythm of the whole. Waiting for scene changes reduces audience attention and concentration because once a production is set in motion, it must continue to move rhythmically. If changes are made on a darkened stage, they must be made in a matter of seconds because waiting in the dark brings an audience back to its own reality, making it self-conscious. The major problem usually is scenery; but costume, light, and sound also require careful designing if the scheme is to work.

Effortless scheme making. Graceful scene changes, if they are visible, are as essential in production as effortless acting. Whatever is done, and this includes visible actors or stagehands making changes, must seem right and inevitable because *the danger lies in making an audience overly aware of the staging effects,* a situation that will reduce their attention and concentration on dramatic action and character. Rhythmic changes tend to enhance the feeling of style because they have been made part of the overall rhythm of the play and are integrally associated with it.

The theatricality of change. Is the change interesting in itself? Without drawing attention to it, does the change provide the dramatic effect of suddenly presenting a new scene, costume, or light? The purpose of scene change is to provide new locales and new time settings and thus new action. However, does the change contain the element of surprise? The style of your production may depend on it. What is the mood contrast in the scene change? Can the dramatic difference be clearly pointed up with dynamic effect? Therein may lie declarations of the production style.

27

Style in Production

Modern Plays

How much of an artistic gambler are you? Unless you are willing to venture as an "idea person" in the theatre, as a "maker of visions," you will never become a stylist and thus will never fulfill your total function as a director. It should be perfectly clear to you by now that taking risks is not done for adventure's sake but out of the strongest integrity and the highest regard for what the theatre as an art form can do. You can move out in an individual way and make something that can be called style.

A director's statement of style is the physicalization of a play in such a way that an audience is lifted into a fresh and exciting perception of that play. Production style excites because it communicates emotionally; it can never be dull because it is a very personal, very intimate statement.

The general treatment in this chapter may disappoint you if you are looking for quick answers about how to effect production style with recent plays, the ones you are probably most interested in. Yet, you should now be well aware that finding style is entirely up to you, that it must grow out of your sensitivity and imagination, and a great deal of hard work. All that can be done here is to alert you to the problems and some possibilities for solving them. *You* must do the rest. And if you do it well, you will see how style in drama shifts from one tack to another, and how, consequently, style in production must also shift to keep abreast of it.

Modern Designations of Style

Although theatre historians and dramatic critics have categorized theatre history in accord with national development or historical eras (for example, Greek, Roman, Medieval, English, Renaissance, Jacobean, Restoration, French Classical, etc.), when designating modern production styles they have tended to use labels often associated with other modern art forms—Naturalism, Realism, Simplified Realism, Surrealism, Symbolism, Expressionism, Formalism, and Theatricalism. Rather confusingly, these forms have been applied to playscripts, as well as scenic investiture, lighting, costumes, makeup, and occasionally acting, although acting cannot easily be forced into formalistic patterns without being self-conscious or stripped of its human qualities.

For all practical purposes, however, there are only two major stylistic designations for modern drama and production that concern the director: (1) Realism and (2) departures from Realism. *These designations assume that Realism is the foundation from which other modern styles depart.* Once you grasp this concept, you will have little difficulty dealing with the jargon that has accompanied modern stylistic descriptions since 1870. Nor will you need to join the labelers of style at this time, but you can devote your energies to making descriptions in your own language on the basis of what you see and hear and thus what you comprehend.

That labeling serves the function of separating differences is, of course, recognized, but the label alone will do no more than provide a general view. Specific designations must be based on analysis. Thus, by dividing all modern drama and production into the two major groups of Realism and departures from Realism, you can proceed to specific labeling as you accumulate knowledgeable experience, not only through the actual process of directing plays but also through diverse theatregoing experiences and through looking at photographs of productions. Do not let yourself be confused by the labeling or the categorizing; learn to make style-analyses by yourself and leave the labeling to others. Eventually, you should become familiar with the labels attached to departures from Realism because they are so widely used and can be confused with each other.

The intention in this chapter is to plant an approach to understanding the differences in modern styles so that you may grow with your knowledge at your own speed.

Realism

The range of Realism has been so wide during the hundred-plus years of its history that it cannot be described easily as one style. But simply stated, it moves from an exact copy of life (Naturalism, or reproducing nature exactly as it is seen with the eye) to a form so simplified that many aspects are only suggested (in production, for example, painted molding is used in place of real molding). Whatever the gradation may be, the intention is to show life as it actually appears to be. *Realism is therefore a style to describe appearances.* Because human beings live their lives surrounded by these appearances, it is assumed that we can understand them as individuals if we can see them in the midst of their specific, viewable surroundings. Most Realistic plays are about families and their problems in living together. This also includes their separations, their violences, their generational differences, and other forces prescribed in the given circumstances.

That this point of view (aesthetic) was seriously open to question is revealed in the fact that no sooner had Realism been established as a style in the 1890s than the new stylists damned it as unpoetic, noncommunicative, inartistic, and simply untrue to life. From that point on, we have had a steady stream of "departures from Realism," though Realism itself, in one modification or another, still remains the dominant style.

Early Realism (1870–1915)

Because much of this book has been concerned with the Realistic style before 1960, further discussion of its general characteristics would be redundant. *But watch out! There are changes within that loosely defined style you must discover for yourself.* And these you can become aware of only through the most careful reading and analysis of the dramatic literature written in this style. Have you read a dozen plays by Ibsen? Another dozen by Bernard Shaw written before 1925? All of Chekhov's and Strindberg's? These are the Early Realists; and to know them well is to make yourself aware of the changes that follow their work, including today's plays.

When it comes to production, you will have many options to consider. Perhaps the biggest problem is that there are so few limitations in producing modern plays, for we are passing through an age that has more diversified staging than any previous period. The problem lies in finding what will work best. This has become increasingly evident as we try to bring the Realistic plays written before 1920 into clearer focus for present-day audiences because their dramaturgical techniques appear dated to us now. We may certainly produce them, as some directors do, in the style of their first performances. But we may very well prefer to look at them in the same way we look at historical drama and to treat them as such.

This means that *a wide range of stylistic possibilities are open to a director in search of fresh meanings,* possibilities that may take him far from the box settings in which most of these plays were originally played. Like the American playwright-adaptors who have worked at transferring the plays of Ibsen, Chekhov, and Strindberg—Arthur Miller *(An Enemy of the People),* Thornton Wilder *(A Doll's House),* Stark Young *(The Cherry Orchard),* and Eva Le Gallienne (much of Ibsen)—U.S. directors feel the pressure for finding fresh stagings. The "historical approach" is a good one because it recognizes that the major problem is audience communication. It is important to remember that these plays appeared on the heels of a Romantic theatre in which acting style by present standards was flamboyant and fully declared. Although the dramaturgy changed noticeably in style from that of Romantic drama, this does not imply that the acting style playwrights had in mind followed the same pattern. An acting statement, then, may lie somewhere between the large, flamboyant acting style of the Romantic theatre and the small, behavioristic pattern of post–World War I Realism. If you look for a larger, more dynamic style for the acting (perhaps something like that in early silent movies) in contrast to what playscripts seem to literally suggest, you may find that these plays can grip audience attention where a more sedate, a more naturalistic style will not.

Another acting problem with these early Realistic plays is finding the decorum of the characters represented. After all, the characters who populate these plays—whether they are Norwegians, Russians, or Frenchmen—are close kin to middle-class Victorians or Edwardians; and because the style is "observed Realism," *a director and his actors must find that outer façade that allows such plays to work. You must never forget that an important part of the style of "observed Realism" is showing a façade that covers up the interiors*—the skeletons in the closet. You must therefore learn to build façades of manners, just as you would for a seventeenth- or eighteenth-century comedy of manners, for you cannot break through them dramatically if they are not demonstrated. How actors walk, sit, stand, talk, laugh, greet others, wear their "clothing-costumes," dress their hair, handle objects, and so on, thus becomes very important. The post-1920 American lower- to middle-class folk drama has so disarmed us about a society in which class distinctions are taken for granted that young directors overlook the necessity of showing the mannered façades of the people in early Realism. *These plays are about environment and how it forces action.* You must give intensive study when producing such plays to how you can reveal given circumstances with the greatest strength.

Departures from Realism

Departures from Realism include all drama and production that moves away from the literal appearance of things. The basic intention of these styles is to communicate through essence rather than through appearance. The audience is given the feeling of something, and thus it is able to receive the communication in direct terms. This aesthetic approach assumes that observed realities do not communicate well because they are so familiar that most people do not perceive them and therefore cannot feel them. Reality is thus given a high degree of symbolization, frequently in abstract terms. On the stage, the designer creates lines and masses that contain essences of real objects, and we are able to *feel* them directly without the distractions of familiarity and everyday use. As viewers, we find these exciting and illuminating, not only because of their direct communication but also because we may actually be "perceiving" the objects for the first time in our lives, not just "seeing" them. Art is an emotional experience and not an intellectual one.

One of the principal points about using such a label as *departures from Realism* for production designation is that it readily parallels departures from Realism in playwriting. We can see the two moving side by side since the 1890s. *But it does not necessarily follow that the departures from Realism in plays will all require departure from Realism in production.* Here is a crucial question about modern style: When can departures in production be used most effectively?

In the 1950s and 1960s, after several decades that thought dramaturgical style should be supported by the same sort of production style—that is, Realistic plays should have Realistic settings, and departure plays should have departure settings—what seemed to be thoroughly accepted has given way to a new style. *Today, we have no confining rules about style because anything goes that will work with audiences.* This flexibility means that Realistic plays can be effectively produced using departure approaches. Thus, dramatic writing and production style are recognized as two separate and distinct areas of theatre as far as style is concerned.

Playwriting Since 1915

The problem facing the young director is always to force himself into a fresh approach for each play he undertakes. We tend to take many plays written in the 1960s and 1970s too much for granted by assuming that because they look like

Early Realism on the outside, they must belong to that familiar category. Therefore, you will need to search out the difference between "outer" Realism and "inner" Realism. Once again, *a director must always do a detailed style-analysis of every play he considers seriously for production, for only through this process can he be sure of a play's potential and thus be able to find a style that would give it life on the stage.*

You must also make your own intensive structural examination of the wide range of *departures from Realism* written since 1915. You should look at the styles of Wedekind, Toller, Andreyev, Kaiser, de Ghelderode, Ansky, Cocteau, Capek, and particularly Pirandello. Similarly, you should know O'Neill's departure drama and what characterizes his style in such plays as *The Emperor Jones, The Hairy Ape, The Great God Brown,* and *Strange Interlude,* as well as his more Realistic style in *Desire under the Elms, Mourning Becomes Electra, Ah, Wilderness!, The Iceman Cometh,* and *Long Day's Journey into Night.* You must also know the Americans—Treadwell, Gertrude Stein, Odets, Hellman, Wilder, Williams, Miller, Albee, Shepard, Mamet, Guare, August Wilson, Kushner, Parks, and Mee—as well as the Irish and English—Synge, O'Casey, Behan, Friel, Osborne, Pinter, Orton—and a host of contemporary writers including Storey, Hare, Churchill, Stoppard, Wertenbaker, McDonagh, and Kane, among many others. The plays of Brecht will attract you, but you will need to give them a hard look to see how they work, as you will with others related to that style, including the plays of von Horvath, Weiss, and Bond. You will need to study Sartre, Ionesco, Genet, Beckett, and Arrabal, and other European playwrights such as Frisch, Durrenmatt, Handke, Havel, Mrozek, Roszewicz, and Mueller, and moving beyond Europe to the plays of Soyinka and Fugard, Mishima, and the other dramatists of Asia and Latin America. And in addition to all this, there is the high-quality musical theater of George Gershwin, Kurt Weill, Rodgers and Hammerstein, Frank Loesser, Leonard Bernstein, Stephen Sondheim, and others. In other words, *you must study all that is considered the best of modern drama. You must know the differences in order to see the likenesses.* But above all, you must become aware of the nature of individuality, the nature of style in playwriting, so that you have points of departure for making style in production.

Your biggest problem, however, may be controlling production, not finding what to exploit in it. Flight must assuredly take place; but to a young director, flight in production too often means making the audience self-consciously aware of the clever staging—an approach that can obliterate the text and all that flows from it.

Stage Limitations and Available Options

The options in staging discussed in Chapters 19 through 21 of this book are the basis for all modern production. Although these options allow great freedom, a director may find himself physically bound by the limitations of a proscenium theatre in which he must produce. However, where this single form has been amplified or replaced in favor of multiple forms, as it has in some educational and nonprofit theatre plants, directors have found new ways of meeting the problem of modern communication. Multiple-production approaches are now possible as never before because we are overcoming the restrictions of theatre architecture and can think more and more in terms of stage-audience relationships and what they can do. Staging has thus become a matter of control of space, with its focus on intensive communication—reaching out and touching. The new freedom has given directors more possibilities for creating dynamic and varied theatre experience than any age has ever had. Whether the director can use it wisely and with sensitive imagination will probably determine his future value in the theatre.

As was noted in Chapter 20, the movement away from the proscenium has also given lighting a new dimension, as the problem is now that of *defining space* in a dramatic way. Although no similar declaration is apparent yet in costuming, the fact that costumes are meant to be seen on many stages "in-the-round" as sculpture, more often than they ever have been before, makes it quite possible that stage wear may undergo pressures that will move it away from the representationalism that has largely confined it since the nineteenth century.

Acting Style of Recent Drama

A major assumption of this book is that the prevailing acting style in the United States, inspired by Konstantin Stanislavski, has placed its primary emphasis on the subtext and its conveyance to audiences with extensively detailed illustration. But by comparison with the "behavioristic" acting of the 1930s and 1940s, there has been an increase in the size and deliberateness of illustration. More recently, greater emphasis has been placed on "delivering" the text, undoubtedly under the pressure of the English tradition and the common necessity for actors to perform in historical drama where concentration on the text is necessary. Thus, this more highly developed process of intensively illustrating the subtext and delivering the text expertly has brought us closer to the historical line of acting as we have watched it shift and change over the period of 300 years.

The acting style for recent drama, then, could be defined as highly illustrated psychological projection of both subtext and text. This style demands the focus of primary attention on character-mood-intensity to bring about "violence levels" in appropriate tempos. The director's best instruction in acting, beyond his own active experimentation as an actor himself, lies in watching the best of contemporary acting—the prevailing general style—for only then will he begin to see how particular actors differ in the way they do things. Eventually, the director will be able to answer for himself why the best actors are the most effective with audiences—that is, what makes them stylists in their acting.

Director's Style

The emphasis up to this point has been on how to bring out the individual work of others. A director's style is the individual product he assembles out of this exploitation. It should now be clear to you that *a director can only be what he is as a person:* the strength of his artistic perception and taste; the strength of his capabilities in being a leader; the strength of his skills in theatre techniques; and, above all, the strength of his quiet, unassuming communication. The individual thing that he wants—the style of his production—can only emerge out of these qualities. Talent in a director, then, means innate possession of some part of each of these qualities; he must then build on his talents extensively through hard work and imagination.

EXERCISES

1. Concentration on plays from early Realism can accomplish a good deal for you simply because it will enable you to see the variations in Realism as a style and why the departures from Realism took place. You should therefore direct a scene from Ibsen, Chekhov, Strindberg, or early Shaw—stay with the masters to learn the most. Study the structures of their plays and isolate their individualities. Scenes from these plays done on the proscenium stage not only will tell you much about them as plays but they will also give you motivations for moving to other stages with later plays.
2. Similarly, concentration on departures from Realism will give you a grasp of these styles. Direct a scene from Wedekind, Pirandello, the German or American Expressionists, or Brecht. Save the "absurdists" until you have done the earlier playwrights. Also save Pinter, Albee, and Shepard until after you understand the others.
3. After you have directed the projects suggested in Exercises 1 and 2, you should try a scene from a play written after 1963 that "looks like Realism." Be certain to note *the shift away from much previous action and the increased allegorical values of the action.* Are the departures still Ibsenite types? Or are they more abstract? Is the emphasis in your play on idea? What is "dark comedy"?

GAME OF VISUAL PERCEPTION: STYLE IN MODERN PLAYS (see Chapter 8)

1. What is "theatrical" in each of photos 59 through 72? What would attract audience attention?
2. Contrast the style of production you see in *Tobacco Road* (photo 62) with that of *The Akhmatova Project* (photo 64) and *Les Cenci* (photo 65). What are the differences in design terms? In terms of what kind of acting and staging are required by the different approaches to style evident in these productions?
3. How do "new" plays from recent years (such as those of Suzan-Lori Parks, Timberlake Wertenbaker, Charles Mee, Jr., and Caryl Churchill, for example) differ from those of earlier decades? What do these differences mean for directors and designers in terms of effectively realizing these styles in production?
4. Choose a play by Parks, Wertenbaker, Mee, or Churchill (or another contemporary dramatist writing in a distinctively "now" style) and present a production approach, including a well-considered scenic plan.

PHOTO 59 *Cowboy Mouth* (Shepard)

PHOTO 60 *Suicide in B^b* (Shepard)

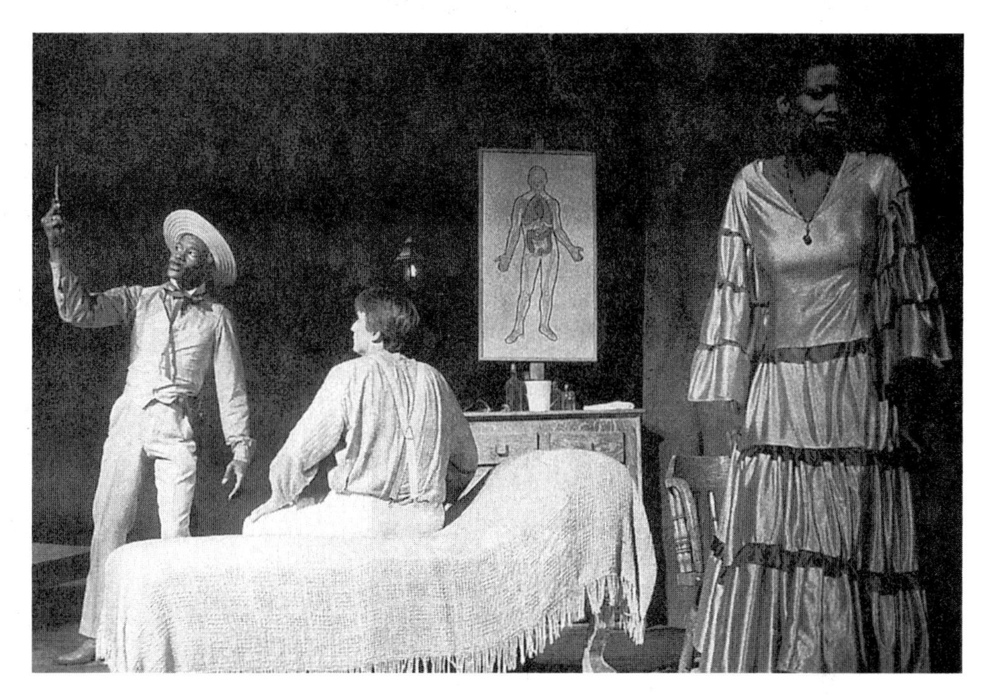

PHOTO 61 *Summer and Smoke* (Williams)

PHOTO 62 *Tobacco Road* (adaptation, Kirkland)

PHOTO 63 *The Little Foxes* (Hellman)

PHOTO 64 *The Akhmatova Project* (Keystone and Critical Mass Performance Group)

PHOTO 65 *Les Cenci* (Artaud)

PHOTO 66 *Heartbreak House* (Shaw)

PHOTO 67 *Antigone* (adaptation, Keystone)

PHOTO 68 *The Adding Machine* (Rice)

PHOTO 69 *The Crucible* (Miller)

PHOTO 70 *Rhinoceros* (Ionesco)

PHOTO 71 *Sticks and Bones* (Rabe)

PHOTO 72 *True West* (Shepard)

28

Style in Production

New Plays

This book takes the position that if a director is not aware of all types of plays, those in past ages as well as those in the twentieth century, he will be far less perceptive of the individual styles and potentials in new plays. The concept expressed in Chapter 1 of this book bears repeating: As the primary theatrical artist, a director is not a playwright, but he helps playwrights clarify their plays, just as he helps actors and designers find more intensive expression in their work. As a master communicator and interpreter of the work of others, a director brings his stage awareness and historical know-how to all the aspects of a production. He serves the play; he does not write it, act in it, or design it. Because he knows how plays are constructed now and how they were constructed in the past, his vision is amplified across the board.

The Evolution of New Plays

Prior to the 1960s, university and community theatres across the United States relied mostly on plays already produced on Broadway to make up their programs. The latest successes were always much in demand as soon as they were released for amateur use. Prominent departments of drama—such as those at Yale, Carnegie Tech, University of Iowa, University of Michigan, and University of Texas—usually included a play from the Shakespearean repertoire or even a Chekhov to enrich their bills, but most of the other plays were warmed-over Broadway. New plays were kept on the back shelf, though occasionally a few playwrights in training were given stagings.

This changed dramatically in the 1960s with the decentralization of Broadway and the growth of regional, nonprofit theatres in major cities across the nation as active competitors of Broadway. But the strongest influences came from the revolt theatre of that period, for its new energies and creative forces moved toward change, and that meant a new perspective on playwrights and their plays. The Broadway theatre, as it then existed, seemed remote to the innovators searching for new expression and new ways of making theatre. Out of these movements came a surge in playwriting that moved sharply away from the limitations and inner focus of Broadway. To get grant money, the regionals were under pressure to do at least one new play each season, and the revolt theatre—ethnic, local, in protest against the existing order—to produce all new plays. The universities soon followed suit, staging the new European drama, as well. In this context, new plays were developed in those university programs in which playwriting was taught, and other institutions began to use the new drama as they never had before. All this rush toward new plays not seen before in this country changed the face of production, as playwrights began experimenting with the options in staging.

The excitement of doing new plays began to push period revivals into the background unless they were adapted to the new thinking and feeling of the times. Doing Shakespeare seemed less important than doing a work by an untried playwright, for the new drama had more potential of exciting youthful audiences. Youthful America was now on the move in the theatre. Changes of all kinds were in the air. In the quest for the relevant, for plays that dealt with the here and now, the old plays began to seem old-fashioned and remote. Not doing them, however, meant loss of skills in all aspects of theatre production, particularly for the director; for the fervent pursuit of the new and the pushing aside of the old with its heritage of other times and cultures meant a much more limited field of choice. So the director's work too began to change. But unless a director could do both the old and the new, he limited himself as a creative artist while also limiting the perspective of audiences.

Because this chapter is based on all the chapters preceding it, understanding those chapters will give you a stance for understanding how a playwright uses new structures, what he expects of the acting, and how he points his ideas. What audiences might regard as innovation in dramatic form today may only be a repeat of that in other ages. One of the changes occurring after 1960 in attempts to compete with motion pictures was a movement toward multiplace, multitime, multiaction drama. With a background in historical drama, a director will see how the Elizabethans and even the Greeks handled this, and thus he will be able to bring this awareness to bear on his vision of a new play. The plays of A. R. Gurney, a prominent Broadway playwright in the 1980s, may appear out-of-date to a young critic today because of their three-act form, their single settings, and their tight unity of action; but this form, as we know from the 1930s, gives room for actors to play characters and not just be instruments in filling out a play's ideas, as happened in the 1960s. By going back to the dominant style of 1920–1960 Realism, Gurney was able to create satires of middle-class life with vision and cohesion. Do you know why Ibsen used five acts to tell his stories or why Tennessee Williams used only two? Does breaking an action into multiple parts in multiple locations help tell a story better? Or is it just a way to keep an audience from becoming bored, by flicking scenes before the viewers—as in television and motion pictures. There were very good reasons for the classical unities. Do you know why? Or why the Pulitzer Prize for

Drama was awarded to Robert Schenkkan's *Kentucky Cycle*, which had not played on Broadway but had been seen in regional theatres in both Seattle and Los Angeles? Or why the Actor's Theatre of Louisville has sent so many good plays to Broadway?

Working with New Playwrights

A novice playwright is exactly like a novice director: Look in the mirror for his image, because he, too, will be striving for exactly the same goals you are—holding an audience tightly with theatrical matter that will move it to laughter or tears or both. When he makes his original improvisation—his scenario—and shows it to you, he is holding his capabilities up for your examination and criticism. Are you sensitive to his fears of what you, as a director, will think of it? Further, what will you do with his delicately devised creation? Will you cut it up, axe parts of it, give it the death blow? Or will you let it live, breathe life into it, and make it fly? Or at least help him do so?

So, your quest in dealing with a new play and its playwright is the same as the one you have learned in dealing with actors and designers: working with a fellow creator in such a way that his great effort is enhanced and not derogated. You must ask yourself, as the objective outsider: Can I help the playwright rework his improvisation to give it the strongest theatrical values it will allow? I am supposed to know how these values work in the theatre, yet am I really more sensitive to them than he is? Have I really examined his vision closely enough to make a judgment on the poem he has written, or do I just want to turn his play into what I would like to make of it? Am I poaching or thieving?

As you can see, these are subjective questions you, as the director, must ask yourself before you reach out to the playwright. Only then will you be able to deal on a one-to-one level and perhaps enhance the play. Such relationships are tender and must be full of understanding on your part, for without closeness and sensitivity, what you intended for help may well turn into confusion and result in becoming "the director's play," not the playwright's. Look before you leap.

Although there is a great deal more that makes a play work than its structure—for example, its imagery, its mood values, its peaks, its understanding of life—the structure is one place to begin your study of the playscript. Because most novice playwrights may not yet be aware of the inner workings of dramatic action and its relationship to character development but tend to see a play more as a literary display through dialogue, you can focus your critical awareness in the usual manner of play-analysis by asking all the necessary questions about workable structure. Do the scene units serve direct functions? Are they sufficient in scope and dynamics to tell the story? Do they move in climactic order from a beginning to a middle to an end? Do they show a change in the principal character; that is, has the character come to any new knowledge and thus declared new directions?

Once you have perceived the weaknesses and *strengths* (this is very important) in the structure, you can then do a style-analysis in the usual manner to see what individualizes the play and really makes it work.

By following these objective procedures, you will not only know a great deal about the play firsthand, but you will have specific points for your talks with the playwright. When you begin these, there is an absolute caution: *You are not the author of this play* but an informed critic who supposedly knows how plays work in the theatre. *Listen! Listen!* to the playwright. Try to discover what he has in mind, for this may reveal to you qualities you may have missed as well as give you jumping-off points in your talk. Your prime action is to communicate, not dominate, for the object is to help the playwright improve his play and not to shape it to your own mold.

Plays are not just written; they are rewritten. You can help this process if you go about your work as a critic, with the same caution and care you give to the creative efforts of actors and designers. Skins in the theatre, no matter how tough they look in public, are very thin, indeed. Be a "heads-up director," not a know-it-all. What makes a play individual and original is your quest. You must be certain to cover all the points about style previously discussed. By searching a play through these techniques, you will be in a position to talk about the play with the playwright.

In your discussions with the playwright, the following plan of action is suggested, and it may work for you.

First Discussion

Do not approach this discussion with negatives about the play; rather, point out all the strengths as you perceive them. This will indicate to the playwright how you feel about his play and make him far more receptive to what you may regard as weaknesses. Do not discuss weaknesses in the first meeting. Let him talk. Try to understand fully what *he* has to say about the play's ideas, its action, its characters, its moods, and its differences from other plays. Question him thoroughly to be sure you understand what he intended to do and how he did it. Do not handle his play; let him do it, for you may discover a great deal you did not see in your study of the piece.

Second Discussion

Before you talk with the playwright again, you must do your homework of placing his concept (based on what you learned in the first discussion) against your own style-analysis. Your job now is to assess the pointing of the play, what makes it theatrical as you see it. With this in hand, you can talk with the playwright again. Does each scene serve a specific purpose in defining the whole? Are the play's beginning, middle, and end clearly marked? In each of these parts are all the scenes present to make it work?

This leads to a review of the characters. Are there definite builds in the actions of the principal character, and is the blocking character or characters fully developed progressively? Do the secondary characters support or block the main character?

Some cautions. Remember this is the playwright's play, not yours; so do not be a second playwright working on the script, but be the critic who can help improve it. And do not fill the playwright's head with your minor suggestions; his work on the major ones may take care of them. Your job is leading the playwright to a better play, not writing it for him. Tightness means economy, climactic points with sure builds, and major parts that are truly meaningful and full of dynamics. Remember: The most highly elevated and therefore exciting moments in the script may not make a good theatrical evening until the quieter scenes, the building scenes that precede or follow, are playable and do their work. Merely exciting an audience is not the problem, but moving it or making it laugh is.

At this point, a play reading with live actors seated around a table, with the actors speaking the roles, can be helpful. Focus the discussion afterwards on major points in the play, asking, among other things: Would they play well? and Is there a sense of build in the play? Actors may want to change lines or speeches, but this is relatively unimportant at this point. What does the play sound like? If guided well, live actors can stimulate the playwright's imagination as well as yours.

Third Discussion

This can only take place after the playwright has worked again on the play. Delay it until he is confident enough either to defend his work against your criticisms and those of the play readers, or to show you how he has handled the suggestions. Now let him lead you. How you give criticism at this point is crucial. You are not writing a review for a newspaper but are giving much attention to the creative work of the major craftsman in a production. Do not try to dominate the playwright, but communicate with him in every way that you can. Your points of criticism may be quite valid, but you must *sell* the idea of change, not force it.

Fourth Discussion

Let the playwright read you his play with the modifications he has made after your critique. Do the same sort of listening to him that you did in the first discussion by not interrupting his reading en route but saving your comments for discussion afterward. If you have observed the procedures outlined here, you can feel free to make your critical remarks and have confidence that they will be listened to. *Once again, you are trying to make a better play as the playwright has written it, not make a new one of your own.*

29

Style in Production

Plays of Past Ages

No young director should tackle historical drama until he has a backlog of experience in modern play production; nor should he venture into this most difficult realm of staging until he has a lively concept of styles in both playwriting and production. Historical play production is not for the novice but for the experienced director simply because, as the previous chapters have pointed out, a mature understanding of play-analysis and a strong sense of what composes individual expression (style) are basic requirements.

Yet, the peculiar paradox is that venturing into production of the plays of past ages is one of the best ways to learn about the modern theatre, because historical perspective lets us see much more clearly the changes and distributions in modern styles of both playwriting and production. This book takes the position that although period play production *for a public audience* should wait until a director has accumulated some experience with modern plays, *training in directing cannot be complete without experimentation with historical drama.*

Thus, laboratory production exercises that can be readily combined with critical discussions are suggested, for a very great deal is to be learned through personal discovery. Like the other arts, play production is discovered in the doing and not in talking about it. Even though such experimentation may turn out poorly, the conscientious student will learn how to use his imagination as well as how to restrict himself.

It follows without question, however, that all such production experience must proceed in the pattern suggested in Part III: first, a style-analysis of the play, then, and only then, a stylistic approach to production. In this sort of laboratory experience, the use of scenery, lighting, and costumes would not usually be available. Yet, much can be done even with these limitations, for you still can decide on an appropriate stage, determine minimum lighting, design a groundplan, and, above all, *work with actors.*

You must learn how to handle essentials before adding other determinants of style. It is quite enough to wrestle with the ideas in an antique play; with what translations or adaptations may be available; with the problems of verse forms; with acting problems of all sorts, including the all-important one of intensive work on delivering the text; with the choice of stage; and with the necessary choreography. Visual designs can wait until later, when you will have much better ideas about their use. Actors like to experiment, too; so learn all you can from them.

The Range of Choice

Plays of past ages, as defined here, include all plays before 1875. This date is, of course, an arbitrary one, but it is used here as it is in most modern drama studies in order to mark the beginnings of Ibsenite Realism, which sets the dramaturgical patterns still dominating our stage.

Although the range of drama throughout the 2,400 years before 1875 is extensive, the actual repertoire of such plays actively produced in America would probably be less than 100, of which only about half are produced regularly, and the other half sporadically. European theatres range more widely because of their national dramas and state theatres.

The following list will give you some idea of the scope of producible plays of past ages. In looking at this list, however, you must keep in mind that many historical plays are given individual productions when directors discover unexpected pertinence in them and that this list contains only the most frequently produced plays.

Historical Plays (before 1875) Produced in the United States in Educational Theatres and Occasionally by Nonprofit Professional Theatres

Fairly Frequently	Occasionally
Oedipus Rex	*The Agamemnon*
Antigone	*The Choephori*
Medea	*The Eumenides*
The Trojan Women	*Electra* (Sophocles)
The Bacchae	*Prometheus Bound*
Lysistrata	*Hippolytus*
The Birds	*Hecuba*
Shakespeare: fifteen of his most popular plays	*The Frogs*
	The Menaechmi
Less Frequently	
The Second Shepherd's Play	Shakespeare: ten of his less popular plays
Everyman	
Doctor Faustus	*The Duchess of Malfi*

Less Frequently

The Shoemaker's Holiday
Volpone
The Alchemist
The Beaux Stratagem
The Country Wife
The Imaginary Invalid
The Bourgeois Gentleman
Tartuffe
The Doctor in Spite of Himself
The Highbrow Ladies
She Stoops to Conquer
The Rivals
The Mistress of the Inn
The Servant of Two Masters
The Inspector General
Woyzeck
A Month in the Country
The York or Chester Cycles
Gammer Gurton's Needle
The White Devil
'Tis Pity She's a Whore
Fuente Ovejuna
Cervantes: Short plays
All for Love
The Way of the World
Love for Love
The Misanthrope
The School for Wives
Maria Stuart
Faust I
The Contrast
The Critic
The School for Scandal
Fashion
Uncle Tom's Cabin
Ten Nights in a Barroom
Across the Country
Rip Van Winkle

Additional Plays Produced Occasionally in Europe but Rarely in the United States

Classical Greek plays other than those noted above (in Greece)
Mandragola (Italy)
Shakespeare: all other plays (England)
The Jew of Malta (England)
Edward II (England)
Lope de Vega and Cervantes (Spain)
Molière: all other plays (France)
Corneille, Racine, Marivaux, and Beaumarchais (France)
Goldoni (Italy)
Goethe and Schiller (Germany)
Nathan der Weise (Germany)
Hugo and de Musset (France)
von Kleist (Germany)

You should note from this list that France and Germany regularly produce a number of native playwrights whose works are little seen elsewhere; Italy and Spain occasionally revive plays by Goldoni and Lope de Vega, respectively; Greece presents revivals of the ancient Greek dramas; and England stages a variety of English plays. Only the United States has no regular productions of native historical drama. Except for *The Contrast, Fashion,* and *Uncle Tom's Cabin,* very few nineteenth-century American plays are staged except in the distorted form of travesties (*Ten Nights in a Barroom, The Drunkard,* etc.).

As a result, *the United States, more than any other nation, is involved in producing the classics from the European repertoire.* This is particularly so in educational theatres, where even Japanese Kabuki plays are produced on occasion. Thus, in search of tradition wherever they can find it, Americans borrow from the English drama and make forays into the French, the German, the Italian, the Spanish, the Russian, and the ancient Greek. Shakespeare is regularly produced in the United States, although the minor plays are less frequently tackled. Jacobean and Restoration dramas are only occasionally produced, for in many ways these plays are deeply embedded in English culture and arc thus more difficult to transfer. The English comedies of the eighteenth century are not infrequently produced, although not without the attendant problems of separated cultures. To see *Lock Up Your Daughters* or *The School for Scandal* in London, where one is surrounded by architectural and historical reminders of the eighteenth century, is quite a different matter from seeing these plays on proscenium stages in New York or Chicago. Nevertheless, the body of producible plays is still a fairly large one, and the director's problems stem mainly from finding ways to tackle each national drama.

The Director Must Have Something to Say

Producing a historical play without having something specific to say will result in vagueness and lack of meaning. Audiences turn away from such productions because they look like dead museum pieces caught up in costume and staging display. To make a historical play meaningful to an audience, a director *must first find and pin down a core idea that is meaningful to him.*

Having "something to say," however, does not mean overlaying a play with a director's own ideas, for his intention is not to act as a collaborative playwright but as an interpreter who wants to bring alive from the printed page what he feels to be moving or amusing in a play's content. The *director's intention, then, is to put on an entertainment that a modern audience can respond to,* and stage it in such a way that the audience will be able to feel and think about what the director has felt and thought about in his association with the play.

This challenge is a difficult one because drama of past ages is truly inert drama—remote in ideas, archaic in language, and even obscure in many actions—until someone comes along with a sensitive perception and a gift for style-making to breathe life into it. "Something to say" in this sense becomes a personal conviction, and out of such a conviction can come clarity and unity.

Once you feel strongly about a play, you must submit yourself to the next personal challenge: Will my ideas mean anything to average theatregoers who have not studied the play carefully? This is a rigorous, direct question because after a director studies a play, he can be easily trapped by the historical context within that play and what surrounds its writing. *The challenge is to place the play in a present-day context.*

Perhaps the challenge will be only that of revealing the blind spots in our present-day way of looking at things. But more than likely, if a director searches deeply enough into a play, an idea will be found that can disturb us into new thinking about the world we live in. Great plays have the capability of revival because they somehow manage to say things about humankind that have been true in all ages. Throughout history, playwrights have been writing about human beings for audiences who have been intensely interested in the dilemmas of other people and how they either were trapped by those dilemmas or escaped them.

The form of drama as human spectacle remains the same, but the immediate contexts in which such actions take place have changed. A director's study of a particular historical drama, then, must proceed on the closest examination of the dramatic action in the context of the given circumstances. Once you comprehend this close relationship, the inner values of the play will become much more apparent to you. In the 1960s, for instance, audiences could better understand violence and revolution in historical drama because of their own similar dilemmas. Not only was that decade actively making new plays that contained these feelings but it also revived a number of old plays that "came into meanings" not previously apparent. Jacobean drama, some of the Greek drama, and even Shakespeare can be cited, along with productions of such plays as *The Duchess of Malfi, The Bacchae, The Trojan Women, Prometheus Bound,* and even Shakespeare's history plays, including *Henry VI* and *Coriolanus.*

These plays seemed to find audience comprehension on the level of feeling because directors found ways to make them speak the "rhythm" of the 1960s. *The premise that historical drama is acceptable to modern audiences whenever the rhythms are closely parallel to modern feelings makes excellent sense.* This theory implies that the dramatic actions in such plays are recognizable and meaningful on the subjective, emotional level.

No matter how a play is reasserted with present-day meaning, however, *a director must believe in that meaning as strongly as he would in that of a recent play based in his own context.* Finding something to say is finding the first point of style on which all other production points will depend.

Arts-and-Crafts Histories and Archaeology as Background Studies for Staging

Because a great deal of a production style is expressed in visual languages, regardless of whether a director deals with modern or historical plays, he must have a sensitive and detailed knowledge of the past. When objects or dress are new, the people who make them use them naturally and freely because they have discerned their need and can take their functionalism for granted. But when historical objects or historical dress are used, if they are to prevent them from "using" the actors (a situation that never fails to draw attention to the objects or dress and away from the dramatic action) someone—and the someone is usually the director—*must know their original need and thus their proper use.* This thinking applies explicitly to set design, whether it is a scenic background, a furniture piece, an entranceway, or a balcony that is being considered. Guessing is no substitute for knowing what is right.

This approach has never been more important than it is today, when historical places are frequently abstracted. The style of presentation may only suggest locations; yet, the design must start from a reality, because all true abstractions are firmly rooted in real-life usage. Conversely, side by side with the "theatre of suggestion" is the "theatre of realistic reproduction," a style that may continue for many decades, as we continue to live in an age of science in which we are very much interested in explicit circumstances.

Of equal importance with scenic investiture is costume. *The history of clothes is required knowledge,* not only for designing stage wear but also for acting in such wear, because real clothes had and have movement of their own making. If you visit the Smithsonian Institution in Washington, DC, you can see over 200 years of women's evening dress in the wax museum of former First Ladies. The fun in viewing this collection lies in imagining how the flowing skirts of the earlier periods moved in contrast to the confined dresses of the 1920s and 1930s. Such knowledge of dress can tell one much about decorum; and because decorum is style, directors can be sure to bring style onto the stage if their awareness of clothing is highly developed. A comedy by Georges Feydeau or Oscar Wilde, for example, would be very poor without such awareness. Actors expect directors to have this information at hand, although they may pursue the subject on their own.

A background for the making of style, then, is the study of archaeology, within which the study of portrait painting, which mirrors the past, may be most rewarding. Everyday crafts also tell us much, as do studies of music and architecture. *A director is constantly on the museum route because his job often requires him to mirror past ages.* He is also an avid reader of social, economic, and cultural history because he must know what a playwright of another age took for granted his audiences would bring to the theatre without explicit mention in the play. The actual style of production may well be far from exact *reproduction* but such stagings all begin with a keen awareness of what real places and real clothes looked like.

The History of Production as Background

Historical play production means the production of plays in their *original context* insofar as that context can be determined. Awareness of theatre architecture and how plays were produced is invaluable simply because playwrights have always taken for granted the stage machine for which they were writing, because they were making skeletons to be fleshed out and clothed by production. The study of the artifacts of theatre history can tell us much about the buildings and the productions in them.

Historical stage costume is much more difficult to ascertain accurately because few records exist to tell explicitly what was worn. Until well into the nineteenth century, actors wore what they considered appropriate from their own wardrobes. Coordination in design had not been established as a premise in staging, as it is today, except in court masques. But it is the rarity of visual historical records that makes this study fascinating. As you continue with directing, you will learn to look everywhere for hints—at paintings of actors (not very reliable), at line drawings and etchings, at brief descriptions some viewer thought worth setting down, and so on. *Your eye for such detail needs careful exercising. Too many students regard theatre history as a peripheral rather than as a central study in their work—a point of view you simply cannot hold if you are to be a director.*

Reaching Audiences

Style in Staging

Once you have found a modern meaning for a historical play you are considering, you are in a position to decide on the physicalization. The problem is the same one confronting the director in finding something to say about a play: *The physical staging must somehow convey modern feelings if the play is to come alive on today's stage.* Archaeological reproduction, as this text has pointed out, is a dead end, and finding other ways is quite necessary. A few possibilities are discussed next.

Adaptations of historical stages. One approach to the design problem is to devise a modern staging that uses the basic elements of the historical stage for which a particular play was written. With this approach, a director has the possibility of finding the inherent physical rhythm of a play, for its production can proceed from its historical environment. Although playwrights have always written for a specific stage, it does not at all mean that they did so consciously, for they probably took the popular stage form for granted; yet, *it is precisely this subconscious assumption of stage "place" that will make the patterns of the play vibrate with life and vitality.* By adapting a stage to incorporate modern feeling in a direct way, a director can meet the inherent demands of a play in its original context and, at the same time, can reach his audience directly, because it will "feel" the stage subconsciously as a part of its own world.

Such staging will involve the use of mass, line, and color in such a way that it will be in keeping with modern rhythms. Thus, the production will look very modern without the playscript actually being so. The use of modern lighting procedures can aid greatly in such staging.

Relocation of a play in an entirely different historical context. Another approach in trying to reach modern audiences is to mount a play with settings and costumes in a completely different period from both the time in which it was first produced and from our own. When the American Shakespeare Festival staged *Troilus and Cressida* in Civil War costumes back in the 1960s, the intention was to place the play in a context U.S. audiences could understand, not that of their own day but that of the country's past history. The New York Shakespeare Festival took a similar approach with *Much Ado About Nothing* in the 1970s by staging it in an

American context of 1900. Such relocating has definite advantages, because it is possible for an audience to see a play imaginatively through its personal feelings about past historical associations. The "something to say" is thus historically placed; but because of the symbolism and mythology surrounding such history, an emotional reaction on the part of the audience becomes possible. (Note how Bertolt Brecht has used something very similar to this approach in his retelling, with modern overtones, of John Gay's eighteenth-century *The Beggar's Opera* under the title *The Three Penny Opera,* and Farquhar's *The Recruiting Officer* under the title *Fife and Drums.*)

Even though costumes and scenic pieces of the relocated period are used, modern lighting effects can still give the production a sense of belonging to the here and now. The challenge in this sort of symbolic transfer is to find an appropriate historical period that will reveal the play, but the director must remember that if he forces such a context, it can be both distracting and confusing.

The use of a neutral stage. Another stylistic approach is an adaptation of a form of staging introduced by Jacques Copeau at the Vieux-Colombier in Paris a century ago. His idea was basically architectural, for it required a single unit setting that could be rearranged via a system of interlocking platforms and steps to become locations for scenes without "representing" them in a realistic way. All recent architectural stages proceed on the same principle: a stage machine that can be easily manipulated.

The neutral stage has many advantages because it leaves the audience's imagination free to create its own places. Because this stage is functional, it offers extensive opportunities for variety in movement and scenic locations. Period costumes on this stage are very effective because they provide "scenery" in a modern, dynamic way. Modern principles of stage lighting can also be used effectively to give a seeming modernity to a production.

Modern dress production. This style can be very effective with highly selected historical plays. The intention is, of course, *to make the play belong to today by giving it the look of contemporary life.* Thus, the choice of stage is modern (perhaps open staging); the properties and costumes are of recent fashion; and the lighting and sound are what we would expect in a contemporary play. Such stagings are not easily accomplished in the United States because of the difficulties in finding gradations in dress to readily delineate class differences that audiences will easily recognize, particularly those of royalty. But even if parallels in dress can be found, forcing plays into this kind of staging does not always help communication. It has worked notably for *Julius Caesar, Hamlet, Coriolanus,* and *A Midsummer Night's Dream* but might suffer badly with other plays.

Acting Styles

As pointed out in previous discussions, the usual approach to acting is to take the given circumstances of a play literally—that is, it is expected that the exterior decorum would be reproduced by the actors. Thus, an actor would illustrate the literal appearances of the social level of his character through his gesture, movement, speech, and use of his costume. And because decorum can mean either control or the lack of it, the actor would move through the action of a play with the literal range of the decorum specified by appearances. The believability of the audience would in this way be satisfied on the basis of appearances. Those plays dealing with nobility would thus have a look of formality, with controlled gestures and movement; and other plays, particularly seventeenth- and eighteenth-century middle- and upper-class comedies, would have varied decorums but would still be near the formal pattern. But no matter how formal or informal the decorum might turn out to be, *we would accept it as Realistic in style* as we would accept Ibsenite drama because the appearances would be all of a piece. Thus, what has been called Realistic acting would support a Realistic interpretation of a play.

A quite different approach to acting historical drama is to overlay the given circumstances, and thus the decorum, with *psychological* acting, which means that the gesture, movement, and so on would be expressive of the inner character and would not merely show the appearance of the literal decorum-character. This approach would allow a great increase in the range of illustration, for control or lack of control would not be determined by the decorum of social level but much more by motivation of the dramatic action. Consequently, another level of Realism in the acting would result, the level on which modern plays are now seen and heard—*inner Realism.* Thus, the actors of the roles of Romeo and Juliet would not be bound by the decorum of the historical social level but would be free spirits in today's society. Or Hamlet would not be a "prince" first and a man with intense feelings second, but vice versa. As you can readily see, quite a different play can result from the use of this style.

Consequently, we cannot say that historical drama is acted Realistically on our contemporary stage without defining the levels of Realistic style. You should be aware, however, that audiences have become so firmly rooted in expecting representational appearances in historical drama that any other stylistic approach may seem a defamation of Shakespeare or of the Greek dramatists. But there is no question that the "modern acting" approach has genuine validity and may be the only way the old plays will continue to find audiences. Your decision on style here is a very crucial matter.

Speaking the Play

Whichever acting style you choose, you must not forget the absolute necessity of finding the violence level in the playing. Plays of past ages are written largely in verse forms in order to allow direct and intense expression of emotions. Character-mood-intensity thus becomes a matter of very great importance, for the *poetic drama sings, surges, and reaches peaks we seldom find in plays written in prose.* You must learn to exploit poetic forms and not to fight them.

Although you may learn fairly easily how to draw the subtext out of actors, *getting out the text* is quite another matter because so much emphasis has usually been placed in modern actor training on "getting across" the subtext. As a result, young actors tend to fight the verse line instead of recognizing that it is their best tool for reaching audiences. A director may need to reorient himself as well as the actors by emphasizing that *the action in such plays lies directly and literally in the lines and not in the subtext,* as in a modern psychological drama. At first, this may seem like a betrayal of modern approaches to acting, but you will soon see how effectively audiences can be held in tension by the force of the spoken word alone. That is how they will experience it if you really believe it yourself and sell it to them.

Careful study of verse structure by a director is essential if he is to get the most from his actors. Neglect of this technical approach can only result in a ragged production, for telling the subtext in verse plays is not nearly sufficient; it is the *way* it is told—*the style of the spoken language*—that makes the difference.

A director's training must therefore include a concentration on the study of verse dialogue and how to exploit it with actors. Such study will make a director aware that his first obligation to an audience is *letting them hear such dialogue with ease and without distraction.* If he does not do this, the dialogue's effect and thus much of the action in a play will be entirely lost.

This is a big order, for verse dialogue, such as Shakespeare's or Marlowe's, often clouds our hearing with archaic words and phrases, lost allusions, inverted sentence structure, and frequent poetic imagery that cannot be received until the previous problems have been navigated. A director does not try to circumvent these problems by removing difficult lines from a playscript; he faces them head on by paying close attention to the mechanics of verse structure, such as punctuation, emphatic words or phrases and where they fall in a line, placement of the caesura, cohesion within a single line or within several lines through proper breathing and the elimination of false pauses, and, above all, the meter.

This last point is important, for the discovery of a line's meaning by an audience may lie much more in its inherent rhythm *when properly delivered* than in its denotative word meanings. To convey to young actors a sense of meter is often like trying to teach people who are tone-deaf how to sing. But without such a sense, an actor cannot deliver verse dialogue with meaning and excitement. Do you sense the musical form of such verse dialogue yourself? If you can "hear" it, you may be able to teach others how to do the same.

Good verse delivery also means careful physical control by actors. As a director, you will learn to insist that actors keep their heads quite still when speaking; that they place the articulated sound as far forward in the mouth as possible; that they do not try to move across the stage when they are delivering a line; that they do not blast into lines with excessive volume, thus producing an in-and-out volume effect; that they keep fairly narrow ranges in pitch variation; that they relax the body and thus the voice to allow easy projection of the lines; that they articulate with great care; that they use pleasing vowel structure; and that they place caesuras where they belong and do not include false pauses. Because verse plays contain high passions that tempt actors to "out-Herod Herod," *you will also learn to insist that textual delivery must take precedence over all subtextual and visual illustrations,* for a passage unheard is a passage that bores an audience and prevents its comprehension of a play.

What to Look for in Historical Play Production

Because the production style of each period will differ in what it emphasizes in form, the study of any particular period will revolve on the basics of all production form: (1) stage shape and audience position, (2) scenic investiture, (3) properties, (4) costuming, (5) lighting, (6) makeup, (7) sound, and (8) acting conventions. The following checklist of what to look for points out the range of your necessary study, because you can apply these questions to any period in theatre history. As a continuation of the material included in Chapter 18, this list encourages you to search out theatre history as explicitly as you can in the interest of discovering the nature of production style. You will certainly add to the list of questions here as you continue to make detailed historical studies on your own.

EXERCISE: CHECKLIST FOR HISTORICAL PLAY PRODUCTION

It is suggested that this checklist be applied to at least two different periods of theatre history so that the production style of each can be seen in contrast. The general assignment can be broken down further by alloting each of the primary areas to a few students who will then pursue the search in detail and report their findings to the class. Make a list of new questions raised in the general discussion.

1. *Stage*
   Where does the audience sit or stand in relationship to the stage? How close?
   Is the stage raised above the audience or lowered below it?
   Is the stage raked? How much?
   Is the stage roofed? If so, what purpose does the roof serve?
   What is the exact shape of the stage? Is there an apron? Is there a proscenium wall?
   Is the stage floor trapped? Why?

2. *Scenery*
   Is the scenery a permanent architectural façade? If so, why? What purpose does such a façade serve? What does it do in terms of line and mass?
   How do actors gain entrance to the stage? How do entranceways affect the speed of entrance and the relationship to action already going on?
   Is the scenery fabricated and changeable? If so, what are the active functions of such scenery? What is done with line, mass, and color? How real is such scenery? How much of the stage is occupied by scenic investiture?
   Are the stage spaces above the usual acting areas used?
   What are the acting areas and how effective are they?

3. *Properties*
   What is the quantity and extent of the set properties? If none are used, why not?
   How real are they?
   Are they carried onto the stage or previously set?
   How often do actors use hand properties in acting? (Confine your answer to historical use, not what you would do as a director.) What kind of properties do they use?

4. *Costume*
   Why are costumes used?
   Is what is worn costume or clothes?
   How are the line, mass, and color employed?
   What is their potential for movement?
   What is the silhouette for both men and women?

5. *Lighting*
   Is daylight or artificial light used? What would daylight accomplish? If artificial, what is the method? What effects can be achieved?
   Where does the light originate?
   Is the audience lighted with the same light as the actors? Why?

6. *Makeup*
   What function does makeup serve?
   What techniques are used? How widely do they range?

7. *Sound*
   What kind of sound is used?
   How are sound effects made?
   Are they live sounds or mechanically reproduced?
   Is music used? How?

8. *Acting*
   How is movement employed?
   What is the size and the scope of gesture?
   What sorts of compositions are used? Is the full stage used or only a portion of it?
   How well is the actor heard? How does he probably project his voice?
   Is speaking the primary theatricality? Why?
   What degree of Realism is employed?

EXERCISE

As was suggested earlier, learning directors should direct scenes from historical drama as a necessary part of their training, for the perception of modern drama and the scope of modern production can be greatly increased with this essential background. Thus, you should now undertake the production of several 10- to 15-minute scenes chosen from the standard repertoire of historical drama. Preparation and production procedures should follow those prescribed at the ends of Part I, Part II, and Chapter 25 ("The Director's Analysis of Style in a Playscript").

One way to start is with a scene from a Greek play, for it will give you an excellent basis for comparison with other period plays in a chronological order. But if scenes from several period plays can be directed, much can be learned by working backward: Do a scene from Ibsen first; then move to the eighteenth, seventeenth, and sixteenth centuries; then medieval, Roman, and Greek periods, in that order. You will then see the relationship of modern drama to all the rest.

Make your choices wisely. Remember that historical drama *requires focus on the text,* which means the most extensive use of actors' voices. Learn all you can about the power of big volume, energy behind acting, and the physical demands on the actor's body.

Your designs for staging a scene from a historical play will give you a far better idea of how to get the best performance from the actors. Do it with imagination and inventiveness. Remember that you must study the original forms of production in order to understand the playscript fully, but your obligation now is to an audience. The question that must be foremost on your mind is: What can I do to make these old plays exciting now?

GAME OF VISUAL PERCEPTION:
STYLE IN PLAYS OF OTHER AGES (see Chapter 8)

1. Can you pick out the elements of style in each of photos 73 through 80? Which element is given the most emphasis?
2. How does the style of each production close the time gap between the historical date of each play and a modern audience?
3. How would *you* stage each play in this section? Can you individualize each one?

PHOTO 73 *Othello* (Shakespeare)

PHOTO 74 *Hedda Gabler* (Ibsen)

PHOTO 75 *Orestes 2.0* (Mee)

PHOTO 76 *Ghosts* (Ibsen)

PHOTO 77 *Fuente Ovejuna* (de Vega)

PHOTO 78 *Elektra Fragments* (adaptation, Hackett and Krajewska-Wieczorek)

PHOTO 79 *Doctor Faustus* (Marlowe)

PHOTO 80 *The Beaux Strategem* (Farquhar)

Major Project 3

Directing with Designers

You are ready to undertake the final project in this study: the directing of a long play. The intention throughout this book has been to guide you, step by step, to this project, where you can demonstrate your mastery of the directing process.

To recapitulate, Major Project 1 provided you the opportunity to work closely with actors in scenes from long plays and Major Project 2 encouraged you to completely design as well as direct a one-act play. Since then, you have navigated the complexities of style and you should now have a good idea of how to give a production your own stamp while also revealing the individualities of the playscript and actors. You are now ready to work with designers and learn how you can free them in bringing about total synthesis.

Play-Analysis and Style-Analysis as the Source of Director-Designer Communication

Just as directors read a playscript visually—that is, with active imagery of what it might look like on the stage—so do designers. In fact, many designers firmly believe that their first impressions are the strongest ones and that their early images, because of their strength and intensity, are those an audience will respond to imaginatively. Consequently, they feel that pursuing a play further in an analytical way will reduce their ability to design freely. There is much to support this attitude, because designing is largely a subjective process, reflecting how one *feels* about a play. However, the danger lies in the fact that the images a designer sees, like those seen by an actor assigned to a specific role, may not only be confined to his own area of design but they may also stem from a reading of a play that is quite different from what you, the director, may have in mind.

Because the main problem in synthesis is to find a total visual statement that will also coordinate with the statement the actors are making, a director's view of a play must be multidirectional and truly comprehensive. In this sense, a director does a total design of a production in his imagination—how he sees it in its entirety. However, as you will read in the next section, *if a director tries to enforce his own specific images on the minds and feelings of his designers,* he may directly inhibit their creative capabilities just as he would those of his actors. Therefore, he must learn how to listen and, further, how to adjust to his designers' needs.

The best approach to director-designer communication is, of course, the director's homework on play-analysis and style-analysis, because they are more objective and rich in ideas than any subjective imagery you may try to convey to a designer. It is also the long way around, but shortcuts can be destructive. *The purpose is to free the designer* (just as you free your actors), not to bind him. The problem in this approach depends on what a designer is capable of in the way of play-analysis and style-analysis. If he understands and works from this position, as many designers do, communication between you and your designer may be relatively easy. If he does not, you may have to work with him on a subjective level, which can be more difficult. Whatever the method, the intention is always the same: to find *neutral* ground that both you and your designer can till together.

Working with Designers: The Process of Design

Understanding the Playscript: The First Discussion

Because the director's intention is to convey *his vision* of a play, a certain amount of controlled discussion with his *group* of designers is absolutely necessary. This means bringing the play to a conscious surface—something of a risk with designers—but it must be done if a multiheaded production is to be avoided.

The problem is how to bring about this mutual understanding without reducing a play to a mere mass of intellectuality that could stultify designers. Yet, the risk must be taken if the neutral-ground approach is to work at all. Too much intellectualizing can be prevented if the director keeps the discussion moving along the story line with concentration on the dramatic action and human elements of character. He can work similarly to the way he handles actors, revealing the action as simply as possible in the interest of arousing spontaneous and inspired illustration. By carefully pointing the emphasis in his storytelling, a director can plant unit ideas and, finally, the main idea itself.

A certain amount of challenging by designers of the director's perception of the action at this point is useful for sharpening emphases and clarifying their necessity. However, the detailed refinement of idea should be carried on in the next major step (separate discussion with each designer) in the interest of preventing overdesign, as delineated in Chapter 18.

The director's procedure in this first group discussion should also be focused on conveying both his own perception of the style of the playscript and the general style of the production he wants to bring about. You should therefore try to convey to the designers the point of style *in the playscript* you think can be developed and emphasized, stylistic points about dramatic action, characters, ideas, dialogue, mood values, tempos, and given circumstances. Only when designers comprehend fully what you see as individual and different in a playscript can they begin to move along the lines of the production style you intend. It must be emphasized again that *overdiscussion of these points by the group can stultify individual designers. The primary emphasis must be on the skillful handling of the story line and the human values in a playscript.*

Individualizing Design: The Second Discussion

After the first general discussion, the director should work separately with each designer, if he has more than one, in order to prevent duplication of emphasis and to bring about desirable counterpoints in design. This procedure recognizes the individuality of each designer and that each has his own way of approaching design as well as an individuality of expression. The second discussion(s) must therefore take the directions desired by each designer.

A designer may want more play-analysis, or more explanation of stylistic emphases declared in the first discussion. Thus, your intention should be the same: to leave the designer as free as possible in forming his visual images while you make certain he understands the playscript as you do. Once this understanding has been achieved, it is possible for you and the designer to discuss his actual images or at least to discuss directions those images may take. You can also present certain images of your own—images that are perhaps highly exaggerated or generalized with the intention of conveying a broad idea of your conception without pinning the designer down to a specific, confusing image.

Some scene designers have been trained to approach the design of a particular play by looking for an overall metaphor (a total visual image) as a way of finding production unity. Now is the time for you to discuss the metaphor the designer may have in mind and to understand thoroughly all of its implications. This understanding can become a basic position of discussion, another neutral ground, because it is a broad imaginative statement of a play. Because the metaphor provides the unusual opportunity of visual projection, both you and the designer can come much closer in communicating with each other.

Other designers do not work from this sort of unity-making device but see design directly in terms of mass, line, color, and physical materials. They are not working from limitations, but they want to imagine the range of expression possible with the ideas of the play in mind. Again, the director can discuss expression of the play through this approach; however, he must be careful not to commit himself on specifics but to help the designer find the *general* range of illustration.

Ideas about Design: The Third Discussion

With a mutual understanding of the play as you see it now in hand, the designer presents some specific design ideas. The third discussion is much like your meeting the actor in a rehearsal and the actor acting out his own understanding of a play while you look on and then respond as a critic to the actor's efforts. In the case of designers, your criticism is aimed at the design's ability to reflect accurately and imaginatively your own perception of the play. If it does, agreement is easy. If it does not, or does so only partially, further discussion is necessary, even acting out a portion of the play for the designer. You are now working closely with the designer, and the result is a collaboration on the designer's visual images.

This is a crucial point in discussion because both director and designer must be tolerant of each other's creative capabilities. If a director does not thoroughly project within his own imagination the ideas of the designer and if he is not genuinely interested in how they differ from his own visual conception, he may be discarding adequate, even exciting, statements because of his own prejudice. On the other hand, if a designer does not give his work freely for inspection with some expectation of modification, no meeting of the two is possible. *All is based on mutual trust and the give-and-take of responsible, creative people.* Without this mutual effort, the creative process in the theatre is impossible.

You can now test the proposed designs in terms of what could happen. In the case of scene design, you would test the compositions and patterns of movement as they could be projected out of the obstacle course proposed by the designer. Some designers work directly from inherent movement principles; that is, in their view, good design proceeds from strong compositions and effective ideas about movement. In this sense, a design is organic. If you work with such a designer, you must analyze a design very carefully to be certain you understand the principles of movement and can readily see their exploitation possibilities. If a designer is not oriented in this approach, you must work out in your own imagination how you can build these inevitable compositions and movements directly into the designs.

Similar *testing* of costume and lighting must also be made, with the utmost attention given to their exploitative possibilities. Discussion with the costume and lighting designers about imagined compositions at the principal climaxes in a play will ensure the types of emphases needed from each medium at those points, resulting in designs that can be "raised" or "lowered" to coincide with those emphases.

It is at this point that you can exercise your strongest control over the counterpoint principle discussed in Chapter 18, because you can strengthen or weaken designs as you see fit, whereas later when they are constructed, changes would be impossible. Only lighting design, and to a lesser degree sound design, as compared to scenic and costume design, has ready flexibility and can perhaps be shifted even in the final rehearsal period. However, the discussion period is the time for planning the number and location of instruments and how these enable certain "looks" because later shifts are difficult and time consuming.

The Decision: The Fourth Discussion

Unlike the director's work with actors, transpiring as it does over many hours of regular daily meetings, which brings about a gradual process of mutual understanding, work with designers must be concluded early in a production period.

This may involve only a few hours of actual director-designer contact. Furthermore, irrevocable decisions must be made because design deals with costly materials and hours of labor, the results of which cannot actually be seen until they are built in their final forms. Modifications in acting can take place through the final rehearsals, but not so with most designs. The director must therefore be able to project fully in his imagination the effect of the designs he may see only on paper or, at best, in scale models. Like all designers, he must be capable of full visualization in his imagination. The strength of his production will be reflected in the degree to which he can exercise this capability.

The *final testing* now takes place. Will all the designs work in counterpointing one another? Does the director thoroughly understand their exploitative possibilities? Will the dramatic action in the playscript actually be enhanced by the designs so that moods will be clear and strong? Will the actors be able to dominate the designs?

Once the commitments to designs are made, the director must believe in them with full knowledge that he cannot change them except for minor details. Fully aware of how he can best make the designs organic in the production, he can then move forward in his rehearsals.

Keeping the Designer Free

The most important aspect in the approach to design is for the director to free his designers and not to entrap them within his own specifically imagined designs. This capability takes a strong director, for a clash in design ideas is as likely as a clash with strong actors over dramatic action and its illustration. *The approach to both designers and actors is identical, because the director's intention is to carry them, through inspiration, beyond themselves.* Any director who fails to see that design exploitation is a major part of his work does not understand the nature of theatre. A play can live with actors alone, but a life of that sort will be anemic without the trappings of theatre. The major problem is the appropriate control of those trappings. Only with that control can an artistic whole emerge.

EXERCISE

Direct a play of your own choosing with the specific help of a designer or designers. The preliminary words of advice are contained in preceding chapters, but here are a few warnings:

- Choose a play of quality by a well-established playwright; this will teach you about structure and style.
- Choose a play commensurate with your production circumstances, with prime attention to the availability of actors and the size of production that can be undertaken. A small cast, one-set play is enough to tackle at this point.
- Choose a play within the scope of your perception and capabilities as a director as well as the capabilities of your actors and designer(s).

- In doing your homework, first reread the chapters on style in Part III and then do a style-analysis and make a production scheme before talking with your designer(s).
- Work with your designer(s) as you would with your actors. Remember that you will fly with a play only as you let your actors and designer(s) fly.

Appendix 1

Musical Theatre and Opera

Although the appetite for musical theatre has nearly driven the speaking play from the Broadway stage, this book would not be complete without considering the "play" director's part vis-à-vis the musical stage form as it began to flourish in the 1940s and 1950s. At first, amateur theatres added musicals to their programs, with many universities and community theatres taking part. But after 1960, as musical theatre became the grand spectacle theatre and became, so it was thought, too expensive and complicated for amateurs to produce, the tight relationship between professional and amateur theatres began to weaken. The speaking theatre became rare on Broadway, with most of it moving to Off-Broadway; and as television developed, a new place was found for speaking theatre.

Although this book is not the place for detailed treatment of the directing of musicals and opera because each is a major study in itself, some mention is needed because every director, sooner or later, will tackle one of these forms. You may have little specialized background for dealing with musicals and operas, but it is nonetheless assumed that you can handle them as part of your job. A young director can feel relatively secure with much of modern drama and even some of the historical, but for many, musicals and operas are off the usual track. They present problems such as: How much do I know about music? About dance? About singing, either solo or group? About leading actors, dancers, and singers in unfamiliar forms? About coordinating a staff of talented specialist directors in these areas?

Musicals

Music in the American theatre evolved from the eighteenth century when the convention of a theatre-orchestra playing "airs," accompanying songs in plays as well as *entr'acte* singing and dancing, and performing operas was in full sway. Later, in the nineteenth century, the orchestra began providing background music to onstage dramatic action, a convention that was continued through the era of the silent movies to the present. The nineteenth century also saw the expansion of songs in plays, especially those with Native American comedians, as well as singing and dancing in great quantity in the minstrel shows.

In the twentieth century, with American George M. Cohan leading the way, the theatre musical came into its own, first in the skits, songs, dances, and production numbers of musical revues, then with *Oklahoma!* and its counterparts in the highly integrated form of musical theatre, with its story told in dialogue, songs, production numbers, elaborate scenery, costumes, and lighting, and with a live orchestra in the pit. The "big musical" of the 1950s had arrived, and with it came a strong need for the stage director. But what sort of director could do the best job became the question: Was it to be a director of plays? Or a conductor of orchestras? Or perhaps a choreographer of dancers?

An important point to remember: Many of the new musicals were adaptations of regular stage plays—for example, *Oklahoma!* from Lynn Riggs's *Green Grow the Lilacs; Carousel* from Molnár's *Liliom; Kiss Me, Kate* from Shakespeare's *Taming of the Shrew; My Fair Lady* from Shaw's *Pygmalion; Cabaret* from Van Druten's *I Am a Camera;* and *The Fantasticks* from Edmund Rostand's *Les Romanesques.* Stage directors thus found a place because the "new-old" form needed acting, extensive scenic development, and coordinated staging. But because the performers were also required to sing and dance, the director either had to be proficient in one of those areas (such as Gower Champion or Bob Fosse, in dance) or serve as a stage director-coordinator (such as George Abbott, Joshua Logan, Moss Hart, or Hal Prince). In later musicals—for instance, *Nine* and *Chicago*—the director's job was taken over completely by choreographer-directors who could handle the extensive use of dance (such as Tommy Tune, Michael Bennet, Susan Stroman, and Graciela Daniele) as well as the acting and singing.

Subsequently, the "big musicals" made room, because of their enormous expense, for the "intimate musical-theatre" of *I Do! I Do!, The Fantasticks, A Little Night Music, Take Me Along, Sweeney Todd,* and *A Chorus Line.* There, the stage director was more assured of a place because the weight of a show now fell on the performance capabilities of the principals in acting, with some singing and dancing. Moreover, they could be produced with moderate expense in nonprofit theatres in universities and regional houses. In the 1980s, musical theatre with some speaking lines had mutated with the inventive help of Stephen Sondheim completely to music, but by the 1990s, even some of these were back in the hands of stage directors. These changes did not take place in the amateur theatre except in those instances where specialty directors were available.

You, then, must ask yourself: What sort of musical can I do? In musicals produced in educational and community theatres, the director is largely a coordinator, and as such he participates in every aspect of the production, from designing to execution. The structure is already firmly established through the book and music, and the director will do well not to tamper with it until he understands the relationships of certain songs to dramatic moments and scene changes. Instead, the director exercises ingenuity by talking music with the conductor; discussing dancing with the choreographer; working out staging with the set, lighting, and costume designers; and closely coordinating plans for use of the stage in "getting out the book" with anyone concerned. Finally, the director will bring it all together—this enormous pattern of dramatic scenes, songs, and production numbers with their dancing and scene changes—and he will set the rhythm and pace the show.

With the intimate musical, the director may participate directly in all aspects of development. So, the questions now become: How much do I know about musical form? About dance? About combining them with dramatic moments? About learning how to respect the creativity of the people in music and dance? These will declare the director's range and scope in the planning and execution. If you can work partly in all of these areas and know how they contribute to the story line and dramatic action—the dominant thing the audience desires and expects—you will know how to raise your creative partners to greater achievement.

The handling of musicals is thus very much like staging plays: The more you understand about style and how it can work for you, the more you will see what you can do. Remember: Music has been a part of the theatre since the days of the Greeks, and its place in today's theatre as a way of communicating form and feeling differs little in function from its ancient forebears. The addition of dance in the twentieth century has added greatly to the musical form. Without a very good choreographer, however, musicals simply do not survive. To understand the American Dream of success, as presented in *42nd Street*, is to understand how each age has always found a way of showing its mythologies and mysteries on the stage, and how it has aroused audiences to high spirits, even exultations, in doing so. Musicals are very much a part of our time and our feelings about life in the United States. Doing musicals is truly a venturing out. It will challenge all your skills in coordinating and finding rhythms in a conglomerate of music, songs, dance, dramatic moments, and staging.

If you are interested in this kind of theatre, be certain to read Tom Jones's *Making Musicals* (Limelight Editions, 1997). Jones not only wrote the book and lyrics for New York's longest-running musical, *The Fantasticks,* to Harvey Schmidt's music but he also kept it alive on the stage as a director while doing other musicals. The motivated director can always find ways to do limited stagings of even the most complicated works such as *West Side Story, The Sound of Music,* and *Guys and Dolls,* if he works well with a choreographer.

Opera

It is important to remember that opera, no matter how it is staged, must always work as a musical event as well as a theatrical event, and the relationship between the director and the conductor and the singers is central to finding success for the whole. Indeed the symbiotic relationship between the theatric and musical components of opera is what makes it so special and from which its great power in the theatre can derive. Though caught in a mesh of tradition for much of its history, opera has steadily developed since the later decades of the twentieth century as one of the most innovative forms of contemporary theatre in terms of design, staging, imagery, and performance, at least in the hands of its most groundbreaking directors, conductors, and designers. Directors such as Peter Sellars, Francesca Zambello, Robert Wilson, Patrice Chereau, and Achim Freyer, along with risk-taking conductors such as Esa-Pekka Salonen and Kent Nagano, musicians who recognize that opera is at its greatest as a theatric as well as a musical form, have vastly expanded what it is possible to do in this marvelous art form. But directors drawn to work in this form must understand that their collaborations with conductors and singers will be as significant, meaningful, and challenging as the experiences they have had in the speaking theatre and in some respects perhaps even more so.

Many directors are drawn to opera because of the conceptual freedom it allows. The expressive power of opera at its most vital can be very strong because of the transcendent power of music combined with visual imagery and the human voice. This means, however, that directors who work in opera must have great sensitivity to the musical dimensions of the work and the production history of particular works. As with plays, directors need to understand the historical background of the particular opera and, unless it is a new work, have some sense of the prior stage life the piece has had. Part of the richness of opera as a form (perhaps not unlike how Shakespeare and other classics are perceived in the speaking theatre) is how contemporary interpretations relate to the traditions that will have inevitably attached themselves to the work. Whether the production you will direct seeks to be "faithful" to a performance tradition or to reinterpret and depart from it, you can be sure that in the world of opera, the directorial interpretation of the work will be seen against a background of how the work has been done in the past. Whether your approach is received positively or not depends, as in most theatre, on how well it illuminates and honors the essence of the work together with the degree to which it entertains, delights, and moves audiences.

In addition to the need for some understanding of performance history and tradition, the director must be open to a significant collaboration with the conductor, because responsibility for the musical dimension of the work rests with this most important collaborator. You should attach the greatest importance to arriving at a shared vision with the conductor of how the two of you, in leading the work of (and in partnership with) the designers and performers, will approach the production. And, of course, as a director of opera, you will need to be sensitive to and appreciate singers and their special needs, which center on the realities of singing, including the particulars they must accommodate having to do with singing with an orchestra, under the baton of a conductor, and in terms of the staging you and the designers propose. Some singers approach the theatrical challenges of singing and acting in a particular production with daring and relish, while others may be more cautious and you may have to adapt some of what you envision to what the singer is able to accomplish under the demands of the score and vocal production. But, as with everything else in the theatre, if you understand the other artist's needs and work constructively, you will accomplish much more than if you attempt to impose solutions.

While the director of opera need not necessarily be a highly accomplished musician, the ability to read music is of inestimable value and should not be underestimated as an educational goal if you are seriously contemplating working in this form. At the very least, the director of opera needs a sensitive ear and as much experience as possible in listening to opera and other forms of serious music. Then there is the matter of language. Opera differs from the speaking theatre in that the works are often (indeed, usually more often) presented in the original language of the libretto rather than in English translation. There are a significant number of important operas in English, ranging from Stravinsky's masterpiece *The Rake's Progress* to the great operas of Benjamin Britten such as *Peter Grimes* and *Billy Budd,* to name but two, and American works such as Gershwin's *Porgy and Bess* and a host of contemporary works by composers such as Philip Glass, Andre Previn, and others. But much of the core repertoire of opera is in Italian, German, French, and Russian, and if you think you might be serious about directing opera, you should acquire knowledge of at least one if not more of these languages. (One young directing student at UCLA knew as an undergraduate that he wanted to work in opera, which prompted his move to Vienna to learn German and observe the opera scene in Europe firsthand. Eventually he acquired a working knowledge of each of the major languages of opera, which, along with directorial talent and skill, has taken him around the world as a director in opera.)

Your work in the speaking theatre with plays, actors, and designers will prove to be an excellent preparation for work you may do in opera, for it is also a dramatic form with action, characters, and particular worlds that must be brought to life. The works of Mozart, Verdi, Wagner, Strauss, Puccini, and others have stood the test of time with audiences, and, indeed, experiencing how the great composers of opera express the human condition in music allied to drama can be one of the most rewarding things theatre has to offer. Your homework of play-analysis and then style-analysis will help prepare you for your interactions with the music people and the intense process of production with designers and singer-actors. Help yourself by closely observing the work of other directors in these forms, particularly noting the ways successful directors find in their stagings of expressing the essence of the music together with the essence of the dramatic situation. (Many excellent productions of opera are available on DVD and videotape, which are superb resources for learning.) The main challenge will center around developing units of action, though character-mood-intensities have been well prescribed by the music. You will learn that you must make climactic illustrations strong enough to match the music and thus capture the overall intent.

Many colleges and universities have opera programs in their music schools. Getting involved with the opera workshop in your university is an excellent way to begin learning your way. Working your way up by doing scenes and then a short opera (there are many good ones) in a workshop setting is a fine way to gain experience and can be a welcome assistance in programs in which participants seek to realize the dramatic as well as the musical aspects of the form. Be inventive with opera, but take care not to destroy its function as a form of music. Attempting to reduce the piece you may be working on to "the play's the thing" can subvert its inner workings in terms of its musical dimension. However, stage directors coming to opera from the speaking theatre will do well if they are sensitive to the dual nature of the form and can draw satisfaction from seeing both the dramatic and musical aspects interact and come to the fullest fruition.

Young people today have the advantage of more opera being done than ever before, particularly in the United States, where there has been a considerable growth of interest in the form. This surge in interest is no doubt due to the increasing number of fresh, effective approaches to production that have come about in recent decades, resulting in stagings that make for good theatre as well as good music. The growth in the use of supertitles (translations of what the singers are singing, projected above the stage, like the subtitles in foreign-language films) has undoubtedly played a part as well, making the opera experience far more accessible to audiences. Going to live opera performances and building up a sense of the art form will be particularly rewarding and will no doubt give you many ideas about what is possible to achieve in production. Worthwhile productions are to be found in many universities and even in some small and medium-size cities, not to mention significant centers of opera production in this country such as New York, Chicago, San Francisco, Los Angeles, Seattle, Houston, St. Louis, and Washington, DC. There are also important summer festivals of opera such as the Santa Fe Opera in New Mexico and the Glimmerglass Festival in New York State. (And all of these are sure to have Internet sites listing their performance schedules.) All of this, combined with the wealth of opera productions available on video, means there is no shortage of examples to get your fantasy and imagination going.

EXERCISES

1. Choose a musical that interests you and, through every resource available, including the book of the musical, the original cast recording, and the score (if available), make an analysis of all the elements that would be necessary to assemble an effective production of the piece. This would include listings of the number and vocal types of principal performers, chorus size, choreography and dance needs (number of dancers with what particular kind of dance skills), music needs (nature of instrumentation required, size of the orchestra, whether the piece can be done in a reduced orchestration or with one or two pianos), and design needs in terms of number of settings and costumes. Repeat the exercise with a very different type of musical to get a sense of the different kinds of needs that come with different shows. (Ideally, your choices should be varied: Perhaps your first project would focus on a traditional musical such as *Oklahoma!* whereas your second project would deal with a piece that makes other demands such as Sondheim's *Assassins* or *Passion* or Adam Guettel's *Floyd Collins.* The goal is for you to gain a sense of the differing demands of different musicals.)
2. Direct a scene from a musical, including singing (and dance if possible) with accompaniment.
3. Choose an opera production on video and analyze what the stage director and designers have accomplished in their interpretation of the work's dramatic dimension. (There are many good possibilities for this, but try to select one of the more innova-

tive choices, such as Peter Sellars's stagings of Mozart or Handel or Patrice Chereau's production of Wagner's Ring Cycle [conducted by Pierre Boulez] or Goetz Friedrich's staging of Richard Strauss's *Elektra.*) Describe how the dramatic and musical dimensions of the work reinforce each other in the particular production. (This exercise should be repeated several times.)

4. Choose an opera that has captured your imagination and come up with a production approach, perhaps even working with your peers in scenic and costume design. Make a presentation of your work to a directing or design class and "make the case" for what you propose, being sure to address the question of how your approach will help realize the musical as well as the dramatic dimensions of the work. (It might be advantageous if your project could be critiqued by a director or other person experienced in opera.)

Appendix 2

The Director and the Dramaturg

In the closing decades of the twentieth century, another figure began to be encountered more frequently in the American theatre—the dramaturg or literary manager. Long a fixture in European theatre, dramaturgs or literary managers began to find a place in America as institutional theatres took hold and became a permanent part of the way theatre is produced in the United States. Today, many of the large and medium-size resident theatres, and even some smaller ones, have a dramaturg or literary manager as a part of the staff. What exactly is this position and what is its relationship to the work of the director? And what is dramaturgy as a specialization within the theatre?

In terms of play structure, the term *dramaturgy* is usually understood as the architecture or strategy a dramatist uses in constructing the play. We speak about the characteristic dramaturgy of Ibsen's middle-period Realistic plays, for example, and how Ibsen's dramaturgy may be different from or related to that of another playwright such as Brecht or Pinter. However, in terms of theatre *production* and the longer-term concern of the overall artistic direction of a theatre company, the term *dramaturgy* has come to include all of the literary-related activities that support both the artistic leadership and the production process itself and even the development of new plays. The elaboration of these activities has led to the development of the function of the dramaturg or literary manager as we have come to know it in the theatre today. For directors, knowledge of the ways directors and dramaturgs interact and collaborate is essential. Knowing how to make the most of the director-dramaturg relationship is crucial, as with the theatre's other primary relationships, for effective collaboration and for realizing the benefits of the resource dramaturgs can bring to the process. Generally speaking, the function of the dramaturg falls into three categories of activity, one having to do with artistic support in a broad sense, one having to do with production support in a very particular way, and one having to do with new play development.

The Dramaturg and the Artistic Director

In the category of activity we might term *artistic support,* the dramaturg works with the artistic director of the theatre in several ways. These include overseeing the life of the theatre's literary office where new plays are received and reviewed after they have been submitted by authors or agents for production consideration. Dramaturgs may also assist by providing a wide range of needed material to those who develop the theatre's programs and educational materials, including background pieces on the play or author or a particular issue focused on in a play. The term *literary management* applies to many of these functions.

A more general but very important function of the dramaturg is maintaining a dialogue with the artistic director of the theatre concerning programming—which plays may be selected for production or put into further development in the case of new works. In the very best examples of these relationships, the director and the dramaturg or literary manager may form productive collaborations in which ideas for upcoming productions or seasons of plays are explored and formulated. This dialogue can be a valuable two-way street, in which the dramaturg may make suggestions the director may find stimulating or useful—and the director may find the dramaturg to be a valuable sounding board for ideas about particular plays, playwrights, seasons, or production approaches. This means the dramaturg must be very familiar with a wealth of dramatic literature from all ages and countries and cultures, including new plays and playwrights (as well as having a highly developed knowledge of theatrical production, including a wide array of artists). Only the most widely read and experienced individual can aspire to fulfill this valuable role in an ideal way. Each director or artistic director will determine the parameters of this relationship according to the needs of the situation and the way the individuals involved work together. On a pragmatic level, the exchange may be as straightforward as the dramaturg or literary manager assisting the director by compiling all of the available translations of a particular play or, more ambitiously, perhaps working with the director and a translator in the evolution of a *new* translation or adaptation for a particular production. But in the most highly developed of these relationships, a director may talk through with a dramaturg, issues as sensitive as particular production approaches or the selection of plays for an entire season.

The Dramaturg in Production Support

In the category of activity we might term *production support,* the dramaturg works on a particular play or project in actual production, providing a broad range of information to all of the creative participants in the effort, including the director, actors, and occasionally even the designers, although the work of the designers may proceed in a different time frame to that of the rehearsal process. For example, for a production of Strindberg's play *The Father,* the dramaturg may provide material on the author, the play, the background of the play and Sweden in the late nineteenth century, including such things as manners, dress, military life, and so on. Even providing visual imagery to help the directors and actors in rehearsal might fall within the support function of a production dramaturg: photographs of small-town life in Sweden or military garrisons such as that where the play takes place or even paintings that evoke the landscape, mood, or style of the world of Strindberg's play. Because these materials can have a powerful effect on the imaginations of the actors, their selection and presentation should be carefully worked through by the director with the production dramaturg. For works such as Brecht's *Mother Courage* and *Galileo,* it is easy to see what a valuable contribution can be made to the rehearsal process by a good production dramaturg in terms of information (both printed and visual) on topics having to do with the Thirty Years War, the early evolution of telescopes, the Inquisition, and even the relationship of Brecht's plays to developments in the twentieth century such as World War II and the invention of the atomic bomb.

The Dramaturg and New Play Development

A third key area of activity for dramaturgs and literary managers, and one in which their efforts have been particularly recognized in the United States, is new play development. As theatres have instituted programs of new play development, much of the activity in these programs is overseen by dramaturgs, often on the staff of the theatre, working with playwrights who have become affiliated with the theatre for a particular production or developmental workshop for new material. Because some theatres commission new plays from promising writers, dramaturgs are often involved in working with artistic directors to determine which writers may be commissioned or which plays will be selected for further development. In some instances, the work on developing a new play may have commenced in the relationship between a playwright and a dramaturg prior to the time when the director who will ultimately direct the play comes into the picture. When the director enters into directing a new play that has been or is being developed with the input of a dramaturg, clearly the situation requires the director to exercise keen judgment and well-honed skills in working with others to ensure that the contributions of all are melded in an optimal way, always keeping in mind the ultimate goal of helping the play fulfill both the writer's vision and the play's fullest potential.

Having an accomplished dramaturg to enrich the work of the collective process of making theatre can prove to be as valuable as having a fine designer or any other highly trained member of the team. As with actors and designers, good directors learn how to take advantage of the particular talents of dramaturgs for the greater good of the collective endeavor. It is important to learn how to make this working relationship be entirely beneficial to the process, but that is true of all of the director's work in the theatre.

Appendix 3

Your Future as a Director

One cannot talk about the future of directing without looking back at how it has operated over its lifetime in the United States. In some ways, it has not changed greatly from those first years at Provincetown (MA), where playwrights directed each other's plays. Eugene O'Neill wanted to call the group The Playwright's Theatre when it found winter quarters on MacDougal Street in Greenwich Village, because playwriting, in O'Neill's view, was its reason for being. But George Cram Cook, who sparked the group into life and directed more than the others, thought The Provincetown Playhouse a better title because it delineated *all* the crafts of the theatre and not just one. When he introduced a "dome" for O'Neill's multiscene *Emperor Jones* and got Cleon Throckmorton, a designer, to help him, the director in him took precedence over his writing self. Robert E. Jones, who was soon to become New York's finest scene designer and occasional director, was soon aboard.

The Theatre Guild, born as the Washington Square Players, began with playwrights in much the same way, but it was more production oriented and brought directors into the group. By the early 1920s, the idea of the director as a separate creative artist took hold, and by the middle of that decade, it was in full swing. In the 1930s, The Group Theatre, a spin-off of the Guild, introduced Stanislavski's method of acting along with new plays with the dedicated purpose of affecting, even changing, U.S. society. Out of this stance came the idea of the director as a teacher of acting as well as a stage director.

With these patterns at its base, art-theatre now flourished, with a playwright in residence as well as actors, scene designers, and directors. This became the pattern for theatres in colleges and universities across the nation, with teachers in all the crafts of the theatre both instructing and doing their own specialties. By 1940, the art-theatre pattern was fully in operation, and it reached its peak in the commercial theatre in the post–World War II years with the work of such directors as Elia Kazan, Joshua Logan, Harold Clurman, Alan Schneider, and others. Outside influences were added in the 1950s, when Tyrone Guthrie set up a theatre at Stratford, Canada, mainly for Shakespeare, and when European playwrights such as Bertolt Brecht, Eugene Ionesco, Jean-Paul Sartre, and Samuel Beckett were produced for U.S. audiences.

During the 1950s, motion pictures flowered on a new level, and television began absorbing audiences that had once gone to see plays. And on the stage, the big musicals began their domination of the commercial theatre, while speaking plays, which had once dominated, took second place.

These later changes affected the course of directing that had, up to this point, held top place in the art-theatre along with the playwright. The art-theatre director—the focus of this book—continued in the regional nonprofits and in educational theatre as before. With the surge of the "new" drama in the 1960s, and experimentation in "improvisational" theatre in which actors alone made up "plays" or composed pieces with a leader in charge, some had begun to question whether a director as he had existed before 1960 in the art-theatre could long survive. But the course was righted again in the 1970s and 1980s with the return to more conventional plays that then included African American as well as female playwrights, Asian American, Latino, and gay and lesbian, among others. Again, the director was much needed as an artistic force.

The growth of educational theatre in the 1960s released a large number of theatre-trainees looking for work, and though Broadway and the regionals were mostly inaccessible to all but unusual talents, a wide avenue of a new kind of community theatre appeared that could be brought to life wherever a group could find an audience to pay attention. With the 1960s as background, this movement spread across the United States, because its form was now multitheatre, multiplay, multiaudience—theatres with a purpose. The theatre as a whole now existed on several different levels: commercial Broadway and its road companies out of New York; regional nonprofit theatres in cities of moderate size; educational training-theatres on the campuses; and multicommunity theatres, some under the auspices of city and state art funds, but many more working on their own. Children's theatre, ethnic theatre, and theatre for seniors also found their places.

In this burgeoning of theatre activity across the nation, the director was much needed as an artistic leader. What he will be like in the future is anybody's guess.

How do you fit into all this? Can you get a job as a director? Every student wants to know what lies ahead. However, if you expect that on completion of your training in directing, you will be entering a plentiful job market, you have not yet faced the realities of trying to work in the highly independent and truly creative world of an art form where everything is pretty much touch and go.

You should also be aware that young people go into directing, just as they do acting, with little or no formal training and go on to successful careers as full competitors. The theatre has no barriers to talent. The only advantage your training has provided is time and place to try your wings in order to uncover your artistic talents and your capabilities in leadership. Beyond that, you should also be able to see the scope of the field of directing and the opportunities for finding your way. You are now on your own, as all artists are, and what you make of your career will depend on you.

What sort of director do you want to be? That is the question you must now face, for there are many routes to travel. Some of these overlap, and it is quite possible that you may be working in two areas simultaneously, and over a period of years you may navigate all of them.

Descriptions of the various areas of employment open to you are given in the following section. For purposes of discussion, they have been gathered under five headings: The Professional Director, The Managing Artistic Director, The Academic Director, The Community Director, and The Artist-Leader.

The Professional Director

Professional directing heads the list of job possibilities because it is a top goal for some directors as the most demanding and most difficult to achieve. What is going on in this field of work can readily be noted when you read the daily theatre ads in *The New York Times,* especially in Sunday editions. The big musicals dominate Broadway, though a few new plays and money-making revivals are also listed. But for the most part, Off-Broadway, where production costs are limited, is the location of new plays in quantity, as are revivals by known playwrights such as Sam Shepard, Samuel Beckett, Eugene O'Neill, Tina Howe, David Mamet, William Shakespeare, and even plays by the latest prize-winners. Other major cities across the United States generally follow this lead. All directors who earn their living directing plays as part of their work are, of course, professionals, but the rarer breed are those who work full time with full-time professional actors and designers. Since the 1960s, with the growth of regional, nonprofit theatres located in major cities across the United States, opportunities at this level have greatly increased. Going to New York may still be the goal of some, but today there are other places where professional directors can earn livelihoods.

What you would find most challenging about these jobs is, of course, their special demand: Everyone you work with knows his job and expects to be creative in his own way. The content of this book has tried to lead you toward this goal, for the process of the director's tasks in production is always the same: freeing artistic talent, no matter what the level. What is different about the professional director's job is that (1) he must have exceptional capability in handling new plays and their playwrights, or in devising new ways for presenting old ones; and (2) he must work creatively with talented actors and designers who will expect independence in their own creativity. This is obviously not a job for a beginner. Experience is a basic requirement for entering the competition at this level—experience that has placed as much emphasis on how to communicate with mature actors as on theatrical schemes and a full awareness of the dynamics of rhythms. Part III of this book lays the groundwork. However, from that point on, if you enter this field you will soon discover that a "talented" professional director is defined largely in terms of his personal attributes as a creative human being who can reach other highly poised creative talents in achieving professional qualities and standards. This is the major league.

Pursuing a professional career in today's art-theatre will make enormous demands on your energies and creativity. This is why, if you intend to go this route, you must direct, direct, direct whenever you can. Remuneration is unimportant; experience is everything. You will become aware that there are many kinds of nonprofit theatres where you could be invited to work as a journeyman. (See *Theater Communications Group* publications.) Some mainly offer programs of revivals and musicals, while others work with new plays entirely or as part of the overall program. Some are pointed toward children's theatre and some target ethnic groups. The range is extensive. Whatever you decide to aim for at the professional level of directing, you must be aware that relatively few jobs exist and that getting one of them may not depend on your talent but on knowing someone as well as being in the right place at the right time. Age is no barrier, for youth is much in demand in the new theatres that developed in the 1960s and 1970s. What you believe in and how committed you want to become may very well determine your status as a potential director in a group that is motivated by a strong central purpose. *Theatre is commitment,* you will discover, has a very special meaning.

If you are serious about pursuing professional directing, you need to give yourself over completely to building that career. Experienced and successful professionals make the point that requisites for success include not only talent but also a deep *need* and strong *will* to express that talent despite any and all obstacles that may be in the way, and the ability to withstand rejection for as long as it takes. Lacking any one of these attributes, the goal of being a professional director is sure to be elusive and heartbreaking. There is no one way to pursue the goal of being a professional director, but there are several things you should consider.

Internships

While you are in school, you should seek out a series of internships that will be invaluable "bridges" as you begin the process of transition from your training program to the professional world. You should seek out internships with the best theatres and the best directors you can arrange. These may be in your own city or region, but you should also set your sights on possibilities in other parts of the country or even in other countries. The goal is for you to see the finest directing being done and learn from the finest directors working anywhere as you develop yourself as a director. In some respects your developing as a director still relates to the journeyman mode through which the aspects of artistic work have long been passed along to succeeding generations.

Networking

Closely allied to the strategy of internships and the many relationships that will flow from them, is the idea of networking, the building up of contacts and relationships with others who already work in the profession or who are making their way as you are. Forming alliances with designers, with actors, and, perhaps most important of all, with writers, is a way to form teams of artists who have an affinity for working together as well as a way to make opportunities for yourself. Getting yourself and your work known is essential in making your way. If you are not willing to pursue networking and the nitty-gritty of career building—all your talent and all your training may not matter in pursuing this particular goal. Theatre is usually an intensely social art in the sense that it is not like writing a book or painting a picture, which may be solitary pursuits. Not only do you need other people to work with, you need to make your way in the social world where theatre is made, for directing opportunities are not at all likely to be given to the persons who have not made themselves and their work known.

Workshop and Bridge Programs

Another of the stepping-stones from academic training to entry professional work may have to do with your participation in seminars and workshops put on by training institutions (director workshops put on by universities and the like), support organizations (such as the Directors Project of the New York Drama League), and theatres (such as the Lincoln Center Directors Lab, hosted by Lincoln Center Theatre). The Society of Stage Directors and Choreographers (SSD&C), based in New York City, is the professional union of stage directors and choreographers in the United States. This organization has a valuable program of associate membership status that allows you to receive its journal, which has many insightful articles and interviews about directing and choreography, as well as providing you with an informative newsletter, which features information about directing workshops and seminars put on by the Society in different parts of the country. Such programs as these provide avenues for emerging directors of talent to show their work and become known. The ambitious young director, committed to networking and building a career, will learn about such opportunities and pursue them.

Directing Your Own Work

Assisting talented and accomplished directors is an invaluable part of virtually every young director's development, and hopefully through internships you will have many such opportunities. However, there is no substitute for doing your own work, directing as often as possible, doing the best, most interesting work that you can, and getting others to come and see it. Good photographs of your work will be invaluable in making your way while you are young, but there is no substitute for getting your work seen by people who may be able to help you. Make your own opportunities to work as an artist and keep at it—for as long as it takes.

There is no one or sure pathway to becoming a professional director. You and your work must make a compelling case for yourself. Remember that you are asking others to entrust you with leadership and the responsibility for the work and viability of an entire collective or organization. You must not be surprised that it takes time to build a career or that your chosen path is a challenging one. But if this calling is really for you, it will be a rewarding journey indeed.

The Managing Artistic Director

A job for the professional theatre director that came into being with the regional nonprofits is that of artistic director. This job was declared explicitly because such theatres could not survive without one, and it is still the order of the day. As the "producer" in these theatres, and usually also a primary stage director, an artistic director can formulate policies; arrange programming; hire actors, designers, and other stage directors; declare the image of the theatre in the public view; and establish activities seminal to the growth of the theatre. He usually works closely in concert with a managing director as his primary advisor on budgetary matters, marketing, public relations, box-office procedures, audience prequisites, rentals and peripheral money-raising activities, financial drives, and the like, but his autonomy is explicit and necessary, answering only to his governing board, who can hire and fire him. Otherwise, a theatre is his to command, including its audience, because he understands its needs and desires. The artistic director projects leadership, because it is through his eyes and visions that audiences will grow in capabilities as well as numbers.

The Academic Director

Compared with the relatively few jobs open to full-time professional directors, there are many others in the academic world. Although most directors work only with actors in training, they can claim the "professional" designation in the sense that they earn their living by producing plays and teaching others how to do so. When secondary and primary school activities are added to those in colleges and universities, the annual number of productions is in the thousands, and their audiences in the millions. Academic theatre is the single largest employer of expert theatre personnel in this country.

Excellent theatre plants are everywhere and the onus is on the director to produce a wide variety of plays, both modern and historical, in varying styles of production. He is the composite leader: the organizer; the producer; the publicist; the primary critic; the scholar; the theorist; the adventurer; the teacher of acting, directing, and other theatre courses; and the prime mover and inspirational force. In fact, so much is expected of directors at the college and university level that it is no wonder good ones are scarce and superior ones as rare as in the commercial professional theatre.

What attracts many people to this area of directing is not only the availability of jobs but also the prospects of a career of varying interests and intensities. There is always the climb up the production ladder from simple to highly complex plays, including the historical drama, but there is also the intellectual and spirit-satisfying compensation of classroom teaching wherein the process of developing young talent can become an end in itself.

The top group of academic theatres in the universities is now as well poised for production in both equipment and design personnel as most professional repertory theatres anywhere in the United States or Europe. That is why the pressure is on directors to work with originality and style. Some not only have graduate student actors to ensure, in the view of some directors, more satisfying casting, but also companies that include one or more professional actors, either as members of the teaching staff or performers hired for particular plays or a season. In these situations, the stakes are high because with so many resources on hand, a director, like a football or basketball coach, must succeed with the public. The emphasis on winning (the commercial goal) may supersede the primary objective of training students in theatre crafts. Consequently, many directors prefer to work in less demanding situations where adventure is possible and "failure" is not demeaning and may even be productive as a learning experience.

The Community Director

The community theatre, sponsored with local and state support, is a product of the increasing emphasis that cities across the United States have placed on recreational facilities since the 1960s. For some, the motivation was sociological, a means of meeting inner-city problems with a recreational resource. With federal grants-in-aid to help some cities increase local funding, theatre participation was looked at as a way of satisfying the needs of the new community groups that had become clearly identified in the 1960s and 1970s as never before, including African Americans, Hispanic Americans, and other ethnic/racial groups. The old community theatre, the one that since the 1920s had satisfied the artistic and social needs of local adult amateurs, was now changed in direction and number, with special emphasis on Children's Theatre, creative dramatics, and Theatre for Youth.

The community theatre director today is identified at several levels. He may be a specialist with ethnic groups, senior citizens, children, or adult art-theatre. In the number of jobs available, this area now holds second place to academic theatre, and it shows a remarkable holding power. In some instances, enough funds are available to employ not only a director but a designer/technical director, as well.

The primary function of recreation, however, does not imply shoddy, amateurish production. The adventurous director can move as he will. Every opportunity to make something the group can be proud of will depend on the vitality and skill of his leadership. Community theatre is still largely unexploited because until recent years it has not had institutional security of the same sort as college and university theatre. However, its potential is great for the enterprising director. Theatre is a sociological institution, and the community is the proper base for its activities.

Community theatre on another level has developed in groups that come together on their own to produce plays, sometimes with a playwright in hand. Directors are involved in leading these groups as both play director and teacher of acting. Some of these local theatres have become successful enough to go "Equity" (actors union) on a specially arranged and modest pay scale. This at once makes such a theatre more permanent in character, but it adds a financial burden to the other expenses of production and usually requires expert business management to succeed.

If you want to work as a community director, you will need to augment your theatre training with exposure to sociology and community dynamics and financial and business management because success in this area combines artistic talent and sound production sense. In most instances, at least early on, you will be more of a producer than director; your growth will lie in your ability to do both effectively. You will also be a teacher in the academic sense, for you will be a developer of talent as well as good community relations.

In many ways, the independent theatre is more satisfying to those who work in it and provides a good job for a young director. "Running your own theatre" is a way of not only finding work but also fulfilling a community's needs, for it is the audience that really matters.

The Artist-Leader

It is perhaps stretching the point to label *improvisational theatre* for audiences "experimental" because it has been around in its present form since the early 1960s. Yet, it is rooted so deeply in the nature of theatre ("two boards and a passion") and has such a noble lineage in the *commedia dell'arte* that it is not at all surprising to find it still operating today. San Francisco's Mime Troupe is an example. This is a director's theatre, for he alone is responsible for its life, its energy, its content, its artistic product, and its overall meaning. However, the word *director,* as defined throughout this book, must be modified because, in practice, improvisational theatricals involve group improvisations, which are not the product of one person's imagination although that individual may lead others into the improvisations and influence their shape. What is made is that which emerges from interchanges within the group. A much better designation is *artist-leader,* simply because it implies both a strong artistic background in theatre as well as exceptional leadership capabilities.

Although improvisational theatricals are group-made, they still have unusual capabilities of conveying intensive dramatic ideas through the elements of visual and aural theatricality, through the variations and unexpected possibilities inherent in improvisation, and through a minimum of improvised words that may or may not employ the interchanges of dialogue. Consequently, such theatricals are not open to "interpretation" by other directors and actors outside of the group because they are the improvised and unique products of the group and its leader who stamp them with the only possible interpretation—the one *they* reveal to an audience. Because all the rules of improvisation apply, the participants are not actors in the traditional sense, nor is the staging in any way restricted to the conventions of established forms.

The intention here is not to discuss the techniques of making improvisational theatricals, for any techniques used in the process can be evolved only by a group itself in the process of effecting its own artistic goals. Furthermore, introducing present means when the range of possibilities can be very great would only confuse what is really important for a director in training to understand as clearly as possible: how the artist-leader differs in his work from the master-craftsman interpretive director.

There is no question that leadership of a very definite sort is involved. In its earliest declarations in the 1960s, this leadership was based in a commitment to social, political, or religious ideas, or all three at the same time. Thus, it was not just the leader's knowledge of the art and craft of the theatre that made him a leader but his belief in a view of life coupled with a dedication approaching that of a reformist—a dedication demanding that he reach and influence people with his ideas and points of view. His intention was not to propagate other people's ideas, such as what the interpretive director does with the work of the playwrights he produces, but to arouse through a group statement the specific point of view he wanted to inculcate. His leadership necessarily involved collecting around him a group that saw eye to eye with his ideas and had a similar desire to propagate them.

Who is this sort of theatre for? Is it primarily for the benefit of the actors who participate in it or for the audience that is also encouraged to participate in it? Expression of audience opinion has been so curtailed in the twentieth century from the general participatory noise of the nineteenth and preceding centuries that more involvement seems possible. And what will the spectators be expected to do? Will they no longer be spectators but actors in the improvisation itself? Will a new audience be found for it, as with the San Francisco Mime Troupe, a primarily youthful audience in contrast to the mature, middle-class audience of the established theatre? Will the new audience demand immediate relevance and commitment? As you can see, improvisational theatre leaves us with many puzzling speculations about the theatre of the future.

Directing as a Volunteer

All of the jobs described up to this point are considered *paid employment*, but not being paid does not make it a lesser job. Many students study directing—like they do acting, writing, music in all of its forms—without setting up professional goals. These people are often natural leaders and are prepared to volunteer if the opportunity arises. These are the people who keep theatre alive in their communities, both as doers and audience members. Use your craft to the best possible advantage. You are needed.

The Director as Ritualist

Finally, it would not be fair to leave the image of the director as only an interpreter-coordinator of the work of others. By giving stage life to the plays he works with, he acts as a ritualist playing out parables in our time in a form dating back to the ancient Greeks. This is a complicated view you will better understand after you have directed a few plays and feel the force you, as leader, have on audiences. Plays are not mere entertainments; rather, they are enveloping experiences. As a ritualist, you bring this about. Playwrights have the poetic vision; directors, through actors and designers, give this vision physical life on the stage. A theatre is not just a place for entertainments but, in its most ideal form, it is a center of community belonging.

Eliot, T. S. "The Function of Criticism," in *Selected Essays.* New York: Harcourt Brace Jovanovich, 1950.

Ferres, John H. *Twentieth-Century Interpretations of* The Crucible. Englewood Cliffs, NJ: Prentice-Hall, 1972.

Forsyth, James. *Tyrone Guthrie.* London: Hamish Hamilton, 1976.

Frankel, Aaron. *Writing the Broadway Musical.* DaCapo Press, 2000.

Gershkovich, Alexander. *The Theatre of Yuri Lyubimov,* trans. Michael Yurieff. New York: Paragon House, 1989.

Giannachi, Gabriella and Mary Luckurst. *On Directing: Interviews with Directors.* Foreword by Peter Brook. New York: St. Martin's Griffin, 1999.

Gielgud, John. *Stage Directions.* New York: Random House, 1963.

Gladkov, Alexander, *Meyerhold Speaks/Meyerhold Rehearses,* trans. and ed. Alma Law. Amsterdam: Harwood Academic Publishers, 1997.

Goodwin, John, ed. *Peter Hall's Diaries.* New York: Harper and Row, 1984.

Gorchakov, Nikolai. *Stanislavsky Directs,* trans. Miriam Goldina. New York: Funk & Wagnalls, 1954.

Grotowski, Jerzy. *Towards a Poor Theatre.* New York: Simon and Schuster, 1969.

Guthrie, Tyrone. *A Life in the Theatre.* New York: McGraw-Hill, 1959.

Hauser, Frank and Russell Reich. *Notes on Directing.* RCR Creative Press, 2003.

Heilpern, John. *Conference of the Birds: The Story of Peter Brook in Africa.* New York: Macmillan, 1978.

Hoover, Marjorie L. *Meyerhold: The Art of Conscious Theatre.* Amherst, MA: University of Massachusetts Press, 1974.

Hunt, Albert and Geoffrey Reeves. *Peter Brook.* Cambridge University Press, 1995.

International Theatre Institute. www.iti.unesco.org

Jones, Tom. *Making Musicals.* New York: Limelight Editions, 1997.

Journal for Stage Directors and Choreographers. www.sdcfoundation.org

Kalb, Jonathan. *Beckett in Performance.* Cambridge and New York: Cambridge University Press, 1989.

Kazan, Elia. "On What Makes a Director." Director's Guild of America, 1973.

———. *A Life.* New York: Doubleday, 1989.

Kiernander, Adrian. *Ariane Mnouchkine and the Theatre du Soleil.* Cambridge University Press, 1993.

Lavender, Andy, et al. *Hamlet in Pieces: Shakespeare Reworked: Peter Brook, Robert Lepage, Robert Wilson.* Continuum Publishing Group, 2003.

Lepage, Robert. *Connecting Flights.* Coach House Press, 1998.

London, Todd. *The Artistic Home: Discussions with Artistic Directors of America's Institutional Theatres.* New York: Theatre Communications Group, 1988.

Lowen, Tirzah. *Peter Hall Directs* Antony and Cleopatra. New York: Limelight Editions, 1991.

Manfull, Helen. *In Other Words: Women Directors Speak.* Smith and Kraus, 1998.

McCabe, Terry. *Mis-Directing the Play.* Ivan R. Dee, Publisher, 2001.

Miller, Jonathan. *Subsequent Performances.* New York: Viking, 1986.

Miller, Scott. *From* Assassins *to* West Side Story: *The Director's Guide to Musical Theatre.* Heinemann, 1996.

———. *Deconstructing Harold Hill.* Heinemann, 1999.

Moffitt, Dale. *Between Two Silences: Talking with Peter Brook.* Dallas: Southern Methodist University Press, 1999.

O'Connor, Garry. *The Mahabarata: Peter Brook's Epic in the Making.* London: Hodder and Stoughton, 1989.

Oppenheim, Lois. *Directing Beckett.* Ann Arbor: University of Michigan Press, 1994.

Quadri, Franco, Franco Bertoni, and Robert Stearns. *Robert Wilson.* New York: Rizzoli, 1997.

Quintero, Jose. *If You Don't Dance They Beat You.* Boston: Little-Brown, 1974.

Rossi, Alfred. *Astonish Us in the Morning: Tyrone Guthrie Remembered.* Detroit: Wayne State University Press, 1977.

Sachs, Harvey. "Profile of Giorgio Strehler." *New Yorker,* May 4, 1992.

Saint-Denis, Michel. *Theatre: The Rediscovery of Style.* New York: Theatre Arts Books, 1961.

Savran, David. *Breaking the Rules: The Wooster Group.* New York: Theatre Communicatoins Group, 1988.

Schechner, Richard. *Public Domain.* Indianapolis: Bobbs-Merrill, 1969.

———. *Environmental Theatre.* New York: Hawthorne Books, 1973.

Schneider, Alan. "What Does a Director Do?" *New York Theatre Review,* Spring-Summer 1977.

———. *Entrances: An American Director's Journey.* New York: Viking, 1986.

Shapiro, Mel. *The Director's Companion.* Wadsworth, 1997.

Shaw, Bernard. *The Art of Rehearsal.* New York: Samuel French, 1928.

Shyer, Laurence. *Robert Wilson and His Collaborators.* New York: Theatre Communications Group, 1989.

Smith, C. H. *Orghast at Persepolis.* New York: Viking, 1972.

Society of Stage Directors and Choreographers. www.sdcfoundation.org

Stage Director's Handbook: 2003–2004: Opportunities for Directors and Choreographers. Stage Directors and Choreographers Foundation. New York: Theatre Communications Group, 2004.

Stanislavski, Konstantin. *Stanislavski on the Art of the Stage,* trans. David Magarshack. London: Faber and Faber, 1950.

———. *My Life in Art,* trans. J. J. Robbins. New York: Theatre Arts Books, 1952.

———. The Seagull *Produced by Stanislavsky,* ed. S. D. Balukhaty, trans. David Magarshack. London: Denis Dobson, 1952.

Theatre Communications Group. www.tcg.org

Thelan, Lawrence. *The Show Makers: Great Directors of the American Musical Theatre.* Routledge, 1999.

Tovstonogov, Georgi. *The Profession of the Stage Director.* Moscow: Progress Publishers, 1972.

Whitmore, Jon. *Directing Postmodern Theatre: Shaping Signification in Performance.* Ann Arbor: University of Michigan Press, 1994.

Willett, John. *The Theatre of Erwin Piscator: Half a Century of Politics in the Theatre.* London: Eyre Methuen, 1978.

———, ed. and trans. *Brecht on Theatre: The Development of an Aesthetic.* New York: Hill and Wang, 1964.

Williams, David, comp. *Peter Brook: A Theatrical Casebook.* London: Methuen, 1988.

———. *Collaborative Theatre: The Theatre du Soleil Sourcebook* (Making Theatre). Routledge, 1999.

Wills, J. Robert, ed. *The Director in a Changing Theatre.* Palo Alto, CA: Mayfield Publishing, 1976.

Wilson, Robert. *The Theatre of Images.* New York: Harper & Row, 1984.

Zeigler, Joseph Wesley. *Regional Theatre: The Revolutionary Stage.* DaCapo Press, 2000.

Acting and the Director-Actor Relationship

Adler, Stella. *The Technique of Acting.* New York: Bantam, 1990.

Adler, Stella and Barry Paris, ed. *Stella Adler on Ibsen, Strindberg, and Chekhov.* New York: Vintage, 2000.

Adler, Stella, et al. *The Art of Acting.* New York: Applause Books, 2000.

Barton, John. *Playing Shakespeare.* London and New York: Methuen, 1984.

Benedetti, Robert. *Seeming, Being, and Becoming: Acting in Our Century.* New York: Drama Book Specialists, 1976.

———. *The Actor at Work.,* 7th ed. Boston: Allyn and Bacon, 1996.

Berry, Cicely. *Voice and the Actor.* New York: Macmillan, 1978.

Boleslavsky, Richard. *Acting: The First Six Lessons.* Routledge, 2003.

Brebner, Ann M. *Setting Free the Actor.* Mercury House, 1990.

Brockbank, Philip, ed. *Players of Shakespeare: 1* and *Players of Shakespeare: 2.* Cambridge and New York: Cambridge University Press, 1989.

Brook, Peter. *The Open Door: Thoughts on Acting and Theatre.* New York: Theatre Communications Group, 1995.

Caruso, Sandra and Paul Clemens. *The Actor's Book of Improvisation.* New York: Penguin, 1992.

Chaikin, Joseph. *The Presence of the Actor.* New York: Atheneum, 1977.

Chekhov, Michael. *To the Actor on the Technique of Acting. New York: Harper & Brothers, 1953.*

Cohen, Robert. *Acting in Shakespeare.* New York: McGraw-Hill, 1990.

Cole, Toby, ed. *Acting: A Handbook of the Stanislavski Method.* New York: Crown Publishers, 1963.

Craig, David. *On Singing Onstage,* rev. ed. New York: Applause Books, 1990.

Green, Ruth M. *The Wearing of a Costume.* London: Pitman & Sons, 1966.

Hagen, Uta. *A Challenge for the Actor.* New York: Scribner, 1991.

Hagen, Uta and Haskel Frankel. *Respect for Acting.* New York: John Wiley, 1973.

Hodgson, John and Ernest Richards. *Improvisation.* London: Methuen, 1966.

Lessac, Arthur. *The Use and Training of the Human Voice.* New York: DBS Publications, 1967.

Lewis, Robert. *Advice to the Players.* Introduction by Harold Clurman. New York: Theatre Communications Group, 1989.

Linklater, Kristin. *Freeing the Natural Voice.* New York: Drama Book Publishers, 1976.

Machlin, Evangeline. *Speech for the Stage.* New York: Theatre Arts Books, 1966.

Meisner, Stanford and Dennis Longwell. *Stanford Meisner on Acting.* New York: Vintage, 1987.

Mekler, Eve. *A New Generation of Acting Teachers.* New York: Penguin, 1987.

O'Connor, Garry. *Ralph Richardson.* London: Hodder and Stoughton, 1982.

Olivier, Laurence. *Laurence Olivier on Acting.* New York: Simon and Schuster, 1986.

Olivieri, Joseph. *Shakespeare Without Fear: A User-Friendly Guide to Acting Shakespeare.* Wadsworth, 2000.

Oxenford, Lyn. *Playing Period Plays.* London: J. Garnet Miller, 1958.

Parrish, Wayland Maxfield. *Reading Aloud,* 4th ed. New York: John Wiley, 1966.

Penrod, James. *Movement for the Performing Artist.* Palo Alto, CA: National Press Books, 1974.

Redgrave, Michael. *The Actor's Ways and Means.* London: William Heinemann, 1953.

Rudlin, John. *Commedia dell'Arte: An Actor's Handbook.* London and New York: Routledge, 1994.

Russell, Mark, ed. *Out of Character.* New York: Bantam, 1997.
Saint-Denis, Michel. *Training for the Theatre.* New York: Theatre Arts Books, 1982.
Salvi, Delia. *Friendly Enemies: The Director-Actor Relationship.* Watson-Guptill, 2003.
Seyler, Athene and Stephen Haggard. *The Craft of Comedy.* New York: Theatre Arts Books, 1946.
Shapiro, Mel. *An Actor Performs.* New York: Harcourt Brace, 1997.
Shawn, Ted. *Every Little Movement.* Brooklyn, NY: Dance Horizons, 1968.
Spolin, Viola. *Improvisation for the Theatre.* Evanston, IL: Northwestern University Press, 1963.
Stanislavski, Konstantin. *Building a Character,* trans. Elizabeth Reynolds Hapgood. New York: Theatre Arts Books, 1949.
———. *An Actor Prepares.* New York: Theatre Arts Books, 1952.
Strasberg, Lee. *Strasberg at the Actors Studio,* ed. Robert Hethmon. New York: Viking, 1965.
Vineberg, Steve. *Method Actors: Three Generations of American Acting Style.* New York: Macmillan, 1991.

The Design Process and Play Production

Appia, Adolphe. *Adolph Appia's Music and the Art of the Theatre,* trans. Robert W. Corrigan and Mary Douglas Dirks. Coral Gables, FL: University of Miami Press, 1962.
Aronson, Arnold. *American Set Design.* New York: Theatre Communications Group, 1985.
———. *The History and Theory of Environmental Scenography.* Ann Arbor: University of Michigan Press, 1988.
Bablet, Denis. *Edward Gordon Craig,* trans. Daphne Woodward. New York: Theatre Arts Books, 1966.
———. *The Revolutions of Stage Design in the 20th Century.* Paris and New York: Leon Amiel, 1977.
Barton, Lucy. *Historic Costume for the Stage.* Boston: Walter H. Baker, 1961.
Bryer, Robin. *The History of Hair.* Philip Wilson, 2000.
Burian, Jarka. *The Scenography of Josef Svoboda.* Middletown, CT: Wesleyan University Press, 1971.
Corson, Richard. *Fashions in Hair: The 1st 5,000 Years,* 2nd ed. Peter Owen, 2001.
Corson, Richard and James Glavan. *Stage Makeup,* 9th ed. Boston: Allyn and Bacon, 2000.
Craig, Edward Gordon. *On the Art of the Theatre.* New York: Theatre Arts Books, 1957.
Davenport, Milia. *Book of Costume,* 2 vols. New York: Crown Publishers, 1948.
Essig, Linda. *Lighting and the Design Idea.* International Thomson Publishing, 1996.
———. *The Speed of Light: Dialogues on Lighting Design and Technological Change.* Heinemann, 2002.
Fraser, Neil. *Stage Lighting Design.* Crowood, 1999.
Fuerst, Walter R. and Samuel J. Hume. *Twentieth-Century Stage Decoration,* 2 vols. New York: Benjamin Blom, 1967.
Gassner, John. *Form and Idea in Modern Theatre.* New York: Dryden Press, 1956.
Graves, Maitland. *The Art of Color and Design.* New York: McGraw-Hill, 1951.
Hainaux, Rene. *Stage Design Throughout the World, 1970–75.* New York: Theatre Arts Books, 1976.
——————. *Stage Design Throughout the World Since 1960.* New York: Theatre Arts Books, 1978.

Hainaux, Rene and Yves-Bonnat. *Stage Design Throughout the World Since 1950.* London: George G. Harrap & Co., 1964.
Henderson, Mary C. *Mielziner: Master of Modern Stage Design.* Watson-Guptill, 2001.
Howard, Pamela. *What Is Scenography? (Theatre Concepts).* Routledge, 2002.
Ingham, Rosemary. *From Page to Stage: How Theatre Designers Make Connections Between Scripts and Images.* Heinemann, 1998.
Jones, Robert Edmond. *The Dramatic Imagination.* New York: Theatre Arts Books, 1941.
Keller, Max. *Light Fantastic: The Art and Design of Stage Lighting.* Prestel, 2000.
Laver, James. *Costume in the Theatre.* New York: Hill and Wang, 1964.
Lebrecht, James and Deena Kaye. *Sound and Music for the Theatre: The Art and Technique of Design,* 2nd ed. Focal Press, 1999.
Moiseiwitsch, Tanya, et al. *The Stage Is All the World: The Theatrical Designs of Tanya Moiseiwitsch.* Seattle: University of Washington Press, 1999.
Palmer, Richard H. *The Lighting Art: The Aesthetics of Stage Lighting.* Upper Saddle River, NJ: Pearson Education POD, 1993.
Pektal, Lynn. *Costume Design: Techniques of Modern Masters.* Backstage Books, 1993.
Pilbrow, Richard. *Stage Lighting Design: The Art, the Craft, the Life.* Design Press, 2000.
Rich, Frank with Lisa Aronson. *The Theatre Art of Boris Aronson.* New York: Alfred A. Knopf, 1987.
Rosenthal, Jean. *The Magic of Light.* Boston: Little, Brown, 1972.
Russell, Douglas A. *Stage Costume Design.* Englewood Cliffs, NJ: Prentice-Hall, 1973.
———. *Theatrical Style: A Visual Approach to the Theatre.* Palo Alto, CA: Mayfield Publishing, 1976.
———. *Period Style for the Theatre.* Boston: Allyn and Bacon, 1980.
Smith, Ronn and Ming Cho Lee. *American Set Design Two.* New York: Theatre Communications Group, 1985.
Southern, Richard. *The Open Stage.* London: Faber and Faber, 1953.
Thudium, Laura. *Stage Makeup.* Backstage Books, 1999.

Dramatic Literature

Anderson, Maxwell. *The Essence of Tragedy.* Washington, DC: Anderson House, 1939.
Bentley, Eric. *The Playwright as Thinker.* New York: Harcourt, Brace, Jovanovich, 1948.
———. *The Brecht Commentaries, 1943–1980.* New York: Grove Press and London: Eyre Methuen, 1981.
Bergson, Henri. *Laughter,* ed. Wylie Sypher. Garden City, NY: Doubleday, 1956.
Brater, Enoch. *Why Beckett.* London: Thams and Hudson, 1989.
Brustein, Robert. *The Theatre of Revolt.* Boston: Little, Brown, 1964.
Butcher, S. H., trans. *Aristotle on Music and Poetry.* New York: Liberal Arts Press, 1956.
Clark, Barret H., ed., *European Theories of the Drama.* New York: Crown Publishers, 1947.
Corrigan, Robert W., ed. *Comedy: Meaning and Form.* San Francisco: Chandler Publishing, 1965.
———. *Tragedy: Vision and Form.* San Francisco: Chandler Publishing, 1965.
Esslin, Martin. *Brecht: A Choice of Evils,* 4th ed. Methuen, 1984.
———. *Theater of the Absurd,* 3rd ed. New York: Viking Press, 1987.
Gussow, Mel. *Conversations with Pinter.* New York: Grove Press, 1996.
———. *Conversations with Stoppard.* New York: Grove Press, 1996.

———. *Conversations with and about Beckett.* New York: Grove Press, 2001.
———. *Conversations with Miller.* New York: Applause, 2002.
———. *Edward Albee: A Singular Journey.* New York: Applause, 2001.
Hart, Lynda. *Sam Shepard's Metaphorical Stages.* Westport, CT: Greenwood Press, 1987.
Kott, Jan. *Shakespeare Our Contemporary.* New York: W. W. Norton, 1974.
———. *The Theater of Essence.* Evanston, IL: Northwestern University Press, 1984.
Meredith, George. *An Essay on Comedy,* ed. Lane Cooper. Ithaca, NY: Cornell University Press, 1956.
Miller, Arthur. "The Family in Modern Drama," *Atlantic Monthly* 197 (April 1956), 35–41.
Moore, Honor, ed. *The New Women's Theatre.* New York: Vintage, 1977.
Tennant, P. F. D. *Ibsen's Dramatic Technique.* New York: Humanities Press, 1965.
Willett, John. *The Theatre of Bertolt Brecht: A Study from Eight Aspects.* New York: New Directions, 1959.

Dramaturgy, Play Reading, and Script Development

Ball, David. *Backwards and Forwards: A Technical Manual for Reading Plays.* Carbondale: Southern Illinois University Press, 1983.
Bly, Mark, ed. *Production Notebooks, Theatre in Process,* Vols. 1 and 2. New York: Theatre Communications Group, 1996 and 2001.
Cardullo, Bert, ed. *What Is Dramaturgy?* New York: Peter Lang, 1995.
Cohen, Edward M. *Working on a New Play.* New York: Limelight Editions, 1995.
Jonas, Susan, ed. *Dramaturgy in American Theatre.* Wadsworth, 1996.
Kahn, David and Donna Breed. *Scriptwork: A Director's Approach to New Play Development.* Carbondale: Southern Illinois University Press, 1995.
Literary Managers and Dramaturgs of the Americas. www.lmda.org
Nelson, Richard and David Jones. *Making Plays: The Writer-Director Relationship in the Theatre Today.* London: Faber and Faber, 1995.
Thomas, James. *Script Analysis for Actors, Directors, and Designers.* Boston: Focal Press, 1992.

Index

This is a subject index. For authors and plays that appear in photographs, see the listings in the front of the book.

Bibliography

Following are listings of books and other sources with which any advanced student of directing should have some familiarity. This bibliography ranges from discussions of directing and directors at work to the director-actor and director-designer relationships, dramatic literature, and treatments of dramaturgy and play development. You will accumulate knowledge of many of these publications as you work through your courses in theatre, but you will need to search out missed works in the interest of giving yourself as complete a foundation as possible for developing your own point of view about directing. In these works you will encounter a range of perspectives on the art form of theater and different approaches to directing. Some may be in certain respects at variance with views expressed in this book and some are even polemical in advocating their point of view. However, all are a part of the discourse of theatre. The more directing experience you have, combined with a thorough grounding in the literature of the theatre, the more you will be able to participate in the dialogue surrounding the art form and chart your course as a contributing member of the theatre community. Directing is not a display of virtuosity but a highly developed craft firmly based in technique and background.

(No bibliography can be definitive on so vast a subject as directing, let alone the adjacent areas of performance, design, theatre history, dramatic literature, and so on. But a good bibliography should get you started on your own personal journey of discovery and eventual mastery. And that is what these listings are meant to do—give you a good start. The rest is up to you.)

Directing

Alberts, David. *Rehearsal Management for Directors.* Portsmouth, NH: Heinemann, 1995.

American Theatre Magazine. www.tcg.org

Artaud, Antonin. *The Theatre and Its Double,* trans. Mary Caroline Richards. New York: Grove Press, 1988.

Ball, William. *A Sense of Direction: Some Observations on the Art of Directing.* New York: Drama Book Publishers, 1984.

Barba, Eugenio. *Beyond the Floating Islands.* New York: PAJ Publications, 1986.

Barrault, Jean-Louis. *Reflections on Theatre,* trans. Barbara Well. London: Rockliff Pub. Corp., 1951.

———. *The Theatre of Jean-Louis Barrault,* trans. Joseph Chiari. New York: Hill and Wang, 1961.

Bartow, Arthur. *The Director's Voice: Twenty-one Interviews.* New York: Theatre Communications Group, 1988.

Beck, Julian. *The Life of the Theatre.* San Francisco: City Lights, 1972.

Benedetti, Robert. *The Director at Work.* Englewood Cliffs, NJ: Prentice-Hall, 1985.

Bentley, Eric. *In Search of Theatre.* New York: Alfred A. Knopf, 1953.

Berliner, Terry and David Diamond, eds. *Stage Director's Handbook: Complete Opportunities for Directors and Choreographers.* Stage Directors and Choreographers Foundation. New York: Theatre Communications Group, 1999.

Berry, Ralph. *On Directing Shakespeare.* London: Croom Helm and New York: Barnes & Noble Books, 1977.

Blau, Herbert. *The Impossible Theatre.* New York: Macmillan, 1964.

Bloom, Michael. *Thinking Like a Director: A Practical Handbook.* London: Faber and Faber, 2001.

Blumenthal, Eileen and Julie Taymor. *Julie Taymor: Playing with Fire.* New York: Harry N. Abrams, 1999.

Boal, Augusto. *Theatre of the Oppressed,* trans. Charles A. & Maria-Odilia Leal McBride. New York: Theatre Communications Group, 1985.

Bogart, Anne. *A Director Prepares: Seven Essays on Art and Theatre.* Routledge, 2001.

Bradby, David and David Williams. *Directors' Theatre.* New York: St. Martin's Press, 1988.

Braun, Edward. *The Director and the Stage: From Naturalism to Grotowski.* London: Methuen, 1982.

———. *Meyerhold: A Revolution in Theatre.* Iowa City: University of Iowa Press, 1995.

———, trans. and ed. *Meyerhold on Theatre.* New York: Hill and Wang, 1969.

Brecht, Bertolt. *Couragemodell.* Frankfurt: Suhrkamp-Verlag, 1958.

Brook, Peter. *The Empty Space.* New York: Atheneum, 1968.

———. *The Shifting Point.* New York: Harper & Row, 1987.

———. *Threads of Time.* Washington, DC: Counterpoint, 1998.

Brustein, Robert. *Who Needs Theatre.* New York: Atlantic Monthly Press, 1987.

Chekhov, Michael. *Director and Playwright,* compiled and written by Charles Leonard. New York: Harper & Row, 1963.

Citron, Stephen. *The Musical from Inside Out.* Ivan R. Dee, 1997.

Clurman, Harold. *Lies Like Truth.* New York: Macmillan, 1958.

———. *On Directing.* New York: Macmillan, 1972.

———. *The Fervent Years.* New York: Hill and Wang, 1984.

Cole, Susan. *Directors in Rehearsal.* Routledge, Chapman and Hall, 1992.

Cole, Toby and Helen Krich Chinoy, eds. *Directors on Directing,* 2nd rev. ed. Boston: Allyn & Bacon, 1963.

Cook, Judith. *Directors' Theatre.* London: Hodder & Stoughton, 1989.

Croydon, Margaret. *Conversations with Peter Brook, 1970–2000.* London: Faber and Faber, 2003.

Daniels, Rebecca. *Women Stage Directors Speak: Exploring the Influence of Gender on their Work.* McFarland, 2000.

Davis, R. G. *The San Francisco Mime Troupe: The First Ten Years.* Palo Alto, CA: Ramparts Press, 1975.

Delgado, Maria M. and Paul Heritage, eds. *In Contact with the Gods?: Directors Talk Theatre.* Manchester and New York: Manchester University Press, 1996.

Donkin, Ellen and Susan Clement, eds. *Upstaging Big Daddy: Directing Theatre As If Gender and Race Matter.* Ann Arbor: University of Michigan Press, 1999.